STUDIES IN EVANGELICAL HISTORY AND THOUGHT

Itinerant Temples

Tent Methodism, 1814-1832

Picture from the *Tent Methodist Magazine* (1823), p.1.

STUDIES IN EVANGELICAL HISTORY AND THOUGHT

Itinerant Temples

Tent Methodism, 1814-1832

John K. Lander

Foreword by T.S.A. Macquiban

First published 2003 by Paternoster

Paternoster is an imprint of Authentic Media,
9 Holdom Avenue, Bletchley, Milton Keynes, MK1 1QR, U.K.
and
P.O.Box 1047, Waynesboro, GA 30830-2047, U.S.A.

09 08 07 06 05 04 03   7 6 5 4 3 2 1

British Library Cataloguing in Publication Data
A catalogue record for this book is available from the British Library

ISBN-10 1-84227-151-2
ISBN-13 978-1-84227-151-3

Typeset by A.R. Cross
Printed and bound in Great Britain
for Paternoster
by Nottingham Alpha Graphics

Series Preface

The Evangelical movement has been marked by its union of four emphases: on the Bible, on the cross of Christ, on conversion as the entry to the Christian life and on the responsibility of the believer to be active. The present series is designed to publish scholarly studies of any aspect of this movement in Britain or overseas. Its volumes include social analysis as well as exploration of Evangelical ideas. The books in the series consider aspects of the movement shaped by the Evangelical Revival of the eighteenth century, when the impetus to mission began to turn the popular Protestantism of the British Isles and North America into a global phenomenon. The series aims to reap some of the rich harvest of academic research about those who, over the centuries, have believed that they had a gospel to tell to the nations.

Series Editors

David Bebbington, Professor of History, University of Stirling, Stirling, Scotland, UK

John H.Y. Briggs, Senior Research Fellow in Ecclesiastical History and Director of the Centre for Baptist History and Heritage, Regent's Park College, Oxford, UK

Timothy Larsen, Professor of Theology, Wheaton College, Illinois, USA

Mark A. Noll, McManis Professor of Christian Thought, Wheaton College, Wheaton, Illinois, USA

Ian M. Randall, Deputy Principal and Lecturer in Church History and Spirituality, Spurgeon's College, London, UK, and a Senior Research Fellow, International Baptist Theological Seminary, Prague, Czech Republic

For my father,
the Revd Thomas James Lander,
a Congregational minister for sixty-two years,
trained at Bristol, the birthplace of
Tent Methodism.

Contents

Foreword

The history and development of Methodism in Britain has been seen to be greatly more complex than the unilinear accounts of earlier commentators who saw it all in terms of the contribution of the Wesleys, as evangelists extraordinaire raised up in the providence of God to spread scriptural holiness through the land. John Munsey Turner's recent analysis has demonstrated that many Methodisms which contributed to a movement which became not one Church but several distinct denominations and groupings. Reg Ward, whose writing inspired this and other books, helped unlock the complex social relationships and tensions which, in the political context of the early nineteenth century, contributed to the schisms and divisions in Methodism after the death of its founder, John Wesley, in 1791.

John Lander concentrates on one such group, the Tent Methodists, of whom no detailed account and analysis has yet existed. He illustrates the complex interaction between the desire for further revival and the need to consolidate the Methodist movement. He assesses the work of George Pocock and John Pyer, two significant figures of the period 1814 to 1825 and their legacy for English religious life. He raises important questions for those who want to investigate the morphology of church growth and decline in relation to social geography and religious belief. The fluidity of a form of Methodism caught in the crossfire of revivalism and revolt, between the need for strong leadership taking on the features of the Wesleyan connexionalism against which it reacted and the inherent congregationalism of local initiatives, is something with which modern Methodism still wrestles, uncertain whether it wants to be a movement for reform and revival or a church distinct and independent. Lander's book takes us to the heart of sociological and ecclesiological questions about Methodist identity still as relevant for us today two centuries later. I commend it to all those who seek to understand the complexities of early Methodist histories and how we are the diverse people we call Methodists today.

T.S.A. Maquiban
Sarum College
April 2003

Preface

This book charts the history of one of the lesser known nineteenth-century secessions from Wesleyan Methodism. Having beeen brought up within a branch of 'Old Dissent', my involvement with Methodism is comparatively recent, and I am grateful to many people who have helped me to increase my understanding of that movement.

The Revd Dr Tim Macquiban has been a constant source of guidance and encouragement from the time that work on the thesis, on which this book is based, began in early 1996. As Director of the Wesley and Methodist Studies Centre at Westminster College, Oxford, now part of Oxford Brookes University, he readily made himself available to me on my frequent visits to the extensive Wesley Historical Society Library. During the research and writing process Professor Reg Ward generously shared his vast knowledge of Methodism with me, and I gained much from his perspective on Methodist affairs and the way he expressed it. Professor David Bebbington has provided me with invaluable advice during the book's preparation, and I am grateful to him for the interest he has shown. I have been exceedingly fortunate in gaining access to the wealth of combined experience that these three esteemed nonconformist church historians have.

Jeffrey Spittal, Honorary Librarian of the New Room Library at John Wesley's Chapel in central Bristol, truly an oasis in the middle of a desert, willingly helped to identify sources of material in and around Bristol from where Tent Methodism originated. The material there, and in many other collections, is of great value to researchers, and I very much appreciate the efforts of all who freely give of their time to preserve priceless local records. I am also pleased to acknowledge the assistance provided by staff at the John Rylands Library, Manchester, the British Library, the Central Library, Bristol, and by archivists at the county record offices in Bristol, Gloucester, Trowbridge and Winchester.

In Julie Jefferies I was extremely fortunate to have a secretary who willingly typed what I had written, and admirably coped with amendments after amendments. Without her skills the exercise, though enjoyable and fascinating, would have been a more arduous one. Finally, and most of all, I owe a huge debt to my family. The book is dedicated to my father who, regrettably, died before the work was finished. My wife, Pat, has given me incredible support in many different ways, and I am exceedingly grateful to her.

Abbreviations

British Library	BL
Bristol Record Office	BRO
Gloucestershire Record Office	GRO
John Rylands University Library of Manchester	JR
Methodist New Connexion	MNC
Public Records Office	PRO
Rules of the Tent Methodists or Agrarian Society for Extending Christianity at Home (1820)	*TM Rules* (1820)
Rules of the Tent Methodists' Society (1824)	*TM Rules* (1824)
Tent Methodist Magazine for 1823 and Register of Events connected with the spread of the Gospel at Home, Volume 1 (1823)	*TM Magazine*
Wesley Historical Society	WHS
Wiltshire Record Office	WRO

Introduction

After John Wesley's death in 1791, schisms from Wesleyan Methodism occurred regularly. These events were not unexpected and the authorities often accepted them with little obvious regret, even if they did not actually encourage them. The first major split took place in 1797 when the Methodist New Connexion was formed, and during the following twenty years further significant schisms led to the establishment of the Primitive Methodists and the Bible Christians.

Other offshoots arose but lasted for much shorter periods. One of these was the Tent Methodists, a group that has been largely ignored by historians. Although some writers have made passing reference to the group's presence in particular localities, the fact that Tent Methodism did not become a major national, or even a regional, body has meant that its significance has not been sufficiently recognized. The primary and secondary material documenting the group's activities has had to be gleaned from many different places and sources. A full length biography of the second most important Tent Methodist was written shortly after his death, but no major work has charted and analysed the group's overall impact. This book is an original contribution to research in the development of Methodism in the early nineteenth century.

The main case to be made in the book is that although the group existed, firstly within the Wesleyan fold and then as an independent Methodist sect, for only approximately eighteen years from 1814 to about 1832, the group's impact in that period was greater than has, hitherto, been acknowledged. Some of the personalities involved went on to serve other denominations with great devotion for many years. From a careful study of the material, it is also possible to compare and contrast Tent Methodism's experience with that of the main groups that emerged from Wesleyan Methodism during the first two decades of the nineteenth century.

CHAPTER 1

The Social and Religious Context of the Conflicts within Methodism from 1791 to 1820

Disputes in Methodism after John Wesley's Death

It has been common ground among many religious historians studying the fragmentation within Methodism which began after John Wesley's death on 2 March 1791 and continued for sixty years, that the frequent and varied disputes and schisms were not unexpected and, indeed, could have been anticipated. John T. Wilkinson has noted that following Wesley's death 'a Connexional crisis was inevitable'.[1] A chapter in *The Methodist Church: Its Origin, Divisions, and Reunion* included a comment when referring to later controversies, that 'the very success of Methodism was making the crisis more imminent'.[2] The leading early twentieth-century Congregationalist, C. Silvester Horne, who wrote about Methodism from a different standpoint: 'it might have been prophesied without difficulty that in the course of time the democratic element would come into conflict with the clerical', and that it was only Wesley's influence and impact that 'had checked certain inevitable developments of Methodism.'[3] Writing from a different perspective, Robert Currie has also argued that divisions were inevitable in the aftermath of Wesley's death.[4]

Wesley had consistently professed his desire that Methodists should remain within the Church of England, although such statements appeared

---

1   John T. Wilkinson, 'The Rise of Other Methodist Traditions', in R. Davies *et al* (eds), *A History of the Methodist Church in Great Britain* (4 vols; London, 1965-88), II, p.276.

2   G.G. Hornby, 'The United Methodist Church', in A.W. Harrison *et al* (eds.), *The Methodist Church: Its Origin, Divisions, and Reunion* (London: Methodist Publishing House, 1932), p.129.

3   C.S. Horne, *A Popular History of the Free Churches* (London: James Clarke, 1903), p.282.

4   R. Currie, *Methodism Divided: A Study in the Sociology of Ecumenicalism* (London: B.T. Batsford, 1968), pp.27-28, 75.

to be less and less convincing as he grew older. He did so as late as 1789, a year in which he frequently drew attention to the possibility that it might be his last.[5] In Dublin, on Easter Day, 12 April, he told the society there that Methodists were 'not to be a distinct party' but were to remain within the Church of England, 'to which they belonged from the beginning'. On the same occasion his personal testimony was that he had always subscribed to the doctrine of the church, but that it was from necessity that he had departed from 'her discipline' so as 'to preach in the open air, to pray extempore; to form societies; to accept the assistance of lay preachers'.[6] A year later he wrote in the June 1790 edition of the *Arminian Magazine*, 'Ye yourselves were at first called into the Church of England; and though you have and will have a thousand temptations to leave it, and set up for yourselves, regard them not. Be Church of England men still.'[7] Hence his frequent claims to be a faithful member of the Established Church.

However, when he registered a Deed of Declaration in 1784 for a group of 100 preachers to be the legislative body after his death, he had effectively established a separate legal position. In addition, he ignored the conventional contemporary view that the vicar of a particular parish managed the Christian activity within it. He preached frequently in the open air partly because for much of his life access to parish church pulpits in many places had been denied to him. By forming, and taking control of, independent societies and local structures for over forty years, by building and licensing chapels, and by ordaining Thomas Coke as Superintendent and Richard Whatcoat and Thomas Vasey as deacons in 1784 for service in America,[8] there had been a steady succession of activities and measures that made a formal separation from the Church of England more likely. It may have been a misfortune that John Fletcher and Charles Wesley, two potential successors as leaders, both died before him by six years and three years respectively. John Wesley's earlier warnings, notably to the conferences of 1766 and 1769, that future

---

5   *Wesley's Journal* entries for 1 January, 9 January, 15 January, 20 January, 1 March, 28 June, 8 August and 23 August 1789 all refer to the possibility of his immiment death.

6   *Wesley's Journal* entry for this date also includes, 'this is done not to prepare for, but to prevent, a separation from the Church'.

7   *Arminian Magazine* 13 (June, 1790), p.289. The extract is from a sermon that Wesley preached in Cork in May 1789. His text was Hebrews 5.4.The quotation was also used in a letter from Mark Robinson to Rev. R. Johnson, '*Observations on the System of Wesleyan Methodist*' (London, 1824), pp.32-33. This letter was principally concerned with Robinson's objections to the steady separation of Methodism from the Church of England.

8   These ordinations took place in Bristol on 1 September 1784. *Wesley's Journal* records that these men were to 'serve the desolate sheep in America'.

disunity was a distinct possibility,[9] were made more likely to come to pass by the decision to appoint a large group of preachers to manage and control Methodist affairs rather than having one acceptable successor, or a much smaller number that would have formed an 'executive council' or 'inner cabinet'.

Disagreement over the extent, timing and pace of separation from the Established Church was one source of argument. That this issue was contentious was not surprising bearing in mind that Dr Thomas Coke had apparently been in favour of a clear separation from the Church of England in 1786, but in 1799 he conducted discussions with the Bishop of London about a formal union,[10] which, however, the Bishop rejected out of hand. Since a man who in some people's eyes had qualifications that made him a possible successor to John Wesley as leader of the Methodists could, apparently, change his mind so fundamentally, it is not unsurprising that other ministers had difficulty in finding a solution which was acceptable to the diverse elements which comprised Methodism as a whole. The other main area that quickly led to friction after 1791 was the question of authority within Methodism. Ministerial control, stemming from its dominating influence at conference at national level and by local district chairmen and circuit superintendents, was challenged by laity and, on occasions, by trustees of buildings. The desire of lay members, particularly local preachers, to have a genuine influence in discussions leading to important decisions, and the insistence of trustees to determine who should be appointed ministers or have authority to preach and administer the sacraments in chapels, were issues that led to many disputes.[11] Robert Currie developed both these areas of controversy—that 'Chapel ownership was a desirable if awesome responsibility', and that 'the position of the minister in Methodism created copious grievances'[12]—at length, although the latter claim has been vigorously challenged by John C. Bowmer.[13]

It was, in the main, church order and government (which included such matters as whether or not there should be a paid ministry) rather than doctrine, that caused friction. One of the earliest dissident groups to become established, however, did come into existence because of a

---

9   See Davies *et al* (eds.), *History of the Methodist Church in Great Britain*, II, p.276, for a fuller explanation of Wesley's concern.

10   Robert F. Wearmouth, *Methodism and the Common People of the Eighteenth Century* (London: Epworth Press, 1945), p.129, succinctly draws attention to these two events.

11   T.S.A. Macquiban, 'The Sacramental Controversy in Bristol in the 1790s', an address given to the WHS Bristol branch, March 1991, *Bulletin* No. 60, sets out the position.

12   Currie, *Methodism Divided*, pp.45-46.

13   J.C. Bowmer, *Pastor and People* (London: Epworth Press, 1975), p.250.

doctrinal disagreement. Joseph Cooke, who had become a local Methodist preacher in 1795 at the age of twenty, was expelled in 1806 as a result of sermons he preached at Rochdale in 1805 during which he questioned the divinity of Christ and, thereby, the doctrine of the Trinity.[14] The Unitarian Cookites became active in Lancashire among 'working men, weavers, colliers, artisans whose means were slender'.[15] After Cooke's death in 1811 the societies he formed developed progressively closer links with the Unitarian movement and eventually either joined it or became independent congregations.

The three main groups to emerge from Wesleyanism during the first quarter of a century after Wesley's death were the Methodist New Connexion, the Primitive Methodists and the Bible Christians.[16] All became significant bodies as they retained independent existences until either 1907 or 1932, produced leaders of great influence, had considerable memberships, albeit concentrated in certain parts of the United Kingdom, and exercised missionary activity abroad as well as at home. The progress of these groups has been carefully documented by many writers who were able to draw on substantial quantities of material, including minutes of meetings, and the personal diaries and correspondence of the key individuals involved. A great deal of information, and a good assessment of their Christian endeavours in the groups themselves, and the wider context into which they conducted their evangelical activities, can be derived from a study of these writings.

However, prior to 1820 many other groups were established. Reference has already been made to the Unitarian Cookites, but bodies such as the Quaker Methodists, the Band Room Methodists of Manchester, the Christian Revivalists from Macclesfield, the Kirkgate Screamers based in Leeds, and the Magic Methodists of Delamere Forest in Cheshire also existed for short periods. Common features of these groups were an unwillingness to accept Wesleyan authority on a variety of issues, including where meetings could be held, and ministerial oversight. They believed 'the saving of souls as of greater importance than ecclesiastical order'.[17] Some of the offshoots that survived became part of the Independent Methodists. There was a significant number of self-governing congregations at this time, particularly in the north west of England, and yearly meetings of Independent Methodists were held from

---

14   D.A. Gowland, *Methodist Secessions* (Manchester: The Chetham Society, 1979), see p.23 for further details of the events leading to Cooke's expulsion.

15   Davies *et al* (eds.), *History of the Methodist Church in Great Britain*, II, p.329.

16   Methodist New Connexion (1797), Primitive Methodists (1811), and Bible Christians (1815).

17   M.R. Watts, *The Dissenters: Volume II. The Expansion of Evangelical Nonconformity 1791-1859* (Oxford: Clarendon Press, 1995), p.138. A brief description of these groups is given on p.32.

1806. At the 1808 conference a membership of 1,219 was reported from sixteen congregations, including those at Macclesfield, Manchester, Warrington, Stockport and Oldham.[18] Eight congregations were represented by thirteen people at the 1813 Yearly Meeting, plus one letter from an absentee, all of them from Cheshire or Lancashire. The meeting was attended by thirty-three local preachers and there were reports of 'several painful circumstances' in Manchester, and of 'preachers neglecting their appointments'.[19] In the introduction to the written report to the Yearly Meeting two years later, it was reported that 'the word Independent among us, signifies no more than each Church has the sole privilege of making its own internal laws'.[20] By then the overall number of congregations had increased by one, including Sheffield and Rastrick, thus extending the geographical coverage into Yorkshire. In addition to small groups, individuals formed their own single societies after being expelled from Wesleyanism. One was in Portland, Dorset, which had been accused of practising witchcraft,[21] and others were in Wiltshire and the East End of London who found unacceptable Wesleyan constraints on their desires to serve local congregations and communities in their own ways. From Methodism's beginnings to the middle of the nineteenth century many groups, some long lasting and many more with only a short independent existence, came into being as the result of a wide range of disagreements.

One of the relatively unknown groups which became active in the second decade of the nineteenth century, and which originated in Bristol, was the Tent Methodists. While brief references to them can be found in some historical and religious works concerned with other Methodist issues, the evangelical activity of the Tent Methodists was more important, lasted for much longer, and occurred in many more parts of the United Kingdom than appears to have been generally recognized up to now.

Many histories of the denomination written after Wesley's death make no reference to Tent Methodism at all. This is true of *History of Wesleyan Methodism* (1872) by Dr George Smith, the *History of Methodism* (1878) by Abel Stevens, *A New History of Methodism* (1909) edited by W.J. Townsend, H.B. Workman and George Eayrs, *A History of Methodism* (1911) by J. Robinson Gregory, *The Spirit of Methodism* (1937) by Henry Bett, and Rupert Davies' *Methodism* first published in 1963. More recently, J.M. Turner's *Conflict and Reconciliation: Studies*

---

18   James Vickers, *History of Independent Methodism* (Manchester: Independent Methodist Bookroom, 1920), pp.9-10.

19   *Minutes of Yearly Meeting of the Independent Methodists* held at Friar's Green Chapel, Warrington, 7 June 1813.

20   *Minutes of Yearly Meeting of the Independent Methodists* held at Sheffield, 15-16 May 1815.

21   Watts, *Dissenters*, II, p.106.

in Methodism and Ecumenism in England 1740-1982, also makes no reference to Tent Methodism. Interestingly, both Eayrs and Davies, at least, were aware of the Tent Methodists as they drew attention to them in local histories they wrote concerning Methodism in Kingswood and Bedminster respectively. A number of other authors seem to underestimate or misunderstand the impact the group achieved, or even dismiss their valuable Christian missionary work with little or no recognition of the significance.[22] There is, however, much available material to study.

One significant secondary source is a substantial biography of John Pyer, one of the two principal people in the history of the movement. This was written by his elder daughter, Catherine, who became known as Kate, in 1865, six years after Pyer's death. Secondary material relating to the other leader, George Pocock, is available, but in the much more fragmented form of pamphlets, articles and local histories. Of particular value is the substantial amount of primary documentation, little of which appears to have been used for any major published assessment. At least two sets of rules were published, four years apart, and twelve monthly editions of the *Tent Methodist Magazine* were published in 1823 which included, among many other articles, details of the movement's progress and activity over a seven year period from early 1814 to the spring of 1821. Several pamphlets which contain the minutiae of two quite separate disputes are available for examination, and there are other primary records, including handbills, indentures relating to land on which chapels were built, and preaching plans. Most of the material is highly subjective in content, much of it favourable to the Tent Methodists, but there is other information, both primary and secondary, to test some of the evidence. In particular, both sides of arguments relating to the disagreements in Bristol during late 1819 and early 1820, and in Manchester between 1824 and 1830, are set out in great detail. Hostile references to the tent preachers were included in the biography of Jabez Bunting, written by his son, and critical comments were made in a near contemporary history of Portland Chapel, Bristol. All these sources of material, and many more, form the basis of this study.

Sect or Denomination?

This book aims to assess the contribution that Tent Methodism made to the religious life of the areas in which it worked, with references and

---

22   See Gowland, *Methodist Secessions*, p.24; T.P. Bunting, *The Life of Jabez Bunting D.D.* (London, 1887), II, pp.170-171, and Bowmer, *Pastors and People*, p.81, are examples.

comparisons, where appropriate, to other groups that emerged from Wesleyanism. In doing so, the experience and influence of other Christian denominations cannot be ignored, nor can the patterns of social and economic development. It is relevant at this early stage to explore whether Tent Methodism should be more properly regarded as a 'sect' or a 'denomination'. The *Oxford English Dictionary* defines a sect as 'a body of persons who unite in holding certain views differing from those of others who are accounted to be of the same religion...deviating from the general tradition'. The Tent Methodists certainly fell within that description. The Clapham Sect, 'a coterie of persons of Evangelical opinions and conspicuous philanthropic activity',[23] is used as an example. Despite 'denominational' being defined as 'belonging to, or of the nature of, a denomination or ecclesiastical sect',[24] there is a tendency for the two words to be interpreted differently. The existence of an organizational structure, including a hierarchy, suggests a denomination. It could be held, therefore, that schisms and secessions from, in this case Wesleyanism, often resulted in sects being formed, some of which later developed into denominations. The Tent Methodists clearly intended to have a formal structure. Two sets of rules and regulations were published, circuit plans were produced for one area and preaching plans for another, quarterly meetings were held for societies in Bristol and Gloucestershire, and at least two annual meetings took place.

Several sociologists have sought to distinguish sects from denominations. Betty Scharf's book, *The Sociological Study of Religion*, refers to Niebuhr's study of religion in America where he claimed 'sect type religion is always transient. A sect either dies or changes into a denomination'.[25] B. Wilson, in *Sects and Society*, classified sects into various types and, again, considered that only some developed into denominations, a view shared by Scharf, who believed that 'all studies show that sects have a high death rate. Few accomplish the transition either to "established sect" or "denomination"'.[26] Some sociologists, including Thomas O'Dea, have characterized membership of sects as being separated from general society, having a degree of exclusiveness and experiencing a conversion, among other features. O'Dea writes that 'the accommodated and routinised sect has been given the name of "denomination" in sociological literature'.[27] However, those two factors are not universally held as being distinguishing aspects of denominations.

---

23   *Oxford English Dictionary* (Oxford: Oxford University Press, 1989), p.842.
24   *Oxford English Dictionary*, p.110.
25   B.R. Scharf, *The Sociological Study of Religion* (London: Hutchinson, 1970), p.105.
26   Scharf, *Sociological Study of Religion*, p.110.
27   T.F. O'Dea, *The Sociology of Religion* (New Jersey: Prentice-Hall, 1966), p.69.

Such diverse religious bodies as the Brethren, Salvation Army, Society of Friends, Christadelphians, Christian Scientists and Jehovah's Witnesses are all regarded as sects by Wilson and Scharf.

It seems clear, therefore, that Tent Methodism cannot be regarded as a denomination. This study will use the word 'sect' to describe the Tent Methodists as it is not felt, in any event, that a sufficiently formal hierarchical structure ever really developed in any of the geographical areas where Tent Methodism was introduced. This was unlike the situation with the Methodist New Connexion, the Primitive Methodists and the Bible Christians. Indeed, it will be shown that the absence of a proper organization was one reason for Tent Methodism's demise. Although the word 'denomination' will not be used in connection with the Tent Methodists, the words 'group' and 'offshoot' will be used as these are more general terms that do not have any technical religious or sociological connotations.

A thorough study of Tent Methodism has a role which is complementary, on the one hand, to the regular, updated general histories of the Methodist denomination as a whole and, on the other, the local histories which concentrate on individual communities in great detail. Some of the works which cover the denominational aspects prominently feature particular issues. For example, the divisions or the class structure of the national church membership are commented upon, and it is the overall progress that is recorded without much reference to the local patterns of penetration and other variations. David Hempton has written 'of the continuing value of micro-histories of Methodist growth in town and countryside to set alongside the burgeoning regional, national and international studies'.[28] Tent Methodism really fell outside all these categories. It became a great deal more than a small, local, temporary phenomenon, but it did not develop into a mainly regional sect in the ways that, for example, the Methodist New Connexion, the Primitive Methodists or the Bible Christians did during the first few years of their existence. While the Tent Methodists became significant contributors to Christian evangelicalism in at least five different parts of the country, the areas were scattered throughout England and there was no coherent pattern of organized expansion.

Social and Economic Background

No activity of the nineteenth century, religious or secular, operated in a vacuum or was unaffected by the immense social, political, economic, as

---

28   D. Hempton, *The Religion of the People: Methodism and popular religion c.1750-1900* (London: Routledge, 1996), p.25.

well as religious developments that were taking place with increasingly rapidity.

The story of Tent Methodism—its establishment, its influence especially among the less fortunate in the communities in which it operated, its geographical expansion, as well as its demise as an independent group—has to be set in the context of several social and religious developments in the early nineteenth century. These developments were complex, intertwined with other issues, and, most significantly, differed in their effect in some parts of England from those in others. In addition, the role of individual Christians, not just those who emerged as leaders, became extremely important. For a relatively short-lived group there were many people from widely different backgrounds who left a significant mark on its activities. Some contributors, supporters but not members, were men of much influence in public life who recognized the value of the tent preachers' work.

The whole story is a mixture of 'macro' and 'micro' issues. At a time when a social class structure was beginning to become more formalized in Britain as a whole, the agricultural workers in parts of the south and some of the industrial employees in the north-west suffered disproportionately as incomes fell at the same time as employment opportunities.[29] On the other hand, there were cities which expanded because of the growing international trade and the need for larger port facilities.[30] Places like Bristol in the late eighteenth and Liverpool in the early nineteenth century, both on the west coast of England, are examples of those cities which achieved material benefit. During the same period pressure was being exerted for the introduction of more democratic procedures, including an expansion of the electoral franchise—not universally but, on the contrary, extremely selectively. Manchester is an example of a city where much agitation for a wider franchise was apparent.

These trends towards what became a capitalist and democratic society were not evenly, steadily or harmoniously achieved. There was much friction which led to widespread unrest, human suffering and economic misery for large numbers of people before, later in the nineteenth century, a more tolerant, economically prosperous and democratic society emerged. Even then there were periods of depression—economic and social—interspersed with a gradual change to better health, housing and education for many. The agricultural crisis of the 1870s caused by the rapid growth of grain imports from North America was one example.

---

29   E. Royle, *Modern Britain: A Social History 1750-1985* (London: Edward Arnold, 1985), pp.82-83, and 94, discusses the growing class issues.

30   M. Dresser (ed.), *The Making of Modern Bristol* (Tiverton: Redcliffe Press, 1996). Chapter 3, and particularly Table 1 on p.55, shows the important relative decline from the mid-eighteenth century.

But in the earlier part of the nineteenth century there was a harshness about the life which most people had to endure. Relationships—between landowner and tenant, employer and employee, magistrate and populace, clergy and parishioner—often lacked any warmth, genuine understanding or sympathy.[31] Most ordinary working-class people, comprising those who were in no regular employment as well as those with relatively low paid jobs in agriculture or industry, and their immediate families, had to cope with many burdens.[32]

The nature of, and reasons for, the problems facing the poor in society were varied. In early nineteenth-century Britain the population grew rapidly. Having approximately doubled in the eighteenth century to reach 10.6 million in 1801,[33] the population continued to expand at the same time that employment prospects were further harmed in 1815 when up to 400,000 servicemen sought civil employment following an end to the long period of war with France. The need for a reasonable wage was exacerbated by the fact that almost half the population was under fifteen years of age and was dependent upon parental income. Not surprisingly, there was intense pressure on the young to gain some form of income from employment.[34] In addition to low incomes for many people, the prices of basic commodities were volatile, often being particularly high in the second decade of the nineteenth century. Furthermore, the government's taxation requirement was excessive because of the need to finance, retrospectively, the cost of the French wars. This burden fell disproportionately on the poor. In agricultural communities 'rural labourers lived in extreme squalor',[35] and in the developing industrial towns and cities living and working conditions for the working classes were also frequently appalling. Indeed, it has been claimed that 'the poorer areas of early industrial cities, where lived the great majority of urban citizens, were citadels of squalor, festering and postulant affronts to a civilized nation. Mere survival was an achievement'.[36] As a fair summary of the overall situation, Ross Poldark, in the eleventh of the Poldark novels, says to the Prime Minister, the Earl of Liverpool, in 1815,

---

31   G.M. Trevelyan, *British History in the Nineteenth Century and After* (London: Longmans, Green, 1937), pp.22-24.

32   P. Mathias, *The First Industrial Nation* (London: Routledge, 1983), Table 23, 'Wheat prices, 1700-1938', on p.441, shows the general increase between 1790 and 1814. They remained high until 1819 before falling temporarily.

33   E.J. Evans, *Britain Before the Reform Act: Politics and Society 1815–1832* (London: Longman, 1989), p.4.

34   Evans, *Britain Before the Reform Act*, pp.4 and 15.

35   R.E. Davies, *Methodism* (London: Epworth Press, 1985), p.22.

36   Evans, *Britain Before the Reform Act*, p.97.

'the labourer, whether in the field or in the factory, should be able to live a decent, honest life. Instead, one sees starvation in the midst of plenty'.[37]

The arrangements in place to alleviate the suffering were unsatisfactory. The Poor Laws were ineffectual, highly restrictive and did not address the real problems.[38] Men and women were not permitted, under the terms of various acts of Parliament (including the 'Six Acts' passed in December 1819), to hold public meetings to discuss action to draw attention to their plight. Very few of those in authority had the will to seek to change the legal regulations so as to achieve meaningful improvements in the conditions of the disadvantaged.

So much for 'macro' factors. What of the more localized 'micro' influences on the background issues? In the first place, although many of the agricultural areas of the south generally suffered greatly, parts of central southern England were less dependent than others on the substantial fluctuations in the price of wheat. Some were engaged significantly in the production of wool and other local industries to provide employment. Wiltshire, where Tent Methodists exercised a significant ministry, was, however, one county where average agricultural wages were, in the early nineteenth century, 8s 6d per week compared with between 10s and 12s in other parts of the south. They remained lower than elsewhere until after 1834.[39]

Bristol, the birthplace of Tent Methodism, had excellent and growing port facilities which, in the late eighteenth century, attracted wealthy merchants to the area. They generated income which was invested in local industries, including coal fields and iron works in south Wales. By 1760 Bristol was the largest city in England apart from London, with a population that had continued to grow from 22,500 in 1700 to 45,000 in 1750, 61,000 in 1801 and 85,000 in 1821. However, in the early nineteenth century the pace of growth became slower than, for example, Liverpool and Manchester.[40] This is not to say that there was a stable, relatively content society. Civil authority in Bristol was challenged many times before the well-publicized events of October 1831 when the Bishop's Palace was burned during riots which followed the defeat of a proposed Reform Bill. In the eighteenth century, disturbances took place in 1749 when tollgates leading to the city were destroyed, in 1753 to obtain the release of a local man who had been arrested, in 1777 and in 1793 when four or five thousand people took part in riots that led to over forty people being killed or injured. Violent objections against the shortage and price of food occurred in 1795. In the early nineteenth

---

37   W. Graham, *The Twisted Sword* (London: Guild Publishing, 1991), p.42.
38   Trevelyan, *British History in the Nineteenth Century and After*, pp.149, 152 and 188, and Royle, *Modern Britain*, p.175.
39   E.J. Evans, *The Forging of the Modern State* (London: Longman, 1983), p.139.
40   Mathias, *First Industrial Nation*, pp.96, 85 and 417.

century the principal focus of unrest by Bristol's citizens was to oppose the growing number of Irish settlers in the city.[41] In the early 1800s, Kingswood, close to Bristol, was described as comprising 'rough cottages, prolific of a rough population'.[42]

The Manchester area of the north west of England exhibited a similar complexity of experience. Parts of the region generated additional employment from the earliest times of the Industrial Revolution, as the Lancashire cotton textile towns were, collectively, the birthplace of industrial capitalism. However, later technological advances led to the decline, for example, in the need for handloom weavers.[43] By 1812 food prices had doubled over the previous twenty years but, over the same period, wages of handloom weavers had fallen to only a quarter of the earlier level. Factory conditions were highly unsatisfactory and in this region much pressure took place for improvements in the working environment and for an expanded suffrage. It was in August 1819 at St Peter's Fields, Manchester, that approximately 60,000 people took part in a vast public meeting that resulted in injuries to 400 and the death of eleven in an event that became known as the 'Peterloo Massacre'. Two years later the Tent Methodists began a much praised evangelical campaign in one of the fast growing parts of the city. There was not, though, a simple division between the social classes, as those agitating for and others against fundamental social and political change often came from the same groupings. The skilled craft employees, for example, held different views from other working class people to calls for action to expand the electoral franchise. Furthermore, the new breed of entrepreneurs included plenty who opposed any increase in the number entitled to vote. Some saw 'the needs of the poor as a threat to their own prosperity'.[44]

Social conditions in London in the early nineteenth century epitomized the need to avoid over simplification of the subject, and the importance of recognizing that these conditions were constantly changing over time and among different groups of people. There was a general feature of high unemployment until the early 1820's as those who had been formerly engaged in the wars with France returned, especially to London, to seek civilian jobs. However, small numbers of

---

41   S. Poole, 'To be a Bristolian: Civic Identity and the Social Order, 1750-1850', in Dresser (ed.), *Making of Modern Bristol*, ch. 4, pp.76-95, gives a fascinating insight into the causes of the civil disorder.

42   W. Arthur, *The Successful Merchant* (London, 1878), p.1.

43   Royle, *Modern Britain*, p.163, and Evans, *Forging of the Modern State*, p.112, both detail the complexities involved with the textile industries, notably cotton.

44   Deborah Valenze, 'Charity, Custom and Humanity: Changing Attitudes towards the poor in Eighteenth-Century England', in Jane Garnett and Matthew Colin (eds), *Revival and Religion since 1700* (London: Hambleton Press, 1993), p.7.

highly skilled craftsmen were well off, both compared with similarly skilled workers elsewhere in the country and labourers in London. The complexity was increased by the presence and continuing influx of immigrants, often refugees from mainland European countries, into selected areas of the capital. Alongside great wealth, one writer of the period noted an 'anonymity, casual contact and lack of social intercourse...a mass of destitute poor, unskilled labourers, casual workers of all sorts...suffering from under nourishment, bad housing, overcrowding, dirt, bad drainage, bad water, adulteration of food and drink, disease'. Furthermore, 'Observers noted the vagrant children, hideous exploitation of juvenile labour, insecurity of life',[45] together with drunkenness, violent crime and other ills. Against that background, Tent Methodist preachers were, from late 1820, to attempt to address the spiritual, if not the material, needs in a small area of east London immediately adjoining the city boundary.

Bristol, Manchester and London were then, like most if not all British cities, places of contrasting wealth and poverty, harmony and discord. Some people had valuable skills, while others had little to no education or training in order to provide self-respect. Some had high expectations for themselves and their families, others had only small hopes of making any meaningful progress in their earthly life.

Institutional Religious Background

If there were significant social, economic and political background issues in the country at the end of the eighteenth and beginning of the nineteenth centuries, the same was true of the religious life of the nation.

It has always been an over-simplification to suggest that the Established Church had a virtual monopoly of religious influence in the mid-eighteenth century. That it 'was more secure than at any time in the preceding century and a half'[46] is, however, accurate enough. The Roman Catholics were small in number and subject to many onerous restrictions, and the various nonconformist Protestant groups were of lesser influence than at the end of the seventeenth century. But, despite a whole range of adverse factors that inhibited their ability to conduct their activities free of hindrance, dissenting groups, congregations and individuals were able to act as spiritual mentors to a significant number of people. One of the most notable of these, until his death in 1748, was Dr Isaac Watts, best known now as a hymn writer, who became concerned

---

45   I.J. Prothero, *Artisans and Politics in Early Nineteenth-Century London* (London: W.M. Dawson, 1979), p.25.

46   William Gibson, *Church, State and Society, 1760-1850* (London: Macmillan Press, 1994), p.4.

'that religion had "decayed" not only among the dissenters, but in the age as a whole.'[47] After the greater persecution during the forty years or so from the Act of Uniformity of 1662 which led to formation of dissenting groups consequent upon the eviction or resignation of almost 2,000 of the more dedicated clergy from Church of England livings, universities and schools,[48] the more tolerant environment that followed created a drift back to the Established Church and a reduced passion for nonconformity. Another leading Independent of the mid-eighteenth century, Philip Doddridge, frequently raised the subject in his writings, including *Free Thoughts on the Most Probable Means of Reviving the Dissenting Interest.*[49] There were, then, some leading nonconformists who not only recognized the decline of 'Old Dissent', but were also considering how best to address the deteriorating interest.

There is plenty to suggest that the Established Church suffered a decline in many aspects of church life from 1700 onwards. Whether or not that decline constituted a 'disaster', as A.D. Gilbert has claimed, is questionable, but the information available is interesting, if not compelling, despite a recognition that the statistical data needs to be treated with care. Gilbert referred to 'an obvious failure of the Established Church to meet the religious needs of the whole society.'[50] The justification for holding that view reflected such things as the lack of numerical growth in human resources to serve a greatly increased population, growing pluralism and absenteeism, insufficient numbers of clergy with a genuine care for the people, and an inability to cater for the needs of the expanding industrial and urban areas. Alec Vidler records that the Church of England at the end of the eighteenth century 'was not asleep, but it was only slowly and in parts rousing itself into activity'.[51] Edward Royle, writing from a social rather than a religious perspective, described what he calls 'the crisis of the established churches'. While detailing many late eighteenth and early nineteenth century weaknesses, he believes the 'story...is not one of entire gloom'. He identifies a greater degree of tolerance than in the previous 100 years, the culture and

---

47   A.P. Davis, *Isaac Watts* (London: Independent Press, 1948), p.142.

48   Horton Davies, *The English Free Churches* (London: Oxford University Press, 1963), see pp.93-96 for a detailed description of the events.

49   Davis, *Isaac Watts*, p.63, for an outline of the relationship between Watts and Doddridge. In addition, see D.W. Bebbington, *Evangelicalism in Modern Britain* (London: Routledge, 1989), p.21, for a general comment regarding the poor state of Dissent.

50   A.D. Gilbert, *Religion and Society in Industrial England: Church, Chapel and Social Change 1740-1914* (London: Longman, 1976), p.3. Royle's *Modern Britain* paints a rather less pessimistic picture of the Established Church's position, pp.284-87.

51   Alec R. Vidler, *The Church in an Age of Revolution* (Harmondsworth: Penguin, 1961), p.40.

learning of some establishment clergy, the poverty of many clergy which 'helped them identify with their parishioners', and a higher level of spirituality than is sometimes recognized. Nonetheless, he claims there was a weakening towards the end of the eighteenth century as growing elitism among clergymen generally occurred at the same time as many of their parishioners were suffering from increasing poverty—the 'social gulf...was getting wider'.[52]

There were, of course, individual establishment clergy who showed immense concern for the problems affecting the poor of the early nineteenth century. Local vicars, such as Arthur Wade when Vicar of Warwick, and members of the church hierarchy, including Charles Blomfield who became successively Bishop of Chester and London, and John Sumner, who succeeded Blomfield as Bishop of Chester and eventually became Archbishop of Canterbury, all made strenuous efforts to ease the social distress of working-class folk. They did so in different ways while holding diverse views about how that pain should be eased.[53]

Bristol Nonconformity

Bristol had played a major role in the development of many dissenting Christian groups, including the Methodists. Long before the origins of Methodism, however, the Quakers had become established in Bristol over eighty years before Wesley first visited the city. In September 1653, John Audland and John Camm, two of the four originators of the sect in Bristol, preached there. Two years later, James Nayler, the former leader of the London Quakers, had made such an entry riding a donkey that the inhabitants were shocked,[54] and George Fox himself made his first visit in 1656. Andrew Gifford was granted a licence to preach as a Baptist in 1672 and he did so with great distinction until his death in 1721. The Pithay chapel was built for Baptist worship in the second half of the seventeenth century, but their affairs suffered periodically until Thomas Roberts became minister. He had such success that within a few years of

---

52   Royle, *Modern Britain*, pp.284-87.
53   Gibson, *Church, State and Society*, p.53, regarding Wade, and p.100 regarding Blomfield. *Prelates and People* by R.A. Soloway (London: Routledge and Kegan Paul, 1969), provides a full account of the Established Church's response to social problems of the period.
54   J.F. Nicholls, and John Taylor, *Bristol Past and Present: Volume 2. Ecclesiastical History* (Bristol, 1881), p.285, and T. Dowley (ed.), *The History of Christianity* (Oxford: Lion, 1980), p.482. See also Ronald Matthews, *English Messiahs* (London: Methuen, 1976), pp.3-42, and Christopher Hill, *The World Turned Upside Down* (London: Temple Smith, 1972), pp.200-202, for further information about the significance of this event.

his appointment 'a capacious Chapel'[55] in Old King Street was built in 1815 and 1816 to replace the Pithay chapel. The Baptist chapel in Broadmead had an outstanding minister in the Rev. Dr John Ryland, beginning in the final decade of the eighteenth century and continuing until his death in 1825. The Independents, who progressively became known as Congregationalists, had some diligent and successful ministers in the early nineteenth century. The Rev. Samuel Lowell at Bridge Street Chapel was one and the Rev. William Thorp who exercised a 'surpassing ministry at Castle Green' from 1806 to 1833[56] was another. Bridge Street Chapel was Presbyterian in 1799 when Lowell was appointed, but it became Congregational during the course of his ministry.[57] Bristol became a centre of Unitarian activity quite soon after the denomination's formal establishment in 1773. Particular importance was attached to instigating the provision of education for poor adults as well as children. The second 'Mechanics' Institute' in Britain was established in Bristol in 1814, and Mary Carpenter, the daughter of Lant Carpenter, the influential minister of Lewin's Mead Meeting between 1817 and 1839, 'devoted her life to the care of poor children in Bristol'[58] until her death in 1877. She has been described as being perhaps 'one of the greatest women of the nineteenth century' having 'boundless enthusiasm, coupled with remarkable powers of organisation'.[59] By the end of the eighteenth century, then, many nonconformist groups had become well established in Bristol and had leaders of distinction.

Nonconformity in Bristol expanded rapidly in the early nineteenth century as, according to one writer, when the century opened, 'the Chapels of Free Churchmen in Bristol might almost have been counted on the fingers of a man's hand'.[60] That claim, however, conflicts with a more recent assessment which indicates a considerably greater presence of dissenters at that time with chapels and meeting houses numbering at least eleven.[61] In any event, by 1821 there were more dissenting places of public worship than the Church of England in Bristol, including five Independent and three Baptist chapels.

The Methodist presence in the Bristol area stemmed from 1739 when George Whitefield and John Wesley preached in March and April. Wesley

---

55   T.M. Williams, *A Short History of Old King Street Baptist Church, Bristol* (Bristol: n.p., 1955), p.12.

56   G.H. Wicks, *Free Church Life in Bristol* (Bristol: n.p., 1910), p.95.

57   Wicks, *Free Church Life in Bristol*, pp.99-101.

58   J. and R. Goring, *The Unitarians* (London: Pergamon Press, 1984), p.31.

59   Elizabeth Ralph, *People Matter*, 'Mary Carpenter', *St Stephen's Review*, Bristol, (December, 1961), pp.6 and 7.

60   Wicks, *Free Church Life in Bristol*, p.142.

61   Madge Dresser, 'Sisters and Brethren: Power, Propriety and Gender among the Bristol Moravians, 1746-1833', *Social History* 21.3 (October, 1996), pp.304-29.

first preached in Nicholas Street, Bristol, on 1 April and on the following day he 'proclaimed in the highways the glad tidings of salvation'[62] to about 3,000 people. The next Sunday he preached three times in the open air, on two occasions at different places in Kingswood. One of them, Hanham Mount, was close to where, eighty years later, one of the first Tent Methodist chapels was erected. In the same year, Wesley incurred the displeasure of Joseph Butler, the Bishop of Bristol, for his preaching activities which were conducted outside the scope of any formal preaching arrangements,[63] but occurred wherever he was persuaded to go. 'I look upon all the world as my parish' were words he included in a letter which he referred to in his *Journal* for June 1739,[64] and were used by many of his followers long afterwards to justify their own Christian missionary activities. There was evidence at the end of the century that Bristol Methodists had a degree of individuality that could cause difficulties for the national Wesleyan authorities. In 1792 an itinerant preacher, Henry Moore, who was later to become President of Conference, administered communion in a chapel several years before the practice became acceptable to Wesleyan Methodists in general. That decision provoked a dispute relating to the respective authority of preachers and trustees. As a result of his action, Moore was refused permission to occupy pulpits in two other local chapels where the trustees retained a belief that Methodism was still part of the Established Church and that, therefore, only episcopally ordained clergymen should administer the sacraments.[65] Two years later, a further dispute arose, this time concerned with who had the authority to appoint ministers. Perhaps it was incidents such as these that caused it to be said that there was 'sometimes friction with the local Methodist community, whose radical outlook and sympathies were often in conflict with the Tory allegiance of the Wesleyan Conference and of the [Kingswood] School'.[66]

By the early nineteenth century Bristol's Methodist communities were at last benefiting from a period of relative calm after the disputes concerning authority in local churches that had arisen in the years

---

62   P.L. Parker (ed.), *The Heart of Wesley's Journal* (New York: Kregel, 1989), p.47.

63   R.E. Davies, *Methodism*, p.65, for a description of the serious disagreement. See also J.F. Butler, 'John Wesley's Defence before Bishop Butler',*WHS Proceedings* 20 (1940), pp.63-66, for another account of this encounter.

64   Wesley's *Journal* entry for 11 June 1739, following a visit to Bath. The letter had been written to a James Hervey, who was described as a pupil of John Wesley. See Nehemiah Curnock (ed.), *The Journal of the Rev John Wesley* (Standard Edition, 2; London: Epworth Press, 1911), pp.216-18, for the full letter.

65   Davies *et al* (eds), *History of the Methodist Church in Great Britain*, II, p.280.

66   A.G. Ives, *Kingswood School in Wesley's Day and Since* (London: Epworth Press, 1970), p.139.

immediately after John Wesley's death. The societies were, of course, very long established by then. In addition to frequent visits by John Wesley until his death, Charles Wesley's home was in Bristol from 1749 until he moved to London in 1771, many annual conferences were held there including important ones in 1745, 1756 and 1786, and John Wesley's school at Kingswood was well known. The latter half of the eighteenth century was not, though, a period of consistent growth and success. Wesley's *Journal* records his concern that several rules of Kingswood School were being 'habitually neglected' in 1749,[67] notes a fire at the school in 1757[68] and his 'Remarks on the State of Kingswood School' in 1783 included complaints about pupils' behaviour and the staff's lack of ability and supervision. In 1748 the Bristol society's membership was reduced from 900 to 730 and there had also been a review of the roll at Kingswood. By 1754, however, Wesley was pleased to report that congregations were 'exceedingly large', with Kingswood membership at nearly 300. From 1801 to 1814 there had been a time of almost unbroken increase in the Bristol circuit membership numbers from 1,450 to 2,040 immediately before a tent was first seen supporting evangelical Wesleyan activity.

---

67   Wesley's *Journal* entry for 25 July 1749 indicates that some of the offenders were expelled for the offences.

68   Wesley's *Journal* entry for 25 October 1757 reports that the roof of a school house was damaged.

CHAPTER 2

Tent Evangelical Activity from 1814 to 1819

This chapter contains profiles of the principal tent preachers, notably George Pocock and John Pyer, and describes and analyses chronologically the progress made up to 1819 in parts of southern England. During this time the evangelical work was regarded as supplementary to regular Wesleyan preaching plan commitments. Reference is made to the opposition that was apparent from time to time and which became more pronounced in late 1818 and throughout 1819. The extensive use of tents is shown to be a vital factor in the widespread missionary activity that was undertaken, normally from Easter to October each year.

The Use of Tents

A tent was first used for preaching by Bristol Methodists on Sunday 24 April 1814. It was constructed as a result of 'two warm hearted local preachers'[1] having difficulty in finding suitable places for preaching in villages just outside Bristol. Although it cannot be definitely established who the second of these two was, it is likely that it was John Pyer who, with George Pocock, became the principal actors of Tent Methodism. The example of Jesus and his disciples motivated these preachers as 'they reflected on the blessed examples of Christ and his Apostles, who went forth and preached everywhere'.[2] They would also have been well aware of John Wesley's and George Whitefield's open air ministries. That a need existed for such an expansion of evangelical effort was suggested by the content of a letter from Bristol in the very year that tent preaching began. People in Bristol, it was claimed, were 'of a dull heavy cast' and in the neighbouring countryside they were 'ignorant, and stupid in a high

---

1   K.P. Russell, *Memoirs of Rev John Pyer* (London, 1865), p.37.
2   *TM Magazine*, p.31.

degree, and seem to have very little religion'.[3] Whether these Bristol preachers would have known of the first English camp meetings at which tents were used to provide shelter in the event of bad weather, and which began in 1807 at Mow Cop on the Cheshire-Staffordshire border organized by those who later formed the Primitive Methodists, is uncertain. There is no evidence that they did,[4] but the expulsion of Hugh Bourne and William Clowes in 1808 and 1810 respectively, and the reasons for them, may have been brought to the attention of Wesleyans in Bristol. Indeed, references to camp meetings appeared regularly in the monthly editions of the *Methodist Magazine*, and the 1807 Methodist Conference minutes included a resolution expressing total opposition to these outdoor events.

The first tent, the size of a marquee as it was initially large enough to accommodate approximately 500 people before being extended two years later to hold 700, was planned and built by George Pocock. It would have been constructed of sail cloth, and it consisted of six sides. There were two inner central wooden poles, with twelve smaller poles around the circumference to which ropes were attached for fixing to the ground. Construction was so arranged that some of the sides at least could be folded or rolled up to allow people outside the tent to be aware of what was going on inside. So as to give further ventilation, a hole was made in the top covered by an umbrella-type arrangement which would also prevent rain entering the tent.

That such a substantial structure was still sufficiently portable to be erected and then dismantled, on occasions, in an evening for transporting and erection elsewhere the next day, said much for the design of the tent, and the dedication of those who were involved in the transport arrangements.[5]

The use of a tent for Methodist services in the Bristol area could have been regarded as an excellent way of responding to a severe national financial difficulty at the time. While there had been periods of economic recession coupled with deflation during the latter years of the eighteenth century, the situation in many years after 1815 was particularly bad. The ending of the long period of conflict with France caused, among other things, reduced demand for some products, such as those made from

---

3   W.R. Ward, *Religion and Society in England 1790-1850* (London: B.T. Batsford, 1972), p.77, letter from John Barber to George Marsden, 22 October 1814.

4   By 1814 the Primitive Methodists were still confined to a relatively small area of Staffordshire and Cheshire. Indeed, H.B. Kendall wrote in *The History of the Primitive Methodist Church*, I, p.163, 'the first few years immediately succeeding 1811 were not marked by any considerable geographical expansion'.

5   A picture of a tent was included at the front of the 1823 edition of the *Tent Methodist Magazine* and is reproduced as the frontispiece of this book. A smaller picture appeared on the class tickets issued by Tent Methodists from 1820 onwards.

iron. This recessionary period coincided with times of poor grain harvests leading to sudden increases in imports and large balance of payments deficits, low wages, high unemployment, and high taxes to recoup the cost of the war effort. That these factors should combine at a time when Methodism had incurred substantial levels of debt to cover the cost of a large scale chapel building programme was particularly unfortunate. Deflation meant that these assets were worth less than when they were built, and the harsh economic circumstances created great difficulties for Methodists to fund the interest liability let alone find the cash to repay loans which had been raised. At the same time the ongoing commitment to pay more and more preachers, a greater proportion of whom were married and entitled, therefore, to larger remuneration, posed great financial burdens. W.R. Ward has described the position that Wesleyanism found itself in: 'What had been a running sore became suddenly a disease of fatal proportions'.[6] The use of tents was a sensible economic response to a serious financial problem which recurred regularly.

It cannot be assumed that George Pocock, in early 1814, understood the cash crisis that was about to become more obvious to Methodists and, as a useful way of alleviating the situation, came up with the idea of a tent to provide cheaper evangelism in places yet to be missioned. However, in 1810 and again in 1812 and 1813 the connexion's large financial debts were referred to in conference resolutions drawing attention to the need to achieve reductions. A letter in 1813 from Joseph Benson, a leading figure in Methodism who had been President of Conference in 1798 and 1810 and was editor of the *Methodist Magazine* since 1803, suggested that the chapel building programme should be restricted as servicing debt was becoming a major problem.[7] In preparation for the 1816 conference Jabez Bunting, then secretary, circulated a letter in which he called for 'prudent retrenchment of expenditure'.[8] In the same year, referring to the financial situation, he wrote to an itinerant preacher 'we are sadly deficient'.[9] The shortage of financial resources for chapel building was still apparent at the times of the 1819 and 1820 conferences. A General Chapel-Fund had been established in 1817 and in response to a question in 1819 regarding the fund's progress, the following answer was given: 'That it shall be considered as an imperative rule, that no chapel, built without the consent of the annual Chapel-Building Committee, if erected subsequently to the first appointment of that Committee in 1817, shall ever, on any account, receive assistance from the General Chapel-

---

6   Ward, *Religion and Society*, p.98.
7   Joseph Benson, letter to (Walter Griffith?), 20 July 1813.
8   Bunting, *Life of Jabez Bunting*, II, p.97.
9   Bunting, *Life of Jabez Bunting*, p.94.

Fund'.[10] In addition to providing a further, flexible tangible resource, tents could have obviated the need for chapels, temporarily at least, in places where demand for preaching services existed, but buildings did not.

George Pocock's Introduction to Methodism

George Pocock (see Appendix A (i)) who, with John Pyer, became the leading and longest serving Tent Methodist, was born at Hungerford in 1774, and was baptized in the local parish church on 29 May. He was the son of a Church of England clergyman, John Pocock, and Mrs Mary Pocock, although his father was not a vicar of Hungerford. His elder brother, also John, born in 1769, became the curate at Frome, Somerset, and they had two sisters, Jemima, who was baptized at Hungerford on 29 March 1772, and a younger one, Elizabeth. By 1796, George Pocock too was living in Frome, as were Elizabeth and his elder brother who had recently taken up the curacy. All four became the close friends of Edward Griffith, a local draper and grocer, who became a Methodist in 1792 at the age of thirty-two, and was subsequently appointed the Sunday School superintendent and a trustee of the chapel. Indeed, in September 1813 he was recorded as being the first named trustee.[11] He was principally known as an extremely active and well respected local preacher, and it was in this capacity that he met John Pocock. When the Pococks' sister, Elizabeth, became seriously ill, Griffith frequently visited her in the month before she died in March 1797, on occasions when George Pocock was present. In the same year, George Pocock first attended the Methodist chapel with Griffith, joined the Methodist society and began to accompany him, not only to class meetings but also on his pastoral and preaching rounds.

On 27 April 1797 George Pocock married Elizabeth Rose in St John's parish church, Frome, thus beginning a long marriage which appears to have been wholly happy.[12] During this period Pocock declined an invitation to follow his brother into the ministry of the Church of England. It is clear from a letter that John Pocock wrote to George in

---

10   *Minutes of Methodist Conference* (1819), p.54. Similar stringent conditions before financial help would be given also existed in 1820, and for several years thereafter.

11   Stephen Tuck, *Wesleyan Methodism in Frome* (London, 1837). This book contains many references to Griffith's valuable contribution to Methodism in Frome and its neighbourhood.

12   Entry No. 1125 in the Frome Parish Church marriage register. The ceremony was conducted by George's brother, and the witnesses were George's sister, Jemima, and a Joseph Rose, presumably a relative of the bride.

1803 that the family as a whole gained no meaningful spiritual Christian convictions under their father's guidance. Hungerford was considered to be an 'infatuated parish, where the name of Christ is seldom used, but for the purposes of blasphemy'.[13] There was, then, no encouragement to John or George from their parents or others in the place of their upbringing to devote themselves to an active Christian ministry.

In 1795, while curate of Frome, John Pocock became Master of the Free Grammar School which, under his guidance, attracted increased numbers of pupils. An extension to the accommodation for educational purposes was necessary and it is probable, though it cannot be confirmed, that George Pocock, at the age of twenty-one, assisted his older brother and so gained the initial teaching experience which he was to use for almost fifty years.[14] George Pocock, together with his wife and first born son, moved to Bristol in 1799 or 1800. After a short period as proprietor of a boarding school, which he may have attempted to run while still living in Frome, he acquired a more suitable property and a playground. Latimer's *Annals of Bristol*, a very substantial and detailed three volume work first published at the end of the nineteenth century, records that Pocock started a boarding school in September 1795, but that school was probably established by a Reverend Daniel Keith, from whom Pocock later acquired it.[15] He opened his own academy in premises previously used as a school for three years, and it became known as Prospect Place Academy. It was located in the St Michael's Hill district, close to the city centre. His previous premises had been considered inadequate, but the new buildings, acquired in 1800, were altogether more appropriate for the type of education Pocock offered. 'His system of education is calculated chiefly for the men of business, and includes penmanship, in all its hands, elocution, arithmetic, mensuration illustrated by globes, accompanied with a general view of the commercial world'.[16] From a study of the *Mathew's Bristol Directory* series, published annually, it is apparent that the St Michael's Hill area of Bristol contained several private schools in the early nineteenth century. Pocock's academy occupied a large and prominent position on Church Lane, just to the west of the southern end of St Michael's Hill itself, and almost opposite St Michael's Church. It was important enough to be marked specifically on Ashmead's 'Plan of the City of Bristol and its Suburbs', published in

---

13   *TM Magazine*, p.25; the same letter also expresses the hope that 'parts of the family, through some of us, be made partakers of at least the knowledge of the way of salvation'.

14   Derek J. Gill, *Frome Schooldays* (Frome: 1300 Publications, 1985), p.76.

15   Elizabeth Ralph, *People Matter*, 'George Pocock': *St Stephen's Review*; Bristol (September, 1962), pp.6-8.

16   *Felix Farley's Bristol Journal*, Saturday 27 September 1800.

1828.[17] Two biographies describe the academy as being 'very large and influential' and 'the most popular private boarding school in the city of Bristol'.[18] In a city well served by private schools, Prospect Place Academy was among the most successful.

The education provided was almost entirely for boys, although in the early years at least it appeared that he taught writing, arithmetic and geography to girls in an hour when his day boy pupils were absent. Full and part boarding, as well as day schooling, was available. Pocock's interest in education was to become a significant feature of Tent Methodism, and it provided a source of considerable wealth which enabled him to support Methodism financially, both before and after his departure from Wesleyanism in 1820.

Pocock's wife also became a member of the Methodist society at Frome soon after their marriage, and when the couple moved to Bristol they joined the membership of Portland Chapel, known as 'The Chapel on the Hill', located in a favoured residential district.[19] At least two of the Pocock's children were baptized in the chapel. Sarah, born on 3 September 1808, and Rachel, born on 30 May 1810, were both baptized on 24 May 1812 by Henry Moore.[20] By 1810 Pocock was clearly a leading local preacher as he hosted meetings early on Sunday mornings which were designed to provide mutual support and encouragement before they set about their preaching responsibilities for the day.[21] Until the relationship with the Methodist authorities turned sour from 1815 onwards, his part in furthering the Methodist cause as a local preacher, for example, was substantial and appreciated. Pocock himself claimed he 'was the primary cause under God of raising not less than ten entirely new societies, and eight new chapels'; providing much financial support for chapel building and many poor individuals; and 'being instrumental in adding several hundreds of members to the Methodist Societies'. He summarized his contribution by asserting that he had spent 'more than twenty years of the most indefatigable and almost unparalleled labour to promote the interest of immortal souls'.[22] These claims were made in 1820 during increasingly vitriolic written exchanges concerning the

---

17   G.C. Ashmead, *Plan of the City of Bristol and its Suburbs* (Bristol, 1828), commenced in 1813, completed in 1828.

18   Russell, *Memoirs of Rev John Pyer*, p.21, and A.G. Powell *et al, The Graces* (Bath: Cedric Chivers, 1974), p.14, and John Latimer, *Annals of Bristol: Volume 2. Eighteenth Century* (Bristol, 1887), p.517.

19   A.J. Lambert, *The Chapel on the Hill* (Bristol: St Stephen's Press, 1929), is a history of Portland Chapel which was dedicated for worship on 26 August 1792.

20   *Portland Chapel Register of Baptisms*. This register covers the period, albeit with some gaps, between 1792-1823.

21   Russell, *Memoirs of Rev John Pyer*, p.21.

22   George Pocock, *A Statement of Facts* (Bristol, 29 March 1820), pp.13-14.

activities of three local preachers who, with others, all withdrew or were expelled from Wesleyan societies in and around Bristol. Before those events, however, much Christian service was undertaken with the help of one tent, with a second used from 1818 onwards, in an increasingly wide geographical area of England and, occasionally, Wales.[23]

The local preachers who travelled with the tents did so in addition to fulfilling the duties allocated to them on the formal preaching plans. They remained, then, entirely within the Wesleyan societies and structure, attending meetings and holding class tickets as evidence of membership. Indeed there were times when senior preachers from the Bristol district demonstrated their support, if not outright enthusiasm, by agreeing to conduct services in a tent. In particular, Walter Griffith, who became superintendent of the Bristol circuit in September 1816 preached a sermon in the tent within two months of his arrival. He did so again at the opening service of the 1817 'season' on Good Friday, 4 April 1817. Already a senior figure in Methodism, having been President of Conference in 1813, Griffith arrived in Bristol after serving for two years as chairman of the Leeds district.

The annual Wesleyan conference of 1814 was held in Bristol and some of the itinerant preachers who were present at it accepted Pocock's invitation to assist in the conduct of worship. The very first services in the tent on 24 April 1814 were held close to what was then the village of Whitchurch, three miles south of the centre of Bristol. In addition to Pocock, John Pyer and James Roberts, who both became regular preachers in the tents, officiated together with other unnamed Wesleyan local preachers. From the start of the tent operations, the intention was to reach 'the wandering, and to save the lost' who suffered 'the perishing condition of the multitudes who were still living without the fear of God'.[24] These people, it was thought, would be reluctant to enter a chapel or meeting house even if such places were available. Despite a fear that the tent's presence might encourage an unruly element to disrupt the proceedings, this did not occur and great satisfaction is recorded of the initial experience.

By the end of 1815, however, there were already signs of opposition to the activities of those who accompanied the tent to lead services and other meetings. These local preachers were not always permitted to take any part in services conducted by the travelling preachers. Converts to Methodism as a result of attending tent services were discouraged from continuing to have contact with tent preachers once they had explained their newly found faith at love feasts or on other occasions. Love feasts in

---

23   Only one visit to south Wales was known to have taken place before 1820, but a further visit took place later and a society was formed.

24   *TM Magazine*, p.31.

particular were times of social exchanges as well as fulfilling spiritual and sacramental functions. Members who attended were encouraged to testify to their personal spiritual experiences. Having described the blessings obtained at tent services, some of the Wesleyan leaders clearly saw dangers if their members maintained contact with the tent preachers. The reasons for these early attempts to discredit the efforts of Pocock, Pyer and others cannot be known with certainty. There might have been jealousy that large crowds were being attracted to services held in a tent capable of accommodating great numbers compared with the much smaller capacity of chapels or other meeting places. Despite the professed absence of any desire by the tent leaders to create any discord among Wesleyans, and a claim by them that many new members were added to the Bristol circuit membership by the end of 1815, it may have been felt in official circles that a split would occur. Certainly, the more flexible and less formalized arrangements, and the apparent lack of consultation with the authorities, were hardly likely to have endeared the tent preachers to the superintendents of the various local circuits.

In addition, the national Wesleyan leadership was anxious not to incur the displeasure of the state authorities at this stage of its post-Wesley development. There had been government threats to curtail any dissenting religious activity which might have been opposed by the Established Church, and by way of response, Methodist conferences were meticulous in reiterating the members' faithfulness to the civil government. This 'loyalist stance was maintained after Wesley's death and undoubtedly helped the Methodists to escape a renewed bout of persecution. Though they came under suspicion the Methodists made repeated and public professions of loyalty'.[25] The official and formal Methodist support was probably the telling factor in deterring the government from imposing harsher requirements on dissenting bodies in 1812. The prospect of restrictions, however, was one reason for the strongly expressed opposition to camp meetings and tent missions as these might have incurred state and Established Church hostility. That the tents were increasingly taken to areas where there were no Methodist meeting places, in locations further and further away from Bristol itself, might be accounted for by a desire to avoid confrontation. In addition, the preachers would have wished to respond positively to specific invitations made by local people who had become aware of their activities.

---

25   John Stevenson, *Popular Disturbances in England 1700-1832* (London: Longmans, 1992), p.41.

John Pyer's Wesleyan Activity

As well as George Pocock, John Pyer was the principal local preacher to accompany a tent in the early years. He was born in Bristol on 3 December 1790 and was, therefore, sixteen years younger than Pocock. Unlike Pocock who did not embrace Methodism until he was in his early twenties, Pyer was admitted to a local Bristol society on Christmas Day 1803 when he was just thirteen. He became a local preacher at the age of nineteen in September 1810, and a class leader and the Secretary to the Preachers' Meeting in 1815 when he would have been twenty-four.[26] Significantly, in the light of events that were to occur later in his life, William Thorp, an Independent minister in Bristol, acted as a mentor to Pyer by instructing him academically as well as becoming a firm friend.[27] At various times, the first occasion being in 1806, he had ambitions to become a missionary overseas, in the West Indies and Ceylon among other places. By 1816 he was on the preaching plans of two other nearby circuits in addition to Bristol itself. There were periods in his life, however, when both his spiritual and secular experiences caused concern, particularly in the years between 1809 and 1817 during which time he lived for short periods in Exeter, Truro, Oxford and London as well as Bristol. He confessed that 'some unpleasant circumstances occurred between me and Mr Harper's children' in 1809, the details of which are not available, and shortly afterwards 'my soul greatly departed from God'.[28] His preaching activities were suspended by the circuit steward in Truro for reasons that are, again, unknown, and in 1812 he was accused of 'saying some disrespectful things of the Preachers'.[29] Pyer, then, even by the time of his early twenties, had experienced contrasting emotions along his Methodist journey.

At the end of 1812 he returned to Bristol, and probably lived and worked for a short time with his brother, James, who owned a druggist business in Redcliffe Street. They were both of sufficient social status to be entitled to vote in Parliamentary elections, and both appear in the October *1812 Bristol Poll Book* as voting for the unsuccessful Whig candidate.[30] He became more acceptable to Methodist authorities for a time as evidenced by the appointments he took on in 1815. Pyer married Mary Smith on 17 June 1813, and they had four children, three

---

26 Russell, *Memoirs of Rev John Pyer*, p.6; before the age of eleven he 'obtained among my playmates the appellation of "Parson Pyer"'.

27 *Congregational Year Book* (1860), obituary of Rev John Pyer, pp.205-206.

28 Russell, *Memoirs of Rev John Pyer*, p.10.

29 Russell, *Memoirs of Rev John Pyer*, p.25.

30 *The Bristol Poll Book being a list of the Freeholders and Freemen who voted at General Election, for Members to Serve in Parliament for the City and County of Bristol* (October, 1812), St Mary's Redcliffe parish.

daughters and a son who was also called John. In early 1817, following the birth of his second daughter, Elizabeth, on 4 July 1816, his wife was ' seized with a distressing mental affliction'[31] and the family moved to Newbury for twenty months so that Mrs Pyer could be looked after by her parents. Her family, including an uncle, Christopher Smith, who was a Member of Parliament for St Albans, and Lord Mayor of London in 1819, seems to have objected to both the marriage and his Methodist activities. They were strong supporters of the Church of England and at one point Pyer himself considered 'Episcopal ordination and admission into the National Church'[32] as Pocock did in about 1797. Although Pyer considered 'his wife's recovery almost hopeless',[33] she in fact lived until 1862, three years after his own death. Their two younger daughters lived with her and their grandparents, while the eldest daughter attended a boarding school run by members of Pocock's family. Pyer eventually sold a business in Newbury, relinquished local preacher responsibilities in the Newbury and Hungerford circuits at the end of 1818, and prepared to become a full time home missionary, based in Bristol, appointed by the other tent leaders without the approval of the Wesleyan authorities. In a biography of her father, Kate Pyer Russell described Pyer's 'amazing energy and perseverance of his early life [which] gave brilliant promise for the future'[34] and claimed that he was 'essentially a man of action' and 'a model citizen'.[35] Pyer himself, however, admitted in 1812 that 'pride has been my besetting sin'.[36] Six years later, however, two supporters of the tent activities said in a letter to him, 'the Lord has peculiarly fitted you for this work, we think it our duty to assure you of our patronage'.[37] Subject to frequent bouts of ill-health, Pyer was a complex character full of energy, but capable of antagonizing, in his younger years, many people.

Evangelical Activity up to 1819

Before it was proposed that Pyer 'might wholly devote himself to the ministry',[38] the original tent, from the end of April 1814 until the onset of winter that year, was taken to various places in east Wiltshire and west

---

31 George Pocock *et al, Facts Without a Veil* (Bristol, 19 May 1820), p.7.
32 Russell, *Memoir of Rev John Pyer*, p.14.
33 Pocock *et al, Facts Without a Veil*, p.7.
34 Russell, *Memoir of Rev John Pyer*, p.13.
35 Russell, *Memoir of Rev John Pyer*, p.vi.
36 Russell, *Memoir of Rev John Pyer*, p.17.
37 Pocock *et al, Facts Without a Veil*, p.8, letter from John Irving and John Gosling dated 13 April 1819.
38 Pocock *et al, Facts Without a Veil*, p.7.

Berkshire as well as to towns and villages nearer to Bristol in Somerset and Gloucestershire. The journeys eastwards from Bristol could have been made relatively comfortably because of the existence of the main road to London which in 1784 was sufficiently improved to have carried the first mail coach in a much reduced travelling time of sixteen hours. Subsequently, improvements occurred in the principal road network as a result of the civil engineering achievements of such people as McAdam and Telford.[39] Although the responsibility for maintaining roads was not always properly carried out, the growing popularity of Bath as a centre for visitors ensured that road transport in the second decade of the nineteenth century between Bristol and London was far better than between most centres of population. It was probably not coincidental that in its first season of use, the tent was taken to Pocock's home town of Hungerford, situated on the Great West Road, and several nearby villages just to the south including Kintbury and Inkpen. It was, however, back in Bristol by the time of the annual conference which began on 25 July 1814. 'High approbation of the measure'[40] was shown, and large congregations were present to see the novel, large marquee-like structure being employed. The available records suggest that the first year was a time of success with large congregations collected in places, but also the appearance of some potential difficulties with the Methodist authorities and local people who did not share the tent preachers' missionary energy. Their success may provide some justification for Robert Currie's view that 'congregations were often dissatisfied with ministers' want of enthusiasm'.[41]

In 1815 the tent was used from May, a rather later starting date than in other years when Easter was normally the time when the missionary activities began. It may be that the delay was caused by the addition of a 'large new wing'[42] to the tent but other evidence suggests that this extension was made before the start of the 1816 season.[43] During the course of 1815, Edward Griffith of Frome, who had maintained and strengthened his friendship with the Pocock family over the previous twenty years or so, agreed to preach in the tent and travelled to Bristol on 5 October and met George Pocock and his family. Griffith spent five days in the company of the preachers and described his experience as 'one of the sweetest, and I hope most profitable visits and seasons of

---

39   Royle, *Modern Britain*. The section in ch. 1 'The Changing Environment', pp.8-10, gives a good account of road transport in the late eighteenth and early nineteenth centuries.

40   *TM Magazine*, p.32.

41   Currie, *Methodism Divided*, p.49.

42   Russell, *Memoir of Rev John Pyer*, p.42.

43   *TM Magazine*, p.34: 'in 1816...the Tent was enlarged and accommodation provided for 700 persons beneath its ample shelter'.

religious privileges I ever was indulged with in public'.[44] Given Griffith's extensive commitment to his Methodist activities in Frome, his concern and support for the tent preaching clearly showed his assessment of its importance. He had previously sought approval for the appointment of a full-time missionary to work in parts of Dorset, Wiltshire, Berkshire and Hampshire to help him in his evangelical activity. After Griffith's death, which occurred in 1816, an obituary included reference to a form of field preaching which he conducted, outside formal preaching plan arrangements, in May 1810. This open air preaching by Griffith may just have been the inspiration for Pocock to build his tent for evangelical work in early 1814. He was, therefore, in any event, likely to be greatly encouraging of any venture which provided greater opportunities for the conversion of non-believers.

The obituary to Griffith also contained the following passage: 'Being ready to every good word and work, he established Sunday Schools, gave his sanction and support to Bible and Missionary Societies, and had a principal hand in erecting several chapels. In his native town he preached more than two thousand sermons. He rode, almost every Sabbath Day, into the surrounding villages, and faithfully preached the Gospel of Christ to the poor; established prayer meetings in numerous places; introduced the gospel into many dark hamlets where it was unknown; and established a regular supply of preachers for them'.[45] In addition to all this work, he twice, in 1815 and again in 1816, supplemented the missionary evangelical work of Pocock, Pyer and others. Had Griffith lived to 1820, he might well have become a man of great stature within the Tent Methodist movement.

Griffith accompanied the tent to Chew Magna, Somerset, in September 1815 before an extended visit in October when he preached in the tent at Bedminster to 500 people—a service which lasted four hours. He also attended meetings at two Methodist chapels in Bristol, and then took part in more tent services on three consecutive days. Three separate services were held on the Sunday, at two of which nearly 1,000 people were present.[46]

At other times during the year, the tent was taken to Brislington, Troopers' Hill, Rose Green, Jeffrey's Hill and Bishport, all places close to Bristol. Rose Green was a particularly significant place as John Wesley had visited there very early in his preaching career on 8 April 1739 and again in May 1739. Signs of great spiritual encouragement were reported during the autumn at Bedminster. Large congregations were recorded, people who were previously sceptical of the work became supporters,

---

44   *TM Magazine*, p.100, letter dated 14 October 1815.
45   Tuck, *Wesleyan Methodism in Frome*, p.105.
46   *TM Magazine*, p.100.

plans were laid to extend the work to the other parts of Bristol, and, apparently, 'at the end of the December quarter, the Wesleyan society in the Bristol circuit received an addition of 220 members; and the income of the Bedminster division rose from 40s to upwards of £12'.[47] Evidence exists of spectacular growth in Sunday School numbers during this early period of tent activity in Bedminster. It was recorded in 1815 that 913 children had been admitted since 1812 and that it 'was by far the largest Methodist Sunday School in Bristol at this time'.[48] Whether tent preachers could take any of the credit for such expansion cannot be known. Four years later, however, in 1819, the vicar of Bedminster felt moved to preach what he called an 'Affectionate Expostulation' in which he complained that only 500 of the 7,979 parishioners 'ever show themselves in the courts of the Lord'. He was 'greatly shocked by a consideration of the fewness of those who attend the public worship of God'.[49] Whether he was referring to all Bedminster churches, or just to his parish church congregations, is unclear.

There appear to have been, in 1815, no excursions much beyond the Bristol area. Some of the Methodist leaders were beginning to show their displeasure at what they saw as unauthorized evangelism. Tent preachers had their activities at services curtailed when itinerant preachers were present. It appeared that verbal expressions of disagreement, if not outright hostility, were shown. The tent preachers, however, consistently claimed to be seeking to work within Wesleyanism 'and ever endeavoured to attach the people to Methodism, by avowing themselves its friends, and by directing those who were seriously impressed under their ministry, to unite with the Wesleyan Society'.[50] At this time there was clearly no intention to secede from Wesleyanism.

The momentum of progress seemed to accelerate from 1816 onwards, the first sign of which was that the tent had been enlarged, presumably by Pocock, over the winter months to accommodate 700 people. Even if, in normal circumstances, no one would be seated in it, and occasionally at least benches were provided for some in the congregation,[51] the size of the tent must have been the equivalent of thirty yards square; a substantial structure. It would have taken considerable skill and human effort to

---

47   *TM Magazine*, p.33.

48   Brian Jefferies, *This House in Bedminster* (Bristol: W.G. Williams, 1975), p.9.

49   Anon., *A Parochial Minister's Affectionate Expostulation, with those inhabitants of his parish who neglect the public worship of Almighty God* (Bristol, 1819).

50   *TM Magazine*, p.34.

51   *TM Magazine*, p.46, in a poem reporting a visit to Marlborough the following lines appear:
    The hardy lads were seated on the ground;
    Benches sufficient for the girls were found.

erect and dismantle the tent, let alone convey it significant distances along some roads that would not have been conducive to easy transportation. Perhaps that is why no particularly long journeys appear to have been undertaken in 1816, but frequent movements were made from just before Easter when the evangelical activity began on 7 April at Bishport, Somerset. On Easter Monday it was moved to Bedminster, a place visited early each year since tent preaching began in 1814, and was there again in 1817 and 1818. After only a day it was assembled at Jeffrey's Hill in Bristol.

Later that month, indicating the growing confidence of the preachers and acceptability to the populace at large, the tent was placed in a field occupied by Pocock where the public execution of a William Carter took place for forgery.[52] For several days before the event and on the two Sundays afterwards 'many thousands were preached to, every evening in the week, three times on the day of the execution, three times on each of the two following Sabbaths, and several other weekday evenings'.[53] There were, apparently, at least 15,000 people at a service on the Sunday evening after the execution. The vast crowds, or 'an immense concourse of spectators' as *Felix Farley's Bristol Journal* described a part of the event in three separate weekly editions, could be explained by the fact that the previous public execution in Bristol took place eleven years before in 1805. The killing took place on Friday, 26 April, but the sentence had been passed two weeks before when William Carter was found guilty of 'uttering a forged £1 Bank of England note'. Unsuccessful attempts were made to obtain a reprieve for him but Methodists, including a local preacher called Bundy, as well as Pocock, provided what comfort they could.[54] Bundy was a well respected local preacher, a feature of whose Christian service was frequent visits to prisons, and, according to his *Journal* '40,000 afflicted persons' until his death in 1818. A lengthy, detailed obituary of Bundy written by Thomas Wood, the Bristol circuit superintendent in 1820, described how he showed 'steady piety and genuine philanthropy—manifested itself especially in his unwearied attention to the prisoners in Newgate, and other gaols in various parts of the Kingdom'.[55]

---

52   Trevelyan, *British History in the Nineteenth Century and After*, p.31, draws attention to the fact that 'two hundred crimes were punishable by death'.

53   *TM Magazine*, p.34.

54   *Felix Farley's Bristol Journal*, Saturday 13 April, 20 April and 27 April 1816.

55   Thomas Wood, 'A Biographical Sketch of the life and character of the late Mr James Bundy', *Methodist Biography* 6 (1820), pp.590 and 609. A fuller biography of Bundy, written by a relative, the Rev. William R. Williams, *The Prisoner's Friend: The Life of Mr James Bundy* (London: Wesleyan Conference Office, 1880), pp.81-85, describes the event, but makes no reference to Pocock's involvement.

In early May the tent was moved to several places to the north of Bristol, almost all of them relatively accessible from the main road to Gloucester. Moving away from the centre of Bristol, Westbury-on-Trym, Tockington, Olveston, Thornbury, and Rudgeway were all villages visited at which 'large and attentive congregations were collected'[56] and existing societies revived. In addition, new societies were established at Compton Greenfield and Milbury Heath.

It was during this period of excursions that Edward Griffith was tragically killed in an accident involving Pocock's carriage. Griffith had, again, spent nearly a week in Bristol supporting the tent preachers and visiting the widow of the Rev. John Pocock, the former curate of Frome who died in 1804, who was living with relatives. The tent, or 'portable Tabernacle' as Griffith himself called it, was at Westbury-on-Trym for three days and then moved to Compton Greenfield for a further two. At both places Griffith had taken part in services and was returning to Bristol with Pocock and John Irving, another tent preacher. Suddenly, at the start of a steep down hill slope, the horse leading the carriage became uncontrollable. Griffith 'jumped out, and the back part of his head was brought with such violence against the ground, as to occasion a fracture of the skull'.[57] Immediate medical attention was provided but he died two hours later. His death was grievously felt by the tent leaders and his very many friends in Frome, 2,000 of whom attended the funeral service. 'Such was the affection of all denominations of Christians for him, that funeral sermons were preached by all the dissenting ministers of the town'.[58] Griffith had written a poem about the tent activities on the very morning of his death. The final four lines were:

> Pocock, PROCEED! and let the desert sing,
> And in thy Tent exalt thy God and King:
> Trophies of Grace will crown the zeal and love,
> And Heaven approving, bless thee from above.[59]

It is somewhat surprising that this significant event is not recorded in the commentary of the 1816 tent activities included in the *Tent Methodist Magazine* for 1823; perhaps reflecting the fact that Pyer was the principal author and editor of the magazine material and that Griffith was Pocock's close friend.

During the remainder of the year requests were received to take the tent to new places, but the travelling preachers became more open in their objections. William Martin, who in April had demonstrated his support by

---

56   *TM Magazine*, p.34.
57   Tuck, *Wesleyan Methodism in Frome*, p.102.
58   Tuck, *Wesleyan Methodism in Frome*, p.103.
59   *TM Magazine*, p.219.

preaching a sermon in the tent, later in the year told Pocock that if he were not a wealthy man he would already have been expelled. Given that Pocock was a trustee of the Westbury-on-Trym chapel that had been built in 1811 at a cost of £1,650,[60] and had just provided the total cost amounting to £353 of a modest new Methodist chapel at Pill,[61] a village on the south side of the river Avon between Bristol and the coast at Avonmouth, the Methodist authorities would probably have been embarrassed and reluctant to lose such a generous donor and energetic preacher. Pill was also noteworthy as being the place, about thirty years earlier, from which the first Methodist preachers left England for America. The insensitive and inappropriate comment by Martin probably reflected the fact that he had only just arrived in Bristol from Cornwall where he had served in various circuits during the eight years since his admittance as an itinerant preacher. He was subsequently transferred to Sheffield, Plymouth and London.

Because of their extensive tent preaching activities, Pocock and Pyer, at two meetings to decide preaching appointments, had requested fewer commitments on quarterly preaching plans. On both occasions, although the local preachers apparently agreed to the requests, publication of the plans revealed that they had been given more engagements than any other preacher in one quarter and a further increase still in the following quarter. This outcome led to more disputes as, although substitutes were found to occupy the pulpits when Pocock and Pyer were preaching in the tent, this arrangement did not satisfy the travelling preachers. All this occurred during the time that Pyer was secretary of the local preachers' meeting for the Bristol circuit. The evidence seems to suggest conflict, not so much between Pocock and Pyer on one hand and the fellow preachers on the other, but between the body of local preachers in the circuit and those people closer to the centre of Bristol Methodist affairs. Despite the clear antagonism that existed it could still be said of 1816 that the tent preachers 'closed this summer's campaign, with gratitude to the Lord of the great gospel harvest, for having blessed their feeble efforts, and with increasing satisfaction at the gracious results which they had been permitted to witness'.[62]

For the start of the 1817 season which began at Bedminster on Good Friday, 4 April, a larger tent still had been constructed, and Walter Griffith, superintendent of the Bristol circuit, and chairman of the Bristol district, preached the opening sermon. During the spring and early

---

60   Laura Hobbs, *A Story of Methodism in Westbury-on-Trym 1805-1989* (n.p.), n.p., records that the chapel was built in 1811 and that Pocock was a trustee by 1815.

61   S.C. Tidwell, *Pill Methodist Church 1757-1982* (Pill: S.C. Tidwell, 1982), p.8, shows that Pocock was the first named trustee in 1819; not surprisingly as he provided the whole of the finance to build the chapel.

62   *TM Magazine*, p.36.

summer, the tent was transported to a greater number of places around Bristol, particularly to new locations within ten miles or so to the north east of the city centre, such as Iron Acton, Rangeworthy, Wickwar and Kendleshire. On other occasions the tent was again taken eastwards, this time as far as Newbury, Berkshire, sixty five miles from Bristol, as well as to Hungerford which was previously visited in 1814. Despite the evangelizing of new places near Bristol, and the undertaking of journeys of considerable distances, Pocock and Pyer still had a substantial number of preaching plan commitments. A preaching plan that has survived for the period from March to June for, it is believed, 1817 shows that Pocock and Pyer each had as many commitments as any other local preacher, including some on weekday evenings, and once in the quarter at meeting houses in the Kingswood circuit.[63]

Other places that received a visit from a tent preacher for the first time were Marlborough, a town that was to become significant in Tent Methodist affairs, and Wanborough and Wroughton, both between Marlborough and Swindon to the north. Pocock's visits to Swindon and Wanborough were, apparently, unplanned and 'at both places he met with ribaldry, outrage and abuse'.[64] Some of the recollections recorded in the book from which that quotation is taken are inaccurate but Pocock, and the tent, clearly made an impact on some of the inhabitants who could, it seemed, recall particular events and sites where the tent was pitched. Hodson, a small hamlet just south of Swindon not referred to in the *Tent Methodist Magazine* account, was said to be the first location in the area that Pocock and the tent visited. A later history of Methodism in Swindon drew attention to Pocock's involvement in the conversion of a man who became a leading Wesleyan for many years. William Noad, a well known businessman, was attracted to a tent service and subsequently allowed his kitchen to be used for services after meeting Pocock.[65] While Swindon is now a prominent manufacturing and business centre, in the early nineteenth century it had a population of little more than 1,000. Indeed, by 1841, just before the town was chosen to become the site of the famous rail engineering works, there were only 2,500 inhabitants.[66] After

---

63   'Lord's Day Plan for the Bristol and Kingswood Circuits', covering thirteen Sundays from 9 March to 1 June 1817.

64   William Morris, *Swindon Fifty Years Ago (More or Less)* (Swindon, 1885), p.395.

65   E.R. Carter, *History of Bath Road Methodist Church, Swindon 1880-1980* (Swindon: E.R. Carter, 1981), p.2. Carter incorrectly refers to Pocock's father as Ebenezer. In fact, Ebenezer was a son who had a school at Bitton between Bristol and Bath.

66   Keith Bassett *et al*, 'Economic and Social Change in Swindon', in James Anderson *et al*, *Society and Social Science: A Reader* (Milton Keynes: Open University, 1994), p.214.

two years when the tent was not taken far from Bristol, 1817 was a year when more extensive journeys were undertaken into Wiltshire.

In June 1817, Pyer had, temporarily, to relinquish his evangelical work based on Bristol as he moved to Newbury because 'of a severe domestic affliction'[67] relating to his wife's health. However, three men in particular, each of whom would have a significant role to play after the Tent Methodist sect was formalized in 1820, accepted additional responsibilities: Samuel Smith, Peter Arrivé and Henry Roberts. Throughout the season until November successful meetings and services took place. It was estimated that 90,000 people had heard the tent preachers in an eight month period of 1817. There appeared to have been no serious conflict with the itinerant preachers, helped perhaps by the manifestation of tacit approval at least from the leading local Methodist, Walter Griffith, in early April.

If 1816 had marked an acceleration in the group's impact, a further quantum leap forward took place in 1818. The middle of April, as in previous years, marked the beginning of the evangelical work which was concentrated upon areas around Bristol, mostly to the north of the city at Milbury Heath, Almonsbury, Olveston and Rangeworthy among other places, but also, yet again, in Bedminster to the south. This activity lasted two months. During that time it would appear that the tent was never away from the Bristol area for more than a week, but in June 1818 a much more ambitious excursion lasting a month was planned and implemented, starting on Friday 12th. The tent had been erected in a field at Marlborough during the morning of the following day. In fact, it is likely that the precise location was a field registered with the authorities to comply with the terms of the 1689 Toleration Act. The records show the registration, on 12 June 1818, of a 'field or close...containing by estimation three acres',[68] owned by John Gosling, at Preshute, a village just outside Marlborough. John Gosling was another man of stature who gave much time, effort and financial help to the movement for several years. He was a banker by profession, being one of three partners of a business based in Marlborough, and had only recently left the membership of the Church of England following a disagreement with his local vicar. This may have been in connection with tithes relating to Gosling's ownership of land in the vicinity.[69] His first direct contact with tent preachers was probably when the tent was in Marlborough in 1817.

---

67   *TM Magazine*, p.53.

68   J.H. Chandler (ed.), *Wiltshire Dissenters' Meeting House Certificates and Registrations 1689-1852* (Gloucester: Alan Sutton, 1982), No. 888, p.86.

69   J.P. Barnett, *Memorials of the late Rev John Barnett of Blaby: 'Faithful unto Death'* (Leicester, 1878). This book provides a valuable further insight into Tent Methodism, particularly in the later years about which relatively little material appears to have survived.

He may well have already known Pocock through their mutual interest and involvement in education and he provided much support to Pyer in later years.

One of the fascinating aspects of the services near Marlborough on Sunday, 14 June 1818 is that one of the preachers, probably Pocock or Pyer, as they both wrote hymns and poems that were published during the following two decades, compiled a poem to mark the occasion. It ran to no less than 464 lines, was serialized in the 1823 *Tent Methodist Magazine* over a six month period, and entered into great detail of the event. The preaching party of three started the missionary tour leaving Bristol on the Friday evening, recording that

> ...Our gospel car ran lightly on the road,
> And soon we reach'd in peace that night's abode...[70]

That was at Bath on a very hot night that prevented the preachers from having much sleep. They arrived at Marlborough before mid-day on the Saturday by which time the tent had already been erected, obviously by others who had travelled separately from Bristol. Gosling and his wife are praised particularly for their work with children in the villages surrounding Marlborough, and for their hospitality from the time that Gosling had been converted. The poem records:

> Oh! may the Lord remember him for good!
> Who call'd him out of darkness into light;
> Who makes him bold to stand, and strong to fight.[71]

Henry Roberts preached the sermon at the morning service which was very well attended by 'peaceful, and cleanly drest'[72] people, including Sunday School children from a wide area, but also by a few who had been asked by others to report back on what they witnessed. These non-attending, but curious people

> Said in effect, 'Pray tell us what thou think'st,
> About this sect, so much declaim'd against?'

As the poem recalls,

---

70   *TM Magazine*, p.23. It is necessary to note that after the first monthly serialization, subsequent instalments incorrectly give 1817 as the year of this visit to Marlborough.

71   *TM Magazine*, p.24.

72   *TM Magazine*, p.46.

Not many rich were there, nor great, nor wise,
Such mighty ones, these feeble things despise.[73]

Following lunch, probably at the Gosling's home, Pocock preached at an
afternoon service, the same poem recalling that he used John Wesley's
own famous words, written in 1739, 'I look upon all the world as my
parish'. Testimonies were heard from recent converts by a large
congregation:

Vast was the multitude, immensely vast,
Who listened with attention to the last.[74]

Attention, it seemed, that had to be maintained until the end of the day
before the service finally finished.

In the following three weeks, the tent was moved to places in Berkshire,
including Lambourne, Wantage, Hungerford and Wycomb Heath, and
southwards to several villages in Hampshire, including Weyhill which
received a further visit later in the year. It is apparent that Pyer
accompanied the party throughout this month-long trip despite his move
to Newbury the previous year because of his wife's illness. The
Hampshire part of the excursion was breaking new ground, and in areas
that were not served by anything approaching a good network of roads.
In addition to Weyhill, Charlton, another village close to Andover,
received a visit as did Vernham, situated mid-way between Hungerford to
the north and Andover. The whole party then moved southwards from
Andover to Lower Wallop, Stockbridge, Winchester and Southampton,
before crossing to the Isle of Wight, where preaching took place at
Newport and Ryde. The progression south was, though, interrupted by a
trip to Kingsclere which is further east than any of the other Hampshire
places visited. Until the second quarter of the nineteenth century the only
substantial Methodist presence on the Isle of Wight was at Newport, partly
because of transport difficulties. For the tent to be erected at Ryde said
much for the determination and commitment of those who made up the
Tent mission. The journey was made by boat from Southampton to
Cowes, thence to Newport, followed by a landward trip eastwards along
the north of the island to Ryde. It was reported that the congregations
'were unusually large, particularly at Southampton, and in the Isle of
Wight; and among the poorer and middling classes'[75] and that initial
prejudices disappeared resulting in many conversions. A substantial work
on the geographic distribution of Christian groups in England claims that

---

73   *TM Magazine*, p.47.
74   *TM Magazine*, p.119.
75   *TM Magazine*, p.54.

'the religious life of the Island was at such a low ebb at the end of the eighteenth century that any new popular approach was assured of success'.[76] It might be expected, therefore, that the impact of the tent preachers' evangelical crusade would have been significant. If that was the case, the overall effect was not sufficient for it to receive a mention in a detailed account written about Isle of Wight Methodism. Furthermore, neither did membership figures increase significantly in the years immediately afterwards, being 300 in 1817, 310 in 1818, and 316 in 1819.[77] A local history of the Methodist Church in Ryde also fails to refer to any Tent Methodist evangelical activity, although Wesleyan chapels were built in 1805 and 1811.[78]

Before 1811 there were just two chapels on the island, but by 1826 'there were eleven Wesleyan chapels, three travelling and twenty-three local preachers, with 430 members'.[79] One of those who supported and accompanied the tent on the ambitious tour to the Isle of Wight was an experienced Wesleyan preacher who was well known in Hampshire. Alexander Weir was appointed to Northampton in 1805 but by 1814 he was at Warminster, and in 1818 he was attached to the Gosport circuit following two years as a preacher in Southampton. Although a supporter of the tent activities during that summer he remained loyal to the Wesleyan cause, ministering in the Andover circuit in 1820 and 1821 before being appointed to serve at Salisbury in 1822. He died in 1838.

The tent was returned to Bristol in mid-July and was deployed in villages in the neighbourhood for the following three months. Given the refusal in 1816 to Pocock's and Pyer's request for fewer commitments on preaching plans, it would be interesting to know what the reaction was to the absence on four Sundays of at least three of the local preachers. No report of any objections is found in the available documentation.

In October 1818 a request was received from a Mr H. Noyes, perhaps one of the 'men of opulence' referred to in the description of the year's events as being 'friends to the spread of the Redeemer's Kingdom',[80] to bring the tent to the Weyhill Fair. It is likely that Noyes had met Pocock and the other preachers earlier in the year when the tent was used at Weyhill, but the fair was an extremely important annual local event, having, it is believed, been in existence from the end of the fourteenth century until it ceased in 1957.[81] The request was complied with and the

76   John D. Gay, *The Geography of Religion in England* (London: Gerald Duckworth, 1971), pp.158-159.

77   J.B. Dyson, *Methodism in the Isle of Wight* (Ventnor, 1865), p.343.

78   Anon., *Ryde Methodist Church 1883-1983* (n.p., n.d.).

79   W.W. Pocock, *A Sketch of the History of Wesleyan Methodism in some of the Southern Counties of England* (London, 1885), p.26.

80   *TM Magazine*, p.54.

81   Richard Cavendish, *AA Road Book of Britain* (Basingstoke, 1995), p.598.

tent was used on a Sunday and several other evenings on a site close to the main fair activities. Noyes, who lived in Thruxton House, a few miles west of Weyhill, does not appear subsequently as a supporter of Tent Methodist affairs, although he had been with the group in Winchester during the summer. He was associated with the Wesleyan chapel at Andover for many years from 1819 and was appointed a trustee of the Wesleyan church building at Nether Wallop in the same year.[82] He intervened significantly in Tent Methodist affairs in 1825.

At the end of October the tent was, for two Sundays, again erected at Milbury Heath where it had begun the season. On 25 October the newly built chapel, established, it was claimed, as a result of the success of tent preaching which first occurred there in 1816, was dedicated in the presence of numbers too great to be accommodated in the combined space of the chapel and tent. Again, there is no report of any conflict regarding the involvement of tent preachers in the formal opening ceremony of what was a Wesleyan chapel.

The apparent absence of controversy would not, however, last for many more months. The tent continued in use in 1818 for longer than had been anticipated, and to a later date than in previous years, as another pressing invitation was made. This time the request was for the preachers to go to visit a farmer at May's Hill, in the Frampton and Coalpit Heath area, about six miles north east of Bristol and four miles south of the village of Milbury Heath where the tent had last been erected. The visit coincided with a fire in one of the local coal mines, which led to several people being killed and many more seriously injured. The fire was first reported in one of the local Bristol newspapers in the form of an extract from a letter written by a coal miner from Frampton. It was discovered on Friday, 13 November and continued for at least two weeks. The newspaper recorded that three people died and another twelve were wounded in 'the alarming conflagration'.[83] Much comfort was provided to those who had suffered in this major local tragedy which seemed to prompt many to consider conversion because 'numbers who formerly idled away the Sabbath, crowded to hear the word of the Lord; and upon the deeply serious, the awfully alarmed and overwhelming multitudes, God abundantly poured out his Holy Spirit'.[84] A lasting impression seems to have resulted from the disaster as two barns were made available in the locality for use during the winter while the weather was unsuitable for outdoor, or tent, activity. One of them, called Algar's Mill, was converted from a barn into a private home only recently, and accounted

82   John A. Vickers, 'Methodism and Society in Central Southern England 1740-1851' (PhD thesis, University of Southampton, 1987), p.277.

83   *Felix Farley's Bristol Journal*, Saturdays 21 November, 28 November and 5 December 1818.

84   *TM Magazine*, p.55.

for the fact that the Tent Methodists were locally known as 'Barn People'.[85] By 1818 the tent preachers' influence and activity had gone beyond the confines of public worship, and had extended to provide real Christian support in a local and socially distressing crisis that was important enough to be reported in three consecutive weekly issues of one of the Bristol newspapers, *Felix Farley's Bristol Journal*.

There was one other fundamental development during the year that had important repercussions in 1819 and 1820. During the summer of 1818 it was decided that the work had become so extensive, and the requests for the tent activities to expand still further into other parts of England were becoming so frequent, that the employment of a full-time missionary was essential. That the time had come to make this appointment was not surprising. Pocock had a large and successful boarding school in Bristol to run, Gosling was a partner in a banking business in Marlborough[86] and Pyer, who had the continuing domestic difficulty of his wife's health, had a business, probably engaged in the wholesaling and retailing of drugs, to control in Newbury.[87] The occupations of some others involved in Tent Methodist affairs at the time, such as Henry Roberts, are not known, but Samuel Smith and Peter Arrivé, both of whom feature significantly for several years, were a poulterer and a customs house official respectively. John Irving, another supporter in 1818, was 'a ship owner and a merchant of wealth',[88] but he did not continue his involvement into 1820, much to Pocock's great disappointment at that time. Pyer was approached and, after consulting friends, agreed to take on the appointment as missionary once he had sold his business and ensured that his wife would be properly cared for by her relatives. His salary was to be £100 per annum, considerably more than many dissenting preachers were receiving at the same time.[89] In 1823 a Wesleyan married itinerant was entitled to £70 per annum, including allowances, but his actual income was often very different. The

---

85   D.C. Hearle, 'The Growth of Methodism in the Frome Valley and South Gloucestershire', address to the WHS Bristol branch, *Bulletin* No. 63 (7 March 1992), p.14.

86   J. Pigot, *Commercial Directory of Cornwall, Devonshire, Dorsetshire, Somersetshire and Wiltshire* (London and Manchester, 1830), p.806. Gosling became a partner between 1819 and 1822, was still a partner in 1830, but his name did not form part of the partnership title in 1842.

87   Russell, *Memoirs of Rev John Pyer*, p.86. In 1810 he joined his brother, and then took over a 'wholesale and retail drug business' in Redcliffe Street, Bristol, in 1812.

88   E. Ralph Bates, 'Portland Chapel, Bristol', address to the WHS Bristol branch, *Bulletin* No. 38 (12 November 1983), p.4.

89   Watts, *Dissenters*, II, pp.238-57, shows that Primitive Methodist married male preachers received £37 per annum in this period until 1845, and Bible Christian married preachers only received £30 per annum in 1837. Salaries for Wesleyans varied greatly.

situation regarding Wesleyan ministerial pay was that 'the individual income of ministers remained subject to the vagaries of economic fluctuations, local circumstances, and lay people's whims'.[90] Indeed, even by 1831 itinerant married male Primitive Methodist preachers only received an annual stipend of £31.4s.[91]

1818 had been the most successful year since the inception of tent activity with large numbers hearing the preachers, the opening of at least one new chapel, the establishment of many classes in new locations, an important geographic extension of the work, and the decision to employ, for the first time, an employee wholly devoted to the work who was 'freed from worldly business'.[92] The appointment of a missionary did not have the specific blessing of the Wesleyan authorities, although no active discouragement is reported as having taken place. It is just possible that the hierarchy was not aware that this important development was being planned, although that was unlikely bearing in mind that Irving, one of the promoters, was already heavily involved in Wesleyan affairs, both in Bristol and as a member of national denominational committees. Furthermore, at about this time he was securing the approval of the authorities to employ another home missionary in the same locality.

By the start of 1819 the storm clouds were gathering for the leading protagonists while at the same time opportunities to expand still further the work were presenting themselves. The appointment of Pyer as the full-time missionary, without consultation with, let alone the concurrence of, the Methodist authorities was a provocative course of action. That the expansion of the work, resulting from the constant requests in 1818 to send the tent elsewhere, could not be handled with the existing resources was clear to all involved. It was a great tribute to the small body of preachers that their growing reputation had prompted these further invitations, which also indicated that the great need for evangelism was recognized by many local Methodists and, indeed, others engaged in Christian witness considerable distances from Bristol. Nevertheless, it is tempting to believe that Pyer's appointment was made deliberately to bring to a head the festering dispute with the itinerant preachers and the Bristol district hierarchy. It may have been a simple, naive step taken with relatively little thought for the consequences, but bearing in mind that many obstacles, some open, others more covertly, had been placed in the way of the tent mission in the first five years that is unlikely. However, while Pyer was ultimately considered unacceptable to Methodist

---

90   Kenneth D. Brown, 'An Unsettled Ministry? Some aspects of Nineteenth-Century British Nonconformity', *Church History* 56.2 (1987), p.218.

91   E. Dorothy Graham, 'Chosen by God: The Female Travelling Preachers of Early Primitive Methodism in England', in T.S.A. Macquiban (ed.), *Methodism in its Cultural Milieu* (Cambridge: Applied Theology Press, 1994), p.41.

92   *TM Magazine*, pp.55-56.

authorities, it was not just his full-time missionary activities that became the focus of the future hostility.

In the meantime, 1819 had begun encouragingly. A second tent had been acquired and Irving and Gosling made significant financial contributions towards its cost. Again the Easter period was chosen as the time to begin the new season and both tents were erected at Frampton, the scene of much successful evangelical work in the last few months of the previous year. Three services were held on Good Friday, Easter Day and Easter Monday with all the leading preachers present. Interestingly, Martin took part in the proceedings despite his disagreeable comment nearly three years earlier that Pocock would have been expelled if he were not such a wealthy man. This was a sign, and there were others, that previous objections to tent activity had been overcome. It was soon clear, however, that the travelling preachers retained their disquiet. They attempted to persuade Irving and Pocock to rescind the appointment of Pyer as missionary, claiming, understandably, that neither conference nor the Bristol district authorities would approve the activity, certainly without prior consideration. However, the preachers agreed that their members would visit Frampton on the occasion of a meeting to be held in both tents where a collection for the Wesleyan Missionary Society would be taken. All the itinerant preachers from the three local circuits, Bristol, Kingswood and Downend, attended and were apparently persuaded to change their collective mind because the results were successful, both spiritually and materially. That the opposition seemed to melt away so quickly is surprising, but harmony lasted some months evidenced by a preacher exchange. Pyer conducted services in the Downend chapel and William Horner, superintendent of the Downend circuit, preached three times on one Sunday in a tent. Horner was a very long standing itinerant preacher, having been admitted in 1770 and had served in several west country counties before becoming Downend's superintendent in 1817. So, although further progress was made in 1819, the early signs that a serious rift was imminent, were also apparent.

At about the same time the superintendent of the Dursley circuit, Richard Wintle, who began his itinerancy in Castle Donnington, Leicestershire, in 1799 and had just arrived after three years in the nearby town of Stroud, requested the presence of a tent for services as the chapel there was to undergo repairs lasting several months. The Dursley chapel had been built in 1802 for a society that was formed in 1799 following the establishment of small Wesleyan groups in nearby communities during the preceding few years. That the building needed extensive repairs relatively soon after it was erected that would render it unusable for a lengthy period, might be thought surprising. It is known, however, that there was a significant level of debt outstanding and this could have made it difficult for ongoing maintenance to be afforded. In fact the chapel subsequently became unsafe and had to be demolished and completely rebuilt in 1863 and 1864.[93] One tent was erected in May 1819 and thus began Tent Methodist work which was to last ten years in various forms. Large congregations assembled, not only in Dursley, but also in the neighbouring villages of North Nibley, Wotton-under-Edge, Cam, Coaley, Uley and Eastington. Four hundred and fifty new members were reported to have joined the society. Membership figures for the Dursley circuit in the years 1818 to 1822 were recorded as 320, 345, 406, 471, and 510 after a period of several years with little numerical change.[94] These figures give some validity to the claims of much evangelical success, bearing in mind that national Methodist membership fell between 1819 and 1820.

During the course of 1819 another man who became an energetic contributor to Tent Methodist affairs, latterly in Dursley and elsewhere, preached his first sermon. John Barnett, who strangely is not mentioned at all by name in the *Tent Methodist Magazine* record of events up to early 1821, first met Pocock in 1817. Barnett had become the manager of a farm owned by Gosling at Ogbourne St George, four miles north of Marlborough and close to Barnett's own home at Mildenhall. Gosling had registered the premises for worship in April 1817[95] and Barnett had become a prayer leader and an occasional preacher. His occupancy of Gosling's farm did not last long, however, as 'we quarrelled, and before the summer [of 1818] was over we parted'.[96] Gosling and Pocock discussed the circumstances and Pocock arranged for Barnett to move to Bristol to help in a number of ways. He lived in the Pocock family home for the next four years, assisted part-time in the Prospect Place Academy, and supervised the transport of the tents—an increasingly complex task.[97] He also undertook much more menial tasks, 'sometimes cleaning knives and shoes, sometimes working in the garden, sometimes brewing beer, sometimes catering in the market for the family' and described Mrs Pocock as 'the best tempered woman in the world'.[98] Significantly, his debut sermon was preached at Whitchurch, the place of the first tent service five years before. Barnett was not to be the only man that Pocock

---

93   *Gloucester Journal* Saturday 4 June 1864. The article deals specifically with the opening of the new chapel, and refers to the previous local history of Wesleyanism, including societies and the earlier chapel buildings.

94   *Minutes of Methodist Conferences* (1816-1823). Membership numbers then fell slightly until rising again in 1826 and 1827.

95   Chandler (ed.), *Wiltshire Dissenters' Meeting House Certificates and Registrations*, No. 856, p.83.

96   Barnett, *Memorials*, p.12.

97   *Baptist Handbook* (1878), pp.330-34, 'Memoirs of Ministers: Obituary of Rev John Barnett' by J.P. Barnett (his son).

98   Barnett, *Memorials*, p.13.

took under his wing and developed into an influential Tent Methodist, before losing them to other nonconformist denominations where they undertook much valuable work for many years.

After a further period at Frampton, a tent was taken out of England for the first time, being transported, at Irving's request, to Swansea, Neath and the Mumbles where it was used for three weeks. Although Pyer's father was Welsh, it is not known what the motivation was to visit this area which must have been exceedingly difficult to reach, complete with a tent capable of accommodating 700 people. The preachers would have passed through Olveston, a frequently visited place of evangelical activity, as it was 'on the highway to the Old Passage. This and its new neighbour New Passage were regularly used by Charles and John Wesley to cross the Severn into Wales'.[99] Hospitality was provided at Neath, and in addition to large congregations in the tent, Pyer preached three times in the Wesleyan chapel at Swansea on 27 June, at the end of the excursion. During the course of that trip the party met 'an excellent Quaker, Elijah Waring'[100] who asked to be sent a history of the tents when published. If this publication ever appeared, no copy seems to have survived.[101] The encounter with Waring was an example, and many more were to follow, of the support of and co-operation with, individuals of other denominations. This was in marked contrast to the souring of relationships with some Wesleyans that was soon to begin in earnest. Waring, born in 1787 and married two years before this first recorded meeting with Pyer, became a leading Quaker in South Wales but indicated a decision to resign in December 1824. He was persuaded to retain his Quaker membership for a short period longer after a delegation of three other Quakers visited him, but he later became a Wesleyan. While it has been recorded that he became a Wesleyan minister,[102] his name does not appear in any of the Hill's *Arrangements*, and a further dictionary reference merely says 'he joined the Wesleyan body'.[103] That Waring became a valuable member of the Wesleyans, nationally as well as in south Wales, can be judged by the fact that he became a lay 'country' member of the denomination's 'Committee for guarding our Privileges' in 1829, retaining this membership up to 1834.[104]

---

99   Christopher Jordan, *Olveston Methodist Church* Bristol: C. Jordan, 1979), n.p..

100   Russell, *Memoirs of Rev John Pyer*, p.59.

101   A reference to this publication appears in Russell's *Memoirs of Rev John Pyer*, p.36, including a record of an incident in the town of Hungerford.

102   T. Mardy Rees, *A History of the Quakers in Wales* (Carmarthen: W. Spurrell, 1925), pp.100 and 241.

103   *Dictionary of Welsh Biography down to 1940* (London: Hon Society of Cymmrodorion, 1959), p.1013.

104   *Minutes of Methodist Conferences* (1829-1834).

When Pyer returned to Bristol, two letters were waiting for him detailing the evangelical revival taking place in the Dursley circuit area, and requesting a further visit with a tent. This began on 8 July and lasted for several weeks. This time work was undertaken in a rather wider part of Gloucestershire, particularly to the west of Dursley reaching the Severn and, indeed, crossing it as Westbury-on-Severn was on the itinerary. Pyer was accompanied by several other preachers, namely Pocock, Samuel Smith, Henry Roberts and an Adam Nightingale, a man not previously recorded as a preacher, but who was the home missionary supported by Irving. 'Vast numbers...were brought out of darkness into marvellous light',[105] but for the first time mention is made of a shortage of human resources to realize the potential that was believed to exist.

At this point, however, there began another concerted attempt to remove Pyer from his appointment despite the indications that his work had been appreciated by at least two local superintendents. Pyer's character was called into question and reports of the evangelical revival at Dursley given at local services elsewhere made no mention of the tent mission's involvement. Pocock attempted to have the tent activity discussed at the annual conference, as he had also done in 1814, but apart from one or two expressions of interest he was unsuccessful in having the whole exercise provided with an official seal of approval. The conference did, however, appoint a travelling preacher, William Jones, to exercise a ministry between Olveston and Frampton, villages five miles apart, in an area which had received much tent mission work in the previous three years. According to the 1819 conference minutes, Jones was appointed to 'Thornbury and its vicinity'[106] and to support the Downend preachers on occasions. The tent leaders were dissatisfied at the conference reaction but Jones did not immediately appear opposed to their work as he wrote to Pocock on 20 September inviting him to be present at Frampton when class tickets were to be issued. That event took place, harmoniously, and there was a short period of co-operation between Jones and Pyer and the other tent preachers.

While many Wesleyans demonstrated varying degrees of opposition over the five and a half years since the first tent service was held in April 1814, there were others who accepted the value of the work without ever offering full time support, or contemplating membership when formal Tent Methodism was founded in 1820. These people came from all levels of Wesleyanism, and included Walter Griffith, a senior figure in the hierarchy, Harry Noyes, a wealthy, influential layman of Thruxton House, and Alexander Weir, a dedicated and loyal itinerant preacher who served in many different circuits.

---

105 *TM Magazine*, p.80.
106 *Minutes of Methodist Conference* (1819), p.11.

From October 1819, however, increasing friction and hostility became apparent which led to long lasting animosity after the exchange of several pamphlets and the occurrence of many personal confrontations. The outcome was the departure of a significant number of men, not only Pocock, Pyer and Smith who featured in the verbal and written barrage, but also several others who had served Methodism with devotion for many years. For them, particularly, the nuances of the fundamental disagreements were of no interest. They found the opportunity to continue Christian witness and service in Tent Methodism as a separate sect. It will never be known how many were disillusioned by the uncharitable exchanges and ceased to have any further involvement in Methodist affairs. The events of the months from October 1819 to the middle of 1820 require a separate chapter.

CHAPTER 3

The Disputes that led to the Tent Preachers' Withdrawal from Wesleyan Methodism

This chapter describes and analyses the events that occurred between October 1819 and May 1820 when the relationships between the various parties became increasingly acrimonious, and there was a marked lack of mutual Christian charity. It was ironic that the bitter exchanges in early 1820 came in a year when the annual conference, concerned at receiving knowledge that Methodist membership had fallen for the first time since figures had been collated, passed a resolution which included the following: 'to avoid a narrow, bigoted, and sectarian spirit... Let us therefore maintain towards all denominations of Christians, who "hold the Head", the kind and catholic spirit of primitive Methodism'.[1] This resolution, among others, was to be read in May each year at district and circuit preachers' meetings. However, by the time George Pocock, John Pyer and Samuel Smith had severed their links, voluntarily or by compulsion, bitterness was unbounded. The situation with each of the three was unique, and their individual departures from Wesleyanism in Bristol came from rather different disputes, despite the timings being almost identical and the fact that it was tent preaching that gave the opportunity to quarrel. Three pamphlets dated between 29 March 1820 and 19 May 1820, that contained a total of ninety-eight pages of intricate detail, set out the two different versions of the arguments.

Samuel Smith and the Methodist New Connexion

The case of Samuel Smith was relatively straightforward, whilst containing some particularly interesting aspects. It was common ground between both sides in the argument that Smith was approached to give advice to a woman called Ann Prestage who had been invited to become a class leader for the 'Kilhamites', formally known as the Methodist New

---

1   *Minutes of Methodist Conference* (1820), p.148.

Connexion. The Wesleyan Leaders' Meeting, having considered the matter, believed that Smith was wrong to have suggested to the woman that she should 'search the Scriptures, pray to God, and act according to the dictates of her conscience', but that he should have actively discouraged her from leaving a Wesleyan society.[2] However, at a meeting to discuss the affair one of his two accusers admitted he had made a mistake in claiming that Smith had encouraged her, with others, to join the new body, while the other accuser did not pursue the claim he originally made. Ann Prestage herself 'cleared Mr Smith from every imputation'.[3] Nonetheless, Smith was censured, though not expelled, and it was said that he should have known enough about the perceived objectionable practices of the Methodist New Connexion to have persuaded Ann Prestage to remain within Wesleyanism. The decision to censure him was by no means unanimous, the vote being passed by thirteen votes to eleven, with Smith protesting that six women were allowed to vote and were among the thirteen. It was clear that Smith was extremely angry at the decision, and while he did not immediately resign as a local preacher or from the society he was a member of, he eventually left after eleven years as a Wesleyan. It is hard to avoid the conclusion that the admonition over the advice he gave was an excuse to make Smith leave, the real dispute being his involvement with tent preaching which he had been undertaking since 1817. He continued to engage in Tent Methodist work, both in tents and in a chapel until, probably, 1829.

The reference to the existence of a Methodist New Connexion society in Bristol in late 1819 and early 1820 is especially interesting. The *Mathew's Bristol Directory* series, first published in 1793, does not show a Methodist New Connexion chapel until as late as 1857, located then at Castle Green, and their annual conference minutes confirm 1857 as the first formal link with Bristol. Before then, the earliest statistical reference to a society anywhere near Bristol was Worcester in 1821 with 111 members. That society seems to have ceased to exist by 1823, but in 1831 there were societies in Birmingham and, again, Worcester. Further to the south west of Bristol there were 100 members in a Cornwall district in 1834. The membership expanded substantially the following year when it had 300 members, eight chapels and nine societies, as a result of the addition of many Wesleyans who fell out with John Baker, the Truro superintendent.[4]

However, the *Tent Methodist Magazine* for 1823 records that 'sometime in February 1820 the Methodist New Connexion formed a

---

2   Pocock *et al*, *Facts Without a Veil*, p.21.

3   *TM Magazine*, p.126.

4   Methodist New Connexion Annual Meeting, *Minutes of 1834 Conference*, and Thomas Shaw, *A History of Cornish Methodism* (Truro: D. Bradford Barton, 1967), pp.79-80.

society in Bristol; a member of the Wesleyan Society who attended their ministry, and some of whose relations were joined with them in church fellowship, was requested to take the charge of one of their classes, but being in doubt as to the propriety of this step'[5] sought Smith's advice. It appeared to be the case that Ann Prestage's father was a member, and her cousin a preacher, of a Methodist New Connexion society in London.[6] There was, in fact, a Mr Prestage who was a local Wesleyan preacher in the London East Circuit in 1816 and it may be the same man who, four years later, had become a Methodist New Connexion preacher.[7] On first examination, therefore, it might be surprising to find the apparent existence of a society in Bristol in 1820 and, of course, it might not have become fully established, or it might have failed very soon afterwards before the annual statistics were collated. However, the Home Mission Committee of the Methodist New Connexion in its report to June 1819 stated, 'the last Conference recognised London and Bristol as most desirable Missionary stations, to be improved as early as opportunity offered'.[8] Good initial progress was made in London where, a year later, seven congregations had been established with 186 members, but no immediate success was achieved at Bristol. Indeed, a resolution passed at the 1820 New Methodist Connexion Conference held at Chester agreed 'That Bristol be considered a Missionary Station: and that the annual committee be directed to send a Missionary to that city, as soon as a suitable person can be obtained'.[9] The search appeared to be unsuccessful as no reference was made to Bristol in the following year's minutes, or for many years afterwards.

There is evidence, however, that the Methodist New Connexion did seek to attract disenchanted Wesleyans in other parts of England before the potential seceders established a separate sect. Pamphlets were issued on several occasions in the early nineteenth century aimed directly at dissidents, including one which was republished in Bristol in 1820 to coincide with the disputes with the men who later became Tent Methodist leaders. The writers of the pamphlets claimed that the Methodist New Connexion was the natural home for those who left Wesleyanism.[10] The author of one pamphlet also claimed that there was a 'very striking

---

5   *TM Magazine*, p.125.

6   Mark Robinson, *Observations on the System of Wesleyan Methodism* (London, 1824), letter written to Rev. R. Johnson, p.66.

7   'A Plan for the Preachers in the London East Circuit', from 2 June to 29 September 1816.

8   *Report of the Committee of the Home Mission established among the Methodists of the New Connexion for the year ended June 1 1819* (Hanley, 1819).

9   MNC Annual Meeting, *Minutes of 1820 Conference*, resolution no. 24.

10   Currie, *Methodism Divided*, p.60, for several examples of the practice of issuing pamphlets at opportune times.

contrast betwixt the excellent civil constitution which we enjoy as Englishmen, and the extremely arbitrary and unequitable ecclesiastical government under which we labour as Methodists'.[11] Their efforts appeared to achieve only modest success as Methodist New Connexion membership growth never reached the rates realized by Primitive Methodists, or the Bible Christians in certain periods. From an initial membership of approximately 5,000 in 1797, Methodist New Connexion numbers actually fell until 1805 before rising to nearly 8,000 by 1812. There then followed three years of decline until good increases were seen in 1817, 1818 and 1819 when membership increased by 19% to 9,672 over those three years. A further fall was recorded in 1820, a good rise was reported in 1821 but from then until 1827 the membership numbers remained static at just over 10,000.[12]

In any event, it seems unreasonable to have expected Smith to know so much about the Methodist New Connexion that he could speak with authority about their perceived unacceptable views and practices. It is just possible that Kilham, its leader for a short time, had retained contact with Bristol after 1793 when he received at least one letter from Bradburn who had just conducted a communion service at Kingswood to the annoyance of those who wished Methodism to remain within the Established Church. Kilham himself died in 1798 and it is unlikely, therefore, that any of his successors would have had any meaningful contact in a city nearly two hundred miles away from the group's centre of activity in an area north of a line from the Potteries to Nottingham.

John Pyer and his Expulsion from the Wesleyans

The dispute with John Pyer was on an altogether different level. It was a much longer running affair than with Smith, and was about various issues. The disagreements were with a man who had served Wesleyanism for many years, in the Bristol area, in Berkshire and elsewhere. The district authorities and some circuit superintendents had attempted to persuade the other Tent Methodist leaders, notably, at different times, Pocock, Irving and Gosling, to rescind Pyer's appointment as a full-time missionary ever since it became effective in early 1819. That

---

11   'A Member of the Old Methodist Society', *An Exposition of the Proceedings of the Old Methodist Conference* (Bristol, 1820), which was printed by Philip Rose who was also the printer for the 'Pocock' pamphlets of 1820. Editions of this pamphlet were also published in Manchester in 1815, Glasgow in 1816, Halifax in 1817, and London in 1821.

12   R. Currie, A. Gilbert and L. Horsley, *Churches and Churchgoers: Patterns of Church Growth in the British Isles since 1700* (Oxford: Clarendon Press, 1977), Table A3, pp.139-140.

appointment sent the wrong signals to official Methodism: firstly, there were by then two large tents in use, secondly, there was the beginning of a separate, formal structure being put in place, and thirdly, the person directly involved was unacceptable to the hierarchy.

Why was Pyer unacceptable? There had clearly been problems in the past with his relationships with other people, some of which have already been recorded. The pamphlets that were produced in early 1820 drew attention to additional incidents where disagreements arose, both in Bristol and in Newbury.[13] The Bristol authorities were not prepared to allow Pyer to act as a local preacher, nor even to be a member of a society. His name did not appear on the preaching plan, issued in early December 1819 at the latest, which covered the first three months of 1820,[14] despite the fact that he had many talents. He was obviously a man of enormous energy and commitment to the cause, he was considered to be suitable for appointment as a full-time employee of the Tent Methodists by men of considerable business acumen and spiritual awareness, and he had, it appears, very great preaching skills. In the obituary of the Rev. John Barnett high praise is expressed of the many qualities of Pyer, and of his sermons; 'a man of remarkable physical, intellectual and moral build, and in his younger days almost as mighty a preacher as George Whitefield'.[15] A high accolade indeed, bearing in mind that it had been said that Whitefield 'was the most popular preacher of his day'.[16] Barnett named his son, who wrote the obituary, John Pyer Barnett so the wording could not be regarded as an objective assessment. Nonetheless there were clearly attributes of value to the church.

There must have been many counter-balancing aspects, probably more than simply that Pyer 'began to excite certain jealousies and prejudices'.[17] A *Correct Statement of Facts*, as the Wesleyan Leaders' Meeting reply to Pocock's original pamphlet was entitled, referred to the necessity to establish 'a Committee to investigate his character, and the circumstances connected with his late painful embarrassments in life'.[18] This enquiry seemed to have consisted of allowing Pyer to explain his position and answer questions, discussions between the members of the committee and correspondence with Edward Millward, the superintendent of the Newbury circuit, where Pyer had served between late 1817 and early 1819. That his character included traits that could cause offence has

---

13   Pocock *et al, Facts Without a Veil*, p.15.

14   'Lord's Day Plan for the Bristol and Kingswood Circuits', covering fifteen weeks from 19 December 1819 to 26 March 1820.

15   *Baptist Handbook* (1878), p.331.

16   J.R. Andrews, *George Whitefield: A Light Rising in Obscurity* (London: 1865), p.30. See also Ives, *Kingswood School*, p.2, and Horne, *Popular History*, pp.265-267.

17   Russell, *Memoirs of Rev John Pyer*, p.76.

18   Thomas Wood *et al, A Correct Statement of Facts* (Bristol, 27 April 1820), p.4.

already been noted. The 'late painful embarrassments' probably related to financial problems connected with the sale of his business and family home in Newbury, caused by an uncooperative mortgagor who was a relative of Mrs Pyer. The make-up of Pyer's personality and character was such that the Wesleyan authorities ultimately found it impossible to tolerate him.

Pyer, after a successful preaching season with the tents in 1819, apparently showed Thomas Wood, the newly appointed superintendent of the Bristol circuit, his latest class ticket and preaching plans as evidence of his involvement in the Newbury and Hungerford circuits. Wood had already been a Bristol preacher for two years, and elsewhere, including London, for thirty years before that. He was subsequently appointed to Sheffield in 1820, to Liverpool in 1823, and died in January 1826. That Pyer's class ticket was not current would have been understandable as he had been away preaching in tents and in Methodist chapels during the preceding six months. He may not have been present on the occasions when the class tickets were renewed. The inability to produce current documentation gave the Bristol authorities the excuse to decline to admit him, either into a society or as a local preacher, both of which he would have been resuming after living elsewhere for a short time. Subsequent events showed an increasing determination to refuse Pyer any of his former involvement, but without providing him with any of the evidence that purported to satisfy the Bristol Methodist authorities that he was not a fit and proper person. The point by point dismissal of the allegations made in the leaders' meeting publication, which was apparently widely circulated to add to the discomfort of the three Tent leaders, was a heavily subjective version. However, as with Smith, it seemed that the means of ensuring that Pyer no longer played a part in Wesleyan affairs, justified the end result. As Pyer is reported as saying in *Facts Without a Veil*, 'the whole of your opposition to me, arises from my connection with Tent Preaching'.[19] So Smith had left in March 1820, and Pyer knew on 13 January 1820 that he was not to be re-admitted into fellowship with official Bristol Methodism. If Pyer's version of the record of the exchanges with Thomas Wood was accurate, it was also acknowledged by the Bristol circuit authorities that it was indeed the tent preaching that was the real reason.

George Pocock—Tents, Chapels and Organ

The situation with George Pocock was rather different. There were no extraneous elements such as business problems away from Bristol, as with

---

19   Pocock *et al, Facts Without a Veil*, p.13.

Pyer, to complicate the issues, neither was he a full-time missionary in a venture that clearly upset the Methodist authorities. He had been, however, the prime mover in all the tent activities since 1814. For a while during the last few months of 1819 and the earliest months of 1820, the aim seemed not so much to expel him or force him to leave, but to persuade him to conform to Methodist rules. The evidence for this comes in part from a study of *A Correct Statement of Facts* where there is shown to be a much greater degree of patience than with Smith or Pyer. The leaders' meeting pamphlet used phrases such as 'much pain to his Christian friends' and said that there was 'an unwillingness to grieve him and a belief that he acted from a desire to do good'.[20] The authorities judged, probably correctly, that if they could induce him to change his mind, the irregular activities could be brought within district and circuit control and Pocock would remain a valuable member of the Methodist community. Indeed, one of Pocock's opponents accepted that he had ' zeal' and 'determined perseverance', and declared that 'when I think of his inclination to do good, I know of no man in this city, no one in the Kingdom, who is fitted to be more useful that Brother Pocock'.[21] As late as 8 January 1820, by which time Pyer was becoming unacceptable, William Jones, the missionary appointed by conference in 1819, wrote to Pocock from Thornbury where he lived saying that Pocock would be welcome to preach in the area, but adding that 'I have no room for anyone but yourself'.[22] The Wesleyan hierarchy recognized that Pocock was a man with much to offer as, among other things, a local preacher and as a generous provider of finance.

Pocock, however, was extremely loath to submit to Wesleyan control the two tangible elements of the evangelical activity he had been leading. Firstly, he saw no acceptable reasons why he should allow the tents, which he probably financed and met the ongoing costs, to be governed under preaching plan type arrangements that would, among other things, determine where they should be used and who should officiate within them. For several years the body of tent preachers had been able to respond quickly to local requests and particular circumstances, and Pocock wished to retain the advantage that the tents had of being flexible in their use. Notwithstanding Pocock's inherent objections, he had reluctantly agreed to the passing of three resolutions which would have given effective control of the tents to the Bristol superintendent. He did so in the belief that justice would be done to Pyer who would be re-admitted as a member and local preacher. Before this issue could be examined again, however, a second dispute with Pocock pre-empted any

20   Wood *et al*, *A Correct Statement of Facts*, p.10.

21   Robinson, *Observations on the System of Wesleyan Methodism*, p.65.

22   *TM Magazine*, p.104.

possible reconciliation. With the clearest of echoes of the disputes that arose in Bristol in the mid 1790's he was not prepared to finance the building of chapels and then have less than full control of them. The Methodist leaders objected to Pocock 'building places of worship in different circuits...without complying with any of the regulations appertaining to that very important branch of our economy' and declaring 'both verbally and in print, that these places shall not be settled on the Conference or Methodist plan'.[23] The question of ownership and control of chapel buildings had not been fully resolved in the 1790's, as the dispute with Pocock showed. He was trustee of at least three Wesleyan chapels, at Westbury-on-Trym since 1811, at Pill for about a year, and at St Philip's in Red Cross Street close to the city centre of Bristol, opened in August 1817 and built at the instigation of people associated with Portland Chapel. A John Hall, a fellow trustee with Pocock elsewhere, arranged the subscription of the entire cost of the St Philip's chapel which amounted to £2,900 and to which, no doubt, Pocock contributed.[24] Pocock came to share the concern of the contemporary writer who claimed 'that when a Chapel is built, or made over, upon the Conference plan, it is theirs [itinerant preachers] for ever',[25] with the trustees' powers being apparent rather than real. In practice, the trustees' concerns were often with high levels of debt rather than with the exercise of authority.

There were, of course, other Wesleyans who supported the refusal to accept Pocock's actions with regard to chapel buildings. A pamphlet written in 1825 includes a footnote claiming that 'Mr Pocock's expulsion was justifiable, by an express Law or Order, enforced by Mr Wesley, in the Year 1782, by which no collection could be made for a chapel, or chapels built, different from the Conference settlement'.[26] However, ten years after 1820 chapel ownership problems still arose. In a letter to Jabez Bunting, the leading Methodist for most of the first half of the nineteenth century, William Leach, who was superintendent at the Langton Street, Bristol circuit between 1829 and 1831, wrote: 'the chapel is in a sad state, unsettled and of course unsafe', meaning that it was 'not secured to Conference by the Model Deed'.[27] This model deed was designed to ensure that effective governance and control of all aspects of

---

23   Wood *et al*, *A Correct Statement of Facts*, p.10.

24   C.J. Spittal, 'The History of Methodism in the Environs of Old Market Street, Bristol 1739-1985', address to the WHS Bristol Branch, *Bulletin* No. 45 (March, 1986), pp.7-14.

25   James Douglas, *The System of Methodism Further Exposed; and the Wiles of Priestcraft Investigated* (Newcastle, 1814), p.10.

26   Charles Welch, *An Investigation of Mr Mark Robinson's Observations on the System of Wesleyan Methodism* (Hull, 1825), p.66.

27   W.R. Ward (ed.), *Early Victorian Methodism: The Correspondence of Jabez Bunting 1830-1858* (Oxford: Oxford University Press, 1976), letter 7, p.7.

premises were retained by conference, membership of which comprised experienced itinerant ministers, not local trustees of the buildings. By late 1819 that model had remained unaltered for thirty one years, and it was not until 1829 that conference established a committee to review the document and up date it.[28]

There was a further, more localized dispute with Pocock that came to a head by the time that, presumably, the authorities finally believed they would not succeed in persuading him to conform to Wesleyan authority. The disagreement is referred to in the three pamphlets, and also in two histories of Portland Chapel, including *The Chapel on the Hill*. What is recorded there as 'the first note of discord',[29] concerned an organ that Pocock had provided for use in the chapel services. It had, apparently, been poorly maintained and he was eventually told by the trustees on 15 March 1820 to take it away. Somewhat petulantly Pocock replied that he, not the trustees, would choose whether the organ stayed or not, but he did arrange for it to be removed. The saga had begun over two years earlier when, at a trustees' meeting on 22 January 1818, four resolutions were passed concerning the organ and 'respecting the Pews occupied by his pupils'.[30] Pocock, then, featured in not one, but two arguments with the Wesleyan authorities.

It is interesting to note that Portland Chapel must have been one of the earliest Methodist chapels to have an organ installed. Another prominent local chapel, Ebenezer, did not have an organ until 1849.[31] Disputes relating to organs had occasionally been raised at annual conferences prior to 1820 considerably before the serious disagreement over an organ installed at Brunswick Chapel, Leeds, in 1827. This argument involved the congregation, trustees and denominational leadership at local and national level and eventually led to the secession of a group which called itself the 'Protestant Methodists'.[32] In 1808, in response to a question about public worship, the minutes record that 'Conference judge it expedient to refuse, after this present year, their sanction or consent to the erection of any organ in our chapels'. A further answer stated that 'where organs have been already introduced, the Conference require that they shall be so used as not to overpower or supersede, but only to assist our congregational singing; and they shall be considered as

---

28   Bunting, *Life of Jabez Bunting*, p.264 n..

29   Lambert, *Chapel on the Hill*, p.50.

30   *Portland Street Journal*, minutes of trustees meetings 1794-1860.

31   T.M. Williams, *A Short History of Old King Street (Ebenezer) Methodist Church, Bristol 1795-1954* (n.p., 1955), p.7.

32   Benjamin Gregory, *Side Lights on the Conflicts of Methodism* (London: Cassell, 1899), pp.48-88, and John T. Wilkinson, 'The Rise of Other Methodist Traditions', in R. Davies *et al* (eds), *A History of the Methodist Church in Great Britain*, II, pp.314-15.

under the control of the Superintendent, or the officiating Preacher'.[33] Pocock was unlikely to have relished the prospect of control by the authorities of his instrument, if they sought to impose it. At the 1820 conference, by which time Pocock had just severed his connection with Portland Chapel and the denomination, consideration was given to the installation of new organs. It was agreed that 'in some of the larger chapels, where some instrumental music may be deemed expedient in order to guide the congregational singing, organs may be allowed, by special consent of the Conference',[34] but only after much intermediate discussion.

It was to be a further five years before the trustees of Portland Chapel decided to try to find another organ. They succeeded but within a year the organist's expenses and salary were already in arrears.[35] Pocock's organ was put in his Prospect Place Academy schoolroom and was regularly used thereafter.[36] This incident suggests that despite the lack of power normally available to local preachers and lay people generally, with authority vested in circuit and district hierarchies, Pocock was able to exercise considerable influence within Portland Chapel whilst not being a trustee. He seems to have owned the organ, played it, and controlled the contribution that music made to the services held in the chapel until his withdrawal. Perhaps it was precisely this power that the trustees, and the itinerant ministers, wished to curtail. The die was cast in March 1820 and despite a Methodist association of almost a quarter of a century, the relationship between Pocock and the Wesleyan authorities had irretrievably broken down. The alienation was, by then, total and mutual.

Notwithstanding all the acrimony during the nine months to May 1820, there were two occasions at least of real Wesleyan support to the Pocock family in that time. Personal suffering occurred twice when two of the Pocock's young children died. Harriet, at the age of only three months, died in October 1819, and Catherine, who was one year nine months old, died just seven months later in May 1820. Funeral services were held in Portland Chapel, conducted by William Henshaw, one of the Bristol intinerants, and both daughters were buried in vaults at the chapel.[37]

The Tent Methodist leaders had always claimed that they wished to cause no schism, but had seen themselves as providing a ministry to help 'the wretched condition of multitudes who are yet perishing for lack of

33   *Minutes of Methodist Conference* (1808), p.29.
34   *Minutes of Methodist Conference* (1820), p.145.
35   Lambert, *Chapel on the Hill*, pp. 66-67.
36   W. Symons, 'Portland Chapel, Bristol, and the Tent Methodists', *Cornish Methodist Church Record* (January, 1893), pp.3-4.
37   *Portland Chapel Register of Burials* (1819 and 1820).

knowledge'.[38] This evangelical mission to the poor later became a central feature and in one of the few references to Pocock in Pyer's biography it was said that Pocock had a 'burning zeal for the ignorant, depraved and neglected population all around him'.[39] The Methodist authorities failed to find a way of utilizing a different, but highly appropriate, means of evangelism. Whether, given the nature of the personalities involved on both sides, a compromise could ever have been reached is not possible to judge, but valuable resources, both in personal and physical terms, were lost to the denomination. It is clear that Pocock, at least, found the gradual relaxation of tight central control happening too slowly and inconsistently, as well as passing it into the hands of local officials who did not share his vision that evangelical activity should be undertaken more widely.

However vitriolic the language was on occasions, the bitter exchanges were expressed in no more extreme wording than when the Methodist New Connexion seceded in 1797. The Bristol Wesleyan leaders claimed, in connection with Samuel Smith's dispute with them, that the Methodist New Connexion leaders 'were using every effort to light the torch of discord, and cause a division in the Society, in order to found another on its ruin'.[40] In terms even more uncharitable, Jospeh Benson, President of the Wesleyan Conference in 1798 and 1810, described Kilham as a 'vile slanderer' and wrote that the Wesleyans were 'well rid of his party of republicans and levellers'.[41] Thomas Coke told a correspondent that the Methodist New Connexion was 'as troublesome a set of people that ever plagued a Church of Christ'.[42] Those who had different views of how to promote and encourage Christian commitment to serve their Lord and their fellow humans were frequently seen as totally unacceptable people.

Other Friends of Tent Activities

Although it would be understandable to concentrate exclusively on the arguments with Smith, Pyer and Pocock, the fact is that Wesleyanism lost many more than three men of high calibre. John Gosling, who had been heavily criticized for providing hospitality to Pyer during a period of illness, left the Wesleyan cause, and other dedicated local preachers including a Victory Purdy and Samuel Bryant, after many years of faithful service were, effectively, expelled.

---

38   *TM Magazine*, p.11.

39   Russell, *Memoirs of Rev John Pyer*, p.21.

40   Wood *et al*, *A Correct Statement of Facts*, p.8.

41   Joseph Benson, letter to William Smith and Michael Longridge, dated 8 November 1796.

42   Thomas Coke, letter to Ezekiel Cooper, dated 12 January 1799.

Gosling became a trustee and financier of several Tent Methodist chapels, and had an overriding concern for the provision of education facilities for the poor who, otherwise, would have probably had none. This social conscience was hinted at in the poem written to mark the evangelical excursion to Marlborough and elsewhere in 1818. During the course of that marathon piece of verse the following lines appear about Gosling's work:

> From village unto village still proceed,
> Till all the children of the poor can read;[43]

His interest in education went beyond his Sunday School activity. In 1816 Gosling applied, with a Thomas Hall, a local Independent layman, to the Society of Friends in Marlborough to use their meeting house 'for the purpose of Educating poor Children on the System of the British and Foreign School Society'.[44] This was a non-denominational group mainly run by Independent and Quaker members, as was the case in Marlborough. Agreement was given on 2 December 1816 for them to teach 'Children in the Lancastrian plan of education',[45] a system of instruction which relied on a monitorial principle, whereby a single schoolmaster was able to use pupil-teachers, sometimes aged only eleven or twelve, whom he had taught. It was an early use of delegation in education that was first devised by Joseph Lancaster, a Quaker educationalist. By 1818 Gosling had also established 'four day schools in Ogbourne St George', four miles north of Marlborough towards Swindon, where '41 children, some from poor families'[46] attended. Why four separate schools were set up in one village by the same person is not known, but Gosling's concern for the academic, as well as the spiritual, training of children is further evidenced. It may be that it was their mutual interest in education that brought Pocock and Gosling together initially in 1817 or 1818, although Pocock had acquired land in Oxford Street, Marlborough, on which a Methodist chapel was built as early as 1811,[47] seven years before Gosling's first known contact with Tent Methodism.

---

43   *TM Magazine*, p.24.

44   Letter of Agreement, dated 2 December 1816, signed by John Gosling and Thomas Hall.

45   *Minutes of Wiltshire Monthly Meetings* (1801 to 1818) of Quakers.

46   D.A. Crowley (ed.), *The Victoria History of the Counties of England: 'Wiltshire'* (London: Institute of Historical Research, University of London, 1983), XII, p.160.

47   Sundry deeds relating, *inter alia*, to propert 'on the south side of Oxford Street' Marlborough. Land was bought by George Pocock for £90 from a William White on 2 July 1811.

The loss to Wesleyanism of these many individual preachers was one it could ill afford. There is certain evidence, quite apart from the testimonies that appeared in the *Tent Methodist Magazine*, to suggest that local Methodist societies had grown at a faster rate up to 1819 than might otherwise have been expected. The statistical data is not wholly convincing or conclusive, but it is worthy of note. A lecture given in Bristol in 1986 drew attention to the fact that the Bristol circuit membership was recorded at 2,006 for 1813, by 1815 the figure was 2,120, but just one year later an increase of 25% to 2,660 was reported.[48] The overall increase in the four years to 1816 amounted to 33% compared with a growth rate of just 6% for the denomination as a whole. The Bristol membership figure then remained almost static to 1819, but the same information for the Kingswood circuit shows a similar position for the corresponding period—an increase from 350 in 1815 to 440 in 1817 and to 490 in 1819, being a percentage rise of 40% in five years. Further corroboration comes from a study of the Dursley circuit statistics. The Dursley area featured strongly in the tent programme for 1819 and there was an increase in membership of 86, from 320 to 406, between 1818 and 1820.

Another indication, albeit grudgingly, of Wesleyan acknowledgement of tent preachers' successes, came from the biography of Jabez Bunting, which recorded 'Certain zealous but heady Methodists in Bristol, laudably anxious to evangelise the dark villages in its neighbourhood, adopted what is not an uncommon practice in these times, and, taking a tent with them, pitched it where they chose, preached the gospel, and, doubtless, did a great deal of good'.[49] Bunting's objection was not so much what the Tent Methodists were doing, although, for several years at least, Wesleyanism's own missionary activity was tending to be concentrated overseas after about 1813, but that it was evangelical work outside the strict confines of central and circuit authority.

There is, then, other evidence to supplement what is reported in the *Tent Methodist Magazine* and the *Memoirs of Rev John Pyer*, the two publications which provide most of the subjective material. The additional benefits that accrued to Methodism during the six years between 1814 and 1819 were substantial. First one tent, subsequently enlarged, and then a second, visited eighty different named places (see Appendix B), mostly small villages, and no doubt very many more that are not referred to by name in either of the principal publications. The vast majority of these places had no existing chapel or meeting house and the tents were, therefore, undertaking genuine missionary work. In other

---

48   Spittal, *History of Methodism in the Environs of Old Market Street, Bristol*, p.14.
49   Bunting, *Life of Jabez Bunting*, pp.170-171.

places former societies were revitalized. In a very real sense the tents were additional resources available to complement existing facilities, and some of the preachers at least worked with the tent mission in addition to maintaining their preaching plan responsibilities. Various references were made to the numbers of people who heard the tent preachers, and the extent to which societies gained new members. Large and increasing congregations were reported, 220 new members were admitted to the Bristol circuit in 1815, 450 to the Dursley circuit in 1819, and it was estimated that 90,000 people heard the tent preachers in 1817. At one gathering there were 'not fewer than 15,000 attentive hearers',[50] and there are two references to 2,000 strong congregations on the Isle of Wight in 1818 and at Hinchcomb Hill, Gloucestershire, in 1819. Even if the numbers were exaggerated, and there is no evidence that they were, the contribution to Methodist missionary life and work was considerable, and probably substantial.

There were other benefits too. The tents encouraged people who would have felt inhibited at attending a chapel, and the tent preachers claimed that many 'old professors'[51] and some who had not attended worship for many years joined the congregations, attracted, perhaps, by the visible, striking presence of a large marquee-type structure. A tent was deemed an adequate substitute for a chapel when the Dursley building was to undergo repairs—ironic then that within a few months of that purpose being served, the tent, and the preachers, were regarded as being irregular and unacceptable. The costs associated with the tents were found entirely by the preachers, principally Pocock in the early years with two other substantial benefactors emerging in 1818. The income generated from collections found its way into Methodist societies. It is not surprising, given the increasing demand, that towards the end of 1819 it was said 'the harvest was great but the labourers were few'.[52] Wesleyanism could ill-afford to lose the services of such a dedicated group of preachers and supporters.

While the departure of the three prominent tent preachers enabled the Bristol authorities to breathe a collective sigh of relief, they might not have expected several other preachers, at least, to leave Wesleyanism, nor anticipated the large amount of sympathy and support from ordinary members of Methodist societies. Indeed they probably seriously underestimated the reaction among their members, misjudged the commitment of many people to continue the tent work, and did not expect the few to be able to establish a new organization quickly. Significantly, bearing in mind subsequent events, a letter from the steward

---

50   *TM Magazine*, p.34.
51   *TM Magazine*, p.33.
52   *TM Magazine*, p.80.

and a trustee of Dursley seeking confirmation, or otherwise, of Pyer's departure illustrated the anxiety of some people to the events. His concern was for the chapel's financial position if collection income fell as there was a large debt following the substantial repairs, but he and many others were readily prepared to acknowledge the contribution Pyer had made to recent successes of evangelical activity.[53] The steward's superintendent was, however, a fierce opponent of any further involvement from Pyer, which indicated that the leaders were not all of the same mind as their members. The last of the three pamphlets charting the course of the events, *Facts Without a Veil*, gave a further impression that more people were siding with Pocock and the other tent preachers than may have been expected. Henry Roberts, like Samuel Smith, a loyal preacher for many years, was going to continue to support the tent mission, as were other local preachers, including a Mr Pring and a Mr Payne, neither of whom had been previously mentioned in connection with tent affairs. Pring was a long standing Wesleyan who had been a Bristol circuit local preacher since 1814,[54] and Payne was shown on the Bristol circuit preaching plan for the early months of 1820.[55] An unnamed class leader and the whole of his class of forty six members had also apparently decided to join the Tent Methodist cause.[56] Thus it was that although the Wesleyans hoped to regain full control in Bristol by removing three individuals from their midst, in fact a much larger number of local lay leaders joined Pocock and his two leading colleagues.

Opponents of the Tent Preachers

As far as can be told from the available material, only two men who had significantly supported tent activities did not continue their commitment after the three leaders left the Wesleyans. Adam Nightingale had only been mentioned once before, assisting an evangelical mission led by Pyer in 1819 to the south Gloucestershire area. He became a Wesleyan minister in 1822 and left for Newfoundland in 1823 as a pioneer of Wesleyanism in that part of Canada. Nightingale was placed on the Bristol preaching plan as a local preacher in 1816 and met John Irving at about the same time. Under the direction of the Dursley superintendent he worked at Arlingham, but in an unusual way. Irving was given 'the sanction of the proper authorities to employ Mr Nightingale as a home

---

53   *TM Magazine*, p.104.
54   *Register of Bristol Society* (1808-1820) (Wesleyan Methodist), n.p.
55   'Lord's Day Plan for the Bristol and Kingswood Circuits', 19 December 1819-26 March 1820.
56   Pocock *et al*, *Facts Without a Veil*, p.48.

missionary, for the benefit of this neglected part of the country'. This was exactly the position Pyer was refused permission to undertake by the same authorities at about the same time, and even though Irving was also involved as a proponent. Nightingale formed a society and erected a chapel at Horsley, six miles east of Dursley, although ten miles from Arlingham. A chapel remained in Horsley for Wesleyan worship until it was closed in about 1899. It was in an area that was being actively evangelized by tent preachers, also with the support of the superintendent—at least while the Dursley chapel was closed for major building work. After two years or so 'it was thought by some who formed a high opinion of his piety and talents, that he ought not to continue in this anomalous position... He was employed by a private gentleman, but was doing the work of a Wesleyan minister without the usual recognition'. In the light of the treatment meted out to Pyer it was not surprising that Nightingale's work had to cease. He met Henry Moore, then chairman of the district, and, quite soon afterwards was ordained at a service in Spitalfields Chapel on 9 July 1823 before going to Canada. He returned to England in 1864 because of failing health and died ten years later aged eighty-four. His obituary recorded that he 'entered on his duties there [Newfoundland] full of heart and hope, and in their faithful and energetic discharge was uninterruptedly engaged for nearly forty years'.[57]

John Irving, who changed sides during the early part of the acrimonious exchanges, was a particularly substantial loss. He became a man of great stature in both Methodist and secular spheres. He had made a significant contribution towards the cost of the second tent, and was one of the small group of people to promote the appointment of Pyer as the full-time missionary. Irving and Pocock would have known each other through their mutual membership of Portland Chapel, of which Irving became a trustee in 1815, a role he still fulfilled in 1843. That Irving had a high regard for Pocock in the earliest days of tent preaching can be supposed by the fact that Irving's son, born on 5 June 1814 and baptized at Portland Chapel on 22 December 1814, was named George Pocock Irving.[58] For many years from 1818 he served as a representative for Bristol on two national Wesleyan denominational committees. He became a very wealthy man, having contributed £1,500, a large sum in relative terms, to the Wesleyan Centenary Fund. Out of the Bristol North circuit's contribution of £3,029 from about two hundred contributors, Irving's donation of one half the total was a substantial benefaction indeed.[59]

---

57 *Minutes of Wesleyan Methodist Conference* (1874), obituary of Adam Nightingale, p.307.

58 *Portland Chapel Register of Baptisms.*

59 *General Report of the Wesleyan Centenary Fund* (Leeds, 1844). Rev. James Wood was general treasurer, and Rev. Francis A. West, Mr John Lomas, Mr T. Percival

Irving had founded a Methodist mission station at Annotta Bay, Jamaica, the scene of a shipwreck he had suffered earlier in his seafaring career.[60] He retained a great interest in overseas missions and through that involvement met and entertained Jabez Bunting in 1837 when they both bid farewell to missionaries as they departed for India. Bunting recalls in a letter to his daughter that he and Irving travelled '35 miles down the Bristol Channel...[and]...returned in Mr Irving's steamer'.[61] What prompted him to change his mind in late 1819 or early 1820 is not known. It was not altogether surprising that some people would fail to take the fundamental step of taking part in a formal separation and the establishment of a new offshoot of Methodism with all the attendant uncertainties associated with that. There was bitterness that Irving did not continue his support, particularly as it did not help Pyer's application to return to the Bristol Methodism fold in the autumn of 1819. It also lost the movement credibility at a time when it was sorely needed.

On the Wesleyan side, it was the Bristol circuit authorities, and Thomas Wood in particular, that had borne the brunt of the hostility of the eight months before the separation. He was, as superintendent, chairman of the leaders' meeting that produced, in April 1820, a twenty page response to George Pocock's first pamphlet. It was that meeting which was the focus for the bitter wrangling, and Wood's role was a difficult one. He was under pressure, not only from other Bristol leaders, but also from stewards and leaders in neighbouring circuits where the tents were frequently to be seen. Very soon after the three Tent Methodists had left Wesleyanism, Thomas Wood produced a pamphlet which was clearly a result of the virulent exchanges that he had been involved in. He expressed his abhorrence of malicious misrepresentation from other professed Christians, and urged restraint on those who had been maligned. In a probable reference to the Tent Methodists who were already becoming a significant force in the Bristol area, Wood acknowledged that 1820 was 'a period when heat and passion, discord and party divisions prevail among the professors of the religion of Jesus Christ, to the great reproach of the Christian name; when new sects are starting up, and misleading those hearts which are not established with grace; when men are more forward to censure than to obey them who are appointed by Divine Providence to have the rule over them'.[62] The fact

---

Bunting, Mr John D. Burton, and Mr John Westhead, were the five general secretaries. See also George Smith, *History of Wesleyan Methodism: Volume 3. Modern Methodism* (London, 1862), p.374.

60   Bates, *Portland Chapel*, pp.4-5.
61   Ward (ed.), *Early Victorian Methodism*, p.198, letter from J. Bunting to Emma Bunting, 6 September 1837.
62   Thomas Wood, *The Spirit of Calumny, Detected and Exposed with suitable advices* (Bristol, 1820), p.5.

was that 'Divine Providence' was not sufficient to retain the unquestioned loyalty of sincere Wesleyans who felt the need to exercise independent judgment in Methodist affairs.

The district chairman, Richard Waddy, did have an involvement, acting as chairman of the committee to examine Pyer's case. He lived in Bristol, and was a man of influence and long experience in Methodist affairs nationally. He had begun his itinerancy at Berwick upon Tweed twenty-seven years earlier, and was to serve in many other places before his retirement in 1847, a career spanning over fifty years. To what extent he was aware of the totality of Pyer's involvement with the Wesleyans is not known, but he does not seem to have emerged from his involvement with much credit. Pyer was not allowed to see correspondence which took place with the superintendent of the Newbury circuit, some of which at least Waddy held, and if Waddy's role was to attempt to find a compromise solution he obviously failed.[63]

In a biography of his son, Samuel, written by a daughter, Richard Waddy is portrayed as a man with very many qualities. His 'disposition singularly gentle and sweet', his 'aim throughout life was to save souls and do his duty', and he is described as a 'courteous gentleman of refined and intellectual tastes...a simple godly man'. He was unable to use these impressive gifts to resolve the situation with Pyer, but it might be that the local hierarchy did not wish to have a solution that suited Pyer and the tent preachers. If so, Waddy's hands would have been tied. There was an ironic twist to Waddy's involvement in the affair. Samuel, his second son, later to become a leading Wesleyan minister himself, left school in 1819 at the age of fourteen but, unable to find suitable employment to satisfy his mathematical interests, returned to the family home in Bristol. In April of that year he 'was sent to Mr Pocock's school to pursue my studies'.[64] It seemed that he went somewhat reluctantly. It is not known precisely how long he was under Pocock's academic influence, but in the light of the events that were soon to unfold from the end of 1819 it was only a few months. Samuel Waddy began an unsatisfactory apprenticeship in January 1820 which also lasted only a brief time as he became a local preacher in 1823 and an itinerant in 1825.

There were others outside the Bristol circuit who had minor involvement. Reference has already been made to the superintendent of the Dursley circuit who became firmly opposed to tent activity, notwithstanding the tangible help it provided early in 1819, and the

63   Pocock *et al*, *Facts Without a Veil*, pp.13-14.
64   Adeline Waddy, *The Life of the Rev Samuel Waddy D.D.* (London, 1878), pp.4 and 13. Samuel was born in August 1804 and was one of the first pupils at Woodhouse Grove which was purchased in August 1811 and opened as a school in 1812. He joined the school roll in May 1813, p.7.

different views held by many of his members. The travelling preacher responsible for the Frampton's End and Olveston area who had previously worked reasonably harmoniously with tent preachers, would from January 1820 onwards only permit Pocock to occupy the pulpits. One other superintendent in the district also manifested his fierce objections to Tent Methodism. His particular opposition centred around the collection of subscriptions for the building of chapels organized by Pocock. Charles Greenly, superintendent of the Downend circuit, came freshly into the controversy having served the previous three years at Shepton Mallet in Somerset, but quickly became a bitter opponent of Tent Methodism. He used several methods of persuasion to discourage people from committing money towards the cost of buildings that Pocock was refusing to have conveyed according to the conference plan. Local congregations, and actual and potential individual subscribers, were all expected to withhold contributions. Pocock's response was to prepare a handbill, dated 23 March 1820, in which he accepted that the agreed denominational arrangements for the ownership of the chapels would not apply, but claimed that the buildings would 'be placed on a foundation which shall secure the privileges of the Poor, and those who, under God, have been the instruments of raising up People and Places'.[65] Reasonable, perhaps, but quite contrary to the rules that were in force. Pocock's concern for the poor at this particular time reflected the fact that many local coal miners, and their family members, gave great assistance in building what became known as 'Colliers' Temple' in Kingswood. At about the same time he was heavily involved in producing the first edition of the *Rules of the Tent Methodists* which made several references to those who were 'receiving relief from the Parish, or who are otherwise in poverty'.[66] They were not to contribute financially to the society, were expected to be taught to read, and at least one third of the society's income was to be used 'for the relief of sick and poor members'.[67] So, Wesleyan leaders outside the immediate confines of the Bristol circuit were equally successful in incurring the wrath of those who became Tent Methodist workers.

So it was that many dedicated, experienced Methodist preachers felt compelled to leave Wesleyanism. If they were not formally expelled they were 'constructively dismissed' by the actions of a local hierarchy that was unwilling to continue to find room for men who had much more Christian service to give. There was no doctrinal disagreement; indeed in the conclusion to *Facts Without a Veil*, in a reference to the preachers,

---

65   George Pocock, handbill headed 'WHEREAS', Prospect Place, Bristol, dated 23 March 1820.

66   *Rules of the Tent Methodists or Agrarian Society for Extending Christianity at Home* (Bristol, 1820), pp.4-5 (hereafter *TM Rules* [1820]).

67   *TM Rules* (1820), p.5.

Pocock writes: 'these ejected ministers are the same characters as they were when in the bosom of the Methodist Society, and their Doctrines are the same'.[68] What could not be accommodated was the individualism of Pocock, the many different facets of Pyer's character, and, equally importantly, the humble but energetic commitment of many local preachers, some of whom featured significantly in the early stages of development of the new group. The dispute locally which had become increasingly bitter in the final months of 1819 and the early months of 1820 was, in one sense, a microcosm of what had happened nationally in the years following John Wesley's death: 'Envy and ambition are formed in all corridors of power, even of church government. The Methodist movement was not exempt.'[69] Using these words, Tim Macquiban discussed the 'jockeying for position' for national leadership that occurred for many years after 1791 and involved a large number of individuals, some of whom, Coke, Mather and Pawson for example, formed themselves into small groupings in attempts to be accepted as 'inner cabinets' and real decision makers. In Bristol there were also men with different agenda. One man, Thomas Harper, apparently harboured a grudge against Pyer for an incident eleven years before.[70] The nature of the problem is not described, but it was probably the one relating to Harper's children that Pyer himself acknowledged in the *Memoirs of Rev John Pyer*. Harper was a man of some influence in Bristol, being for a few years secretary of the Strangers' Friend Society which was founded in Bristol in 1786, and a trustee of Portland Chapel in 1815,[71] remaining so until his death in 1832.[72] Others, however, including a James Wood, described as 'a respectable druggist',[73] endeavoured to find a compromise. In the end, however, the personal animosities and entrenched positions taken by the various parties within Methodism were such that there could be no meeting of minds.

The focal point for all the troubles that culminated in challenges to Methodist authority was the tent activity. John C. Bowmer described 'an innovation which, not being under the jurisdiction of the leaders' meeting, was immediately frowned upon with suspicion'.[74] He could well have been describing the Bristol district hierarchy's view of Pocock's tents, but in fact it was the room used by those who became the Band

68   Pocock *et al*, *Facts Without a Veil*, p.49.

69   T.S.A. Macquiban, 'Ministerial or Lay Aristocracy? A Study of Methodist Church Polity, its Antecedents and Development from the Death of Wesley to the Form of Discipline' (MA thesis, University of Bristol, 1986), p.25.

70   Pocock *et al*, *Facts Without a Veil*, p.20.

71   Bates, *Portland Chapel*, p.4.

72   Deed dated 8 December 1832.

73   Robinson, *Observations on the System of Wesleyan Methodism*, p.iv.

74   Bowmer, *Pastor and People*, p.71.

Room Methodists in 1805 after a Mr Broadhurst was expelled that is the subject of his remarks. Wesleyan officialdom dealt promptly with the Manchester Band Room issue, whereas it took six years to achieve the withdrawal or expulsion of the tent preachers. It was not clear in March, April and May 1820 how the situation would develop, but the various disputes involving chapels, tents, an organ and the whole question of the influence of lay people that surrounded the individual issues had culminated in a serious rift in Wesleyan affairs. The consequences of the rift are described, analysed and assessed in the following chapters.

CHAPTER 4

The Formal Establishment of the
Tent Methodists in 1820

Following the departure of several men, all of whom had made significant contributions to Wesleyanism for a number of years, various courses of events were possible. The one chosen was to establish a separate sect, retaining Wesleyan doctrine, very much at the instigation of George Pocock. This chapter examines the ways in which, within just a few months, a formal structure, incorporated in a set of rules and regulations, had been set up, and describes the very early results. It will be shown that Tent Methodism was both reformist and revivalist in character. It was reformist by virtue of rules that were, in some respects, materially different from the Wesleyans, and forms of government that allowed much more lay participation. It was also revivalist in the sense that its emphasis on outreach, notably among poorer communities, was greater than exhibited by the Wesleyans during the 1820s.

Bristol Methodism had experienced controversy and dissension before the events that led to the formation of the Tent Methodists. During the final decade of the eighteenth century what has been called 'The Sacramental Controversy' took place.[1] There were similarities between the two disputes quite apart from the city in which they arose. No fundamental theological differences were involved in either case. Other common aspects were the underlying complexities of the issues that became the focus of attention, and the length of time that the controversies took to be debated and decided. There were, though, important differences in the two situations. Firstly, in the contentious exchanges of the 1790's it was conference authority that was being threatened and national leaders of the time who were the principal participants in the feuding. The Tent Methodist disputes, however, mainly involved district and, particularly, circuit leadership. Secondly, and more importantly for this work, the earlier controversy did not lead

---

1   T.S.A. Macquiban, 'The Sacramental Controversy in Bristol in the 1790's', address given to WHS Bristol Branch, *Bulletin* No. 60 (March, 1991), pp.1-20.

immediately or directly to a formal separation, although Alexander Kilham was kept informed of the progress of the dispute by correspondence with Bradburn, one of the protagonists in 1793. It is just possible that the secession of 1797, at which time Kilham became leader of the Methodist New Connexion for a very short period before his death, indirectly resulted in part from the earlier problems in Bristol. This did not happen, however, for several years whereas the Tent Methodists formed themselves into a separate society without delay.

Tent Methodism was not, therefore, a secession like that which created the Methodist New Connexion twenty-three years earlier. Then, officially at least, it was the lack of a sufficient decision making role for lay people and impatience at the slowness of the progress towards separation from the Church of England that caused Kilham to lead about 5,000 Wesleyans into the new sect.[2] Indeed, conventional wisdom up to now has suggested that Tent Methodism was not a secession, as such, but the result of a schism. A judgement will be made later in the chapter as to whether a 'schism' or a 'secession' is a more accurate description of what occurred. Certainly there is no evidence to suggest that Pocock had any interest in changing the established rules of government of Methodism apart from those connected with the ownership of chapels and control of tents. He appeared to be unconcerned about the denomination's relationships with the Church of England. In addition to Pocock, Pyer and Smith who were effectively expelled after the bitter verbal confrontations and exchange of pamphlets, at least five other prominent local Wesleyans and other lesser important men, either resigned or were dismissed during the same period. Of even more significance is that sections at least of local societies left Wesleyanism and became Tent Methodists at the time of formation or within a few days.

According to E.P. Thompson, a historian mostly critical and unsympathetic to Methodism, Wesleyan Methodism, especially in the first three decades of the nineteenth century, was more in tune with 'self-made mill owners and manufacturers, and to foremen, overlookers, and sub-managerial groups', than the lower working-class communities. In these categories Thompson includes miners, weavers and rural labourers.[3] If that was true of Wesleyanism, it was certainly not the case with Tent Methodism. From an examination of the rules, the tenor of remarks quoted in the *Tent Methodist Magazine* for 1823, and many statements of the leaders in the pamphlets that were published, it is clear that Tent

---

2   G. Packer (ed.), *The Centenary of the Methodist New Connexion, 1797-1897* (London, 1897), sets out the background to and formation of the Methodist New Connexion. An interesting primary source is Anon., *An Apology for the Methodist New Connexion* (Hanley, 1815).

3   E.P. Thompson, *The Making of the English Working Class* (London: Penguin, 1991), pp.390-91.

Methodism sought to help working-class people. This was so both for the 'new proletariat' and those in more traditional working-class environments, such as coal miners in Kingswood, Bristol, agricultural labourers in Wiltshire, and those from inner city areas of parts of London, Manchester, Liverpool and Birmingham. The offshoot's keen desire to particularly serve and spiritually help the poorest in society began in earnest after the separation in 1820, albeit immediately, rather than before. Wesleyans did not have much inclination to make missionary activity among the poor a priority at that time. Julia Werner's observation that 'Bible Christianity and Primitive Methodism were *of* the people; Tent Methodism was *for* them'[4] is an accurate enough statement as the leading Tent Methodists were all, it seems, educated, professional men, some of whom had considerable wealth and social influence.

There were several features in the chain of events that led to the establishment of the Tent Methodists that paralleled those that occurred in the years preceding the formation of the Primitive Methodists and the Bible Christians. All the offshoots that were formed between 1810 and 1820 disagreed, to a greater or lesser extent, with Wesleyan policy and practice of substantially greater authority being given to superintendents and itinerant preachers than to local preachers. This was one reason why Pocock insisted on retaining control of the chapel premises he had arranged to be built and financed. Indeed, it was not only Tent Methodists who claimed that some local preachers who whole-heartedly supported Wesleyan doctrine were excluded from pulpits. Hugh Bourne and William Clowes of the Primitive Methodists and William O'Bryan of the Bible Christians all fell foul of local superintendents. In addition, all three groups were formed after the key individuals who had, initially at least, no desire to leave Wesleyanism, became involved in personal disputes with Methodist leaders. Part of the difficulties with the authorities was the preaching and evangelical activity which went beyond the confines of chapels and meeting houses on formal preaching plans. Other common features were the apparently limited long-term ambitions at the establishment of the sects, the relatively closely defined geographical areas where the work was undertaken in the groups' early years, and the limited nature of competition with Wesleyanism after the initial separation. Of particular importance was the concentration of effort with working-class people at a time when it was felt that Wesleyanism was becoming more middle class in its emphasis. The evangelical work coincided with the emergence of a clearer sense of class distinction as the Industrial Revolution developed. Furthermore, the groups were formed in a period of ten years when the influence of Jabez

---

4   Julia S. Werner, *The Primitive Methodist Connexion: Its Background and Early History* (Madison: University of Wisconsin Press, 1984), p.21.

Bunting was becoming extremely important in the Methodist hierarchy, and issues of discipline and a curtailment of individual initiatives were dominant. Bunting became secretary of the Wesleyan Methodists in 1814 and was president for the first time in 1820. This was a period when Methodists were beginning to 'concentrate...energies on disciplining the converted rather than extending even farther the nominal sway of the Connexion',[5] and from about 1813 onwards expand and promote missionary work overseas rather than in the United Kingdom. Tent Methodists, together with the Primitive Methodists and Bible Christians, were particularly keen to take the Christian gospel to the working-class populations of both industrial and rural areas where their respective strengths lay.

Tent Methodism had to establish itself quickly as a quite separate organization if the work was not to cease after six years of growing influence within Wesleyanism. To retain the commitment of people they had converted in parts of Bristol, and towns and villages such as Dursley and Frampton Cotterell, in the face of concerted attempts to persuade them to return to the Wesleyan fold, the leaders needed to maintain frequent contact. To do this a formal structure was required so that people could join a distinct body and feel a sense of belonging and support. In this respect two favourable factors were apparent. Firstly, Pocock, who became a close friend of Henry Moore,[6] one of the principal actors in the disputes of the 1790's, rapidly produced a set of rules, and secondly, an important local chapel, Pithay, became available for use.

Pocock proceeded with quite amazing speed. While he may have anticipated the final separation which was progressive rather than occurring on one particular date, he must have been spending much of his time planning the future. That this could happen while Pocock, 'a self-made man, who conducted successfully for half-a-century a large boarding school',[7] gives a clue to his enormous appetite for action in 1820, although this became less apparent later in the decade. This statement comes from an article written by a man who, together with his father in earlier years, was a pupil at the Prospect Place Academy and would therefore have had great knowledge of its impact in the local community. Within six days of Pocock's response by way of the publication of a handbill to Greenly's attempts to curtail fund-raising activities for chapel building, he was announcing the beginning of the 1820 season. 'The FIRST PUBLIC MEETING for Field Preaching this

---

5   B. Semmel, *The Methodist Revolution* (London: Heinemann Educational Books, 1974), p.137.

6   Vickers, 'Methodism and Society in Central Southern England', p.277 n..

7   W. Symons, 'Highways and Byways of the Connexion', *Bible Christian Magazine* (April, 1884), p.179.

Season, will commence on GOOD FRIDAY next, March 31st, 1820, at SHEPHERD'S PITS, in the vicinity of Kingswood' was the statement expressed in confident terms in a further handbill dated 29 March.[8] Pocock was not only a busy man, but he was also managing a highly complex and constantly developing situation. He was already signing class tickets as a Tent Methodist in March,[9] yet the last of the three pamphlets relating to the disputes with him, Pyer and Smith did not appear until 19 May, two months later.

Pithay Chapel, Bristol

By that time, the Pithay chapel, a former Baptist church, had already been acquired and used for a month. This building was to play a significant role in the life of the Tent Methodist movement, becoming its headquarters for eleven years. Its acquisition also indicates Pocock's remarkable influence on the affairs of the time. The use of the building just before 1820 is not entirely clear as the available evidence is somewhat conflicting, but its earlier history is well documented. The first chapel was built in about 1653 and was the centre of activity for Andrew Gifford's Baptist ministry until his death in 1721. In 1791 and 1792 the chapel was 'rebuilt and made larger',[10] but by 1814 it was again too small to accommodate the great congregations attracted by the Rev. Thomas Roberts who became minister there in 1807. In 1814 'the desirableness of a larger place became the subject of anxious deliberation',[11] and the congregation moved to bigger premises in Old King Street in 1816. The final Baptist services at Pithay took place on 27 October 1816. It is the use of the building between then and April 1820 that is in some doubt. Gordon Hamlin records that it ' was used by a group of Congregationalists who had separated from Castle Green Church'.[12] It is probable that this group is the one that the *Mathew's Bristol Directory* simply describes as 'Christians' in the 1818 edition. The information would have taken some time to obtain and include in the directory following the change of congregation worshipping at Pithay.

---

8   George Pocock, handbill headed 'The Tent', Prospect Place Bristol, 29 March 1820.

9   See copy of class ticket signed 'Geo Pocock' and issued to Mrs Ann Smith in March 1820; A.J. Lambert, *The Chapel on the Hill* (Bristol: St Stephen's Press, 1929), p.54.

10   Gordon Hamlin, 'The Pithay Chapel, Bristol', *Baptist Quarterly* 15 (1953-54), p.378.

11   J.G. Fuller, *A Memoir of the Rev Thomas Roberts M.A.* (London and Bristol, 1842), p.105.

12   Hamlin, 'Pithay Chapel, Bristol', p.378.

Hamlin further reports that, on a date which is not recorded, another Baptist group used the building when the previous occupants moved to new premises. It is likely that he was referring to a Welsh Baptist group that took over the building in 1831 or 1832. The Tent Methodists occupied the chapel in the intervening period.

Again using the *Mathew's Bristol Directories* as the main source, it is known that the 'Christian' group moved to Alden's Court, Broadmead, some time before publication of the 1820 directory. Ministers of congregations were not recorded in earlier editions, but in 1822, and probably before, the pastor of this group was a Mr H.C. Howells. This man may have been the key link to explain the availability of Pithay Chapel for Tent Methodist use. Howells is first recorded in the *Mathew's Bristol Directory* of 1812 as a 'Writing Master, 1 Somerset Square', moving to 31 St James's Place by 1814. Of particular significance is the 1818 edition's report that he had a boarding school at 36 St James's Place which, by 1828, had become the West Park Academy in Cotham.[13] Howells could have known Pocock for many years because of their mutual experience in the provision of boys' boarding education in Bristol. At the time, then, when the Tent Methodist issue was reaching its climax, Pocock may well have been aware from Howells, either that his congregation had already vacated Pithay, or that it was soon to do so. Whatever the precise circumstances were, the availability of a prominent, city centre building, described as 'of no means of small dimensions'[14] and 'spacious and beautiful',[15] was an extremely important and encouraging development. It was located immediately to the north of the only bridge, at the time, that crossed the river Avon in the city centre. The chapel was bought, presumably by Pocock, for £900 and 'a considerable sum has been expended in fitting it up'.[16] It is not known exactly how many people could be accommodated in the building but it had been used for regional Baptist denominational events when large numbers of representatives would have been present. On 1 and 2 June 1814, for example, the annual meeting of the Western Association of Baptist Churches was held there. That body consisted of sixty-three Baptist congregations in the counties of Cornwall, Devon, Somerset, Dorset, Wiltshire, Hampshire and Gloucestershire.[17] On the first Sunday that it was used by the Tent Methodists for public worship, 23 April 1820, all four services attracted large congregations.

---

13   *Mathew's Bristol Directories* which were produced annually from 1793 have provided valuable information, particularly those between 1812 and 1830.

14   Fuller, *Memoir of the Rev Thomas Roberts*, p.28.

15   *Mathew's Bristol Directory* (1793-94 edition).

16   *TM Magazine*, p.173.

17   Record of the Annual Meeting of the Western Association of Baptist Churches, held at Pithay Chapel, 1-2 June 1814.

The First Set of Rules

Having acquired an eminently suitable building to provide a clear sense of separate identity, Pocock and the other leaders felt the need to establish an administrative structure without delay bearing in mind that the main preaching season using the tents had begun. In this respect Pocock would have been greatly assisted by the arrival in Bristol from Marlborough at the end of March of John Gosling, a wealthy and influential local banker with a special interest in educating the poor, as the previous references to him have shown. He was to become the promoter of the Tent Methodist expansion in one area of east Wiltshire bounded by Marlborough to the north and Salisbury thirty miles to the south, but in the meantime he had travelled to Bristol to give important support. He had resigned from the Wesleyan society in Marlborough following criticism by the local superintendent of his actions in providing hospitality to Pyer for three weeks during an illness, and for accepting him as a preacher despite his expulsion from Wesleyanism. Gosling had objected to receiving the censure from anyone concerning his private friendships. Considering that he had been instrumental in providing and financing premises for Wesleyan use in two nearby villages in 1817 and 1818, such action seemed unduly insensitive and unnecessary.

A set of rules, to be replaced by another much more comprehensive one in 1824, was produced, probably in the spring of 1820, although no precise date appeared on the document.[18] The inclusion of the words 'Agrarian Society' in the full title reflected the frequent visits and the importance of the work in the rural areas to the north of Bristol and elsewhere since 1814. Many villages between the river Severn to the west and such places as Dursley and Wotton-under-Edge some ten miles to the east had received much attention from tent preachers over the previous six years. It was only from 1820 onwards that the Bristol city centre and the inner suburbs received much evangelical activity once the Pithay chapel had been established as the group's centre of operations.

The rules show signs of hastiness in their preparation. They exhibited an intense concern to produce arrangements that would avoid some, at least, of the difficulties that had occurred in the last few years of the leaders' involvement with Wesleyanism. In particular, specific reference is made to a proper procedure for anyone who was criticized or suspended to defend or explain their action or behaviour before final decisions to expel them were made. Additionally, deacons of congregations had to be re-elected annually rather than continue in office for longer periods. The use of the word 'deacon' is interesting. It was a familiar word in

---

18   *TM Rules* (1820). This document was eight pages long, published in Bristol and was sold by a Philip Rose who became a trustee of some Tent Methodist chapels.

Independent and Baptist denominational terminology to describe lay leaders, but not in any of the Methodist groups at the time, including the Primitive Methodists and Bible Christians, as well as the Wesleyans. It should be noted, however, that the word was used for the title given to several men in December 1784 when Dr Thomas Coke ordained Francis Asbury, John Dickens, Caleb Boyer and Ignatius Pigman as deacons to provide ministerial and pastoral leadership on the formal establishment of the Methodist Episcopal Church in America.[19] It perhaps provides an early indication of the direction that part of the offshoot would go as the decade progressed, and probably resulted from Pyer's continuing friendship with William Thorp, an influential Independent minister in Bristol. Furthermore, and most significantly, consultation would occur before preaching plan proposals were implemented, thus avoiding the objections that Pocock and Pyer voiced in 1816 when they were given more preaching appointments than they wanted because of their involvement with tent activity. As far as premises were concerned, trustees would own the buildings, but they would be chosen from members of societies by one of the numerous committees that were to be established. Chapels could only be acquired or built if at least one half of the expected cost had already been subscribed, in an effort presumably to try and limit Pocock's personal financial commitment to future chapel expenditure. The Tent Methodists, then, were determined to give greater involvement in their affairs to local lay members.

Several of the biblical texts used to justify the rules did not seem to be entirely appropriate for the specific situation referred to. For example, the need for members 'to evidence an earnest and sincere desire for the salvation of their souls'[20] is cross-referenced with Acts 2:37. In fact verse 38 is more relevant. The verses read: 'Now when they heard this, they were pricked in their heart, and said unto Peter and to the rest of the apostles, Men and Brethren, what shall we do?' (verse 37), and 'Then Peter said unto them, Repent, and be baptised every one of you in the name of Jesus Christ for the remission of sins, and ye shall receive the gift of the Holy Ghost' (verse 38). Intriguingly, John 5:39 ('Search the scriptures, for in them ye think ye have eternal life: and they are they which testify of me') was the text used to justify instructing those who could not read to learn to do so. The rules referred, with great feeling, to Ezekiel 34 in which there are described shepherds who fail to care for the flocks of sheep in their charge. In verse 16, God will 'seek that which was lost, and bring again that which was driven away, and will bind up that which was broken, and will strengthen that which was sick: but I will

---

19   George Smith, *History of Wesleyan Methodism: Volume 1. Wesley and his Times* (London, 1859), pp.514-515.

20   *TM Rules* (1820), Rule No. 12, p.4.

destroy the fat and the strong; I will feed them with judgement'. The Tent Methodists believed that they had been harshly treated, but expressed in the conclusion to the 1820 rules a determination to serve their members and adherents and to become 'a Branch, however insignificant, of that Mighty Tree which is to fill the whole earth'.[21] They wished to put the period of bitter disputes behind them and make a positive contribution to the evangelizing of the areas in which they worked.

The overall impression of the rules is of a cumbersome set of procedures, produced in a great hurry, and lacking clarity for anyone seeking to interpret the document. Indeed, the printed copy of the rules held at the British Library shows ink alterations where cross references to other rules were originally incorrect. The copy held at the Library of the New Room, Bristol, is identical except that the necessary corrections had been made. Reference is made to a yearly meeting which would take place at Easter, but the only two annual meetings that are known to have occurred were held at the end of May 1822 and the middle of June 1823. There were many committees to be established, some of which may have been the same committee but with different names in different places of the document. For example, there was to be held weekly a preachers', pastors' and deacons' meeting, and a missionaries and resident preachers' meeting which may have been one and the same. There was also a pastors' meeting and a preachers' meeting, the purposes of which were not made entirely clear. On the other hand, specific rules were made regarding financial matters which were to be organized on a formalized basis and in a clear fashion. Five of the ten general rules dealt directly with money matters, of which the first was that 'The Missionaries or Itinerant Preachers shall have nothing to do with the management of financial affairs'.[22] A financial committee was to control the finances, and as an indication of the immediate concern for the poor, 'any member of this Society receiving relief from the Parish, or who are otherwise in poverty, shall not be allowed to contribute anything to the funds of the said Society'.[23] Furthermore, one third of the income was to be used 'for the relief of sick and poor members'.[24] While the rules may have been produced with undue haste, there was a clear intent to manage the sect's financial affairs efficiently and to be acutely conscious of the position of the less fortunate members of their societies.

It is likely that the rules were prepared by Pocock, Pyer and Gosling very soon after the new group was established. Certainly the same person was employed to print the rules who printed two of the three pamphlets

---

21 *TM Rules* (1820), p.7.
22 *TM Rules* (1820), Rule No. 6, p.3.
23 *TM Rules* (1820), Rule No. 18, pp.4-5.
24 *TM Rules* (1820), Rule No. 20, p.5.

that detail the disputes with Pocock, Pyer and Smith. More significantly, the rules document only referred to the first pamphlet published on 29 March 1820, and at the very end it is reported that a history of the activities over the previous six years would soon be issued. Given that tent activity began in April 1814, the spring of 1820 rather than a later date is, therefore, the probable publication date of the rules.

If it was indeed the case of early publication, it was a very different experience from that of the Primitive Methodists. It was two and a half years after the first Primitive Methodist class tickets were issued before the formal rules were accepted when 'laid before the Quarterly Meeting of January 3rd 1814'.[25] They were perceived to be 'well drafted, quite remarkable for their agreement with Scriptural principles, are pervaded by a liberal spirit, and lay down a broad basis for a democratic Church'.[26] Hugh Bourne, one of the founders, 'had discussed the proposed regulations with almost every person in the community'.[27] Bourne, apparently, had 'peculiar law-making ability'.[28] That was not the case with the writers of the Tent Methodist rules. They were not 'well drafted', nor was there, probably, much consultation, but they seem to have been prepared as a result of a perceived need to publish regulations promptly. There did, however, appear to be opportunity, like the Primitive Methodists, for ordinary members to have the ability to choose members of committees and office bearers. If the Tent Methodist rules were produced hastily, and the Primitive Methodists waited for over two years and engaged in substantial consultation during that period before their rules were formally approved, the Bible Christians also waited two years after formation of the sect before producing 'Rules of Society'. There does not, however, appear to have been much consultation with members, the document being the joint work of William O'Bryan and James Thorne. The reason for the delay was probably that O'Bryan regarded himself as its undisputed leader and felt that rules were of much less importance than a concentration of effort on committed evangelical activity.

Absence of Women Preachers

The differences between the three groups as to the perceived relative importance of many issues, including the early production of regulations,

25   H.B. Kendall, *The Origin and History of the Primitive Methodist Church* (London, [c.1906]), I, p.170.

26   Kendall, *The Origin and History*, I, p.171.

27   Werner, *Primitive Methodist Connexion*, p.78.

28   B. Aquila Barber, *A Methodist Pageant* (London: Holborn Publishing House, 1932), p.131.

are interesting. There was another matter about which the Tent Methodists seem to have taken an opposite approach to either the Primitive Methodists or the Bible Christians. These two groups welcomed the involvement of women as itinerant preachers particularly in the early years, sometimes expecting them to travel and work long distances from their homes. Of the twenty-nine itinerants recorded at the Bible Christians' first conference held in August 1819, no less than fourteen were women, and a few years later when there were between two and three hundred local preachers, nineteen of the forty-three itinerants were women.[29] The Primitive Methodists had some distinguished and dedicated women preachers during the early years. They included Sarah Kirkland, considered to be the first travelling preacher, who worked in Cheshire, Nottingham, Derby and Yorkshire, Jane Brown in Hull, and Elizabeth Johnson who at the age of only sixteen began her travelling preaching commitments and became the mother of three future Mayors of Walsall.[30] In 1818, 20% of all Primitive Methodist preachers were women, though most were local preachers, not itinerants. Furthermore, while they were welcome as evangelists, their voting and speaking rights at meetings were not equal to their male counterparts until much later in the nineteenth century.[31]

There is no indication, however, that when Tent Methodism was formalized in the spring months of 1820, women had any preaching part to play. A possible reason was that both Pocock and Smith strongly objected to the role that women took in their departures from Wesleyanism. This may have coloured the views they held as to the contribution that women could make. Smith drew specific attention to the fact that of thirteen people who voted against him, six were women. Pocock had disparaging words for women at the time of his withdrawal. He strongly objected that the 'Leaders' meeting composed of so many females, some of whom were young enough to be his daughters, who had it in their power to judge the ministers of Jesus Christ'.[32] In his later pamphlet he referred scornfully to 'a female Leader, little more than twenty years of age'.[33] Pocock's most caustic comment 'spoke of the impropriety of females being called upon to hold up their hands in such

29   Robinson, *Observations on the System of Wesleyan Methodism*, p.69.

30   Joseph Ritson, *The Romance of Primitive Methodism* (London: Primitive Methodist Publishing House, 1910), ch.7, pp.133-159, highlights the contributions made by many early women preachers. See also E. Dorothy Graham, 'Chosen by God: The female Travelling Preachers of Early Primitive Methodism', paper presented to Centenary Conference of WHS in conjunction with the World Methodist Historical Society entitled *Methodism in its Cultural Milieu*, 26-30 July 1993, in Cambridge, England.

31   Werner, *Primitive Methodist Connexion*, pp.142-143.

32   Pocock, *Statement of Facts*, p.12.

33   Pocock *et al*, *Facts Without a Veil*, p.5.

cases, pointing out that it was unbecoming, indecorous, and ill suited to their characters'.[34] He also said that 'Ladies...must be taught...to stay at home and mind their own sewing business'.[35] It is, therefore, not surprising that of a total of approximately twenty preachers referred to by name or initials in the *Tent Methodist Magazine*, and elsewhere, as being involved with Tent Methodism in the spring and summer of 1820, not one is a woman (see Appendix D). The *Tent Methodist Magazine* for 1823 contains eight obituaries, two of which concern ministers of other dissenting denominations. Of the six Tent Methodists, three are women and although they are referred to with great affection, none of them appear to have held any position of leadership.

In other parts of the country Wesleyanism had had first hand experience of the effects of new Methodist sects by 1820, but in Bristol this was not the case. Primitive Methodism was then still mainly contained in the north Midlands and was not, for several more years, to move substantially southwards. The Bible Christians, whilst beginning to expand outwards into Somerset from their initial areas of activity in Cornwall and Devon, did not become firmly established in Bristol until much later. The Methodist New Connexion, despite the earlier reference to an apparent society in Bristol in early 1820, the Unitarian Cookites, and the various strands of Independent Methodism, were all firmly based in the northern half of England. It was understandable, then, that Bristol Wesleyans, especially because of the antagonism that had occurred from time to time in previous years, were quick to oppose the newly created society. They were used to co-existing with long established dissenting groups including Roman Catholics, Moravians, Unitarians, Jews and French Protestants as well as Quakers, Presbyterians, Independents and Baptists on the one hand, and the Church of England on the other, but this breakaway organization was felt to be a much more direct threat. The written exchanges in pamphlet form seem to have ceased in May 1820, but the verbal confrontations continued.

Early Geographical Expansion

With a chapel acquired, and a set of rules and regulations in place, the evangelical activity could resume for the 1820 season. It was fitting that the three men who had been subjected to the cross examination and bitter hostility of former spiritual colleagues should be the ones who led the opening services at the Pithay chapel on Sunday 23 April. They were well supported by friends from beyond Bristol in addition to local people who

---

34   Pocock *et al*, *Facts Without a Veil*, p.33.
35   Pocock *et al*, *Facts Without a Veil*, p.31.

combined to form very large congregations. That Christian charity had not returned was evident as 'a busy host of determined calumniators were not deficient in their attempts to blast our reputation'. 'Bitter Speeches, unmerited reproaches, confident and vaunting prophecies of our speedy extinction, were heaped upon us'.[36] There were other measures which were designed to prevent the new group from expanding and consolidating the position it had established with those people who had been converted by the evangelical work of previous years. Perhaps it was because it was known that the first society of thirty-one members with four preachers had already been formed at Pithay, that such vitriolic language was used. The local Wesleyan hierarchy had decided that any of their members who showed support should be dismissed. The ability to establish a society so quickly at Pithay is particularly interesting as the evangelical work of the previous six years had been carried out away from the city centre. It is probable that the group was formed from Pocock's supporters among the Portland chapel membership, as a late nineteenth century manuscript history of the chapel records that 'a few office bearers and several members'[37] left the Wesleyans to join the Tent Methodists. There is further evidence for this as a picture of a Tent Methodist class ticket, signed by George Pocock, appears in a later history of Portland chapel. It was issued in March 1820 to a Mrs Ann Smith, not known to be a relative of Samuel Smith, but who was the grandmother of a Simon Smith who was a trustee of Portland chapel in 1929.[38] There were, perhaps, also people who had been in membership at other churches who were aware of the long running hostilities. A Bristol Wesleyan itinerant, in a letter to Jabez Bunting in October 1820, bemoaned the fact 'that so many good men have left us'.[39] The various acrimonious meetings, of which there were very many, were held at King Street vestry in the centre of Bristol and the on-going disagreement was well publicized among Methodists. It is clear that several dedicated men, including Victory Purdy and Samuel Bryant, refused to accept such provocation, and became local preachers for the Tent Methodists.

Within a very short time from mid-April 1820, the most likely date that can be given for the actual establishment of the sect of Tent Methodists, a

---

36   *TM Magazine*, p.174.

37   Anon., *A Short History of Portland Street Wesleyan Chapel, Bristol, and its surroundings with brief notices of some of the principal persons and events connected with Methodism in the City* (n.p., n.d.). This thirty-eight page manuscript records events up to 1878. From this, and other information contained in it, it can be surmised that the work was written in c.1880.

38   Lambert, *Chapel on the Hill*, p.54.

39   W.R. Ward (ed.), *The Early Correspondence of Jabez Bunting 1820-1829* (London: Royal Historical Society, 1972), p.54, letter from Joseph Sutcliffe to Jabez Bunting, 31 October, 1820.

number of societies had been formed. In the main the societies emerged quite naturally from the evangelical work of previous years, notably at Frampton, Dursley, Wotton-under-Edge, Bath and at several places in the Kingswood area. Subsequently, chapels were acquired, and Soundwell, Kingswood, seemed to have the distinction of having the first newly built chapel for Tent Methodism, followed by Frampton and Dursley very soon afterwards. It is clear from the many subsequent references to the 'Colliers' Temple', as the Soundwell chapel was known, that it had a central role in Tent Methodist affairs and was a place of great blessing in the coal mining communities of the neighbourhood. In an area a few miles to the north in the more rural parts of south Gloucestershire, people who had received Pocock, Pyer and other tent preachers from 1817 onwards also sought chapels so that they could have more permanent places of worship. These requests for chapels to be erected were agreed to by Pocock, the original members of the societies being former Wesleyans and those of no previous Christian belief. However, several prominent local Wesleyans, including William Jones, the itinerant preacher appointed by the 1819 annual conference, and Irving and Nightingale, both former supporters of tent preaching, attempted to dissuade people from joining the Tent Methodists or subscribing financially to the building programme. Notwithstanding the pressure, an unnamed leader with twenty-six years of Methodist service resigned from Wesleyanism and brought his class of forty-six members into Tent Methodism at about the same time. So it is claimed, did others.[40] At most other places it is not known how many joined the societies, but it is recorded that 'nearly forty gave us their names as members of Society'[41] at Dursley in April. Overall, rapid progress was made, especially in the transition of what had been informal groups into structured societies.

It is no wonder that the final pamphlet in the series of three, *Facts Without a Veil*, closes with an apology by the three authors for the delay of three weeks in replying to the one produced by the Methodist Leaders' Meeting. The delay, readers were told, was 'solely occasioned by their extensive and numerous engagements'.[42] The pace of activity between the very end of 1819 and the end of May 1820 was astonishing and it is not surprising that such a detailed response, running to fifty pages, had to take second place to such encouraging initial evangelical progress.

---

40   Pocock *et al*, *Facts Without a Veil*, p.48.
41   *TM Magazine*, p.175.
42   Pocock *et al*, *Facts Without a Veil*, p.50.

Additional Resources

There were several other factors that contributed to an auspicious start to Tent Methodism as a formal, separate body. The commitment, enthusiasm and shrewdness of Pocock was probably the principal one. He was, by then, well known in Bristol, having lived and worked there for twenty years. Quite apart from his support for Methodism, including his financial generosity, his boarding school was well established in 1820 by which time he was forty-six years of age. He had assistance, certainly from John Barnett who was by then an active Tent Methodist, but probably also from one or two of his sons. Schools in those days had two holiday periods, one of which, fortunately in view of the timing of events, was in the early summer. The regular local newspaper advertisements for the Prospect Place Academy included, for example, on 10 July 1824, a notice that pupils would return on 19 July 1824.[43] The reopening of schools took place at about that time every year, so Pocock could give substantial amounts of time during June and early July to establishing the movement. His school was successful, and apart from occasional tribulations such as a break-in and robbery in 1813,[44] no longer took all his energy. His business colleagues would have, as has been shown, provided him with useful contacts and information, including the availability of Pithay chapel, and he would certainly have had access to printing facilities. With at least twelve and possibly as many as fifteen children, several of whom became involved in running their own schools, he had other responsibilities to fulfil, but he received great support, particularly from his wife and his eldest daughter, Rose.[45] A man used to gaining his own way, any attempts by the Wesleyan authorities to curtail Pocock's activities and make him conform to established rules and practices he disagreed with would have been unwelcome to him. It is, however, inconceivable that he would have gone to the lengths he did to establish a new sect without a genuine desire to extend the kingdom of God, in accordance with Methodist doctrine, particularly focusing on his interest and belief in the value of education, and his concern for the poor. Edward Griffith, five years earlier, had spoken to a number of Pocock's pupils at Prospect Place Academy about his Christian commitment, and Pocock was later to publish a book of poems and hymns especially for young people.

Pocock was ably assisted, not only by the other existing Tent Methodist preachers, most of whom continued their support of earlier years, but also

---

43   *Felix Farley's Bristol Journal*, Saturday 10 July 1824.
44   *Felix Farley's Bristol Journal*, Saturday 26 June 1813.
45   Dorothy Vintner, *More Kingswood Stories* (Bristol: Central Press, 1951), 'The Cleft in the Rock', p.19.

by new followers, some of whom had been faithful, long-time, local Wesleyan preachers. Pyer, Smith, Roberts and Gosling were all people who had been involved for some time and mentioned in *Tent Methodist Magazine* record of events, but Barnett, Pring and Payne were three others who, freed from their Wesleyan responsibilities, entered fully into the Tent Methodist cause.

There were two more, at least, who came into group at about this time. Samuel Bryant and Victory Purdy had been valuable workers in Wesleyan societies, Bryant for three years in Kingswood and Purdy for no less than forty-nine years as 'he preached his first sermon in 1771'[46] when he was twenty-four years of age. Purdy received a letter from John Wesley in February 1784 which drew attention to the support and friendship Wesley and Purdy's father had enjoyed. Both Bryant and Purdy fell foul of the 'edict...passed by the official characters among them [Wesleyan leadership], prohibiting their members either praying, or any way exercising their gifts in any of the Tent places of worship, or services of the Tent Missionary Society, on pain of expulsion'.[47] Purdy, also in 1820, had written a pamphlet which criticized the actions of travelling preachers, sought permission for local preachers to attend the annual conference and, on the final page, wrote prophetic words which were soon to come to fruition: 'But if you cannot receive them [local preachers], there are others that can and will'.[48] He had served the Downend circuit for many years but frequently showed his dislike for formal denominational distinctions.[49] In a letter written in 1809 he said 'I am neither a Wesleyan, nor a Whitfieldite, I am not in connection with any religious body of people whatever. I am a Dissenter from the Church of England, though not a rigid one'.[50] It was with understandable sadness that after refusing to undertake to have no contact with Tent Methodists 'he returned his preaching plan and society ticket, accompanied by a note to the superintendent of the Downend circuit'.[51] Humble, largely self-educated, dedicated men like Bryant and Purdy gave Tent Methodism a practical, down-to-earth element which complemented the education interests and business skills of men like Pocock and Gosling.

---

46   Victory Purdy, *The Poetical Miscellanies* (Bristol, 1825), p.iv (published posthumously).

47   Anon., *Memoirs of the Life and Character of Samuel Bryant, a Kingswood Collier* (Bristol, 1827), p.7.

48   Victory Purdy, *Thoughts on the case of the Local Preachers in the Methodist Connexion* (Bristol, 1820). [The pamphlet incorrectly shows 'Vicary' not 'Victory'.]

49   John B. Edwards, *Victory Purdy, 'The Kingswood Collier'* (Bristol: New Room, 1984), pp.11-12.

50   Anon., *The Life of Victory Purdy* (Methodist Biography No. 6, n.d), p.453.

51   Anon., *Some Account of the Life, Ministry and Writings of Victory Purdy, the Kingswood Collier* (Bristol, 1822), p.24.

The combination of all those attributes, together with Pyer's full-time commitment to the cause, was another reason for the encouraging beginnings.

It would seem that the attitude and actions of the local Wesleyan leadership were counter-productive and actually contributed to Tent Methodist early success. That men like Bryant, Purdy, and others, felt forced to leave Wesleyanism had a double effect—a loss of valuable resources for them and a clear gain to their new friends and spiritual colleagues and fellow workers. None of the local circuit superintendents seemed able to look beyond the disputes that climaxed in 1820 and see the effects that losing such useful men would have in the longer term. Henry Moore returned to Bristol in 1820 and became chairman of the district. According to a letter written by Joseph Sutcliffe, an itinerant preacher in the circuit, to Jabez Bunting later that year, Moore believed the affair leading to the departures of Pocock, Pyer and Smith had been badly handled and could have been avoided.[52] Moore was a man of great experience who was, by that time, an elder statesman of Methodism. Born in 1751, he was at various times a biographer of John Wesley, a trustee of both Kingswood and Woodhouse Grove Schools, and President of Conference, but was quite prepared on occasions to voice views that were contrary to contemporary official Wesleyan thinking. Had he been appointed to return to Bristol a year or two earlier the whole hostility might not have occurred. However, the dogmatic, uncompromising views of Wood, Greenly and Wintle, superintendents respectively of the Bristol, Downend and Dursley circuits, supported by the other members of the Bristol leaders' meetings, were ultimately determined to see the back of the Tent Methodist leaders. They did so at significant cost to Wesleyan affairs in and around Bristol, and further afield, as the third decade of the nineteenth century progressed.

Another factor which was helpful in the immediate aftermath of the separation was the existence of two tents, supplemented by at least one more within a short time. With only a few chapels under their control in 1820, the use of tents as additional places of worship would have assisted the group to serve the local societies that had already become established. Tents could have been employed at short notice, quickly erected, dismantled and moved elsewhere, and were used as well as private houses, and barns. Seven hundred people were capable of being accommodated in one or more of the tents and structures of that size were an obvious, tangible advertisement that tent preachers were to conduct services. Congregations of up to 2,000 were attracted, but to ensure that the tents were available for worship to those people living close to Bristol, no

---

52   Ward (ed.), *Early Correspondence of Jabez Bunting*, p.54, letter from Joseph Sutcliffe to Jabez Bunting, 31 October 1820. *TM Magazine*, p.102.

excursions of any distance took place for several months. Bradford-on-Avon and Warminster were the furthest places visited until a highly significant visit to London was undertaken in September 1820.

The final helpful feature in establishing the group quickly was simply the momentum that had been steadily building up, particularly since the second tent was brought into use in early 1819 which coincided with Pyer's appointment as a full-time missionary. Some areas around Bristol had received much evangelical attention for several years and this was a beneficial factor in sustaining interest while new parts of Bristol and places much further afield were being opened up for missionary work. That this momentum followed the efforts that Pyer and others were making was clear from letters that were received around the end of 1819. In addition to two letters from the superintendent and the circuit steward of the Dursley circuit at the end of June 1819 before the rapid deterioration in the relationships, others were sent from a nearby circuit six months later to Smith and Pocock. John Palser, a leading member of the society at Wotton-under-Edge, wrote to Smith on 1 December 1819 and to Pocock on 19 December 1819. He acknowledged the contribution that previous visits to the area had made by saying that 'the work continues in a prosperous state', and he fervently hoped for other visits from any of the preachers who could be spared. Significantly, one of the letters sought 'a little more of that heavenly fire which used to descend, while worshipping under the Tent'.[53] By January 1820 reports of Pyer's effective dismissal from Wesleyanism were clearly circulating in the Dursley neighbourhood as a letter to Pocock from John Cook, the Dursley steward and a trustee, showed. It was with great distress that Cook had heard the news and wrote, 'when I see the spot where the Tent stood, or only hear the name of the Tent, I cannot help dropping a grateful tear to the great Author of all our mercies'.[54] Very many Dursley members, he claimed, would send their support. Cook recalled the provision of a tent nine months before while the chapel was undergoing major repairs and expressed the view that 'hundreds of precious souls have reason to praise the Lord, on account of your great kindness'.[55] While there was a revival which had resulted in increased membership at Dursley, Nibley and Wotton-under-Edge, among other places, the authors of those letters recognized that it would only last for a limited time before the effect wore off and the memories were forgotten.

There were, of course, many places away from Bristol that had only been visited once and there is no evidence of any permanent increase in Methodist membership figures in these towns and villages (Appendices B

---

53   *TM Magazine*, pp.102-103.
54   *TM Magazine*, p.105.
55   *TM Magazine*, p.105.

and C). The excursion which included Winchester and the Isle of Wight was not repeated and reference to the island's membership figures suggest no lasting impact from the Tent Methodist mission in 1818. Similarly, the visit to south Wales the following summer appears not to have led to the establishment of any new societies in that particular part. The effects in many places were, no doubt, ephemeral but such experience was not confined to Tent Methodism. The quality of the preaching and the genuine concern of the leading tent preachers, travelling with the familiar, distinctive sight of what was a large marquee, generated the response from some people by way of a commitment to the Christian way of life. The greatest results were achieved in those areas where regular and relatively frequent visits had occurred. The villages to the north east of Bristol as far as Dursley, including Frampton, Rangeworthy, Olveston and Wotton-under-Edge were examples. They became centres of future valuable evangelical work, as did Marlborough, another place to have benefited from tent evangelical missionary work each year from 1817.

Schism or Secession?

It is now possible to form a judgement as to whether the events of late 1819 and early 1820 should be described as a 'schism' or a 'secession'—a word that has rarely, hitherto, been used to describe Tent Methodism's withdrawal from Wesleyanism. While John Bowmer's brief reference to Tent Methodism in *Pastor and People* includes the word 'secession', he goes on to say that it 'did no damage to the Wesleyan cause',[56] a view that is certainly open to debate. Definitions of the two words are necessary, but dictionaries' distinctions between them are not particularly helpful. Various versions define a 'schism' in similar terms: 'A breach in the unity of the visible Church' from *The Oxford English Dictionary*; 'division within or separation from an established Church, not necessarily involving differences in doctrines' from *The Collins Concise Dictionary*. For 'secede', however, the dictionaries record, for example, 'The action of seceding or formally withdrawing from an alliance, a federation, a political or religious organisation, or the like' from *The Oxford English Dictionary*. *The Collins Concise Dictionary* and the *Chambers 20th Century Dictionary* define the word similarly. Common usage in the context of nonconformity and the fragmentation of Methodism and among other denominations does attempt to produce a rather clearer distinction between the two words. Both 'schism' and 'secession' indicate disagreement and then withdrawal from a religious

---

56   Bowmer, *Pastor and People*, p.81.

body. 'Secession', however, implies that an organized withdrawal takes place by a group, or a collection of individuals, which then as a conscious next step forms or joins a new body. Bible Christianity would, if this distinction is accepted, be correctly regarded as resulting from a 'schism' because, in the main, those people who joined in the initial stages did not leave Wesleyanism but came from a significant variety of denominations, including the Church of England, and none. The position with Primitive Methodism is not so clear cut, but should probably be regarded as a secession as several societies and classes rejected Wesleyanism to form the new group when it was established in May 1811.

The contention in this work is that Tent Methodism should be considered a 'secession', albeit a minor one. Although the evidence for this view is principally derived from Tent Methodist sources there is more objective material that tends to give support to this opinion. It has already been noted that several classes left Wesleyanism and became Tent Methodist groups either at the time of the formation or very soon afterwards. There were others who joined later, but in addition to the society formed in the middle of April 1820 and based at Pithay chapel it has been recorded that at least five others were created within relatively short distances from Bristol. In addition, as the next chapter will show, an existing Wesleyan group not previously connected with the Tent Methodists left a London circuit and joined the newly formed sect in late 1820 or early 1821. At all these places chapels were available at the time the societies were established or quite soon afterwards. Pocock's introduction to the 1820 version of the rules, and indeed the 1824 edition, and the final pages of the final pamphlet of the three written in 1820, all claim that considerable numbers of people and groups left Wesleyanism to join Tent Methodism.

There are also indications from Wesleyan sources that a secession took place. Jabez Bunting had his attention drawn to the Tent Methodists on several occasions and in the biography written by his son, the word 'secession' is used, referring in a footnote to a description of the Bristol events, 'this was an inconsiderable secession'.[57] 'Inconsiderable' it may have been, but the membership statistics for the local circuits in the Bristol district for the relevant years make interesting scrutiny. At a time when the national membership figures declined by 4,100 (2%) between 1819 and 1820, the fall in the Bristol circuit was from 2,690 to 2,523 (6.6%), in Kingswood circuit from 490 to 460 (6.5%), and in the Downend circuit from 460 to 432 (6.5%)—not conclusive evidence, perhaps, but supportive of the claims that some groups of former Wesleyans in several places joined the Tent Methodists.

---

57   Bunting, *Life of Jabez Bunting*, II, p.170 n..

A modest secession, then, occurred. While fundamental disagreements among Methodists were not as commonplace as Pocock claimed when he wrote 'in almost every circuit through the whole kingdom, discontents, discords, and divisions are spreading and multiplying to such a degree, that the Fabric of Methodist Government is tottering on every side',[58] much dissension was apparent. It was an early twentieth-century author of a book about a long established Methodist London community group who wrote: 'the Church of God need never fear enemies outside, but ever since its earliest formation in the first century, dangerous and hostile foes have arisen within its own borders sowing error, causing dissensions and stirring up discontent, which have been far more harmful and ruinous than any attack from its avowed opponents'.[59] It was a year too late when Joseph Sutcliffe, a preacher in the Bristol circuit between 1820 and 1822, wrote to Jabez Bunting on 31 October 1820 and told him that 'Mr Moore thinks the preachers imprudent for bringing Pocock's case at all into the Leaders' meeting. Others lament that so many good men have left us, and think that things might have been better managed'.[60] Contemporary Bristol Wesleyans also seemed, therefore, to acknowledge that a secession had occurred, and some at least regretted that outcome which, by the time of that letter, was seven months after the event.

Having prepared a formal set of rules which contained a structure of sorts, the Tent Methodists nonetheless relied extremely heavily on Pocock for leadership and, probably, day to day organization. It is likely that he was supported in this aspect of the work, not so much by Pyer who was engaged in the evangelical activity on a full-time basis, but by Gosling. After a time in Bristol, he returned to Marlborough to continue to run his banking partnership and, as will be shown in the next chapter, to establish a significant number of Tent Methodist chapels and meeting houses in east Wiltshire. While Pocock would have been eminently capable of making decisions, quickly and with little consultation, his school was back in operation by the end of July 1820 and he had other matters to deal with from that time onwards. There was much success to follow, but seeds of future problems were already sown. His inability, or more likely his unwillingness, to spend much time away from the Bristol area, his increasing interest in several mechanical inventions that were to emerge over the next few years, his domestic responsibilities as the father of a large family and perhaps, a lack of harmony with Pyer, all, in due course, were to present difficulties.

---

58   Pocock *et al*, *Facts Without a Veil*, p.49.

59   E.C. Rayner, *The Story of the Christian Community 1685-1909* (London: Memorial Hall, [c.1910]), p.50.

60   Ward (ed.), *Early Correspondence of Jabez Bunting*, p.54, letter from Joseph Sutcliffe to Jabez Bunting, 31 October 1820.

The biblical text which appeared on the class tickets indicated a recognition that the evangelical work must be God inspired: 'If this counsel or this work be of men, it will come to nought: But if it be of God ye cannot overthrow it'. It was a significant quotation to use from Acts 5:38-39. Firstly, there was a hint that constant attempts would continue to be made to discredit the group. Additionally, and of particular note, the two verses immediately preceding verse 38 draw attention to two men who attempted but failed to establish new sects: Theudas, and Judas of Galilee who 'drew away many people after him: he also perished, and all, even as many as obeyed him, were dispersed' (Acts 5.37). There was clearly a confidence that the evangelical missionary work was supported by God, and a certainty that Pocock and the other leaders were not false prophets who would quickly fail. Furthermore, bearing in mind that the words 'Goodwill to Men' were shown in capital letters in the top right hand corner of the class tickets, there was a claim by them that no hostility was felt to their former Wesleyan friends.

Orthodox, Not Extreme

There was a keen desire by Pocock to be considered the leader of a mainstream Methodist group. He believed that there was no need for the Wesleyan leadership to be obstructive or to object to his evangelical activity. The whole tenor of the final pamphlet, *Facts without a Veil*, sought to establish the reasonableness of the leadership as well as a desire to compromise and continue to serve Methodism. There were, so Pocock claimed, others in the Bristol district that were also conducting Methodism outside a strict interpretation of the rules. 'Rule, Rule, Methodist Rule "Conformity or Expulsion"'[61] was a cry of Pocock's without, he insisted, any account being taken of scriptural guidance, or any flexibility to take account of practical considerations. In the same pamphlet, Pocock complained that a local preacher was guilty of breaking an instruction given by John Wesley, and others were collecting funds without following laid down procedures. None, however, had received the censure of the local hierarchy, let alone been excluded from Wesleyanism. The concluding sentences of the last pamphlet in the written exchanges highlighted the claim that tent preachers' activity was recognized as valuable by a wide variety of Christian groups, and others. 'While the Magistrates, the Gentry, and respectable housekeepers in every direction; while the Friends, the Dissenters, and even the Clergy of our venerable establishment have the candour to acknowledge the

---

61   Pocock *et al*, *Facts Without a Veil*, p.32.

reformation and piety which have followed the labours of the Tent Preachers; and while thousands who know themselves to be sinners, and are seeking mercy, and are saying "come again", the leading men among the Methodists are the only Class of persons...who...are becoming persecutors',[62] was the final point that the three writers, Pocock, Pyer and Smith, wished to make to the Wesleyan leaders and all the others who would read the series of pamphlets. The last one was published in mid-May 1820, by which time the first set of rules had been prepared which contained further evidence of a concern to be regarded as an orthodox group. The words 'equity and moderation' were used in the concluding section together with an assertion that the regulations had a 'close analogy to the Scriptures'.[63] Furthermore, the doctrines that were set out for the members to follow were entirely consistent with the beliefs of Wesleyan Methodists. It became clear that although personal animosities remained between individual Wesleyans and Tent Methodists, the sect itself was never regarded as extreme by any of the Methodist groups.

Pocock was keen to show his knowledge of, and indeed his agreement with, Methodist regulations when it suited his argument and opinions. He objected to Thomas Wood using the prefix 'Reverend' which, he said, was contrary to the instructions in 'Large Minutes, section 29, page 54', quoted as 'Nor shall gowns or bands be used among us, or the title of Reverend be used at all'.[64] Nonetheless, Pocock himself was, apparently, using the word 'Reverend' within the next two years. There were other references to the members of the Wesleyan hierarchy in Bristol departing from the official rules in the treatment of Smith, and to the claim that another rule was broken by preachers who conduced services in chapels that were 'Not settled in a proper way'.[65] Furthermore, Pocock quoted from the works of Jonathan Crowther, a prolific writer on Methodist affairs, who was especially concerned with the justification and interpretation of internal rules and regulations. He was a significant Wesleyan figure from the end of the eighteenth century until well into the nineteenth, and was president of the Wesleyan Conference in 1819. Pocock was determined to portray Tent Methodism as a fully acceptable way of developing mainstream Methodism so that it continued the evangelical activity along lines that would have been wholly condoned by John Wesley himself.

Indeed, the very fact that the word 'Methodist' invariably appeared in all references to the group showed a determination to retain an orthodoxy which, by 1820, was associated with Wesleyanism. It would also have been used to counteract attempts that were made by the Bristol

---

62   Pocock *et al, Facts Without a Veil*, pp.49-50.
63   *TM Rules* (1820), p.7.
64   Pocock *et al, Facts Without a Veil*, p.9.
65   Pocock *et al, Facts Without a Veil*, p.39.

authorities to convince people that the Tent leaders were opposed to Methodism. Smith continued: 'to act so hostilely to Methodism in regard to the Tent business'[66] was an allegation made by the Wesleyan leaders. Pyer was accused of being 'disaffected to Methodism', but he insisted he had 'preached Methodist doctrines, maintained Methodist discipline, and gave the fruits of his labour to Methodist Travelling Preachers'.[67] As a result of his friendship with Moore, Pocock may well have been advised to avoid the eccentric edges of Methodism and could have been warned of the consequences of alienating the bulk of the leadership, both central, and at district and circuit level. It is likely that Pocock genuinely believed his views would, given time, be accepted and he worked hard to persuade the authorities. His attempts to gain the approval of those attending the 1814 and 1819 annual conferences in Bristol were, however, never likely to succeed in the absence of a much more encouraging climate for laity to influence policy. In 1820 a 'top down' bureaucracy was in place in Methodism which was not conducive to being influenced by lay people, even respectable, long serving, energetic men such as Pocock.

He clearly wished to distance himself from some of the fringe religious groups that existed in some parts of the country in the early part of the nineteenth century. As Tent Methodism's concern for the poor became an increasing feature of the evangelical activity, there would probably have been an anxiety that the perceived extreme views of such people as Joanna Southcott should not permeate the movement. Although she had died in 1814, it has been claimed 'that the Southcott cult wreaked great havoc in the Methodist camp, notably in Bristol',[68] where, during her lifetime, she had a chapel. Southcott had been associated with the Methodists in Exeter in her youth and found much of her support from the 'working people of the west and north'.[69] In addition to holding views that E.P. Thompson describes as 'cranky',[70] she was able to produce hysterical reactions to her messages and to gain, temporarily at least, a great deal of support, mostly in the West Country and in parts of Lancashire and Yorkshire. After her death others continued to develop the messages she proclaimed and 'her voluminous writings became the gospel of sect after sect of religious eccentrics'.[71] Although Pocock and the other tent preachers were keen to encourage their hearers to seek forgiveness of sins and to embrace a personal commitment to the Christian message, they did not wish to have any connection with

---

66   Wood *et al*, *A Correct Statement of Facts*, p.9.
67   Pocock *et al*, *Facts Without a Veil*, pp.11 and 9.
68   Thompson, *Making of the English Working Class*, p.426.
69   Thompson, *Making of the English Working Class*, pp.421-22.
70   Thompson, *Making of the English Working Class*, p.420.
71   Ronald Matthews, *English Messiahs (Studies of Six English Religious Pretenders 1656-1927)* (London: Methuen, 1936), p.46.

successors to Southcott or with similar bodies that arose from time to time. It would have been partly for that reason that the set of regulations was quickly produced, showing that the movement was 'founded upon the doctrines and duties of the Holy Scriptures'.[72] In the event, as will be confirmed, the future support for the group came, particularly in Manchester, from mainstream denominations, and individuals who were very highly regarded within their own spheres of activity.

Differences with Wesleyanism

With the group having been fully established by the middle of 1820, it is relevant to recognize the differences between the operation of Tent Methodism and Wesleyanism. Although there were no theological disagreements, there were matters of organization and emphasis where distinctive practices emerged. Bearing in mind that Wesleyanism had been developing for eighty years by the time that Pocock, Pyer and Smith left, it is not surprising that some dissimilarities were apparent. Even taking this fact into account, however, the practices and priorities of Tent Methodism showed significant variations.

From a careful study of the first version of the rules a number of differences are apparent. In the first place any Methodist model deed for holding the legal title to chapel premises was clearly not going to be acceptable to Pocock. A very early example of the hostility that this was to cause occurred with premises at Rangeworthy. Pocock went into great detail to describe how he was approached to provide a chapel for those people who had heard tent preachers for several years. Rangeworthy had been a regular recipient of a tent since 1817 and a Mr Bedggood made the request 'to assist the poor people there in getting a place of worship'.[73] Bedggood provided a plot of land which was a part of his garden, and Pocock instructed the builders, became responsible for payments, and supervised the building work. He insisted that it was understood from the beginning that the Methodist model deed would not be used so that the tent preachers could officiate at services, but the legal formalities had not been completed promptly. The local superintendents apparently persuaded the local people to insist on the conference agreed documentation being used. Pocock was not aware of this manoeuvre until he was finalizing the transaction with his attorney. The Tent Methodist rules provided for the members of the individual society to choose the trustees of buildings, not to have them imposed by the dictate of the circuit authorities, frequently the superintendent alone. Rule 34 of the

---

72   *TM Rules* (1820), p.3.
73   Pocock *et al, Facts Without a Veil*, p.35.

1820 version states: 'The Trustees of Chapels or other buildings for religious worship, shall be chosen from among the members of the Society by a special meeting of Official Characters'. The ownership and day to day management of chapels was undoubtedly a sensitive issue in the light of Pocock's objections to Wesleyan practice, but he did not insist on having the controlling influence written in to the rules.

Tent Methodism became a mission to the poor to a greater extent than appears to have been the case with Wesleyanism. This was evidenced by evangelical work being undertaken in some city centres where living and working conditions were often appalling, and rural areas where agricultural wages were lower than the norm elsewhere. In this, the sect shared the same concerns as the Primitive Methodists and the Bible Christians at a time when there seemed to be a feeling that Wesleyanism was becoming more middle class in its outlook. While the common claim that there was an increasing middle-class trend must remain a subjective judgement, Bunting's support for Tory politicians as well as his famous words 'Methodism was as much opposed to democracy as to sin',[74] both created an impression among the less well off in society that official Wesleyanism was less concerned with their lot than the various offshoots. The final pamphlet castigates the Bristol authorities for a lack of sympathy and practical help to the poor, and the Tent Methodist regulations contained several rules designed to alleviate the burden on poor members. Pocock and his fellow preachers did not accept 'the natural, habitual poverty of the working-man',[75] words spoken by an Anglican mill-owner in Charlotte Brontë's *Shirley*, but sought to improve their material and spiritual lot.

Understandably, the formality and relative inflexibility of preaching plans did not suit the Tent Methodist missionary zeal in the very early period although at least one area was using preaching plans by the middle of 1822. There continued to be need to respond quickly to opportunities to take one of the tents to meet requests, and this would have been inhibited by a close adherence to a preaching plan, covering a three month period, the details of which would have been worked out considerably in advance. Whereas Wesleyanism was beginning to become rather more inward looking as far as home missionary efforts were concerned, the second 'General Rule' of Tent Methodism was that 'the Gospel shall be preached whenever, and wherever Divine Providence may open their way'.[76] Using verses from Luke 16 as the scriptural justification, evangelical effort would occur relying upon the 'power of God' as well as the activities of the tent preachers. As the following

---

74   Jabez Bunting, *An Appeal to the Members of the Wesleyan Methodist Societies in Great Britain* (Leeds, 1827), p.6.
75   Charlotte Brontë, *Shirley* (London: Penguin, 1985 [1849]), p.99.
76   *TM Rules* (1820), Rule No. 2, p.3.

chapter will describe and analyse, 'divine providence', and the influence of men who had been converted by the preachers, led Tent Methodists to several different parts of England over the following few years, as well as extending the activity in the Bristol neighbourhood.

Not surprisingly Tent Methodism had a much greater role for laity to play although Pocock's personal influence remained immense in the immediate period after 1820. There were structures within societies, and a format which would have served if a district or circuit arrangement became fully operative. There was not, however, anything approaching a 'Legal Hundred' or a national hierarchy that could impose policy stemming from an annual conference. Although Pocock was, at this time, the undisputed leader, the general tenor of the rules he was instrumental in producing was that only after much consultation within the movement would decisions be made. There was a role for a 'Yearly Meeting' but 'all the official members of this Society'[77] would attend so ensuring a much greater degree of lay participation. While this may have been a deliberate policy, it was also necessary because there was simply an insufficient number of dedicated leaders with the time, ability or inclination to contemplate, discuss and implement general policy.

Tent Methodism's clear mission was to fulfil evangelical aspirations to local communities, particularly to the poor, comprising those out of regular work and their dependants who were often badly housed, badly fed, and in poor health. Those communities were located in several different parts of England. They were missioned as a direct result of invitations received from individuals who had been made aware of Tent Methodist work, or who had already received much personal blessing from Tent Methodist preachers. Several years of expansion and progress were enjoyed, despite the facing and overcoming of immense difficulties. There was not a steady, immediately logical geographic development as with the Primitive Methodists and Bible Christians—outward from Bristol, for example—but, on the contrary, there was no coherent pattern to the evangelical work that was undertaken. That is not to say that there were not good reasons for the decisions made, and the following chapter will describe and analyse the process of expansion.

---

77   *TM Rules* (1820), Rule No. 8, p.3.

CHAPTER 5

The Geographical Spread of Tent Methodism

From the start of 1820 and for the following six years there was much encouraging progress. Geographical expansion took place which opened up new areas of Christian evangelicalism to the less well off in society, both in urban conurbations and in rural communities. The impact of Tent Methodism, albeit in localized parts of England, and in one small area of south Wales, became substantial until it faded in a variety of ways and for a number of reasons.

The initial advances of the group happened despite some considerable handicaps. Firstly, it was clear that anyone in the Bristol area who associated with the group in any way was liable to be expelled. There was an instruction to all the local circuits that 'none of their members should assist us [Tent Methodists] in any of our religious services upon pain of being excluded from the Methodist Society'.[1] Apparently long since forgotten was the resolution passed at an annual conference: 'We cannot, however, we will not, part with any of our dear flock, who loves God and man, on account of unessential points'.[2] That statement was made in 1793 during the period immediately after Wesley's death when it was already feared that secessions would occur, and long before the quite different climate engendered by the impact made by Jabez Bunting. While Bunting remains a controversial figure, with church historians far from unanimous in their assessment of him, it is universally acknowledged that he had great influence through an authoritarian approach and a powerful personality. It was he who, in a response to the superintendent of the Hungerford circuit in 1820—two days before Christmas Day—wrote: 'There is no rule directly against wearing a fool's cap in our pulpits, but he who did so would be properly and legally excluded'.[3] The context of that letter was an an urgent concern that there

---

1   Pocock *et al*, *Facts Without a Veil*, p.5.
2   *Minutes of Methodist Conference* (1793), p.292.
3   Ward (ed.), *Early Correspondence of Jabez Bunting*, p.55, letter to Jabez Bunting from William Griffith, 20 December 1820, endorsed by way of reply by Jabez Bunting on 23 December 1820.

were defections to the Tent Methodists. It underlined the atmosphere and tone of Wesleyanism when disagreements arose. What effect the expulsion threats had cannot be known, but they provided further evidence that local Wesleyans were disturbed at the prospects.

That obstacles were likely to be placed in the way of the Tent Methodists can also be gathered from the study of a letter addressed to George Pocock and John Pyer from Elijah Waring dated 28 May 1820. News of these potential difficulties had clearly reached south Wales a year after Waring had been deeply touched by the tent visit to the Swansea and Neath area. He was still in fellowship with the Quakers at the time, and for a further five years before he joined the Wesleyans, but he wrote, 'May you be preserved in meekness, in long-suffering, with patience rejoicing in the truth, whatever discouragements may assail you'.[4] It is clear, then, that knowledge of the initial difficulties with the Wesleyans soon reached areas well beyond Bristol.

The second problem which had to be overcome was a potential shortage of preachers. In this respect the early signs were promising. With the attraction of well respected former Wesleyans, the work in the Bristol area could proceed with familiar local preachers gaining the confidence of local congregations. Appendix D is a significant list of preaching talent, and includes one name that was to become very well known in Congregational circles from the 1830s onwards: George Smith. It was in 1820 that Pocock first met Smith, then a youth of only seventeen, who already had a 'desire to win souls to Christ'. Pocock, presumably using his school master's insights, 'saw in him a young man of great promise: his mental capacities were superior, his ready and lucid utterance remarkable, his earnest and fervent piety of no common type. He [Pocock] took, therefore, a special interest in his welfare, and, after a course of theological instruction, he was sent out to preach in the neighbouring villages'.[5] The nature and the extent of the 'theological instruction' is not known, but it might have come from Pocock himself or, perhaps, the Rev. William Thorp, an Independent minister in Bristol, who had guided Pyer from time to time over many years.

The overall preaching resources available to the Tent Methodists in the second half of 1820 could well have been greater than that available to the Wesleyans in the Bristol area, bearing in mind the defections and new talent such as that provided by George Smith. W.R. Ward has drawn attention to a shortage of adequate Wesleyan ministerial talent 'in the country where the supply of preaching was less in both quantity and professional quality than in the towns'.[6] John Vickers, in 'Circuit Life in

---

4   Russell, *Memoirs of Rev John Pyer*, p.60.
5   *Congregational Year Book* (1871), p.346, obituary of Dr George Smith.
6   Ward , *Religion and Society in England*, p.50.

1825', refers to the inconsistent pattern of ministerial care in places in southern England. From a careful study of circuit preaching plans, he is able to say that 'morning and evening services at Salisbury were conducted entirely by ministers', but at other Wesleyan chapels, particularly in the relatively isolated country districts, 'between one third and one half of the preaching places had no Sunday services conducted by ministers'.[7] David Hempton also draws attention to 'the decline of rural itinerancy'.[8] In a reference to Wotton Bassett in the Spring of 1820, a place that does not subsequently feature in Tent Methodist accounts, Pyer's *Memoirs* describe an occasion when he had preached 'to a small company of people, left as sheep without a shepherd, not having had any preaching for some time'.[9] It would seem, therefore, that the demand for preachers was much greater than the supply of them, and that the Tent Metodist preachers were fulfilling a real need in the locations that they selected for missionary activity.

Bristol City Centre, Kingswood and Gloucestershire

With a group of preachers of ability, great energy, and, in some cases, wide experience of both tent preaching and Wesleyan circuit plan preaching, Pocock, Pyer and the other Tent Methodists were able to set about expanding the work and influence in an ever-widening geographical area. If a substantial proportion of their time continued to be spent in the rural districts, a significant commitment was also given, for the first time, to parts of inner cities beginning with Bristol. Wesleyans were urged in the annual address at their 1820 conference, 'Let us, dear Brethren, "renew our strength by waiting upon God", and redouble our efforts to instruct the ignorant, to reclaim every wanderer, to make manifest in every place the savour of the knowledge of Christ'.[10] The Tent Methodists certainly worked with the evangelical fervour sought by the Wesleyan hierarchy of their preachers. The locations that attracted Tent Methodists to preach and minister had certain similarities with those, in different parts of the country, of the Primitive Methodists and Bible Christians in the early stages of their development. The Bible Christians 'filled in the gaps in Wesleyan activity in Cornwall, and particularly in

---

7   J.A. Vickers, 'Circuit Life in 1825', in Macquiban (ed.), *Methodism in its Cultural Milieu*, p.163.

8   David Hempton, *Methodism and Politics in British Society 1750-1850* (London: Hutchinson, 1984), p.110.

9   Russell, *Memoirs of Rev John Pyer*, p.73.

10   Jabez Bunting (President) and George Marsden (Secretary), 'Annual Address to Societies', given 7 August 1820, in *Minutes of Methodist Conference* (1820), pp.159-167.

Devon',[11] both counties with large rural areas. Primitive Methodists succeeded, too, in country districts such as Lincolnshire and Wiltshire in the late 1820s although much of their very early work was undertaken in manufacturing areas such as the Potteries in Staffordshire—Burslem and Tunstall for example—and, a little later, Derby and Nottingham. They were not so much inner urban areas of the major cities, but more the expanding townships of the Industrial Revolution.

A significant new development was the beginning of evangelical activity in central Bristol once the Pithay chapel was acquired. This work was conducted with particular emphasis on the conversion of unbelievers in the poorest parts of the city. Local preachers had rarely been appointed by the Wesleyan authorities to officiate in the principal city centre chapels. Two of the 'Lord's Day Plan for the Bristol and Kingswood Circuits' documents survive for the periods from March to June 1817 and from December 1819 to March 1820. On these plans no local preacher's name appears at all for either Portland Street Chapel or Ebenezer Chapel, King Street, the first two chapels listed.

Although the middle months of 1820 appear to have been spent mainly consolidating the earlier work in south Gloucestershire, from August a concentrated evangelical effort was focused on Bristol itself. Brandon Hill, close to the city centre, became a notable preaching place from mid-August onwards. Pyer, with initial reluctance at having to forgo an appointment elsewhere, preached in the morning of Sunday 13 August, and later in the day a Rev. G.C. Smith, a Baptist minister from Penzance, preached to a 'multitude...perhaps not less than 10,000 persons'.[12] The impact was sufficient to warrant an interesting newspaper report. 'Brandon-hill, which is famous for being the scene of "open-air" political meetings and pugilistic contentions, has now become the resort of the followers of the Cross, and a place of righteousness. Last Sunday afternoon several thousand persons assembled there, to hear the Rev Mr Smith, of Penzance, preach on the doctrine of Christ's atonement for sinners: and in the evening a vast concourse listened to the exhortations of one of the Agrarian Ministers. A large and handsome tent was pitched opposite Queen's parade, but was found incapable of containing any considerable proportion of the numbers assembled'.[13] The word 'Agrarian' was sometimes used to describe Tent Methodist preachers, and was included in the title of the first, but not the second, set of rules. Another newspaper reported a congregation of 14,000. A further large gathering met on the following Tuesday when, encouragingly, there was

---

11   Ian Sellers, *Nineteenth-Century Nonconformity* (London: Edward Arnold, 1977), p.52.
12   *TM Magazine*, p.198.
13   *Bristol Mirror and General Advertiser* Saturday 19 August 1820.

'plenty of help'.[14] The actual size of the congregations might have been exaggerated, but there seems little doubt that very many people witnessed the impact the Tent Methodists quickly made.

This George Charles Smith, known as 'Boatswain Smith' because of his particular concern for the seafaring communities throughout Great Britain,[15] returned to Penzance at the end of August after assisting the Tent Methodists at services on the Quay. Two separate issues of *Felix Farley's Bristol Journal* refer to him addressing a meeting of the Bristol branch of the Seaman's Friend Society, which he formed, and preaching frequently on board ships.[16] He had spent over a month in Bristol and expressed himself 'highly delighted...with the life and zeal which appeared to prevail among us, etc; and exhorted us all to do the work of the Lord with greater faithfulness than ever'.[17] There was evident confidence to preach at familiar Bristol landmarks, and it might have been Smith's interest in evangelical activity in the Bristol docks area that prompted the Tent Methodists to take up the work there with enthusiasm, again in an inner city environment. They had established a 'Seamen's Prayer Meeting'[18] by the end of August when Pyer first visited it, and he was again at the docks twice on the following Sunday. He and Pocock were there at the same times on the next Sunday when the congregations 'greatly outnumbered those of the preceding Sabbath, especially in the evening, when I scarce ever beheld a more imposing sight'.[19] Between 10,000 and 12,000 people were, apparently, present. Only occasional further reference to the docks ministry is made in the *Tent Methodist Magazine* record which goes on to March 1821, but that was probably because other pressing commitments caused Pyer, Pocock and others to give their main attention elsewhere.

Real evidence of a concern to convert those from the poorest parts of the city comes from the record of the ongoing work in the Poyntz Pool district of Bristol, just east of the city centre. A pamphlet on *The History of Methodism in the Environs of Old Market Street, Bristol, 1739-1985* refers to the area around George Street, and draws attention to the results of a study on population in 1781.[20] In a district of poor housing, 'the very worst local conditions were to be found at Poyntz Pool...where there

---

14   *TM Magazine*, p.198.
15   *Baptist Handbook* (1864), p.121, memoir of Rev. George Charles Smith.
16   *Felix Farley's Bristol Journal* Saturday 12 August and Saturday 26 August 1820.
17   *TM Magazine*, p.198.
18   *TM Magazine*, p.199.
19   *TM Magazine*, p.202.
20   Spittal, *History of Methodism in the Environs of Old Market Street, Bristol*, p.3, quoting J. New, 'An Account of the houses and inhabitants in the parish of St Philip and Jacob' (1781).

was a residential density of 10.36',[21] being the average number of occupants per dwelling. There are many references in the *Tent Methodist Magazine* to the state of the local population; 'multitude of poor neglected people'[22] and 'most abject of the children of men...covered with rags and dirt', but it is with obvious pleasure that Pyer records that 'they hear the word of God with eagerness, and manifest the greatest respect they are capable of'.[23] Following one service, many 'with clean faces and hands'[24] later attended a service at Pithay. The Wesleyans had a chapel close to Poyntz Pool at 'George Street', as it was shown in 1817 preaching plan, but this was no longer in use by December 1819.[25] Neither was a preaching place at Jacob's Well that held two services each Sunday in 1817 but did not feature in the 1819-1820 plan. On the other hand, St Philip's Chapel, of which Pocock was one of twenty-six trustees, a large building seeking to serve the poor in the community in that area was opened in August 1817.[26] Interestingly, Pyer claims to have preached 'at a new place in St Philips' on 28 September 1820 and 'formed a class of eleven persons'.[27] This would not have been in the Wesleyan chapel, but followed several weeks of open air preaching in the neighbourhood 'of this poor neglected parish'.[28] There is reference to preaching in a 'poor house' in the district, and two months later at the end of November, the Tent Methodists 'agreed to rent a small chapel capable of holding about 350 persons situated in West Street'.[29] This was in the same area which 'is inhabited by persons in the lowest walks of life, most of whom are remarkable for nothing but extreme poverty, ignorance, and vice. Prostitutes, thieves, and vagabonds crowd the miserable dwellings'.[30] All the preaching places that featured strongly in Tent Methodist work in this inner city urban quarter were served by many local preachers, but Pyer appeared to be the principal person involved.

While much evangelical activity was being undertaken in the poorest area of Bristol, Pithay Chapel, first used by the Tent Methodists on 18

---

21   Spittal, *History of Methodism in the Environs of Old Market Street, Bristol*, p.3.

22   *TM Magazine*, p.199.

23   *TM Magazine*, p.200.

24   *TM Magazine*, p.201.

25   'Lord's Day Plan for the Bristol and Kingswood Circuits', one covering thirteen Sundays from 9 March 1817 to 1 June 1817, and another covering thirteen Sundays from 19 December 1819 to 26 March 1820.

26   Spittal, *History of Methodism in the Environs of Old Market Street, Bristol*, pp.7-11.

27   *TM Magazine*, p.223.

28   *TM Magazine*, p.224.

29   *TM Magazine*, p.227.

30   *TM Magazine*, p.228.

April 1820, had become the sect's centre. It was the base for the original society of four local preachers and thirty-one members, and immediately attracted very large congregations. There were occasions when many could not get into the chapel and they heard Pyer who 'stood on the end of an empty waggon [sic], in All Saints Street, and preached to all who were willing to hear'.[31] *Mathew's Bristol Directory* for 1822, with information collected the previous year, first records the Pithay chapel as being occupied by Tent Methodists and, already, Sunday services were held at 7 am, 10.30 am, 2.30 pm and 6 pm, with a service also on Wednesdays at 7 pm.[32] Given the length of time services frequently took, there would be barely a time on Sundays when the chapel was not being used. Indeed, there is specific reference to one 10.30 am service not finishing until 1 pm. None of the Wesleyan chapels shown in the 1819-1820 preaching plan had more than two services on any Sunday. Even on a Monday evening in August 'every part was crowded to excess; whilst many surrounded the doors and windows, and many others went away not being able to come at all within hearing'.[33] The spectacle of an active chapel congregation and a city centre building with vast numbers of people frequently present could not fail to have been a noteworthy sight to Bristol's population in general, and its religious communities in particular. The chapel was, naturally enough, the one chosen to hold the quarterly meetings, the first held on 3 August 1820, and the various committee meetings.

In addition to the regular meeting places throughout the year, the Tent Methodists were active during special or annual events. Reference has already been made to tent preaching while an execution of a local man was being considered and carried out in 1816, and the annual fair held over a weekend in September each year was a recurring event. Large numbers of people were present, some, seemingly, bent on causing 'riot and dissipation' and 'wantonness and folly',[34] but the fair's location close to the Pithay Chapel was an opportunity when several preachers attempted to undertake evangelical activity. So it was that during the course of 1820, from only tenuous links with central Bristol communities at the beginning of the year, a substantial Tent Methodist presence was established. Pithay Chapel was the focal point and several other parts of Bristol received tent preaching, particularly in poor areas. While Pyer and Pocock were the principal advocates and workers, Brother Pring and a Brother H., nowhere else fully identified, also made positive contributions. One other valuable preacher, at least, promoted the Tent Methodist cause. Victory Purdy had been a Wesleyan local preacher for

31   *TM Magazine*, p.173.
32   *Mathew's Bristol Directory* (1822), p.13.
33   *TM Magazine*, p.198.
34   *TM Magazine*, p.201.

many years and had drawn attention in a pamphlet published in 1820 to the valuable role played by local preachers and the unacceptable exclusion of them at conference and district meetings.[35] He had objected to the treatment of Pocock, Pyer and Smith, and 'when he could no longer reconcile his mind to remain a member of that body',[36] he left to become an extremely valuable Tent Methodist preacher after more than fifty years as a Wesleyan local preacher. Purdy died at the age of seventy-five in June 1822 but 'it was very evident to his friends that for the last two years he discharged his ministerial labours with increased cheerfulness and satisfaction; and as he had frequent opportunities of addressing large congregations in Bristol, at the Pithay Chapel, he considered that his gracious Master had put honour upon the declining years of his ministry'.[37] Experienced, highly regarded preachers such as Purdy provided vital support to the leaders in Bristol and further afield.

At a time when national Wesleyan membership was increasing, by 29 per cent in the decade between 1820 and 1829, the Bristol circuit's figures were static. From a recorded figure of 2,690 in 1819, membership actually fell in several years and was 2,590 in 1829, the last year before the circuit was divided into two (see Appendix G). If the national pattern had been followed, membership in 1829 would have been 750 higher at approximately 3,440. It would seem, therefore, that the Tent Methodist activity had drawn some support away from Wesleyanism, as well as attracting new converts with no previous religious conviction.

At the same time as the evangelical activity was taking place in the city centre, the outskirts of Bristol and many parts of south Gloucestershire were also places of missionary initiatives in the second half of 1820. Initially, the tents were used as preaching stations but as time went on chapels were acquired or built. More information is known of some places than others as the surviving material is fragmented, and, of course, only partial. While the *Tent Methodist Magazine* for 1823 and Pyer's biography are the principal sources, there are other documents available which help to provide a picture of what occurred in various places.

The Kingswood district to the north-east of the city centre was an area of great evangelical activity frequently visited by Pocock. A society was formed at Soundwell on 16 April 1820 when 'fifty came forward, almost

---

35 Victory (Vicary) Purdy, *Thoughts on the case of Local Preachers in the Methodist Connexion by an Old Preacher* (Bristol, 1820). This was printed by Philip Rose who appears to have become a Tent Methodist himself as he was a trustee of the Dursley and Hanham chapels.

36 Anon., *Some Account of the Life, Ministry and Writings of Victory Purdy, the Kingswood Collier* (Bristol, 1822), p.24.

37 Anon., *Some Account of the Life, Ministry and Writings of Victory Purdy*, p.25. See also F.A. Wilshire, 'Victory Purdy', *WHS Proceedings* Vol. 22 (1939-40), p.37, where it is recorded that Purdy was buried in Stapleton churchyard on 2 July 1822.

all of whom are newly brought from darkness to light'.[38] Soundwell had
been described as 'a district of Kingswood, very thickly inhabited, but
throughout which no place of worship was found'.[39] Here, certainly, was
a place where tent preaching was filling a gap where Christian witness was
not evident. From the autumn of 1819 and throughout the following
winter and spring people met, in a tent until the weather became too bad,
and then in three separate places in the neighbourhood. The notice which
announced the start of 'Field Preaching' on 31 March 1820 also
reported that colliers had 'been lately brought out of the horrible Pit of
Sin, and out of the Miry Clay of the vilest Practices. These lately
reformed Sabbath-Breakers and Thieves...are in the Act of Building, for
themselves and Children, a Place for a School and for Religious
Services'.[40] One hundred and twenty people contributed towards the cost
and many more indicated their desire to be taught to read, a number
which soon reached over 300. At Soundwell, very early in Tent Methodist
existence, Pocock was able to combine his ambition to help the poor with
his professional educational interest. Several local historians of the late
nineteenth and twentieth centuries have referred to Pocock's contribution
to Kingswood's religious life. He became affectionately known as
'Grandfer' Pocock, and was frequently accompanied by one of his
daughters, 'Bessie',[41] on his regular visits. Pocock would have supervised
the building which became known as 'Colliers' Temple', and he found
the balance of the monies required, although much of the construction
was undertaken by self-help. While no records remain of the type of
building that was originally erected, it has been said that 'its appearance
as two cottages may have been intentional, and examples exist of
buildings built in this manner for protective as well as prudential reasons.
No details survive of its interior, but the two storey building suggests a
possible gallery, with columns supporting the valley beam in the centre of
the building'.[42] George Pocock developed an intense concern for this
part of the Bristol area which continued long after Tent Methodism as a
sect had folded.

By the beginning of August the society was well established and class
tickets were being renewed to almost 100 people. They are referred to
with great affection by Pyer, having 'a clear knowledge of the pardoning
love of God'. At a meeting the next day 'the testimonies borne by the

---

38   *TM Magazine*, p.175.

39   *TM Magazine*, p.128.

40   Geo Pocock, *The Tent* (handbill, Prospect Place, 29 March 1820).

41   George Eayrs, *Wesley and Kingswood and its Free Churches* (Bristol: J.W.
Arrowsmith, 1911), p.216, and A.E. Jones, *Our Parish, Mangotsfield* (Bristol, 1899),
p.72.

42   Ron Martindale, 'The Architecture and History of Nonconformist Chapels and
Meeting Houses of Kingswood' (unpublished MS, c.1990), p.8.2.3.

people to the power of divine grace,—the prayers which God put into the hearts and mouths of his servants,—the singing,—the exhortations, were such as exceeded description'.[43] Both Pocock and Pyer preached frequently at the Colliers' Temple, one of Pyer's services lasting two and a half hours, causing him to rush to his afternoon engagement. The society flourished for at least seven years, as Pyer, returning from Manchester to Bristol for a visit in February 1827 at the time of his younger brother's death, commented on the large congregations.[44]

After the middle of 1821 when Pyer's energies were first devoted for several weeks to the Manchester cause, Samuel Bryant became the main support to Pocock at the Colliers' Temple. A contemporary account of Bryant's life described how he 'was proposed...to be the pastor of a little flock which had been as sheep straying in that wilderness, 'til the instrumentality of the Tent had gathered them'.[45] Initially reluctant to take on what he knew to be a heavy responsibility, he was persuaded to do so by the members. A recent study of the social state of the area notes the distressing conditions at the time and the need for real Christian witness,[46] and Bryant had the qualities required to provide spiritual blessing. He was born in 1792, married in 1811 and was converted in 1817 following his attendance at a Wesleyan prayer meeting. A miner for many years, he became 'bailiff to the works at Soundwell',[47] a relatively senior position with considerable authority, and this, combined with his dedicated service at the Colliers' Temple, caused him to be highly regarded and well known in the local community. He later became an exhorter, and then a preacher among other Tent Methodist societies, but that was only a short time before he was killed on 12 January 1827 while entering the mine where he worked.

There were other parts of Bristol's hinterland quite close to Kingswood where the Tent Methodists became active. These were on the north east and east sides of the city, but other places near Bristol did not seem to receive the attention that they did in earlier years. Bedminster and Brislington to the south and Shirehampton and Westbury-on-Trym to the north, are examples. Some of the places that became important in the life of Tent Methodism were venues that Wesley and Whitefield visited in the very early days of Methodism. On Sunday 8 April 1739 Wesley preached at both Hanham Mount and 'in the afternoon at Rose-Green (on the

---

43 *TM Magazine*, p.197.
44 Russell, *Memoirs of Rev John Pyer*, p.28.
45 Anon., *Memoirs of the Life and Character of Samuel Bryant, a Kingswood Collier* (Bristol, 1827), p.7.
46 Peter Brown, *The Bristol and South Gloucestershire Coalfield* (Bristol: n.p., 1994), p.43.
47 Anon., *Memoirs of the Life and Character of Samuel Bryant*, p.8.

other side of Kingswood)'[48] where about 5,000 people heard him preach. He preached at both places again on Sunday 13 May 1739. At Hanham a Tent Methodist chapel was built. It was claimed by a pupil of Pocock's academy that Hanham was the first chapel to be constructed. He wrote: 'when the writer was at the School, Mr Pocock had only one chapel under his care at Hanham, near Kingswood. It was at the head of a rocky valley leading up from the Avon'.[49] In fact this chapel was built a year after Colliers' Temple and, perhaps, several others, as Hanham is not mentioned at all in the *Tent Methodist Magazine* that records events up to March 1821. In another article the same pupil of Pocock's recalls that 'sometimes Mr Pocock's pupils were invited to accompany him there on a fine Sunday, and, boy-like, we were always ready to do so, provided with picnic dinners'.[50] Pocock clearly devoted much attention to Hanham from 1814 and eventually bought land on which then stood 'two dwelling houses...a brew house, stable'.[51] The price he paid was £75.5s, and a chapel was built (which still exists, now incorporated into the rear of Hanham United Reformed Church), measuring approximately 60 feet by 30 feet. It was erected by the side of what would then have been the village square, and known locally, not surprisingly, as 'Pocock's Chapel'.[52]

At about the same time as the chapel was built, a local resident, John Horwood, was convicted of the murder of 'his sweetheart, Eliza Balsam'.[53] He had thrown a stone at her from a distance of, apparently, over forty yards, injuring her forehead. She died six weeks later from the effects of the injuries. As with the case of William Carter five years earlier, this criminal conviction and the carrying out of the execution of John Horwood on 13 April 1821 caused great agitation in the hearts and minds of many local people. The work of the tent preachers had led to the conversion of Horwood's brother, Joseph, several years before, and John Horwood himself claimed that 'their preaching in the Tent had been a great blessing to my soul'.[54] Pocock, together with Pyer and

---

48   Parker (ed.), *Heart of Wesley's Journal*, p.48, Sunday 8 April 1739.

49   W. Symons, 'Highways and Byways of the Connexion', *Bible Christian Magazine* (April, 1884), p.179.

50   W. Symons, 'Portland Chapel, Bristol and the Tent Methodists', *Cornish Methodist Church Record* (January, 1893), p.4.

51   Indenture dated 23 August 1822.

52   For this information I am indebted to Mrs Diane Comley, who in 1998 was researching the history of Hanham United Reformed Church.

53   Vintner, *More Kingswood Stories*, p.18.

54   Anon., *A Short Narration or Circumstances Connected with the Life and Death of John Horwood who was executed at Bristol, Friday April, 13 1821, aged eighteen years and two days* (n.p., n.d.), p.9. It is clear that this pamphlet is written by a Tent Methodist supporter but not, it seems, Pocock or Pyer.

Thomas Roberts, minister of King Street Baptist Church, made strenuous efforts to alleviate the spiritual distress. They held three services at Jeffrey's Hill, Hanham, on the Sunday following Horwood's death. Large congregations were present on each occasion, 9,000 attending the afternoon service. From the record of the events, it is clear, firstly, that Tent Methodism was prepared and able to exercise a significant missionary ministry outside the confines of chapels and tents, and, secondly, that by this time there were three tents in use. Pocock referred to this incident in a letter to the vicar of Bitton in 1842 when he recalled that the services held on Jeffrey's Hill following Horwood's execution 'produced an unprecedented effect throughout the neighbourhood, for which many individuals, and some whole families, thank God to this day'.[55] Pocock was frequently in the area, preaching three times on a Sunday, twice in the chapel and once in the open-air, though not apparently, in the mid-1820's, in a tent.[56]

Rose Green was a place where Pyer preached on occasions, and where there must have been a society as Samuel Bryant is recorded as being a class leader, conducting his last meeting on 7 January 1827.[57] Bryant was also associated with a group that met at Fishponds where 'he engaged in prayer'.[58] Pyer preached there at least three times, being accompanied by Quakers from Bristol on one occasion when, he hoped, 'the whole service...will be made a peculiar blessing'.[59] On his last recorded visit, however, on 27 December 1820, he 'found a sort of liberty, but it was only liberty to reprove. Oh that these dry bones may yet live!'.[60] At two other places in the Kingswood area, Clay Hill and Staple Hill, Pyer had successful preaching visits. The chapel at Clay Hill was crowded on Monday 20 March 1820 with 'those who gasped for the water of life'[61] at a service which lasted two hours, and Pyer was there again in August. At about the same time a chapel was under construction at Staple Hill which was nearing completion at Christmas. On Christmas Day 1820, Pyer preached at Pithay at 5 am, Colliers' Temple at 10 am, and at Staple Hill twice, at 2 pm and 6 pm. Bearing in mind that he had preached at Bath twice the previous day before returning to Pithay to conduct the 'Lord's Supper' in the evening,[62] the extent of his preaching commitments in support of Tent Methodist endeavours is clear. The chapel at Staple Hill was in use by 1 March 1821 when Pyer preached,

---

55 George Pocock, letter to Rev. H.T. Ellacombe, Bitton, dated 13 October 1842.
56 Vintner,*More Kingswood Stories*, p.19.
57 Anon., *Memoirs of the Life and Character of Samuel Bryant*, pp.18 and 21.
58 Anon., *Memoirs of the Life and Character of Samuel Bryant*, p.16.
59 *TM Magazine*, p.223.
60 *TM Magazine*, p.249.
61 *TM Magazine*, p.175.
62 *TM Magazine*, p.249.

and for several years after that Samuel Bryant was a class leader in addition to other responsibilities, including those at Rose Green and, especially, at the Colliers' Temple.

The Wesleyan Kingswood circuit membership seemed to suffer an initial fall as Tent Methodist influence adversely affected the figure in 1820, but thereafter the number grew modestly, until a substantial jump occurred in 1828, to 640 from 520 in the previous year.

Frampton Cotterell, a mining and hatting community eight miles north east of Bristol, was another place where a society was quickly formed in 1820. This was not surprising as tent services had been held regularly there for three years. In addition to the use of tents, services were held in barns when none of the tents was available, and the members 'were urged by necessity to desire the erection of a suitable chapel'.[63] At nearby places, Nibley and Coalpit Heath for example, large congregations were present on occasions. A society had been established in the latter place at least, as reference is made to 'an agreeable hour with the pastors, and was comforted to find the good work of the Lord going on among them',[64] and in October class tickets had been renewed.[65] Brother H., possibly John Hollister, previously associated with Pithay Chapel, was now the local pastor and he reported at a watch-night service of the progress being made at Coalpit Heath. By early 1821 there seem to have been two classes at Frampton Cotterell, one led by Samuel Long, who was to become a trustee of the chapel. Although a request for a chapel had been made in the spring of 1820, the beginning of a subscription list for contributions did not occur until 1 February 1821[66] and the building was not completed until later that year. That date is shown under the eaves of what is now 153 Church Road, Frampton Cotterell. It is situated on the top of a hill, a quarter of a mile east of the centre of Frampton Cotterell, among what would have been a group of cottages and farm buildings. The barns that had been used for services could well have been close by. From an Indenture dated 12 April 1832 it is known that there were fourteen Tent Methodist trustees, two of them, including Samuel Long, from Frampton Cotterell itself, but most from Bristol, among them George Pocock who headed the list.[67] While it might be imagined that Pocock financed this chapel building as well as others it is interesting to note that Resolution 8 of the 1823 Tent Methodist annual meeting stated 'That the net proceeds of the Annual Collections be equally divided

---

63   *TM Magazine*, p.128.
64   *TM Magazine*, p.197.
65   *TM Magazine*, p.225.
66   *TM Magazine*, p.270.
67   Indenture of Bargain and Sale dated 19 September 1827 (Documents held with Charge Certificate Title No. AV149486 deposited in 1997 with the National Westminster Bank Home Loans).

between the Frampton Chapel in the Bristol District, and the Stretford Chapel in the Manchester District'.[68] This shows that Pocock did not finance all the chapels erected after 1820 and also confirms that he did not become the controlling trustee but shared the authority and responsibilty.

Further away still from Bristol, to the north east, was another area of much activity. Before the dispute with the Wesleyans reached its climax in early 1820, a part of south Gloucestershire, north from Frampton Cotterell, encompassing Iron Acton, Rangeworthy, Rudgeway, Olveston, Milbury Heath, Wickwar and Wotton-under Edge, all in the direction of Dursley, had been frequent recipients of tent visits in 1819. The places were mostly on, or just to the east of the main road leading from Bristol to Gloucester, and were coal mining communities. From the middle of 1820 onwards, some of the villages did not seem to receive visits, but several others were centres of missionary work, especially those within about three miles of Dursley itself. A number of the places were in the Downend circuit where the Wesleyan membership was static throughout the third decade of the nineteenth century. If the national pattern had been shown, an increase of approximately 120 should have been expected, suggesting some modest transfer of allegiance to the Tent Methodists from the Wesleyans.

Between Frampton Cotterell and these small communities close to Dursley was Rangeworthy where occurred an example of the hostility with the Wesleyans described in the pamphlets that were issued earlier in 1820. Pocock had been asked to provide a chapel on land owned by a local man called Bedggood, but the local superintendents persuaded him and the local members to have the model 'Conference Plan' used as the documentation. Pocock, then, found himself as the facilitator of a chapel over which he ultimately had no control. This all became evident to Pocock on Monday 1 May 1820,[69] and he was careful not to allow that situation to arise again. It is doubtful whether the Rangeworthy chapel was ever home to a Tent Methodist group, although one of the trustees in 1837 was a William Ovens[70] who, according to an 1820 handbill, was one of a group authorized to receive subscriptions towards the cost of building Colliers' Temple.[71] Rangeworthy was not the only place where Tent Methodists sowed but Wesleyans reaped. Olveston, a village north west of Bristol, had seen much tent preaching since 1816, but it was a Wesleyan chapel that was built after approval was given between the 1819 and 1820 conferences. The note of authorization appeared as follows:

---

68   *TM Magazine*, p.150.

69   Pocock *et al, Facts Without a Veil*, pp.35-36.

70   Anon., *Rangeworthy Methodist Chapel 1820-1970: 150 Years of Christian Worship* (n.p., n.d.), p.1.

71   George Pocock, *Whereas* (handbill issued by 23 March 1820).

'Olveston, in the Thornbury Circuit. The purchase of Houses etc £200. Expense of building the Chapel £200—subscriptions £150—the rent of a house £6 per annum; and seventeen trustees engage to provide the remaining interest money. Wm Jones, Supt'.[72]

At several places, though, along the western-most ridge of the Cotswold hills which runs in a north-south direction around the west side of Dursley, much encouraging progress occurred from the middle of 1820 onwards. A society was formed at Wotton-under-Edge (variously spelt 'Wooton', Wootton' or 'Wotton') in April, and a further seventeen joined in August. Interestingly, Pyer 'obtained the consent of Mr P [Pocock] to become their Pastor'.[73] He spent many Sundays and weekdays ministering to the society thereafter at least until the spring of 1821, sometimes helped by Samuel Smith and a Brother R..The Wotton society, on 16 October, obtained the use of a chapel: 'Providence has wonderfully provided for us and our little flock at Wotton, by putting into our hands the old Baptist chapel, which having been comfortably fitted up, we this day solemnly dedicated to the worship and service of our adorable Lord and Master'.[74] What the reason was for that chapel being available is not known, but as with the Pithay Chapel in Bristol, it may have been that the Baptist congregation outgrew its premises and moved to a larger chapel. There was certainly a Baptist chapel at Wotton-under-Edge six years later in 1826, when the pastor was a Mr Thomas.[75] The opening services were conducted by Pocock and Samuel Smith as well as Pyer, and during the following week tickets were renewed to members.

Wotton-under-Edge is three miles due south of Dursley and Pyer and his preaching colleagues made frequent visits at various places along the ridge of the Cotswold hills. Waterly Bottom, a hamlet in a valley just a mile south of Dursley, Nibley and Stinchcombe, villages on hills overlooking the town, and Cam just to the north, all received the attention of tent preachers. The tents were used on occasions but at other times open-air services were held, and at Nibley Pyer preached ' in Farmer M's large kitchen'. At Stinchcombe Hill in September 'the Tent was well filled',[76] and at Waterly Bottom at the end of January 1821 'never before had so many people there, except when preaching in the Tent or in the open air'.[77] None of these small hamlets, though, supported a society.

---

72   *Register Book for Chapels, built, enlarged or purchased since the Conference held at Sheffield in 1817* (n.p., n.d.), p.10.

73   *TM Magazine*, p.199.

74   *TM Magazine*, p.225.

75   *Baptist Handbook* (1878), p.331.

76   *TM Magazine*, p.222.

77   *TM Magazine*, p.270.

Several references were made in the *Tent Methodist Magazine* account to the successful evangelical work undertaken during 1819 when tent preachers were supported by John Irving and Adam Nightingale who, just a year later, were dissuading local people from joining the Tent Methodists. The rural communities around Dursley could not fail to have noticed the missionary zeal of Pyer and several of his fellow preachers, including both Samuel Smith and John Barnett. The road from Wotton-under-Edge to Cam followed the contours of the hills and would have become extremely familiar to them. Many times services were held at three different places on one Sunday, and weekday meetings were also regular events. That road passed to the west of Dursley, but in 1823 there was further expansion of work in two places to the east. At Horsley, a village five miles from Wotton-under-Edge, the Tent Methodists acquired the 'Free School' which was to be controlled by Samuel Smith. This might have been work started by Adam Nightingale, who had by 1823 left for Newfoundland as a Wesleyan missionary. Further still to the east, but still in south Gloucestershire, the market town of Tetbury was visited in May 1823, and a house registered for worship.[78] By September 1823 the society formed there had fifty five members, indicating rapid progress in a town which, at that time, had no Wesleyan presence.[79]

Tent Methodist influence in Dursley and the immediate neighbourhood was substantial, both in terms of time and the intensity of the activity. It had previously epitomized a fundamental dilemma within Wesleyan Methodism, with help and co-operation from willing volunteers among the laity quickly turning to open hostility when they fell out with the local hierarchy. The over-riding mission to extend Christian belief among the local population which was the starting point for tent preaching in Dursley in 1819 was lost sight of as the bitter dispute, which began in earnest at the end of that year, developed. Tent Methodism flourished for several years, despite the hostility, as a direct result of a specific invitation by the Wesleyans for the use of a tent.

On the surface Dursley itself did not fit comfortably into either of the categories that became the focus of the evangelical effort. It was neither an inner urban area of a large city nor a rural district with much agricultural based poverty and little Wesleyan impact. Cloth making prosperity had existed for centuries, encouraged by favourable natural resources in the form of clear running water in the nearby valleys and a humid local climate. 'In time, however, steam replaced water as a source of power; labour was cheaper further north; and high taxes on wool combined with consumer preference for lighter cotton textiles to drive

---

78   R.B. Pugh (ed.), *The Victoria History of the Counties of England: Volume 2. Gloucestershire* (London: Institute of Historical Research, University of London, 1976), p.281.

79   Barnett, *Memorials*, p.25.

Dursley's mills out of business'.[80] Former economic wealth, therefore, had by the beginning of the nineteenth century turned to far less happy conditions, although there was no direct relationship between the changing economic conditions and tent preaching in the area.

Methodist and other older dissenting groups were well established there by 1819. Dursley was the centre of a Wesleyan circuit formed in 1800, and the Independent chapel was well supported, although this feature was partly based on past prosperity. Fewer local difficulties over the acquisition of land from landowners for chapel building had also helped. Thirty years later, the Independents, by then known as Congregationalists, accounted for as many as twenty per cent of the population at the 1851 census calculation,[81] a level of support only reached in a few parts of the country, notably in Essex and Suffolk. A leading Independent layman, William King, was a prominent promoter of the early Sunday School movement at the end of the eighteenth century. Indeed, it was suggested that he had 'a stronger claim to having started the Sunday School movement than Robert Raikes in nearby Gloucester',[82] and a biography of Raikes acknowledged the role that King played in persuading him to establish Sunday Schools after a visit to Gloucester gaol and a meeting with him.[83] Nonetheless, there were still occasions when local magistrates refused to grant licences to local dissenters intending to register premises under the terms of the Toleration Act.[84]

Against this background valuable evangelical work had begun in 1819 when at the end of April 'the Superintendent Preacher of the Dursley Circuit, wrote to say their Chapel at Dursley was about to be repaired, on account of which it would not be used for some months, and requested the Tent might be sent to their assistance'.[85] With a passage of just a year, however, help was no longer required or, indeed, welcomed by the authorities, although several leading individual Wesleyans wished to remain associated with Pyer and Pocock. John Cook, who had been a trustee of the Wesleyan chapel since it was built in 1800 and 1801[86] was one. He remained a trustee until at least 1833, but in January 1820 he was also a steward and wrote to Pocock as he wished 'to inquire...concerning

---

80   Christopher Catling and Alison Merry, *Gloucestershire and Hereford & Worcester* (Harmondsworth: New Shell Guides, 1990), p.58.

81   Watts, *Dissenters*, II, p.39.

82   Richard Sale, *The Visitor's Guide to the Cotswolds* (Ashbourne: Moorlands Publishing, 1987), p.105.

83   Frank Booth, *Robert Raikes of Gloucester* (Redhill: National Christian Education Council, 1980), pp.64 -65.

84   Watts, *Dissenters*, II, p.386.

85   *TM Magazine*, p.79.

86   James Alderson, *Dursley Methodist Church Centenary: Historical Souvenir, 1864-1964* (n.p., 1964), p.5.

a report which is privately circulating in Dursley and its neighbourhood to the pain and disquietude of many sincere friends'[87] that Pyer had been expelled. Three months later, on 19 April 1820, Pocock and Pyer visited Dursley again and formed a society consisting of nearly forty people.

On Friday 21 July 1820, a date which 'will be remembered by many through time and eternity',[88] and after a service attended by 300 people, Pocock and Pyer laid the foundation stone of a chapel. The legal documentation was not completed until 17 July 1821 and while most of the trustees were not from Dursley, one name was locally significant. William Elliott of Cam was one who, while being a trustee of the Wesleyan chapel since 1801 became a trustee, not only of the Dursley Tent Methodist chapel, but also of the Hanham and Frampton Cotterell chapels. The indenture reveals that £140 was paid to a Thomas Richards for the land, then containing fruit trees, and the Tent Methodist chapel measured 137 feet by 60 feet.[89] This was a very large building by contemporary standards, being 60 feet longer than the chapel built a year later in Ancoats, Manchester, which was capable of holding 1,200 people 'chiefly on forms and closely disposed'.[90] The building, known as Hill Road Chapel, took six months to complete and during that time Pyer, particularly, but also Pocock and John Barnett, were frequently at Dursley and nearby villages. Barnett had moved out of Pocock's house to live in Dursley during March 1821. In addition to a tent, the preachers also used a chapel 'lent us by some kind friends till our building is completed',[91] meeting there, on one occasion at least, at five in the morning. Pyer also spent time 'begging for the chapel',[92] and 'collecting subscriptions for and managing the business of the new Chapel'.[93] Several other local preachers, including Samuel Smith and a Mr Roberts, shared in the missionary endeavours. The borrowed chapel was well filled but there were frustrations at the delays in finishing their own new chapel. Pyer spent most of a week just before Christmas and a further time early in January 1821 ensuring the completion in time for the opening services which were held on Sunday 14 January. Services took place in the morning, afternoon, and at six in the evening, and the impact in Dursley must have been substantial. Four different events took place on the following day, and the preachers came 'to this unanimous conclusion...

---

87   *TM Magazine*, p.104.
88   *TM Magazine*, p.177.
89   Indenture dated 17 July 1821.
90   B. Nightingale, *Lancashire Nonconformity* (6 vols; Manchester, 1890-1893), V, p.181.
91   *TM Magazine*, p.178.
92   *TM Magazine*, p.199.
93   *TM Magazine*, p.227.

that we never had known two such blessed and happy days'.[94] Thirteen more people became members later the same week.

There is supporting evidence of the successful nature of the Tent Methodist presence in Dursley, but one account portrays a different impression. Erroneously stating that 1823 was the year that 'three Wesleyan Evangelists from Bristol' began a mission, the record goes on to mistakenly report that the superintendent 'did not wish them to do so, and persuaded his members not to support the project'. Pocock, Pyer and Smith are correctly identified as the leaders, but the pamphlet states that 'it is not known whether any Wesleyans left their own chapel to join this group, or whether its support came from the converts of the Mission'.[95] It has, in fact, been established that several leading Wesleyans joined the Tent Methodists, some of whom became trustees of the Hill Road Chapel.

A more detailed and recent local history, on the other hand, provides an altogether different account. For a time the Tent Methodists, it is claimed, 'had a larger following than the Wesleyans'[96] and Wesleyan membership figures tend to corroborate that trend. Between 1822 and 1825, Wesleyan membership numbers in the Dursley circuit were as follows:

> 1822 — 510
> 1823 — 504
> 1824 — 490
> 1825 — 500

a decline of 2 per cent in those four years. During the same period the denomination's Great Britain membership rose by 8.1 per cent from 211,392 to 228,646. It is not possible to find evidence that the Tent Methodists had a membership of over 500 in Dursley at that time, although the building which may have accommodated over 1,500 people was described on occasions as 'much crowded' and 'crowded in every part'.[97] In fact, numbers in the society were normally said to be forty or fifty, rather than a much greater number. Even allowing for a normal pattern of 'hearers' often being four or five times the number of members, a congregation of approximately 500 appears unlikely.

Once Pyer concentrated his time, for a while at least in late 1821, in Manchester, John Barnett and, later, Samuel Smith seem to have had principal oversight at Dursley. Barnett had, for four years since late 1817 when he was twenty years of age, lived and worked with Pocock. In 1821, having no doubt served a full apprenticeship, and having worked 'with

---

94   *TM Magazine*, p.269.
95   Alderson, *Dursley Methodist Church Centenary*, p.10.
96   D.E. Evans, *As Mad as a Hatter: History of Nonconformity in Dursley* (Gloucester: Alan Sutton, 1982), p.120.
97   *TM Magazine*, p.269.

extraordinary zeal, and enjoyed a popularity second only to that of the eminent man above named [George Whitefield]' he moved to Dursley. There 'he spent part of his time in teaching boys, and the remainder in conducting meetings in all parts of the neighbourhood, where 'Tent Mission' chapels were built with remarkable rapidity'.[98] The boys he taught were in another school controlled by Samuel Smith, though no doubt under Pocock's guidance, and his experience at Pocock's academy would have prepared Barnett for the work which filled the daytime hours. Samuel Smith (but not John Barnett) was a trustee of the chapel and when the deed of Indenture was completed in 1821 he was described as a 'poulterer'. By 1825 he was shown in a Manchester document setting out all the trustees as, like John Pyer, a 'Dissenting Minister' of Bristol. It is likely that he had some form of supervisory function over Barnett before becoming more closely involved in 1826 for reasons that will be analysed and described in a later chapter. Barnett, in fact, had been asked to become a full time missionary in October 1823 but it was not until January 1826 that he finally agreed—an appointment he never actually took up.[99]

Before analysing the group's progress to Bath and then further eastwards into Wiltshire, there were two other places, one in north Gloucestershire and the other in south Wales, that received Tent Methodist attention. At the end of February 1821 Pyer received a letter asking him to go to Cheltenham, an invitation he accepted although, it appears, he went without a tent. He preached on 26 February in the home of a Mr Rose, and later described his experience: 'Multitudes of persons of all descriptions are living without God, and without hope in the World, and for the lower classes in particular, no man appears to care. A month's visit with the Tent would be the means of doing great good'.[100] The population of Cheltenham was expanding rapidly at this time, having grown from only 3,000 in 1801 and would reach nearly 23,000 by 1831. Wesleyan circuit membership fluctuated between 100 and 280 in the years from 1818 to 1828, the main chapel being Ebenezer Chapel in King Street. This was opened in 1813 but for a long time had a membership of just twenty, and the whole circuit in about 1820 consisted of only five societies with a combined membership of 133. Soon after that, in the 'ten years from 1822 fifteen societies were formed, many of them companies of people meeting in cottages and farm kitchens... Many of them did not exist for more than a few years'.[101] It is not known whether any of these societies were Tent Methodist groups formed after

---

98   *Baptist Handbook* (1878), p.331.
99   Barnett, *Memorials*, pp.29 and 33.
100   *TM Magazine*, p.272.
101   Dorothy Myatt, 'The Development of Methodism in Cheltenham', address to the WHS Bristol branch, *Bulletin* No. 74 (5 October 1996), p.5.

Pyer's visit which lasted only two days, but there is no record of any Tent Methodist chapel being acquired, or even society formed.

South Wales, Bath and Wiltshire

Earlier in February, Pyer had spent a five day period in south Wales, travelling to Newport, Monmouthshire, by scheduled mail coach and then enduring a journey of several hours to Cwm Dws. He had a younger brother, George, who lived in Newport at that time and who died in February 1827.[102] It is known that Pyer was 'of Welsh extraction on his father's side, and descended from a wealthy family in Pembrokeshire, that once inherited a valuable estate in that county'.[103] Although this was the earliest recorded Tent Methodist visit to that part of south Wales, there was already a society in Cwm Dws that was 'assembled and waiting for me',[104] and he gave tickets to sixty-three members during his visit. There is no obvious reason why this part of south Wales should have attracted the Tent Methodists and which led to the establishment of a society. It is possible that Elijah Waring who, in 1819, wrote in glowing terms of a visit to the Swansea area, had contacts in this district, but in the early 1820's it was almost entirely Welsh-speaking, a language not known to have been spoken by Pyer. Barnett spent two months in south Wales during February and March 1821 preaching 'in private houses, and I hope not altogether in vain'.[105] Pyer's visit might have been the prelude to Barnett's work, although there had clearly been evangelical activity before then which had led to the formation of a society. It was a coal mining, iron ore and stone quarrying area, and Pyer gave a graphic account of the appalling conditions underground. 'What can more resemble the infernal abodes than these subterraneous regions', and he went on to describe the miners as 'a set of God-insulting wretches, who, discoverable only by the faint glimmer of a candle fastened upon their heads, pop about, regardless of all danger, angrily cursing one another, and horribly blaspheming their Maker'.[106] This was an occasion when Pyer clearly displayed his concern for the less fortunate in society, as he did at other times, especially in connection with the east end of London inhabitants. In addition to two services on a Sunday, he preached at a funeral, and generally undertook much pastoral work during the time he was there.

---

102 Russell, *Memoirs of Rev John Pyer*, p.128. See also the list of subscribers towards the cost of publishing the poems and hymns written by Victory Purdy.
103 Russell, *Memoirs of Rev John Pyer*, p.1.
104 *TM Magazine*, p.270.
105 Barnett, *Memorials*, p.21.
106 *TM Magazine*, p.270.

It is not known how long the society survived, but the two places mentioned by Pyer, Cwm Dws and Abercairne, now have different names—Abercairne being an anglicized version of Abercarn. Cwm Dws was an area of woodland and small farms in which deep coal mines were being developed, two miles north-west of Abercarn, and one mile to the west of Newbridge, in the Ebbw river valley. Its name changed to 'Cwm Dows' in the middle of the nineteenth century having been known as 'Cwm Dous' in 1830, again reflecting the increasing influence of the English who were drawn to the expanding coal mining industry. The 'Cwm Dows' coal mine had become disused by the end of the century although it reopened for a short period during the early part of the twentieth century. In addition to coal mining, several stone quarries were worked, but the employees came from a large number of scattered cottage communities in the neighbourhood.[107] Whether the society was formed by somebody who went from the Bristol area to work in a local mine and invited Pyer to visit is not known, but it is the most likely explanation.

In many ways Bath was an unlikely place for a Tent Methodist society and, later, a chapel. It was neither a rural village, nor a city with a large part of its population living in poverty. Indeed, it had been described as 'the most elegant town in the country' and 'from 1725, becoming the most fashionable resort...[with]...miles of Georgian houses, mostly in terraces, looking much as they did when Jane Austen or Gainsborough visited'.[108] Wesleyans and Independents, in particular, were strong and long established with noted ministers serving their respective congregations. It fell between, on the one hand, the country agricultural areas where Wesleyans came to exercise little itinerant pastoral care[109] and 'the neglect of their rural ministry',[110] and, on the other, the desperately poor and squalid inner city districts such as Poyntz Pool in Bristol, Spitalfields in London, and Ancoats in Manchester. Bath, though, had become a frequent preaching place of Tent Methodists from 1820 onwards, having been first visited in 1814.

A society had been formed at Bath in the spring of 1820 soon after the leaders had severed their links with the Wesleyans. Pyer later preached twice on Sunday 25 June, without assistance from other preachers, in a tent which was erected near the Angel Inn.[111] Local directories, providing

---

107 I am grateful to a number of local people for information in this paragraph. Messrs Fox, Williams, Taylor and Lloyd, in particular, responded most helpfully to a letter published for me in selected local south Wales newspapers.

108 Richard Cavendish (gen. ed.), *AA Road Book of Britain*.(Basingstoke: Automobile Association, 1995), p.78.

109 Vickers, 'Circuit Life in 1825', p.160.

110 Ward, *Religion and Society*, pp.99-101.

111 *TM Magazine*, p.175.

much information on early nineteenth-century Bath, show two inns with the name 'Angel'. One of them was located on 'Old Bridge' and was not in existence by 1837. The other 'Angel Inn' was on Westgate Street, close to the town centre and described as 'Commercial, from where Coaches start'.[112] It was probably the more important of the two, and is likely to have been the one referred to in the *Tent Methodist Magazine* account. Pyer was again at Bath on 28 August where he preached in a room before returning to Bristol. Despite an increasingly hectic schedule, Pyer went there on two days in quick succession on Thursday 5 October and Sunday evening 8 October. He 'renewed the Society tickets' to a considerable number, three quarters of whom were 'the immediate fruits of our missionary labour, all of them having received their first religious impressions while attending the services in the Tent'.[113] Further preaching engagements at Bath took place on Christmas Eve, making at least six occasions when Pyer himself went to Bath in about eight months. It might be assumed that other preachers had also been to nurture the society. Pyer returned early in January 1821 and 'gave tickets to about thirty of the members'[114] and on Thursday 15 February went again, and recorded: 'We greatly need a Chapel here, and today we have been taking steps towards getting one; but we do not yet see our way clear'.[115] Precisely when the chapel was opened is not known, but one had been acquired within a year, and certainly by the time the *Gye's Bath Directory* was prepared for publication. Directories for 1820, 1821 and 1823 have not been found, but the following entry appears for 1822: 'Independent Methodist Chapel, Corn Street. Divine Service every Sunday at eleven in the morning, and at six in the evening. Rev Mr Pocock, minister'.[116]

There are a number of interesting features of this announcement. Firstly, in some places where buildings for worship were acquired to obviate the need for a tent to be the principal vehicle for preaching, the word 'Independent' rather than 'Tent' was being used. The same practice was adopted at times in Wiltshire. Secondly, Pocock was, apparently, prepared to give himself the prefix 'Rev.' despite his earlier strident criticism of Wesleyans who did the same. Thirdly, it would appear that Pocock was less involved in travelling to other chapels and with a tent, but spent more time in Bath than elsewhere. It may not be entirely coincidental that at Fieldgrove House, Bitton, on the main road midway

---

112 A considerable number of Bath Directories compiled by H. Gye, J. Keene, and H. Silverthorne for years between 1819 and 1833 are available. Some editions are missing and publication was not quite an annual event. It is known, for example, that there was no edition published in 1825.

113 *TM Magazine*, p.224.

114 *TM Magazine*, p.268.

115 *TM Magazine*, p.271.

116 *Gye's Bath Directory, corrected to January 1822*, p.11.

between Bristol and Bath, one of his sons, Ebenezer, established his own school.[117] It was a highway that Pocock would regularly travel along as the third decade of the nineteenth century progressed when he developed a variety of inventions designed to propel carriages using kite-like structures.

By 1824 the congregation had vacated the Corn Street chapel and had moved to one in Wells Road. Two years earlier a Welsh dissenting group had used the Wells Road chapel with two Sunday services, but it seems to have ceased to exist soon afterwards as no reference appears in any Bath directories later than 1822. Corn Street was, and still is, situated on the south-west side of the city centre and quite close to Westgate Street where the Angel Inn was located. Wells Road, however, is on the other side of the river Avon and was then the south western most extremity of the town. Why Pocock's congregation moved is not known, but several different religious groups met in the vacated premises thereafter. The Corn Street chapel had become home to an Independent congregation by May 1826, and having been 'taken for Rev Dr Cracknell, and put into complete repair, was re-opened for public worship'.[118] It was used by a Baptist congregation in 1833. Later still, it was referred to as Bethesda Chapel in 1837, but the name of the denomination was not shown in the directory, and, in 1846 the same building became a 'Jews' Synagogue'.

Despite the presence and preaching of Tent Methodists for ten years to 1824, and the references in two directories to a chapel in two places in the latter part of that period, the authors of the most recent account of Methodism in Bath make no reference to the group.[119]

Apart from noting the numbers to whom class tickets were issued in 1820 and 1821, no later membership statistics are available. In addition, no information can be found regarding the size of the Wells Road chapel, although it might be assumed that it was not substantial, nor did it last for long. However, that a chapel was believed to be necessary in early 1821 to provide a more permanent presence than a tent to contain the society, and that the appointment of Pocock to be minister was considered appropriate, suggests that he, at least, felt it was a significant Tent Methodist society. In any event, the Bath Wesleyan circuit membership grew rapidly during the early 1820's, from 780 to 1,290 by 1825, although there was then a modest decline in the second half of the decade. This reduction, though, was unlikely to have been the result of Tent Methodist successes.

Tent Methodists continued to extend their influence eastwards from Bath. On Sunday 25 June 1820, Pyer and Pocock had preached at Box,

---

117 Vintner, *More Kingswood Stories*, p.15.

118 *Evangelical Magazine* (May, 1826), p.349.

119 Bruce Crofts (ed.), *At Satan's Throne: The Story of Methodism in Bath* (Bristol: White Tree Books, 1990).

six miles east on the main road which led, in due course, to Marlborough and Hungerford, two places that were particularly familiar to Pocock. For most of the following week, the three Tent Methodist leaders took one of the tents in a south-easterly direction to Bradford-on-Avon, Trowbridge and Warminster,[120] all towns in Wiltshire. The working population of Wiltshire suffered from lower than average wages throughout the first part of the nineteenth century. Perhaps because the 'Wiltshire agricultural labourer earning below 10s a week' was relatively much worse off than elsewhere, the county's population fell in absolute terms during the early 1800s, one of only a few to do so.[121] Inhabitants also suffered 'much persecution from squire and parson'.[122] Parts of the county gave strong support to Baptists, particularly in the Melksham and Westbury areas,[123] and to Independents, but the Wesleyans did not appear to be active away from the main centres of population. Indeed, John Vickers refers to 'the dissatisfaction and frustration felt by laymen at the slackening of evangelical outreach in the Wesleyan Connexion'[124] as a reason for Tent Methodism's progress.

Plans to visit Warminster were interrupted as Pocock, Pyer and Smith were persuaded to stay at Bradford-on-Avon to hold a service in a tent. They had to arrange for it to be brought from Trowbridge, but at 7 pm a large congregation of 2,000 people, including some from other Nonconformist denominations, attended a service at which all three leaders took a part. The following day they continued their journey to Warminster and preached on two successive evenings, before beginning the journey to Dursley.[125] There is no record of any societies being formed in this western part of Wiltshire.

Marlborough, in the east of the county, had been, and continued to be, a frequent venue for the preachers. It was a regularly used stop on the way to, or from, London, as was the case when Pyer preached in September 1820. Pyer was there again in early November when he stayed with Gosling, and preached at Lockeridge. This was at a property owned by Gosling, and acquired under protest from the Wesleyans as it had been registered as a Wesleyan dissenter meeting place in June 1818. Under the terms of the Toleration Act of 1689 Dissenters from the Church of England were required to register premises that were to be used as places of worship. For Wiltshire very many of the registration documents survive and they have been carefully analysed by John Chandler. In this

---

120 *TM Magazine*, p.176.

121 Royle, *Modern Britain*, pp.101 and 59.

122 J.M. Turner, *Conflict and Reconciliation: Studies in Methodism and Ecumenism in England 1740-1982* (London: Epworth Press, 1985), p.85.

123 Watts, *Dissenters*, II, p.40.

124 Vickers, 'Methodism and Society in Central Southern England', p.273.

125 *TM Magazine*, pp.176-177.

particular case the premises comprised 'three tenements and gardens adjoining'.[126] The Tent Methodists opened a chapel in Marlborough on 5 January 1821 and this, too, is confirmed by a registration: '3 Jan 1821 (13 Jan 1821). Marlborough. A chapel and premises adjoining, in the occupation of John Gosling esquire, in St Peter's parish. Independent Methodist. William Sanger of Salisbury, gentleman'.[127]

The date in parentheses is the date the certificate was issued and the registration request was lodged by William Sanger, an attorney practising in Salisbury whose name often appeared on other applications. Despite many objections to the Tent Methodist presence in Marlborough, Pyer was able to record 'the Lord answered for himself, and gave such evident proofs of his approval as were sufficient to silence our fears'.[128]

Apart from Pocock and Pyer who had had close associations with the Marlborough district for several years, the principal Tent Methodist there was John Gosling. He had been one of the two proponents (John Irving was the other) of Pyer as a full-time home missionary at the end of 1818, and was a leading figure in the events that led to Pocock, Pyer and Smith leaving the Wesleyan connexion. He had acted as chairman of a meeting held at the end of December 1819 at which it was hoped to reach a compromise with the Wesleyan authorities concerning the future use of the tents. During March 1820 he had left the Wesleyans and became a firm supporter of Tent Methodism, for several years at least. He was a partner in a banking business based in Marlborough which was named in the *J. Pigot, Commercial Directory, of 1822,* as 'King, Gosling and Tanner'. The same trading name is used in the 1830 edition, and in 1831 he, and his two partners, were parties to a lease transaction in connection with a High Street, Marlborough property.[129] In December 1822 the banking partnership provided mortgage funds of £400 towards the cost of building the chapel at Dursley, of which Gosling was a trustee, as he was also of Hanham. The business clearly survived the many bank failures during 'the terrifying crisis of 1825'. The banking problems continued up to February the following year 'with banks still disintegrating after the panic of the preceding December'.[130] Gosling was a man of considerable influence locally, partly, no doubt, because he owned several properties and parcels of land, and also because of his

---

126 Chandler (ed.), *Wiltshire Dissenters' Meeting House Certificates and Registrations*, No. 886, p.85.

127 Chandler (ed.), *Wiltshire Dissenters' Meeting House Certificates and Registrations*, No. 957, p.92.

128 *TM Magazine*, p.268.

129 Lease of property in High Street, Marlborough. John Gosling, Stephen King and William Tanner, 28 May 1831.

130 L.S. Pressnell, *Country Banking in the Industrial Revolution* (Oxford: Clarendon Press, 1956), pp.12-13.

banking business. In December 1832, and in 1833, he was on the electoral roll of both Marlborough and the nearby parish of Preshute where he was one of only seventeen people entitled to vote. He was the Proposer of Sir Alexander Malet who sought to become one of two Members of Parliament for Marlborough in December 1832. Sir Alexander Malet was a graduate of Oxford University and later had a distinguished career in the diplomatic service, but he was the one unsuccessful candidate in the election.[131] Bearing in mind his status locally, Gosling's support for, and membership of, the Tent Methodists would have been helpful in the expansion phase.

The earliest record of Gosling providing premises for the Wesleyans was in April 1817, with another registration the following year in the Hampshire village of Bramley.[132] Both these registrations occurred very soon after his departure from the Church of England. In 1818, in addition to the property in Lockeridge that Pyer preached in during November 1820, he registered 'a field or close...containing by estimation three acres' at Preshute, this registration request being made by, among others, Pyer.[133] In 1820 and early 1821, Gosling provided two sets of premises in Marlborough, and in March and November 1825 two more, one in Preshute, on the outskirts of Marlborough, and the other at Milton Lilbourne, a village six miles south of Marlborough.[134] Milton Lilbourne was a place well known to Gosling as it was in the parish church there that he married a Miss Monk on 13 September 1795.

From a careful study of Chandler's analysis of the dissenter meeting place registrations it is possible to obtain an idea of the importance of Wiltshire to Tent Methodist work. Including those premises already referred to as being associated with Gosling, Chandler identifies a total of twenty-five registrations that were made on behalf of Independent or Tent Methodists. It would be presumptious, however, to believe that all the places registered were regularly used for public worship as some may only have had an occasional service. In addition, four others were previously registered for Wesleyan use, at Ogbourne St George, Lockeridge, Preshute and Marlborough, but were under Gosling's

---

131 'The Poll for Electing Two Burgesses to Serve in Parliament for the Borough of Marlborough, Wiltshire: Taken before Thomas Halcomb Esq, Mayor, on the tenth and eleventh of December 1832', and *Alumni Oxonienses 1715-1886* (4 vols; London, Joseph Foster, 1887), III, p.905.

132 A.J. Willis, 'Dissenter Meeting House Certificates in the Diocese of Winchester 1702-1844', in *A Hampshire Miscellany'* (4 vols; Folkestone, privately published, 1963-1967), p.81.

133 Chandler (ed.), *Wiltshire Dissenters' Meeting House Certificates and Registrations*, No. 888, p.86.

134 Chandler (ed.), *Wiltshire Dissenters' Meeting House Certificates and Registrations*, Nos 940 on p.91, 957 on p.92, 1108 on p.107, and 1142 on p.110.

control and might be regarded as Tent Methodist preaching places from the second half of 1820 for the following five years at least. The Marlborough premises might have been superseded by the chapel in January 1821. This chapel was, in fact, the first registration as an Independent Methodist building in Wiltshire. Over the following five years until November 1825 a wide variety of places were registered for worship. They were all located in a narrow band approximately twelve miles wide from east to west, and thirty miles long from north to south— Marlborough in the north and Salisbury to the south. The peak period was in 1823 when twelve of the twenty-five certificates were issued, nine of which were between the end of March and the middle of October. There were 185 Dissenter registrations recorded by Chandler in the years 1821 to 1825, of which 13.5 per cent were Independent Methodist or Tent Methodists—a significant proportion bearing in mind that all the dissenting denominations contributed to the total. Seventy-three, for example, were either Baptist or Independent ones. Seven of the Tent Methodist registrations relate to chapel buildings, fourteen relate to parts, or the whole, of houses, and the remainder relate either to land: for example 'orchard of 1 acre', 'field called Horse Pits (6 acres)', or rooms in commercial premises. One of these, in Freemason's Hall, George Yard, High Street, Salisbury, was used by several different groups within a very short time. It would appear from the registration documents that the Baptists used the hall from 1817 until the Tent Methodists took it over in 1823. They, though, apparently only had access to it for two years as 'the New Jerusalem in the Revelations' were the registered users in December 1825 and occupied it for the following four years.[135]

The majority of the Tent Methodist meeting places were in small villages where there were no other dissenting groups represented. They were locations where poverty was often very evident. 'Much of the worst rural poverty was found in the southern most districts of the country, in a belt stretching from east Kent westwards to Hampshire, Dorset, southern Wiltshire and parts of Devon...little industrial development was taking place to provide surplus labourers with alternative employment, and where the labourers themselves were firmly anchored in their parishes by the operation of the settlement law, and even more effectively, perhaps, by their own poverty and ignorance'.[136] Most of the meeting places were in the occupation of tenants, rather than the owners, men whose names are not otherwise identified in any Tent Methodist context. They are likely to have been agricultural labourers who had been converted by the preaching of Pyer, Gosling and others in the previous few years. The

---

135 Chandler (ed.), *Wiltshire Dissenters' Meeting House Certificates and Registrations*, pp.83-111.

136 G.E. Mingay, *Rural Life in Victorian England* (London: Heinemann, 1977), p.48.

earlier registrations were mostly described as 'Independent' Methodists, but from August 1823 onwards the word 'Tent' was increasingly, though not invariably, used.

Two of the chapels are recorded as being owned by John Pearse Sweetapple and he is referred to several times in Wiltshire and Hampshire registration documents. In February 1819 he registered for Wesleyan use a property at Shipton Bellinger, Hampshire,[137] and in June 1820 he was shown as owning a Wesleyan chapel at Netheravon, Wiltshire. It would seem that he left the Wesleyans soon after then because he was the owner of chapels at Urchfont and Chisenbury—a neighbouring village to Netheravon—used by the Independent or Tent Methodists. A further indication that he joined the Tent Methodists comes from the record of the annual meeting held in Manchester in 1823. He attended that gathering and seconded one of the resolutions which referred to 'the labours of the Home Missionaries'.[138] His departure from Wesleyanism is acknowledged in a biography of Jabez Bunting where, following reference to the Tent Methodist secession, it is written 'there was another [secession] as feeble, about the same time. An excellent brother, Sweetapple by name, formed a society of his own, the members of which were called Sweetappleites'.[139] By 1825 he controlled 'six chapels eight local preachers two hundred and seventeen members'[140] in the Devizes area of the county. It is likely, though not entirely certain, that Sweetapple should be regarded as part of the Tent Methodist evangelical mission in Wiltshire. Further evidence that Sweetapple became a prominent Tent Methodist comes from the knowledge that Pocock 'opened Mr Sweetapple's Chapel, at Salisbury' on 8 January 1824.[141]

The activity extended into western Berkshire where two registrations were made on behalf of Tent Methodists in 1824. In Newbury 'Union Chapel', Bartholomew Street, was registered for the Independent Methodists just three months after a field called 'Daisy Meadow' had been registered on behalf of the Tent Methodists, in both cases by Sanger.[142] There is evidence of other Tent Methodist work in Berkshire. The Bunting biography claimed that 'two local preachers in a Berkshire circuit persist in giving their services to the new sectling of the "Tent Methodists"',[143] and an exchange of correspondence between Jabez Bunting and William Griffith, the superintendent of the Hungerford circuit, gave further detail. Griffith wrote to Bunting on 20 December

---

137 Willis, *A Hampshire Miscellany*, p.136.
138 *TM Magazine*, p.154.
139 Bunting, *Life of Jabez Bunting*, II, p.170 n..
140 Harry Noyes, letter to Jabez Bunting, Thruxton, 19 January 1825.
141 Barnett, *Memorials*, p.29.
142 Vickers, 'Methodism and Society in Central Southern England', p.278.
143 Bunting, *Life of Jabez Bunting*, II, p.133.

1820 and after confirming 'you are aware that Mr Pocock is endeavouring to enlarge his borders and he has a party in Marlborough' goes on to say that an exhorter 'has engaged to assist them [Tent Methodists] once a month' at a place 'they have gotten from us, and another of our local Preachers is disposed to assist them'.[144] Bunting's response referred to 'a party avowedly opposed to us, which has in print calumniated us, and which is trying to divide our people'.[145] Griffith had only recently arrived in Hungerford, Pocock's birthplace, and was clearly troubled by the Tent Methodist progress.

With activity spread among a number of Wesleyan circuits, it is difficult to judge the extent to which Tent Methodist progress resulted in loss of Wesleyan membership. In Great Britain membership rose from 191,217 in 1820 to 245,194 in 1828, an increase of 28 per cent. Hungerford circuit's membership actually fell over that period, from 355 to 334, whereas a 'natural' increase of ninety-nine to 454 would have been achieved if the national pattern of membership had been followed. On the other hand, the Newbury, Andover and Salisbury circuits all exhibited good rates of growth. In the absence of any record of Tent Methodist membership figures in east Wiltshire and west Berkshire, only a tentative assessment can be made. It is difficult to come to any other conclusion than that the Hungerford Wesleyan circuit, which included the Marlborough area, did suffer defections. However, Tent Methodist growth elsewhere was achieved in places where there was little or no Wesleyan activity, and the tent preachers attracted people who had no previous religious allegiance. That would, therefore, constitute genuine missionary activity which should have evinced universal Methodist support. Jabez Bunting, and others in the Wesleyan hierarchy, failed to recognize that, preferring to concentrate on what they saw as threats to its authority.

Robert Currie believed that this part of England, 'the Berkshire–Wiltshire–Gloucestershire area',[146] represented both a gap in Wesleyan coverage and the main area of Tent Methodist influence. Certainly, with something approaching thirty places where preaching and pastoral work was carried out all within a reasonably small area, the first half of the 1820s would have seen much evangelical work. Pocock was frequently in and around Marlborough up to 1822, working mainly, it would seem, with John Gosling and John Sweetapple as his main advocates, both of whom lived in the immediate vicinity. Pyer from early 1821 onwards, was

---

144 Ward (ed.), *Early Correspondence of Jabez Bunting*, p.54, No. 21, letter from William Griffith to Jabez Bunting, Hungerford, 20 December 1820.

145 Ward (ed.), *Early Correspondence of Jabez Bunting*, p.55, endorsement to letter No. 21 dated 23 December 1820.

146 Robert Currie, 'A Micro-Theory of Methodist Growth', *WHS Proceedings* 36 (October, 1967), p.71.

more involved in Gloucestershire and then Manchester. One of the tents was known as the 'Marlborough and Bristol Tent' and would have been very fully employed in the ministerial work to the local agricultural communities. Currie's assessment, however, failed to recognize the extent of evangelical activity in other parts of England, notably a small district of east London, a rapidly growing industrial area of Manchester, parts of Liverpool and Birmingham, as well as Bristol.

East London

The first extension of Tent Methodist activity away from the steady geographical expansion northwards into Gloucestershire, southwards into Somerset and eastwards into Wiltshire, was to London in the final months of 1820. While there is no record of a September trip in Pyer's *Memoirs*, a two day visit was undertaken on 20 and 21 September where, although only the initials of the parties involved were shown, Pyer, Pocock and Gosling met a Mr J.. This is likely to have been Mr Jeffs who, from a surviving Tent Methodist London preaching plan for 1822, was then at least, the first named local preacher and one of only a few who conducted Communion Services and officiated at love feasts. Three Tent Methodist leaders went to London following a written invitation to do so, and the significance of the visit can be judged by the fact that all the leaders, except Samuel Smith, made the journey. Apart from the month long excursion away from Bristol in 1818 when several preachers took part, this prospect of expansion of the work into London was considered of sufficient importance for all the main decision-makers to go. Pocock and Gosling rarely ventured beyond their home territories of Gloucestershire, including Bristol, and Wiltshire respectively, and this underlined the anticipated value of the meetings they were to conduct in the Spitalfields district of east London with Jeffs.[147]

This part of London seemed to have become difficult territory for Methodists. At the 1786 annual conference, John Wesley was able to say 'No parish-church in London or Westminster could contain the congregation',[148] but while Methodist membership numbers nationally trebled between 1800 and 1830, the position in London by 1820 was very different. Edward Royle records that Methodism was poorly supported in London,[149] and Michael Watts refers to an 'extraordinary weakness of Methodism'[150] of all varieties in 1851. Watts also claims that 'densely populated areas with a high level of poverty...such as the east

---

147   *TM Magazine*, p.223.
148   *Minutes of Methodist Conference* (1786), p.191.
149   Royle, *Modern Britain*, p.299.
150   Watts, *Dissenters*, II, p.132.

end of London...proved as difficult for the Non-conformist churches as for the Church of England to penetrate in the first half of the nineteenth century'.[151] These assessments seem to confirm that the various branches of Methodism all found it difficult to make much headway in the east end of London.

Several interviews took place with Jeffs who, with others, was active in establishing Sunday schools in the Spitalfields area, and in preaching in the evenings to the parents of the Sunday school scholars. Two chapels were used, one of which was in Webb Square, very close to Shoreditch, the main thoroughfare at the time in that part of London, and near to Shoreditch parish church.[152] Pyer and Pocock participated in a service at the Webb Square chapel in an evening at the end of the two day visit in September 1820, following which 'Mr J offered himself and his two classes to us, and hoped we should henceforward consider them a part of our Society'.[153] The absence of any obvious enthusiasm in the record of that excursion belied the events of the following two years. The report did not indicate why the request from Jeffs to join the Tent Methodists was made, or whether it was accepted, but it can be presumed that it was agreed, as in late November an exchange of preachers took place—Pyer to London, and, probably Jeffs, to Bristol. Jeffs, in pursuing his, apparently, independent role of evangelism outside the confines of Wesleyanism may well have been made aware of the events in Bristol and felt an inherent affinity with the tent preachers.

Pyer's second trip to London two months later lasted nine days and is extensively commented upon in the *Tent Methodist Magazine*. The reference in the *Memoirs of Rev John Pyer* specifically draws attention to those who were 'anxiously concerned for the poor of the metropolis',[154] and Pyer spent much of the time in contact with those who lived in squalid conditions. In particular he referred to Cooper's Gardens, an area of 'three or four acres of ground covered with about five hundred or six hundred huts; and hovels of various descriptions'.[155] This was the district that the Primitive Methodists first missioned two years later when they sent Messrs Sugden and Watson from the Leeds circuit.[156] The Tent Methodists succeeded in forming a Sunday school there, and laid a foundation stone for the building on 27 November 1820, but the depressing environment for the poor and destitute deeply affected Pyer.

151 Watts, *Dissenters*, II, p.110.
152 Richard Horwood's map of London, *A Plan of the Cities of London and Westminster, with the Borough of Southwark including their adjacent Suburbs* (London, 3rd edn, 1813).
153 *TM Magazine*, p.223.
154 Russell, *Memoirs of Rev John Pyer*, p.144.
155 *TM Magazine*, p.145.
156 John Petty, *History of Primitive Methodist Connexion* (London, 1860), p.191.

During the remainder of Pyer's time in London he frequently preached at the Webb Square chapel, and at Harefields Chapel, probably the second chapel mentioned in the reports of the earlier visit. Services were well attended, a number of local preachers were exercising a good ministry and wished to expand the operations, and a society of about forty members had their tickets renewed. Much progress was being made and Pyer was moved to record 'and this closed one of the best Sabbaths I ever enjoyed'.[157] Pyer left London on Tuesday 5 December 1820, greatly encouraged by the overall advances being achieved.

At about the same time the Tent Methodists were joined by up to three former leaders of the Christian Community, a Wesleyan Methodist group consisting of 'a band of strong, zealous, spiritual men, doing such magnificent work for God and Methodism'.[158] The Christian Community preachers exercised a valuable ministry in the Bethnal Green area, 'visiting the sick and instructing the poor in the work houses',[159] and was 'a mission to Workhouse paupers and vagabonds'.[160] The society was 'sanctioned by the founder of Methodism',[161] used a vestry of the City Road chapel on Sunday mornings with John Wesley's approval, and was regarded highly for nearly fifty years from its formation in 1772. However, the combination of Jabez Bunting, who had been appointed to the London east circuit in 1818, and Charles Atmore, the superintendent, succeeded in disrupting the work and causing several of the preachers to leave the Wesleyans. E.C. Rayner's *The Story of the Christian Community* is a subjective account of the dispute but less biased versions, including general histories of the denomination, testify to the value of the Christian Community's work.[162] Stevenson refers to 'young men, who commenced their active Christian labours in the Community, and who afterwards became useful, active and even distinguished preachers of the gospel'.[163] Here was a group of Methodists who seem to have succeeded in finding a way of bringing the gospel message to a section of the poorest inhabitants of east London.

Atmore and Bunting wished to exercise complete authority over the activities of the Christian Community by taking on to the circuit plan the

---

157 *TM Magazine*, p.246.

158 E.C. Rayner, *The Story of the Christian Community 1685-1909* (London: Memorial Hall, [c.1910]), p.50.

159 G.J. Stevenson, *City Road Chapel, London and its Associations* (London, 1873), p.509.

160 Rayner, *Story of the Christian Community*, p.32.

161 Stevenson, *City Road Chapel*, p.509.

162 Stevens, *History of Methodism*, and Myles, *History of Methodism*, both refer to the valuable work of the society, although the biography of Jabez Bunting by his son does not, despite Bunting's direct involvement in the dispute.

163 Stevenson, *City Road Chapel*, p.509.

'best of the Community preachers',[164] fully to control a chapel in nearby Globe Road, 'which had been built principally through their [Christian Community] agency ',[165] and generally remove any decision-making power from the local preachers. There were, therefore, close parallels with the situation in Bristol with Pocock and the other two leaders at a similar time. A Christian Community business meeting at the end of 1818 was interrupted by the arrival of five itinerants, including Atmore, who 'took the chair somewhat rudely...then spoke to the effect that he possessed authority to dissolve our Community, and had come to the meeting for that purpose' because it was 'a self-governed and irresponsible body'. The leaders of the Christian Community were accused of being arrogant, insubordinate, and lacking 'deference and respect'.[166] Thus it was that the exercising of valuable Christian service to the more deprived in London society was considered of less importance than its organizational position in the denomination's structure. Stevenson concluded his reference to the disagreement by saying, 'This conduct, on the part of the preachers, served to break up the Community for some time; but instead of being a benefit to Methodism, it created a spirit of resistance, and was a source of much disquietude and ill-feeling for several years'.[167] It was exactly the use of this kind of belligerent authority that caused antagonism and, in some cases, secessions.

The disruption led to significant departures from Wesleyan Methodism, including a 'Brother Thomson...grieved in spirit, the severance cast him adrift, and he eventually became a Baptist minister'.[168] A future chairman of the Community, Mr Webber, later left to join the Methodist New Connexion. At least two of the other leaders who refused to accept the prospect of operating within the regulations that Atmore and Bunting imposed left the Community. Brother Woodland was one who became a Tent Methodist local preacher. The report of Woodland's departure in Rayner's account does not specifically mention the Tent Methodists, but records that 'he and a few others opened a chapel in Squirries Street, Bethnal Green Road, where many from Wilmot Gardens attended his ministry'.[169] 'A Plan for the Preachers, Exhorters and Prayer Leaders of the Independent or Tent Methodists, London' for several months of 1822 shows Woodland as a preacher, and a chapel in Squirries Street where he preached regularly.[170] Another Christian Community leader, a

164 Stevenson, *City Road Chapel*, p.190.

165 Rayner, *Story of the Christian Community*, p.51.

166 Rayner, *Story of the Christian Community*, p.51.

167 Stevenson, *City Road Chapel*, p.190.

168 Rayner, *Story of the Christian Community*, p.53.

169 Rayner, *Story of the Christian Community*, p.52.

170 'A Plan for the Preachers, Exhorters & Prayer Leaders of the Independent or Tent Methodists, London', 28 April to 25 August 1822.

Brother Lea, who was also present at the fateful meetings with Atmore, Bunting and the other members of the Wesleyan hierarchy in London, later joined Woodland. The combination of the timing of the schism within the London East circuit, the name of 'Woodland', the chapel he was associated with, and the appearance of his name on a Tent Methodist preaching plan for a period shortly afterwards, is conclusive cumulative evidence that the Christian Community's loss was Tent Methodism's gain.

The precise date that these preachers left the Christian Community is not known with certainty, but Woodland and the Squirries Street chapel appeared on the Wesleyan preaching plan which covers the period from 28 November 1819 to 2 April 1820. It might, therefore, be presumed that Woodland, if not other former Christian Community workers, joined the Tent Methodists soon after Pocock, Pyer and Gosling's visit to London in September 1820. In fact, another account of the problems that the Christian Community suffered reported that 'Mr Jeffs MD, and Mr Lindsey, a feather bed maker, preached under a tent, which resulted in the establishment of Tent Street Chapel'.[171] This suggests that the original visit to London by Pocock and his colleagues was actually prompted by the schism which affected the Christian Community. Yet a further Christian Community worker, a Mr Palmer, left having been held 'in high esteem among the paupers'.[172] A 'Palmer' also appears on the 1822 Tent Methodist preaching plan, although it cannot be automatically assumed that they were one and the same. Several references survive of Tent Methodist activity in 1821. In May 'a Tent visited the Metropolis, and was employed for six weeks in Hare Street Fields, with very evident tokens of success'.[173] Another man who benefited from Pyer's preaching during that period was a John Parkhouse. He was brought up in the Church of England, but accepted deist beliefs for a time before hearing Pyer preach, following sight of an advertisement for tent preaching. Parkhouse became an exhorter and prayer leader a year later.

If the various accounts of the qualities and commitment of the Christian Community workers who joined the Tent Methodists were accurate, they comprised a particularly valuable evangelical resource. 'Superior talent', 'great devotion' and 'affectionate in demeanour' were phrases used to describe Woodland. Lea 'possessed a gigantic mind' and his preaching was characterized by 'mature wisdom', and Palmer's work was 'constant and indefatigable as well as efficient'.[174] The loss from

---

171   Anon., *Historical Sketch of the Christian Community AD 1818-1826*, by 'one of its members' (London, 1868), p.30.

172   Anon., *Historical Sketch of the Christian Community AD 1818-1826*, p.29.

173   *TM Magazine*, p.90.

174   Anon., *Historical Sketch of the Christian Community AD 1818-1826*, pp.25 and 28.

Wesleyanism of people such as these could have been ill-afforded, but Tent Methodism benefited from their dedication to provide spiritual help to poorer people in a part of east London.

At about the same time the early Bible Christian leaders had contact with the Tent Methodists in London at least a year before the Bible Christians themselves began their missionary work in the capital. Not all histories of the Bible Christians acknowledge the fact that Catherine Reed, who was later to marry James Thorne, the Bible Christian leader, visited London in late April 1821. She did so at the invitation of a Mr Gunn, who 'had been a Methodist travelling preacher but at this time he was connected with the Tent Methodists' of Bristol'.[175] The only reference to a 'Gunn' in Hill's, *An Alphabetical Arrangement of all the Wesleyan-Methodist Preachers and Missionaries* published in 1827, was a Robert Gunn who was admitted on trial in 1803 and subsequently served as an itinerant in Kettering and Oxford until he was expelled in 1808. Whether or not this was the man who became a Tent Methodist is not known, but Catherine Reed 'heard from Mrs Gunn a glowing account of the glorious work the Lord was carrying on in Bristol'.[176] Pyer was also once again in London in the spring of 1821 and preached, apparently, to as many as 10,000 people in Hare Street Fields.[177] Catherine Reed preached in the Webb Square chapel, in the open-air at Harefields and, on the same evening in the Harefields Chapel. Her visit finished on 4 May 1821 when a larger chapel adjoining Bunhill Fields Burial Ground was used to preach to more than 1,000 people. Bunhill Fields Burial Ground was a significant place in dissenter history. It was large and long established and contained 'many of the ministers ejected in 1662, who were refused burial in the City churches',[178] together with other famous Nonconformists such as George Fox, John Bunyan and Isaac Watts. It was indeed a 'burial place of godly men and worthy citizens'.[179] Later the same year James Thorne himself preached in the Webb Square chapel on 12 October, and Catherine Reed preached on the two following days, in both Webb Square and Harefields chapels, and in a tent. At two different times, then, during 1821, two leading Bible Christians assisted established Tent Methodist evangelical activity.

Tent Methodist progress clearly continued into 1822 as can be deduced from the information available from a study of the preaching plan which covered the period of eighteen weeks between 28 April and

---

175 F.W. Bourne, *The Bible Christians: Their Origin and History 1815-1900* (London: Bible Christian Book Room, 1905), p.109.

176 Bourne, *Bible Christians*, p.110.

177 Russell, *Memoirs of Rev John Pyer*, p.95.

178 Anon., *History of Bunhill Fields Burial Ground* (London, 1887), p.13.

179 Anon., *History of Bunhill Fields*, p.5.

25 August 1822.[180] The year 1822 does not appear on the face of the
plan itself but on the reverse is written, in manuscript, 'Mr Lindseys Plan
1822'. On the plan itself 'Lindsey' is consistently spelt 'Linsey' and this
may be a significant name. A.J. Linsey appears in several minutes of
Methodist New Connexion annual conferences, representing London in
1802, and paying subscriptions in 1805, 1807 and 1810. After 1810,
there is no record of any Methodist New Connexion activity in London
until 1819, and it is just possible, therefore, that the 'Linsey' who was a
leading London Tent Methodist preacher in 1822 was a former member
of the Methodist New Connexion.

An analysis of the 'plan for the Preachers' provides much information
to suggest that Tent Methodism had a significant role in east London
evangelical activity. In the first place preaching took place at fifteen
different venues, including three tents. This is the only certain evidence
that three tents were ever in use—they were designated 'new', 'old', and
'small', and were used on every Sunday between 2 June and 25 August
at least. The 'small' tent had been in London throughout the period
covered by the plan. Although the preaching places were concentrated in
an area just to the east of the 'city' boundary in Spitalfields and Bethnal
Green, two other places, Lambeth and St Clement Danes, among several
more, appear on the plan as locations for prayer meetings. For fifteen
places there were only twelve preachers, suggesting a particularly heavy
commitment for them all. They were supported by five exhorters and
twenty-five prayer leaders, five of whom were also exhorters, but while
four men were shown as being on trial, three more were to be needed to
fulfil all the commitments. It was not surprising that the statement that
was normally found on Wesleyan Methodist plans instructing preachers
to find alternatives from the list of preachers if the appointed person
could not undertake the engagement, did not appear. The human
resources were simply not sufficient to allow that luxury. Most of the
meeting places had more than one service each Sunday, and many also
had mid-week services. Of significance, in the light of Pyer's wish in late
1820 that the preachers find opportunities 'to hold meetings in different
directions from house to house',[181] prayer meetings were held in nine
homes in addition to the fifteen places where services were held. Overall,
there is plenty to suggest that mid-week evangelical activity was regarded
as extremely important.

The available material does not enable an assessment to be made of
how long after August 1822 progress continued. A resolution passed at
the 1823 annual meeting instructed 'a Committee consisting of the

---

    180   'A Plan for the Preachers, Exhorters, & Prayer Leaders of the Independent or
Tent Methodists, London', 28 April to 25 August 1822.
    181 *TM Magazine*, p.245.

brethren Pocock, Pyer and Arrivé be appointed to answer the letter of the acting member of the London District'.[182] It would be too presumptuous to read much into the word 'District'. There is no evidence that London ever had more than one circuit, although the same annual meeting 'received the most cheering and satisfactory accounts of the prosperity of the work of God in several societies'.[183] On the same occasion calls were made for more helpers to be found to help realize the potential that was believed to exist. Certainly, London seemed to be one place where there was the need for 'the Lord [to] raise up and send forth faithful and efficient labourers'.[184] Support was given from time to time by the group's leaders to supplement the local preacher resource. During 1822 and 1823 Pyer spent time in London, although probably not much as he was also in Bristol, Birmingham, Manchester and Liverpool.[185] In a letter from John Parkhouse which was published in the April 1823 edition of the *Tent Methodist Magazine*, he refers to Pyer's 'excellent friend Mr Smith'.[186] This is unlikely to be Samuel Smith who was by this time mainly based in Dursley, Gloucestershire, but probably George Smith who may well have accompanied and assisted Pyer as part of his training before being sent to Liverpool in September 1823. It might be that Smith's experience in London, and later in Liverpool, was a contributory factor in his decision in 1842 to begin a long and successful ministry at the Trinity Congregational chapel, Poplar, a district of east London close to where the Tent Methodists had worked.[187]

There are no available membership figures for Tent Methodist societies in London. Forty tickets were renewed by Pyer on 3 December 1820 and services were reported to be well attended during his visit at that time, but no statistics have been discovered. From an analysis of the 1822 preaching plan it can be assumed that there must have been nine societies in the middle of the year as tickets were to be issued at that number of services on Sunday 9 June. It is known, however, that Wesleyan membership in the London East circuit reduced significantly from 4,500 in 1820 to 3,862 in 1823, despite a 15% increase in overall Great Britain membership numbers during the same period. There was a small drop between 1820 and 1821 at the time that the dispute with the Christian Community leadership had occurred and the Tent Methodists were becoming established, but national membership increased by 9,000 or 5% in that year. The biggest annual London fall was evident in 1823 when there was a reduction of just over 800, but this might be accounted

---

182 *TM Magazine*, p.150.
183 *TM Magazine*, p.150.
184 *TM Magazine*, p.150.
185 Russell, *Memoirs of Rev John Pyer*, p.119.
186 *TM Magazine*, p.90.
187 *Congregational Year Book* (1871), p.347, obituary of Dr George Smith.

for by a redistribution of societies between circuits as the London East circuit had just been divided to create, for the first time, a London North circuit. Even after this separation, however, London East membership numbers remained static while steady progress was being made nationally. In 1825, London East had recorded 2,030 members, but by 1830 the figure was 1,900. Expressed another way, London East contributed 0.88 per cent of national membership in 1825, but it fell to only 0.76 per cent in 1830, while London North's share of national membership increased during those years.[188]

It is not, of course, possible to draw meaningful conclusions about Tent Methodist support in London from the Wesleyan membership statistics. Bearing in mind, however, that the tent preachers were also attracting those who had no previous Wesleyan allegiance, that they certainly built up a significant number of preaching places quickly between the end of 1820 and the middle of 1822, it is reasonable to believe that they made an important impact in a small part of east London, occupied by a large number of 'the lowest and most abject of the poor'.[189] Pyer, at the end of 1820, described an example of living conditions thus: 'the whole apartment consists of one room from eight to ten feet square, serving as a place of residence and rest for two, three, four and in some cases, five or six human beings...each exhibiting nothing but a varied scene of human wretchedness and woe'.[190] Here, again, is an example of the increasing concern to serve the poorest in the local communities becoming a distinctive feature of Tent Methodist work.

Manchester

Much is known about the sequence of events and factors leading to the establishment of Tent Methodism in Ancoats, Manchester. While the name of who it was that invited Pocock and Pyer to visit with a tent is not recorded, it can be deduced. Both W.R. Ward, in *Religion and Society in England 1790-1850*, and D.A. Gowland in *Methodist Secessions*, refer to the presence of the group in Manchester, but not how it arrived there.[191] It is, in fact, possible to determine why the Tent Methodists went to Manchester, but not why they set up their evangelical activity in Ancoats, a location immediately to the east of the city centre. There was no

---

188 Annual Wesleyan Methodist Conference membership statistics from 1820 to 1830.
189 *TM Magazine*, p.244.
190 *TM Magazine*, p.244.
191 Ward, *Religion and Society*, p.83; Gowland, *Methodist Secessions*, pp.24 and 45.

geographical logic to the expansion of the work to the north west of England, but rather it was a response to a pressing appeal from one man.

Peter Arrivé is first mentioned as a tent supporter in the record of events in 1817. That he became a man of some influence in Bristol can be inferred from the entry of his name in the annual *Mathew's Bristol Directories* from 1814 to 1817. He was the only son of Peter and Elizabeth Arrivé who lived in the Channel Islands. His mother joined the first Methodist class on Guernsey in 1785 and her Methodist service was sufficient to warrant a lengthy 'Memoir' in the *Methodist Magazine* editions of April and May 1820.[192] In that obituary it is reported that Peter became a pupil of Kingswood School, then still in Bristol. After he left 'he lost all relish for Divine things, and fascinated with the pleasing habits of sin, was carried away with the allurement of the world, and went with the giddy multitude to do evil'. That was in about 1800, but later on 'he left the ways of sin and iniquity to serve the living God'.[193] He was to serve the Tent Methodists, initially in Bristol and later in Manchester, with great commitment.

Under a heading in the 1814 *Mathew's Bristol Directory* 'names arrived too late for insertion in regular alphabetical order', he is described as a 'Commission Merchant, 28 Quay and Upper Berkeley Place'.[194] In 1817 he was living at 10 Upper Berkeley Place, an elegant four storey house, still surviving at the end of a row of ten houses, situated now close to West End car park, and within half a mile of the Cathedral and University. Arrivé's involvement with the tent preachers in the Bristol area was short-lived as there is no entry in the *Mathew's Bristol Directory* of 1818, and it is recorded in his mother's 'Memoir' that shortly before her death he arrived from Manchester in May 1818.[195] In the biography of John Pyer it is noted that he was invited to Manchester by 'a gentleman of French extraction formerly (we believe) resident in Bristol',[196] and that on Friday, 17 August 1821, Pyer, and one other, met and stayed with Arrivé. At this time Arrivé was a Wesleyan local preacher in Salford.[197] On his arrival in Manchester after a two day journey from Bristol, via Birmingham, Pyer was concerned to find 'only a handful of people holding a prayer meeting' in the Methodist chapel in Oldham Street. It was 'in search of their friend',[198] that prompted Pyer and his companion, probably Samuel Smith, to go to the north east of the

---

192 William Toase, 'Memoir of Mrs Elizabeth Arrivé', *Methodist Magazine* (April and May 1820), pp.290-298 and 368-379.
193 Toase, 'Memoir of Mrs Elizabeth Arrivé', p.369.
194 *Mathew's Bristol Directory* (1814), p.154.
195 Toase, 'Memoir of Mrs Elizabeth Arrivé', p.372.
196 Russell, *Memoirs of Rev John Pyer*, p.102.
197 Gowland, *Methodist Secessions*, p.24.
198 Russell, *Memoirs of Rev John Pyer*, p.102.

Manchester centre, rather than Salford, where Arrivé lived. It was, however, in the fast expanding area of Ancoats just south of Oldham Street that the tent was first erected, on Sunday 19 August 1821.

Ancoats had been a medieval hamlet, but by the seventeenth century it had become part of Manchester itself. At a time of food shortage in 1812 'strong and alarming appearances of rioting took place at Ancoats'.[199] In 1821 the population of Manchester was 108,016[200] and expanding very rapidly. Still standing in the Ancoats area, although now derelict, is the massive eight storey Royal Mill, built in 1797, and situated in Redhill Street, formerly Union Street, which contained many huge factory buildings in the 1820's. Friedrich Engels claimed that Ancoats contained 'the largest mills of the town...many streets unpaved and unsewered...and cottages...of very flimsy construction'.[201] In the 1820s 'action against noisome and noxious fumes and vapours emitted by a manufactory of sal ammoniac at Ancoats Bridge' had to be taken.[202] In the middle of the second decade of the nineteenth century richer families were moving 'to the "posh suburbs" of Chorlton-on-Medlock',[203] but 'round about the year 1817, many of the large mills and work-shops were built in the district of Ancoats and for the many work-people, provision had to be made by the building of cottage homes, schools and places of worship'.[204] By 1821, apparently, in the Ancoats area there was a 'population of 20,000 souls, (chiefly poor) who were destitute of any place of worship whatever'.[205]

Arrivé, 'deeply concerned for the masses of factory operatives, who at that period seemed grossly neglected, as far as regards religious teaching',[206] persuaded Pyer to make the journey to Manchester with a tent. While it was claimed that the area with 20,000 or 30,000 people was devoid of religion,[207] the evidence actually suggests a rather different picture. At the time the main Methodist chapel was in Oldham Street, and

---

199 Arthur Redford, *The History of Local Government in Manchester: Volume 1. Manor and Township* (London: Arthur Longmans, 1939), p.248.

200 *Pigot & Co National Commercial Directory: Cumberland, Lancashire, Westmoreland for 1828 & 1829*, p.178.

201 Friedrich Engels, *The Condition of the Working Class in England in 1844* (London, 1845), quoted in Arthur Redford, *The History of Local Government in Manchester* (2 vols; London: Green, 1939-40), II, pp.138-139.

202 Redford, *History of Local Government in Manchester*, I, p.42.

203 E.A. Rose, *Tell It How it Was, 'Oldham Street 1781-1883'* (Manchester: n.p., 1981), p.6.

204 *Souvenir Brochure of the Opening and Dedication of the New Methodist Church, Ancoats*, Saturday 30 May 1964.

205 *Imperial Magazine* 4 (1822), pp.363-368, letter by Philanthropus, Manchester, 9 March 1822.

206 Russell, *Memoirs of Rev John Pyer*, p.102.

207 Russell, *Memoirs of Rev John Pyer*, p.104.

a surviving Wesleyan preaching plan for early 1821 shows other preaching places in New Islington, Jersey Street and Pollard Street, all in the Ancoats area.[208] By 1822 the Jersey Street preaching station was no longer used but Oldham Street chapel 'was well attended'[209] despite the experience of Pyer finding only a very few there on the Friday evening of his arrival in Manchester.

Tent services began with great enthusiasm and frequency. A man who later became embroiled in a bitter dispute with Pyer felt bound to record about the tent preachers that 'in labours they were abundant—preaching almost incessantly—generally four or five times on the Sabbath, and almost on every night in the week'.[210] Congregations of 4,000 were attracted and, significantly 'Methodists of the Old and New Connexion, Band Room and Primitive Methodists, Baptists and Independents, and scores of no Society at all'[211] were present. Services of that size were rarely witnessed in Manchester and, for about a month, the Tent Methodists clearly made a great impact with their tent.

In parallel with this evangelical activity, discussions were taking place with prominent Dissenters in Manchester as to the future scope of the work. There was an attempt, presumably by Arrivé, to obtain Wesleyan support to the venture and to accept converts into Wesleyan societies. Not surprisingly, if the official version of the Bristol acrimonious exchanges had reached Manchester, Pyer was informed 'that the Wesleyan Travelling preachers...had unanimously determined to have nothing to do with the Tent, nor would they receive into their society those persons who had been reformed and reclaimed by means of Tent Preaching'.[212] In addition, Arrivé himself was effectively expelled. A resolution passed in December 1821 required him to 'give up preaching for others' by the next quarterly meeting. In a written response to William Myles, the chairman of the local preachers' meeting, Arrivé claimed that he had never missed a preaching assignment or a class meeting and refused to relinquish his involvement with the Tent Methodists. As a result, the meeting passed a resolution on 1 January 1822 that 'this meeting considers Mr Arrivé has formally withdrawn from the local preachers of the Salford Circuit'.[213] So much, once again, for Christian charity, or any recognition that there was a role in Methodist evangelical work for activities which took place outside the strict confines of the preaching

---

208   'Plan for the Preachers in the Manchester Circuit', 21 January to 15 April, 1821.

209   Rose, *Tell It How it Was*, p.6.

210   S. Stocks Jr, *A Reply to the Rev. John Pyer's 'Few Plain and Indisputable Testimonies* (Manchester, 1830), p.4.

211   Russell, *Memoirs of Rev John Pyer*, pp.110-111.

212   *Imperial Magazine* 4 (1822), p.365.

213   *Congregational Magazine* (1822), pp.107-108.

plan system. Pyer and Arrivé were, however, making a most favourable impression with Baptist and Independent leaders, both ministers and laymen, as well as a few individual Wesleyans.

The positive reputation of Tent Methodist work elsewhere, notably in and around Bristol, must have preceded the visit to Manchester because within a few days of their arrival the tent preachers had met at Arrivé's home with several men who were to give initial support. Prominent among these were lay people well known in the Manchester district. One such was William Wood of Bowdon who was particularly associated from 1820 onwards with the movement to prohibit the use of young boys as chimney sweeps. Wood eventually became a Congregationalist, although not until September 1848. He had been a Wesleyan member since about 1804 and was a class leader in 1813. He had lived in the Ancoats area, and owned his own woollen manufacturing business nearby.[214] This association might provide another reason for Ancoats being chosen as the centre of Tent Methodist missionary activity. He first met Pyer on 23 August 1821 and became a trustee of the chapel that was subsequently built, while remaining a Wesleyan class leader until at least 1824. How much of an active part he played in Tent Methodist affairs is not known, but he eventually left Wesleyanism at the time when a serious dispute arose in Manchester in 1834 when Samuel Warren, the Oldham Street superintendent, fell out with the national leadership. Wood had, apparently, 'impeccable credentials as a rebel' and was 'a keen advocate of disestablishment'.[215]

Another who was present at Arrivé's house on that occasion was Samuel Stocks, Jr, who was much later to be engaged in a bitter clash with Pyer. Stocks, a cotton manufacturer, largely financed the building of the Tent Methodist chapel and was a member of the building committee, having 'dissolved my connection with the Wesleyan Methodist Society'[216] on 3 November 1821. For three years he was actively involved in Tent Methodist affairs, being chairman and treasurer of the trust.

The most important layman involved in the early weeks and months was George Hadfield. Hadfield was born in Sheffield in 1788, qualified as an attorney in 1809 and set up business in Manchester in the same year. He eventually became Liberal Member of Parliament for Sheffield retaining the seat until 1874 when he announced 'I consider it my duty to intimate respectfully that it is not my intention to seek re-election'[217] at the General Election called in that year. He died in April 1879.

---

214 Marjorie Cox, *William Wood of Bolton: Champion of 'Climbing Boys'* (Manchester: Lancashire and Cheshire Antiquarian Society, 1995).

215 Gowland, *Methodist Secessions*, p.45.

216 Stocks, *A Reply*, p.4.

217 *Manchester Guardian* 22 April 1879, obituary of George Hadfield.

Throughout his adult life he was a member of the Congregationalists, being 'associated with almost every important Congregational movement in the county during the period of his long and most striking career'.[218] He was secretary of the Lancashire Union of Independents from 1811 to 1817, and was a generous financial contributor to Congregational causes, including a gift of £2,000 towards the construction of a ministerial training college in 1840, and to several other chapel building projects. It was he who was the prime mover in the decision to establish a Tent Methodist chapel. When it was decided in early September 1821 that the tent which had been used extensively for evangelical activity would soon have to be returned to the Bristol area, he discussed with Pyer the benefits of building a chapel. Hadfield 'conceives that a good plain building, capable of holding 2,000 people, might be built for £1,000'.[219] This was an early indication of his thinking, as was a similar comment on 9 September when he 'expressed his convictions that something should be done to perpetuate the work so blessedly begun'.[220] There were other issues, though, to be addressed before any definite measures could be taken.

In addition to the prominent lay people who quickly became aware of the evangelical successes, several leading dissenting ministers from the Baptist and Independent denominations provided support to the venture. For example, the Rev. John Birt, the newly appointed Baptist minister at the chapel in York Street, Manchester, met Pyer before the end of August. He gave encouragement throughout the following months and preached the first sermon in the Tent Methodist chapel when it opened, having chosen not to have a service in his own chapel that evening. Birt, an author of several religious works, arrived in Manchester at the age of thirty-four, and remained there until he moved to Oldham in 1842.[221]

Significantly, in the light of subsequent events, several local Congregational ministers were also actively supportive of Pyer's work. The most important of these in the earliest weeks that formulated much of what was to follow was the Rev. William Roby. He became minister of Cannon Street chapel, Manchester, in 1795, formed an academy for the training of ministers in 1803, and 'had a passion for evangelising—in the country districts by itinerating, in the towns by opening-air preaching... and in the wider life of the whole Church of Christ by his co-operation

---

218 B. Nightingale, *The Story of the Lancashire Congregational Union 1806-1906* (Manchester:Lancashire Congregational Union, 1906), p.76.

219 Russell, *Memoirs of Rev John Pyer*, p.106.

220 Russell, *Memoirs of Rev John Pyer*, p.111.

221 *Baptist Handbook* (1864), 'Memoirs of Baptist Ministers Deceased', pp.117-118.

with other branches of the Church'.[222] In 1821, Roby, who had moved, with most of his congregation, to Grosvenor Street was described as 'the loved and venerated minister'. It was not surprising that he should encourage evangelical effort in a new, expanding part of Manchester, albeit by a group not, then, of Independent persuasion. Another prominent Congregational minister, the Rev. Dr Thomas Raffles who also became secretary of the Lancashire Union, serving in this capacity from 1826 for no less than thirty-seven years, preached in the newly opened chapel on Christmas eve 1821. Raffles later became chairman of the Congregational Union of England and Wales, and has been described thus: 'if not the greatest figure in Liverpool nonconformity, certainly occupies a conspicuous place in any local Dissenting pantheon'.[223] Roby and Raffles were two among several Congregational ministers who were held in high regard by the denomination's membership and who significantly influenced Pyer in future years.

The impetus to build a chapel increased once it was decided that the tent was to return to Bristol and it became known that Manchester Wesleyans were to oppose the evangelistic activities. 'A universal burst of joy broke out'[224] when Pyer gave the news on 10 September 1821 that a chapel was to be built. J. Pigot's 1821 map of Manchester shows that Ancoats still barely stretched eastwards beyond Great Ancoats Street, but Canal Street was one such road and within a few years the whole area became built up. On the corner of Canal Street and Horne Street ' a suitable spot was secured'.[225] A large plot of land was bought from a Mr Boothman,[226] and within three weeks a building contract had been entered into with a firm of builders, Petty and Son. The chapel was to measure seventy-eight feet by sixty feet and was to cost £900.[227] To celebrate the event, the tent was erected on the site and a service held which was conducted by John Birt, again indicating Baptist denominational approval. Present at the service was a Mr Brookes, a local banker, who 'sent his compliments afterwards, with an offer to advance all the money required'.[228] The construction period was only seventy-two days, helped by the fact that 140 people 'in the short space of five hours, with cheerful gratuity, dug the foundations and otherwise prepared the

---

222 W. Gordon Robinson, *A History of the Lancashire Congregational Union 1806-1956* (Manchester:Lancashire Congregational Union, 1955), p.30.

223 Ian Sellers, 'Liverpool Nonconformity, 1786-1914' (PhD thesis, Keele University, 1969), p.86.

224 Russell, *Memoirs of Rev John Pyer*, p.113.

225 Russell, *Memoirs of Rev John Pyer*, p.114.

226 Stocks, *A Reply*, p.4.

227 Russell, *Memoirs of Rev John Pyer*, p.114.

228 Russell, *Memoirs of Rev John Pyer*, p.115.

ground for the erection'.[229] Understandably, perhaps, the building was later described to be 'in a very rough condition' and in use although 'the walls were not yet plastered'.[230] Nonetheless the first services were held on Sunday 23 December 1821, the building being known as the 'Poor Man's Chapel'.[231] On Christmas Day there were 300 communicants, including Wesleyans, Baptists and Independents. The *Evangelical Magazine* carried a report of 'crowded and deeply attentive congregations'[232] at the first services. Hadfield had contributed £100 towards the cost and on the evening that the subscription list opened 100 people had provided sums varying from £5 to 5 shillings.[233]

So it was that in only four months from Pyer's arrival in Manchester, a large chapel had been built to serve one of the town's growing residential and manufacturing areas. The Wesleyans had preaching stations nearby and a year later the Primitive Methodists built their first chapel in Manchester in Jersey Street, on the northern edge of Ancoats. This was to supplement their evangelical work carried on in a ' very large room [that] was taken over a factory in New Islington in June or July 1820'.[234] New Islington was barely a quarter of a mile from where the Tent Methodist chapel was built and Jersey Street, where the Wesleyans had a station for a time up to 1822, was only a half a mile away from the 'Poor Man's Chapel', on the other side of the Rochdale Canal. It would appear, therefore, that Ancoats could not quite be regarded as an area of no religious activity, but it was a district where 'misery was accentuated...by the introduction of machinery into many textile trades. The old hand-loom weavers, and other workers, lost their means of livelihood; and hungry, desperate men...were ripe for bloodshed and revolution'.[235] Into this environment, then, prompted by men of influence who were concerned for the spiritual well-being of the poorest in society, came the Tent Methodists who gave energetically to provide Christian teaching.

In 1822 and 1823, Pyer spent much of his time in Manchester, where he had succeeded in establishing 'a flourishing society...a large congregation gathered in the midst of a long neglected neighbourhood... a powerful impression...upon the poor of our teeming population' and, what the writer of a letter recalls as 'one of the greatest blessings which

---

229 *Imperial Magazine*, p.366.

230 Stocks, *A Reply*, p.4.

231 Russell, *Memoirs of Rev John Pyer*, p.116.

232 *Evangelical Magazine* March 1822, p.114.

233 *Imperial Magazine* 4 (1822), p.366.

234 Michael, Sheard, *Primitive Methodism in the Manchester Area 1820-1830* (WHS Lancashire and Cheshire Branch, Occasional Publication No. 4, 1976), p.3.

235 William Barker, *The Mother Church of Manchester Primitive Methodism* (Manchester: n.p., 1928), p.13.

Manchester ever witnessed'.[236] The author goes on to express the hope
that in subsequent years there would be more visits with tents and more
chapels. Those wishes were not fully accomplished and, perhaps because
Pyer had other responsibilities elsewhere, the work did not prosper as had
been hoped. Pyer himself claimed that between 1821 and Christmas 1823
the chapel was well attended and when, in early 1824, he 'returned to
Bristol, he left a large congregation and a flourishing society of more
than 300 members'.[237] The early years in Ancoats for Tent Methodism
seem to have been highly successful.

An annual meeting of the Tent Methodists was held in Manchester in
June 1823. On the Sunday before the business meetings began, 'the
congregations that attended...services were large and serious' and
'multitudes of all descriptions and characters flocked'[238] to services in
two tents that were erected nearby. A public meeting held the following
day to form a 'Home Missionary Society for the Manchester District'
was told of the success of those who 'had raised many of the wretchedly
fallen, from the dunghill of human degradation'.[239] All seemed well; a
'large commodious chapel', many members, and a significant amount of
support from leading people in other denominations. Although no
formal Tent Methodist membership figures seem to have been reported,
their presence failed to have any materially adverse effect on Wesleyan
numbers. Wesleyan membership in Manchester rose only marginally
from 3,206 to 3,288, 2.5%, between 1822 and 1824, whereas nationally
membership rose by 7%. During the same period Methodist New
Connexion membership in Manchester showed an actual fall of 80 from
473 to 393, so no firm conclusions can be drawn. Primitive Methodist
activity had just begun in the early 1820s and little significance can be
attached to their initial membership growth in the Manchester circuit.

Not long after the 1823 annual meeting there was a move to persuade
Pyer to become the full-time minister in Manchester. That the decision
whether or not to accept the invitation was a tortuous one to make could
be judged by the fact that it was not until 'the summer of 1825, Mr Pyer
acceded to the wishes of the people of Canal Street, and settled
permanently among them as their pastor'.[240] The chapel was adapted to
contain congregations of well over 1,200, living accommodation for Pyer
and his younger sister was built, and he was paid £120 per annum by way
of stipend. This was a considerable sum in relative terms, particularly so
in comparison with itinerant preachers in other Methodist groups. From

---

236 *Imperial Magazine* 4 (1822), p.366.
237 John Pyer, *Six Letters to a Trustee of Canal Street Chapel, Manchester....*
(London, 1830), p.5.
238 *TM Magazine*, pp.149-150.
239 *TM Magazine*, p.151.
240 Russell, *Memoirs of Rev John Pyer*, p.120.

extracts that exist of the minutes of meetings held between 5 January 1824 and 6 June 1825 it is clear that much time elapsed between the decision in principle to extend the chapel, provide a Sunday School room and build a house, and the final agreement to proceed. Significantly, in the light of subsequent events, during January 1825 it was agreed that the 'church declares itself independent of any other whatsoever, and forms rules and regulations for its own government'. A footnote stated that the name 'Tent Methodist' was retained,[241] but it was not long after the middle of 1825 that there began a long running dispute, described in a later chapter, which led, unhappily, to the demise of Tent Methodist activity in Manchester.

While Ancoats was the centre of Tent Methodist activity in Manchester, there seems to have been at least one other chapel in the city for a time. Manchester was a 'district' in the Tent Methodist organization and in a resolution passed at the 1823 annual meeting, it was agreed that a half of the collection taken for missionary expansion should be used for a chapel at Stretford. Stretford was to the south west of the city closer to where Peter Arrivé lived. It is also recorded elsewhere that when Pyer returned to Manchester on a full-time basis in 1825 it had been agreed that he would 'preach at Canal Street morning and evening, and in Oxford Road, or elsewhere, in the afternoon'.[242] Oxford Road was a major thoroughfare close to Stretford and might have been where this chapel was located. Two other contemporary records of Christian denominations written in the 1820's by Charles Hulbert and Mark Robinson that refer to the Tent Methodists also suggest that there were other preaching places in Manchester.[243]

Liverpool and Birmingham

The extension of Tent Methodism into Liverpool is inextricably linked with one man, George Smith, who later became the most well known Nonconformist to have been a member and preacher with the Tent Methodists. Before George Smith was sent to Liverpool in 1823, Pyer had visited the town on at least two separate occasions. During the hectic activity in Manchester in the final four months of 1821, he travelled with a tent to Runcorn, Warrington and Liverpool, probably in late October or early November.[244]

---

241 Stocks, *A Reply*, pp.16-18.
242 Pyer, *Six Letters*, p.10.
243 Charles Hulbert, *The Religions of Britain: or a view of its various Christian Denominations* (Shrewsbury, 1826), p.42; and Mark Robinson, *Observations on the System of Wesleyan Methodism* (London, 1824), p.68.
244 Russell, *Memoirs of Rev John Pyer*, p.116.

It was on Thursday 19 June 1823 that Pocock and Pyer left Manchester at the end of the annual meeting 'to open a Mission in Liverpool'.[245] It is not known how long Pocock and Pyer stayed, but in September George Smith 'took up his abode in that city'[246] and began to work with great energy, using a tent 'in a poor area of the town'.[247] Although Pyer was, according to the writer of Smith's obituary, his main adviser at this time, it was Pocock who had guided Smith a few years earlier and, once in Liverpool, he received much support and advice from Dr Thomas Raffles. That Smith would have needed help from experienced colleagues was understandable as he was barely twenty years old when he was sent to Liverpool, and his conversion to Christianity had taken place only three years before.

The great promise that Pocock had previously identified was, no doubt, fulfilled as he 'soon gathered around himself a congregation, of which he was requested to take the "entire oversight"'.[248] His obituary writer recorded that 'He threw himself into this mission with all the ardour of his heart. Such was the success that attended it, that many souls were brought to Christ'.[249] While a tent was used in the initial stage a room in Heath Street became the meeting place for services. Heath Street was a relatively minor thoroughfare in the Toxteth Park area of Liverpool and was, in the early 1820's, at the southern extremity of the town. A map published in 1825 shows a chapel in Heath Street but without a designation, and it is uncertain whether this was the building used by the Tent Methodists. Once again, no records are available that show Tent Methodist membership numbers, but the Wesleyan membership in Liverpool declined every year from 1821 until 1827 when it began to rise again. The Tent Methodist work continued for several years until, as in Manchester, events and personalities combined to change the direction of the society in Liverpool.

There was one other place that was missioned but where progress was hard to achieve, if it occurred at all. Birmingham is not referred to in the *Tent Methodist Magazine* and it can be supposed, therefore, that no activity began before the middle of 1821. The *Memoirs of Rev John Pyer* report that in 1822 and 1823 'his time was divided between Bristol, London, Birmingham, Liverpool and Manchester, in each of which towns the Tent was used with much success'.[250] That 'success' was not readily recognized by Barnett who spent two months in Birmingham in 1823 and where he was beset with difficulties. It is known that a chapel was

---

245 *TM Magazine*, p.155.
246 *Congregational Year Book* (1871), p.346.
247 Sellers, *Liverpool Nonconformity 1786-1914*, p.94.
248 Nightingale, *Lancashire Nonconformity*, VI, p.170.
249 *Congregational Year Book* (1871), p.346.
250 Russell, *Memoirs of Rev John Pyer*, p.119.

acquired in 'Rea Street, near to Moseley Street'[251] in the parish of Aston—streets that still exist just to the south east of the city centre—but attempts to undertake profitable tent preaching on adjacent ground proved exceedingly difficult. Barnett recorded in a letter to Pyer that 'the rabble was so numerous and behaved so badly'[252] over several successive days in September. The church authorities refused to 'certify any piece of waste ground as a place of Religious Worship, unless there is a Building on it'.[253] Barnett left behind him a William Williams to continue missionary work, but Pocock was displeased that Barnett had given up without persevering for longer.[254]

So it was that in only three years from the middle of 1820, the Tent Methodists had become established in several widely scattered parts of England, and in one small area of south Wales. This progress had been achieved as a result of the substantial commitment of its leader, George Pocock, its only full-time missionary, John Pyer, and a considerable number of dedicated men who undertook significant roles, of whom George Smith and John Barnett became the most well known. The geographical expansion, though, had no immediate logic or pattern to it, and in most cases at least, happened because specific invitations had been received from individuals who knew a little of Tent Methodism and its personalities, but wished to enlist their help to extend evangelical activity still further.

---

251 Barnett, *Memorials*, p.28.
252 Barnett, *Memorials*, p.27.
253 Barnett, *Memorials*, p.26.
254 Barnett, *Memorials*, p.29.

CHAPTER 6

Tent Methodism's
Progress up to 1825

It is now relevant to examine other features of Tent Methodism during the years of expansion. The structure and organization developed quickly, there was a significant amount of written material produced, and the steady acquisition of chapels reduced the relative dependency on tents. Much has been written about the preachers involved but an attempt will be made to assess the relative progress of the sect overall during the first half of the third decade. While most of the information is from supportive sources which are highly subjective there is also some objective evidence to use.

The 1824 Version of the Rules

The original administrative structure set out and adopted in the 1820 version of rules was the starting point from which subsequent changes occurred. The first set of rules was produced before much of the expansion was anticipated, let alone took place, and there seems to have been a particular emphasis on ensuring that the rules addressed the issues that caused the withdrawal or expulsion of the three leaders in 1820. It has already been noted that the first version was published in a hurry, and it is known that Pyer spent most of Christmas Eve in 1821 'revising and new modelling our rules'.[1] Another, more comprehensive set of regulations was published in 1824. It might be assumed that the amendments that Pyer was working on at the very end of 1821 subsequently emerged as the 1824 arrangement. Even the first *Rules of the Tent Methodists or Agrarian Society for Extending Christianity at Home* clearly envisaged the development of a significant body. A structure of committees was identified, and various titles for officials with distinct duties were described, including an assumption that there would be a number of 'Itinerant Preachers', 'Missionaries', and 'Resident Preachers' as well as, for example,'Exhorters', 'Pastors', and 'Trustees'.

---

1   Russell, *Memoirs of Rev John Pyer*, p.116.

The 'Yearly Meeting' was, among other things 'to devise plans for extending the work of God'.[2] There was considerable work to be done in updating the original rules in the light of the early experience.

By the time the 1824 version of the rules was published the words 'or Agrarian Society for Extending Christianity at Home' had been deleted. This clearly reflected work then taking place in the inner city areas of Bristol, London, Manchester, Liverpool and Birmingham, and meant that it was no longer appropriate to draw particular attention to the original activity in rural areas. Three or four years of experience led to other changes in the rules.

Not surprisingly, the 1824 version of the rules was much longer, consisting of twelve pages instead of eight, and the doctrinal statement at the beginning was expanded. The Arminian principles were confirmed, and added to in some subtle as well as some obvious ways. Justification was by faith alone, the word 'alone' being added to the original wording, and the doctrines were 'believed' as well as taught. The word 'believed' was not included in the first version of the rules. The doctrinal statement was expanded by the inclusion of three new features: 'The being and attributes of God; the supreme divinity of the Lord Jesus Christ; the personality and influences of the Holy Ghost'.[3] The absence in the first edition of any reference to 'The Holy Ghost' probably had no doctrinal significance; rather it is further evidence that the original version was prepared in great haste.

Understandably, there was a change of emphasis reflecting the increased number of chapels, a standard form of legal ownership of buildings had been prepared, and no chapel acquisition could proceed until approval had been given in the quarterly district meeting. A previous requirement that at least half the cost of new building or purchase must be subscribed before a chapel was built or acquired was not included in the later version. Robert Currie claimed that Pocock retained personal ownership of at least one chapel for 'nearly a quarter of a century',[4] but it has not been possible to confirm that statement. Indeed, as far as is known the last chapel was disposed of by Pocock in 1832, having acquired it in 1821.[5] More stringent requirements were introduced before full membership was permitted, and special reference was made to the need for regular pastoral instruction and weekly meetings with pastors. The role of trustees had been altered in that only those who were members of the society were authorized to attend the weekly meeting of each chapel's officials. Perhaps reflecting the much

---

2   *TM Rules* (1820), p.3.
3   *TM Rules* (1824), p.4.
4   Currie, *Methodism Divided*, p.56.
5   Indentures dated 1 April 1833 and 2 April 1833 set out, among other things, the arrangements for the sale of the Hanham chapel.

greater geographical spread of the societies some of the meetings were held at less frequent intervals. To address concerns sometimes expressed in Wesleyan circles, any member could attend the annual meeting, although only authorized representatives were entitled to have their expenses paid and vote. References were made to 'several districts' with Bristol, London and Manchester districts being mentioned by name. Wiltshire is likely to have been a fourth. Overall, the later document is a much more understandable one, reflecting more care in its preparation, the progress made in the intervening period, and the time that had elapsed since the bitter events of late 1819 and early 1820.[6]

In both sets of rules there were indications that later Congregational influences and directions were already inferred. The Wesleyan rules, and even more significantly, the ones issued by the Methodist New Connexion, the Primitive Methodists and the Bible Christians, made no use of the word 'deacon'. The Tent Methodist rules, however, show a significant role, akin to a 'steward' in the other sects, as the deacon had a duty to 'report the state of each Church'[7] to every quarterly meeting. In addition, the church meeting had a prominent place in the structure of meetings and organization, particularly so as there was no place for circuits. That might, of course, reflect the relatively small number of societies, but there would, in fact, have been a logic for a greater number of circuits as each district, except London and Manchester, covered a wide geographical area. Pyer, who was later to join the Congregationalists, had regular contact with a leading Congregational minister in Bristol from the early days, and it might be that he, rather than Gosling, was the architect, with Pocock, of both sets of rules, and not just the second one. Certainly, there was greater autonomy for local congregations, including more enquiry and scope for discussion before expulsion of individual members took place.

Co-operation with other Dissenting Groups and Individuals

Perhaps because of the continuing friction with Wesleyans, the Tent Methodists developed close relationships in places, and for certain purposes, with leaders in other denominations. In addition to Pyer's links with William Thorp, the Independent minister at Castle Green, Bristol, he established many points of contact with several other Independent ministers as well as George Hadfield, a leading layman, in and around Manchester. As early as September 1820, the Tent Methodists were instrumental in forming a Bible Association in the Kingswood area of

---

6   *TM Rules* (1824), particularly pp.5-12.
7   *TM Rules* (1824), p.6.

Bristol, the chairman of which, S. Prust, was a leading lay Independent who later served on national denominational committees.[8] They co-operated with the Quakers who also undertook preaching work in the Bristol docks area, and who accompanied Tent Methodist preachers on occasions. Elijah Waring, the south Wales Quaker who later joined the Wesleyans, gave support in various ways. Several Baptists in the Manchester area were instrumental in encouraging the construction of the Ancoats chapel. In Bristol, at the time of the trial and execution of John Horwood in 1821, a leading Baptist as well as Pocock was involved in providing Christian support. Thomas Roberts, the successful minister at Old King Street, Bristol, 'was also a frequent visitor to gaols and as a result of his labours John Horwood, a condemned murderer was converted before his execution'.[9] For the greater benefit of ecumenical progress individual Wesleyans were prepared to co-operate with the Tent Methodists, of whom Samuel Budgett was one. He was well known in the Kingswood area. Born in 1794, he prospered as the result of the 'management of an extensive mercantile establishment', and his obituary made a particular point of describing him as 'Loving all who love our Lord Jesus Christ in sincerity'.[10] He, too, was involved in the formation of the Bible Association in Kingswood and served on the organizing committee, but there is no evidence that he supported Tent Methodism's own missionary work.

The receptiveness to ecumenical co-operation was also shown in the contents of the *Tent Methodist Magazine* for 1823. In addition to the extensive information provided on Tent Methodist matters, there was room for articles concerning several other denominations, and material relating to leading Wesleyans. There was for example, over a three month period, a verbatim record of John Wesley's funeral sermon following the death of George Whitefield, a comment by Dr Adam Clarke on some verses from a chapter in Proverbs, and a review of a book by James Macdonald on the life of Joseph Benson, a leading Wesleyan. Several obituaries of other denominational members appeared, one of a young Wesleyan woman, another of a Baptist minister who had been an overseas missionary, and a third of an Independent minister from Bristol. Perhaps because of Pyer's earlier ambitions to become a missionary himself, there were several contributions about foreign countries, many of them

---

8   *TM Magazine*, p.201.

9   Robert W. Oliver, *The Strict Baptist Chapels of England: Volume 5. Wiltshire and the West* (London: R.F. Chambers, 1968).

10   *Wesleyan Methodist Magazine* (1851), p.606. A comprehensive biography of Samuel Budgett's life and work was written by William Arthur, first published in 1852 only a year after Budgett's death, entitled *The Successful Merchant*. There is no evidence that, despite his undoubted generosity, Budgett supported the Tent Methodists directly, either financially or spiritually.

concerning the work of Christians in those parts of the world. Four short articles written by Dr Isaac Watts, the leading Independent minister, were included, as were others written by ministers of several other denominations, including the Church of England. It was quite normal for religious periodicals to contain articles by or about members of other persuasions and it was, therefore, not unexpected that the Tent Methodists should also pursue that policy. The type of material included in the monthly editions of the 1823 *Tent Methodist Magazine* followed closely the pattern of the *Wesleyan Methodist Magazine* for the same period.

There was a period of national, as well as local, calm before further schisms occurred later in the decade. The annual address to the Wesleyan societies at the 1824 conference included the following optimistic, though cautionary, section: 'The general absence of all strifes and divisions throughout our now widely-extended Connexion, is another circumstance on which we congratulate you... This blessing we have long enjoyed, and we rejoice in the prospect of its permanence; though attempts, arising out of offences, peculiar views, and other motives, may occasionally be made to divert the attention of the unwary from the great ends of our common vocation, and to sow discord among brethren'.[11] The disputes which had resulted in the Tent Methodists becoming established as a formal sect in 1820, as well as the earlier ones which resulted in the formation of the Primitive Methodists and the Bible Christians in the previous decade, were a relatively distant memory.

Although provision was made for several 'home missionaries' to be appointed, John Pyer was the only full-time paid official of the Tent Methodists. Despite bouts of ill health, he showed enormous energy and worked extremely hard for the cause. While Pocock was the man who directed the proceedings, especially in the early years after 1820, Pyer was the man who implemented plans and travelled thousands of miles to promote, manage, and guide the day to day affairs. It was not just his preaching and pastoral activity that gives justification for that judgement. He was joint editor of the *Tent Methodist Magazine*, he was probably the reviser of the rules, and he, jointly with Pocock, published *A Collection of Hymns*, and wrote the preface to it.[12] All these things were undertaken in addition to his domestic family responsibilities which would have been more difficult as he did not have regular companionship and support of his wife who, because of continuing ill health, lived with her relatives in Newbury. His obituary referred to this: 'patiently and bravely did he endure this long fight of affliction'.[13] He always provided a home to one of his two daughters until she died in 1837, and gave board and lodgings

11   *Minutes of Methodist Conference* (1824). 'Annual Address to Societies by Robert Newton, President, and Jabez Bunting, Secretary' (London, 1864), p.525.

12   John Pyer and George Pocock (eds), *A Collection of Hymns* (Bristol, 1825).

13   Russell, *Memoirs of Rev John Pyer*, p.300.

to a nephew while he was in Manchester. The various responsibilities he undertook, including an active involvement with the teetotal movement, were undertaken wholeheartedly.

The Hymn Book, and the History of the Early Years

The hymn book contained several features of significance in Tent Methodist affairs. Firstly, its production had been urged on Pocock and Pyer at the 1823 annual meeting. Indeed, it was supposed to have been ready for printing by that time. The fact that two more years elapsed before actual publication indicates that Pyer and Pocock had more urgent responsibilities to fulfil. Some of the hymns included were written by well known authors such as Watts, Doddridge, Cowper, Luther, Toplady, and Charles, John and Samuel Wesley, but others were written by Tent Methodists. Pocock, Purdy and Roberts, in addition to Pyer, all had contributions, and one, in particular, reflected the concern for the poor and the use of tents. The editors did not attribute authors to individual hymns, but two verses of one, probably written by Pyer and included in a section for hymns suitable for 'opening ceremonies of places of worship', read:

Verse 1:   Behold, a great effectual door,
            Open before God's servants stands;
            Witness this temple for the poor—
            This monument of mercy's hands:
            Witness these crowds, these prayers, these cries.
            This sounding praise which rends the skies

Verse 5:   Then, like thy servants sent of old,
            Our power receiving from on high,
            Forth would we go divinely bold,
            And spread thy truth through earth and sky.
            Our Tents should other churches raise
            and other courts should sound thy praise.[14]

The reference to 'Tents' being the precursor of other churches in the penultimate line of the hymn is consistent with rule 32 in the 1824 version: 'From Easter to October, providing convenience will allow, there shall be preaching once on each Sabbath day at least, in the neighbourhood of each chapel or preaching house, either in the open air

---

14   Pyer and Pocock (eds), *Collection of Hymns*, No. 964, p.491.

or under a Tent'.[15] This must have been an increasingly difficult requirement to comply with as the number of preaching places grew in number over a wide area. It is believed that there were never more than three tents, one of which might have been permanently based in London.[16]

In Pyer's preface to *A Collection of Hymns*, he explains the reason for each hymn being on one double page: 'While engaged with God in praise, the worshippers have been often disturbed by the turning over of leaves throughout the congregation',[17] an intriguing insight into Pyer's character that shows his close attention to detail. By analysis of a book that Pocock later published entitled *Sacred Lyrics for Youth*, it is known that Pocock, too, wrote hymns. Four of the hymns in the *Collection* appear in Pocock's publication, the content of which covered a wide variety of topics. Victory Purdy was also an author—indeed as he is reputed to have written 1,853 verses[18] it would not have been difficult to find some that were considered to be appropriate. One of Purdy's hymns included a verse:

> O make us of one Spirit, Lord,
> Simple in thought and deed and word:
> Nor may we ever disagree,
> But all be love and harmony.

It might be thought that that verse has more than a passing resemblance to two written by Charles Wesley:

> Jesus, Lord, we look to Thee
> Let us in Thy name agree;
> Show Thyself the Prince of Peace;
> Bid all strife for ever cease.
>
> Make us of one heart and mind,
> Courteous, pitiful, and kind,
> Lowly, meek, in thought and word,
> Altogether like the Lord.[19]

---

15   *TM Rules* (1824), p.12.

16   The Tent Methodist preaching plan for London between 28 April and 25 August 1822 shows '1st tent (new), 2nd tent (old), and 3rd tent (small)'.

17   Pyer and Pocock (eds), *Collection of Hymns*, Preface.

18   John B. Edwards, *Victory Purdy, 'The Kingswood Collier'* (Bristol: The New Room, 1984), p.13.

19   The hymn is to be found in many hymn books, including *Congregational Praise*, as well as Methodist hymn books.

Paraphrasing the work of other hymn writers was not an uncommon practice. It might have been the events of 1819 and 1820 leading to the formation of the Tent Methodists, following the bitter personal enmities, that prompted Purdy to paraphrase Charles Wesley's famous hymn.

None of the hymns written by Pyer, Pocock or Purdy seem to have been used for more than a few years, although it is not possible to be sure as many hymn books of the time did not record the names of the authors. Composers of the tunes, however, were normally shown. It is known that three collections of hymns produced at various periods after 1820 from sources that would have been considered sympathetic to the Tent Methodist cause did not consider any of Pocock's hymns worthy of publication. William O'Bryan published a comprehensive set of hymns for the Bible Christians in 1825, a Joseph Reynolds produced at a similar time a collection 'designed for a body of Independent Methodists', and an unknown compiler published *The Tent Hymn Book* in 1873.[20] None include any that can be definitely attributed to Pocock or Pyer. It may be that the earlier two were published before their hymn writing was known about, and by 1873 Pocock and Pyer had been forgotten and many more famous authors had emerged.

At the 1823 annual meeting the first resolution referred to the need to complete the production of the hymn book which was to be introduced into the societies as soon as possible. Pyer and Pocock's *A Collection of Hymns*, while not specifically named as a Tent Methodist publication in the hope of generating sales from other groups, was nonetheless clearly compiled for Tent Methodist use. It was a massive and impressive work which helps to explain why it took so long to appear. There are no less than 1,091 hymns on 555 pages and in addition to a preface of some length, there is a comprehensive index of first lines, scriptural texts and subjects.[21]

The third resolution at the same annual meeting was 'That the brethren Pocock and Pyer be earnestly requested to finish the Tent History without fail'.[22] Several previous references had been made to this publication and, bearing in mind that the final pamphlet in the series of three issued in May 1820 included an announcement that 'Speedily will be published, A History of the Tent or Itinerant Temple',[23] it was not surprising that its non-appearance after a period of another three years should prompt a

---

20   William O'Bryan, *A Collection of Hymns for Arminian Bible Christians* (Stoke Damarel, 1825) is a substantial publication. Joseph Reynolds, *A Selection of Hymns and Spiritual Songs, designed for a body of Independent Methodists* (Cambridge, 1822), is a much more modest publication.

21   Pyer and Pocock (eds), *Collection of Hymns*. The title and general layout is remarkably similar to that produced by O'Bryan for the Bible Christians in the same year.

22   *TM Magazine*, p.150.

23   Pocock *et al*, *Facts Without a Veil*, p.50.

plea for it to be completed and published without any further procrastination. The delay was certainly caused by the many more pressing day to day issues of a group that had grown substantially over that period. It did eventually become available as there are two references to it in the *Memoirs of Rev. John Pyer*,[24] and another in an early history of Portland Chapel, but no surviving copy has been found. There is another publication that was produced but appears to have been lost. A *Tent Methodist Magazine* for 1824 was certainly issued as there were two references in it to the death of Pyer's mother which occurred on 6 March 1824.[25] That publication would, no doubt, also provide further information about the sect's progress in the early 1820's.

It is believed that annual meetings took place in 1822 and 1824, in addition to the one held in Manchester in 1823 and extensively reported in the magazine for 1823. Robert Currie refers to 'The Rules of the Tent Methodist Society, Adopted at the First General Meeting of Representatives Held in Bristol, May 27th and 28th, 1822',[26] but no minutes or information about that meeting have been traced. That it did take place can also be judged by the fact that the account of the 1823 Meeting begins, 'According to the appointment of the previous year'.[27] If a meeting took place in 1824, on the first Monday in July, as suggested by resolution 10 of the 1823 Meeting, again no information is available.

The absence of much detail of the events of the middle years of the 1820s does make it more difficult to assess the full contribution of Tent Methodism in that period. If any of the missing material is ever uncovered, scholarly assessment would be considerably aided. It might simply be that the on-going work precluded the production of minutes and notes, but it is more likely that they have been lost through the passage of time.

Pyer was instructed, by resolution passed at the 1823 annual meeting, to spend half his time in the Manchester district and the balance in the Bristol district. That left a considerable number of places without his services and, in any event, during 1824 he began to devote more and more time to his Manchester work. The day to day activity in the large number of places in the southern half of the country was having to be directed by Pocock himself and a number of local preachers. With the increasing number of congregations to receive pastoral care, spread

---

24   Russell, *Memoirs of Rev John Pyer*. References appear on pp.36 and 42, the latter reference quoting *The History of the Itinerant Temple*, p.89.

25   Russell, *Memoirs of Rev John Pyer*, pp.2 and 121. On p.2 it is said that John Pyer wrote a 'sketch' of his mother's life that was published in the 1824 edition of the *TM Magazine*. Similarly, on p.121 it is noted that Pyer published a 'memoir' of his mother, also in the 1824 *TM Magazine*.

26   Currie, *Methodism Divided*, p.143.

27   *TM Magazine*, p.150.

geographically along a narrow band eastwards from Bristol, those involved worked with very great commitment.

Lack of Competition with other Dissenters

The growth that was achieved occurred, in part at least, because many of the places where Tent Methodist missionary endeavour took place were in areas where little dissenting presence was evident. Dursley, Bath and parts of Bristol were some of the exceptions to that, but the information that is available of Methodist and 'Old Dissent' chapel building in the period suggests very little activity during the first half of the 1820's. Examination of *Nonconformist Chapels and Meeting Houses in South West England*[28] does not indicate any real chapel building programme in those places where Tent Methodists were active. The records of the Wesleyan authorities show only agreement to a chapel at Roadley, in the Dursley circuit, and one at Fisherton, Wiltshire, in the Salisbury circuit, in 1821 and 1823 respectively, in districts where Tent Methodists were present.[29] On the other hand, there is plenty of evidence that Tent Methodists were active in many places that were devoid of Wesleyan presence. Inner city areas of Bristol, where housing provision was particularly poor, Kingswood and Tetbury, in Gloucestershire, were examples, as was Cwm Dws in south Wales and a large number of the agricultural communities in Wiltshire. It cannot be known with certainty whether this was a deliberate policy so as to avoid confrontation with the Wesleyan authorities and to undertake real missionary endeavour, or whether it was accidental. This feature of little competition mirrored, to some extent, the Primitive Methodist experience and, particularly, the Bible Christian one.

Primitive Methodist evangelism in the fifteen years or so from its establishment in 1811 took place in both urban and rural areas. In some places not only were Wesleyans at work but so too, especially when expansion reached the urban districts of Yorkshire and Nottinghamshire, were Methodist New Connexion societies. Although there was a considerable degree of overlap geographically, and also competitiveness, the Wesleyans did, during that period, tend to reduce their involvement in rural areas throughout the country. To a significant degree this was for financial reasons and occurred despite resistance by itinerants from time to time. One in the north riding of Yorkshire 'warned that abandoning small societies in order to cut costs would be "exceedingly painful" to

---

28   Christopher Stell, *Nonconformist Chapels and Meeting Houses in South West England* (London: HMSO, 1991).

29   *Register Book for Chapels, built, enlarged or purchased since the Conference held at Sheffield in 1817* (n.p., n.d.), pp. 13 and 35.

loyal Wesleyans, however [much] this might please the Ranters who preach in every place in the circuit'.[30] The Primitive Methodists, it has been said, 'excelled at village evangelism and followed up their field and street preaching with cottage prayer meetings'.[31] There was, then, a close similarity with the areas actively worked by the Tent Methodists.

That was also the case with the Bible Christians. Despite the long history and numerical strength of Wesleyanism in the West Country counties, especially Cornwall, the evangelical efforts of William O'Bryan, the founder, and his fellow preaching colleagues in the early years, was concentrated in pockets of north-east Cornwall and north-west Devon where there were relatively few Wesleyan societies. Tiny villages such as St Neot, Week St Mary and Bridgerule in east Cornwall, and Cookbury, Bradworthy and Shebbear in north Devon all feature in the first few years' history of the Bible Christians. There was no Wesleyan presence in these places and the Church of England too, it was claimed, 'was generally without a living ministry'.[32] The Bible Christians expanded their geographical coverage, especially in Devon and Cornwall, with considerable success, although there is less evidence of open air or field preaching.

The Methodist New Connexion, however, did come into greater conflict with the Wesleyans during the period under examination. Being a secession from Wesleyanism, disputes were probably inevitable. Much antagonism between the two groups duly took place, including some that related to the ownership and occupation of chapel premises. Bitter wrangling and legal actions adversely affected their relationships for many years.

It can be claimed that much of the Tent Methodist growth was achieved in places where there was no competition with Wesleyans, an experience it shared to a similar degree with the Bible Christians, to a lesser extent with the Primitive Methodists, but not with the Methodist New Connexion. They were, then, filling gaps in the Methodist coverage of England, particularly in rural districts. That this is the case provides further justification for the predominant historical view that some, but not all, Wesleyan offshoots developed their contacts and influence in parts of the country left alone by the Wesleyans. Even so, Robert Wearmouth has claimed that 'as late as 1830 many of the agricultural areas would be correctly described as a "Methodist wilderness"', although 'after 1830, all the various sections of Methodism began to invade the rural areas'.[33]

---

30   Werner, *Primitive Methodist Connexion*, p.181, quoting letter to Jabez Bunting from Zachariah Taft, May 1822.

31   Werner, *Primitive Methodist Connexion*, p.183.

32   R. Pyke, *The Golden Chain* (London: Henry Hooks, 1915), p.14.

33   Robert F. Wearmouth, *Methodism and the Working-class Movements of England* (London: Epworth Press, 1937), pp.214-215.

The Tent Methodists' movement into rural areas had all taken place before 1830, but the Primitive Methodists and Bible Christians certainly continued their expansion into country districts well after 1830.

While there is scope for more detailed research to test the evidence further, it is probably also true that much of the missionary activity in rural areas occurred without competition from other dissenting groups. This is not to say that there were often formal ecumenical agreements, but simply that local evangelists focused their attention on places where no missionary work was regularly undertaken. Although this was probably so in the areas where Tent Methodists operated, other parts of the country including parts of the south Midlands, did develop structured approaches to ecumenism so as to use more effectively the resources available.

It is difficult to assess to what extent Tent Methodist success was due to the perceived inward looking trend and the apparent middle class focus of Wesleyanism. W.R. Ward noted that 'there was a tension between the Methodist ideals of an evangelistic mission, and of a pietistic society set apart from the world in pursuit of sanctification'.[34] Gay claimed that the divisions within Methodism were caused by an 'underlying motive in each case...to recover the flexible and democratic spirit of early Methodism which was fast fading in the increasingly conservative main body of Methodism'.[35] It is a subjective judgement as to how relevant these features were to Tent Methodist growth, but in all that has been written about them in contemporary accounts the following quotation does seem to summarize the position: in 'small communities the denominational label counted for less than the simplicity of the religious forms and the social bonds of membership'.[36] That was a strength in the period under review, but it became a weakness in the following few years.

Tent Methodism's Numerical Membership

The absence of any national Tent Methodist membership figures being discovered for any year makes it difficult, on one potential measurement of the influence, to assess the significance of Tent Methodism's impact in the 1820's. This is regrettable as each quarterly meeting was charged with the responsibility of reporting 'the number of members in each church throughout the District'.[37] All that is available are references to the number of class tickets issued and renewed, the trend of Wesleyan

---

34   Ward, *Religion and Society*, p.135.

35   John D. Gay, *The Geography of Religion in England* (London: Gerald Duckworth, 1971), p.148.

36   David Hempton, *The Religion of the People: Methodism and Popular Religion c1750-1900* (London: Routledge, 1996), p.54.

37   *TM Rules* (1824), p.6.

membership during the 1820s in the places where Tent Methodists were active, and even more tenuous indicators such as the size of chapels that were acquired. It would be especially dangerous to equate any substantial movement, up or down, in Wesleyan circuit membership against the national trend, solely to the results of Tent Methodist activity. Appendix G sets out the Wesleyan Methodist position in the relevant circuits between 1819 and 1831 and significant variations can be found. A number of important factors, other than Tent Methodist influence, may explain the discrepancies. First, there was the expansion or contraction of circuits with societies being formed or others ceasing to function. Secondly, there were constant changes in the make-up of circuits with societies transferred in or out. In addition, internal disputes leading to loss of membership numbers, the effect of other schisms, and less than total accuracy in recording and reporting the annual figures would all have been relevant.

Taking into account the information that is capable of being used, and aggregating it to obtain a cumulative figure, it is possible to suggest, nothing more, the following membership totals, reflecting the timing of the expansion into the various geographical areas:

December 1820 —   700
December 1821 — 1,500
December 1822 — 2,000
December 1823 — 2,500
December 1824 — 3,000
December 1825 — 3,500

There is little evidence to corroborate these figures. Pyer's daughter in her *Memoirs of Rev John Pyer* tells of a district meeting held at Cleve-Wood, near Bristol, on Easter Monday 1821 when 600 people were present. This meeting would have been held at the place where Pocock's 'two eldest daughters conducted an Establishment for the education of young ladies',[38] located between Downend and Frenchay to the north of Bristol. The house had been in the family's occupation since 1816 at least as it was visited in May of that year by Edward Griffith who went to see George Pocock's sister and sister-in-law just a week before his fatal accident.[39] Making assumptions that most of those present at the 1821 meeting would have been members, that a relatively large proportion of local members in Bristol and Gloucestershire would have attended, and that in Bath, Wiltshire, London, Manchester and south Wales there would have, in total, been several hundred more members, it is possible to make

---

38   Russell, *Memoirs of Rev John Pyer*, pp.93-94.
39   *TM Magazine*, p.217.

a reasonable assessment of 1,500 members by the end of 1821. At that time there was still much expansion to come—some of it in other areas in Gloucestershire, Wiltshire and London, and part of it in areas not then influenced by Tent Methodist preachers, including Liverpool and Birmingham.

In addition to Wesleyan concern at Tent Methodist growth, in the form of letters to or from Bunting, there are a number of other pieces of more objective contemporary information. A Mark Robinson wrote a letter to his superintendent in 1824 which was principally concerned with his desire that Methodists should rejoin the established Church by pointing out the defects that he perceived existed in the Wesleyan system. That seventy-two page letter contained an Appendix in which he set out the position as he believed it to be regarding the Tent Methodists and other groups that had been formed after schisms from Wesleyanism. Interestingly, he discussed the Tent Methodists and their progress after the Primitive Methodists, but before the Bible Christians and Methodist New Connexion. He wrote that Tent Methodists 'have numerous and increasing societies in the west of England' and that 'many hundreds of persons have been converted by their preaching'.[40] He was writing that in 1824 when, apparently, expansion was continuing, and although it is not possible to deduce actual membership numbers from Robinson's comments, they do confirm a general picture of increasing numbers in the early years.

A second source of contemporary material comes from a substantial book written by Charles Hulbert which was published in May 1826. In it he described a large number of dissenting sects, including the Methodist offshoots that existed at that date. About the Tent Methodists he wrote that other societies had been established in the Manchester vicinity and that there were 'many respectable members and preachers'.[41] Sixty years or so later, but still of significance, Mark Guy Pearse referred to the formation of the Tent Methodists. Pearse was an eminent Wesleyan who was for a time minister at Portland Chapel, Bristol. He published two articles in the 1884 monthly editions of *The Wesleyan-Methodist Magazine*, and in one he wrote that Pocock left the society there 'taking with him many sympathisers; so that there was a considerable rent in the Society'.[42] It does seem that most of the growth had been achieved by the end of 1825 and the following chapter will describe and analyse the events of the second half of the third decade of the nineteenth century.

---

40   Robinson, *Observations on the System of Wesleyan Methodism*, p.68.

41   Charles Hulbert, *The Religions of Britain, or a view of its various Christian Denominations; .... and the History of the British Church* (Shrewsbury, 1826), p.299.

42   Mark Guy Pearse, 'Portland-Street Chapel, Bristol', *The Wesleyan Methodist Magazine* (September, 1884), p.656.

It is interesting to attempt to compare the Tent Methodists' possible growth in numerical strength during the first five years to 1825 with that achieved in the early years of Methodist New Connexion, Primitive Methodists and Bible Christians. The Methodist New Connexion was established in August 1797 with approximately 5,000 members who had seceded from the Wesleyans. The English membership figures for the following five years to 1802 show an actual decline. From an estimated 5,380 in 1799 the membership total fell to under 5,000 in 1801 and did not rise above 5,000 again until 1806.[43] A fascinating contemporary view of the Methodist New Connexion early experiences comes from a pamphlet written in 1815 by 'a trustee and layman'. The anonymous author records that in 1800 there were about twenty preachers but is quite open about the difficulties encountered in the early years.[44] Several specific factors conspired to restrict the growth,[45] some of which were later to be mirrored in Tent Methodist experience. The Primitive Methodists did not record their membership figures annually until eight years after their establishment. In 1820 when the number was 7,842, it was reported that 'there is reason to believe that about one half had been added during the preceding year'.[46] If that is so, the membership in 1819 after eight years of existence was less than 4,000. Bible Christian membership was recorded quarterly in the period immediately after formation in late 1815. The following figures are quoted from the minutes:

January 1816	—	237
April 1816	—	412
July 1816	—	496
October 1816	—	567
January 1817	—	920
October 1817	—	1,146
Christmas 1817	—	1,522

A short gap then occurred in reporting the figures, but for 1819 membership was minuted as being 2,839, which increased to 3,118 in 1820, and 4,146 in 1821, six years after formation.[47]

---

43   Currie, Gilbert and Horsley, *Churches and Churchgoers*, Table A3, p.140.

44   Anon. ('A trustee and layman'), *An Apology for the Methodists of the New Connexion illustrating the origin of the Division in 1797, its commencement, progress, present state, influence and prospects* (Hanley, 1815), pp.33-38.

45   Davies *et al* (eds), *A History of the Methodist Church*, II, pp.290-294, set out the difficulties encountered by the Methodist New Connexion in the early years.

46   Petty, *History of Primitive Methodist Connexion*, p.137.

47   *Digest of Rules and Regulations* (London: Bible Christian Book Room, 7th edn, 1902).

From these figures it can be seen that in the period immediately after the groups were established, no dramatic surge in membership occurred. It might even have been less substantial than that which the Tent Methodists experienced. That is not a position that has been recognized up to now by historians who have studied and written about the Methodist schisms of the first half of the nineteenth century. Given that the number of 'hearers' was normally regarded as being four or five times the number of members, there would have been large numbers of people who were influenced to a greater or lesser extent by the tent preachers, and, later, by those who were more permanently based in the chapels and meeting houses. It is the purpose of the following chapter to attempt to explain why, unlike the Methodist New Connexion, the Primitive Methodists and the Bible Christians, all of whom progressed into the twentieth century, the Tent Methodist expansion was halted and then fell into a decline which led to nothing less than disintegration during the second half of the 1820's.

CHAPTER 7

The Years of Decline

There are two quite separate requirements to be met in this chapter. Firstly, it is necessary to describe the process of decline, as far as it is possible to do so. The steady reduction in Tent Methodist influence occurred in different ways, with different results, and at different times in the various parts of the country where it had been active. Secondly, and of even more significance given the progress that other offshoots of Wesleyanism continued to achieve after the first few years, it is important to attempt to explain the reasons. On the surface, the many promising features that were apparent between 1820 and 1825 were still relevant at the end of that period.

It is a matter of regret that less material is available to analyse Tent Methodism's decline than of its expansion. However, as far as primary or near contemporary information is concerned, it should never be overlooked that relatively few people in early nineteenth-century Britain could read or write. Indeed it was for these folk that the Tent Methodist leaders primarily worked. Of those who could write, such as the Tent Methodist leaders, few had the time or inclination to record events and feelings in diaries. Even fewer of those documents that were compiled have survived. That is a shame as the fragments that are available to researchers give a fascinating insight into the impact that Tent Methodism made—for a short time and in a few places. With the notable exception of Manchester, the demise in other parts of the country has to be explained with the benefit of comparatively little direct information. There is, however, some fragmentary documentary evidence, and there is more knowledge of the key people involved. This does significantly help to explain what happened in the second half of the 1820's. In addition, there is a useful amount of primary material in the form of indentures and notices that detail the course of events regarding some of the chapel premises. On the other hand, some properties were held on such informal arrangements that no records would ever have existed which would assist in knowing the occupancy after the Tent Methodists ceased to use them.

The disintegration of the Tent Methodist movement has, therefore, to be assessed using a wide variety of available material.

The Loss of John Barnett to the Baptists

The decline in the Bristol and south Gloucestershire area probably began in 1826 and was given a significant impetus, if it did not actually begin, as a result of John Barnett's decision to leave the Tent Methodists and join the Baptists. It would appear to have been a sudden doctrinal change of heart to reject the practice of infant baptism. At the end of January 1826 he recorded that he returned from 'a good Quarterly Meeting' in Bristol where 'the brethren were all of one mind in almost everything', and that he was to become a full time missionary. Only two months later, however, he had been baptized as a Baptist and joined the congregation at Wotton-under-Edge. That decision was badly received, but probably only by Pocock, as Barnett remained firm friends with Pyer until the latter's death in 1859. The biography of Barnett, though, refrains from naming the individual who had 'not treated him as a brother'[1] over his departure. It is unlikely to have been a coincidence that Barnett's resolve to join the Baptists marked the start of a steady decline in Tent Methodist influence.

It is clear from the biography written by his son that Barnett's spiritual life was marked by periods of uncertainty and depression, but there were probably other reasons too for his decision to reject Tent Methodism. He, like other preachers, had worked extremely hard for the cause and he had calculated that in a period of twelve months to May 1824 he had 'preached 219 times, and to do this I have travelled 1,880 miles, chiefly on foot'.[2] During that year he had certainly been regularly to the Marlborough area, Tetbury and Birmingham. That sort of commitment could only be sustained for a short period without an adverse affect on health, and there were times when illness forced him to curtail, temporarily, his evangelical work. Other factors emerged that may have prompted his determination to continue his Christian service elsewhere. In the first place, some dissension was apparent within the sect as a whole from time to time. For example, his decision not to continue his work in Birmingham was criticized by Pocock in 1823. In October 1823 he recorded that in a 'Quarterly Meeting...there is not the forbearance among the brethren I should like to see'.[3] A very serious and damaging dispute occurred in Manchester, although he did not become directly involved in it. Secondly, the Dursley chapel had much debt associated

---

1   Barnett, *Memorials*, pp.33-34.
2   Barnett, *Memorials*, p.30.
3   Barnett, *Memorials*, p.29.

with it and Barnett was one of those who attempted to raise funds to clear the borrowing. He might well have found that distasteful. He certainly found the exercise dangerous as he and a friend were nearly drowned in the river Severn near Blakeney,[4] while touring the neighbourhood seeking funds to reduce the debt. A further factor was that Barnett received no payment for his work. 'I have not received a penny from the people'[5] was a plaintive cry, particularly as he incurred personal debts that were not repaid for several years. Indeed, he and his wife had to sell furniture to repay their creditors, including the local doctor whose bill was not finally cleared until eight years later. He was a great loss in March 1826 as he was a dedicated evangelist, and had 'worked with extraordinary zeal, and enjoyed a popularity second only to that of the eminent men above named [Pyer and George Smith]'.[6] Very soon after his change of belief to a doctrine of believer's baptism he was ordained a Baptist minister at Appleby, Leicestershire, at a salary of £40 per annum. He served there for eleven years before becoming minister of Blaby Baptist Church, Leicestershire, for thirty-seven years until his death in 1876.

Decline in Southern England, including Bristol and Wiltshire

Barnett's Tent Methodist ministry had been concentrated at Wotton-under-Edge, Dursley and Tetbury where he seemed to serve under the day to day guidance of Samuel Smith. Smith managed at least two day schools, at Dursley and Horsley, in addition to his ministerial duties. The chapel at Dursley, built with so much effort in the second half of 1820, remained a place of Tent Methodist worship for six years at least. In 1826 it was, apparently, taken over by a group who had left Dursley Tabernacle. The Tabernacle had originally been used by Calvinistic Methodists but most of the members had become Congregationalists in 1825, and they established a separate congregation in the former Tent Methodist chapel.[7] The Tent Methodists had been unable to clear the capital expenditure debt associated with the building. The total cost of the land and chapel is not known but a mortgage of £400 was provided by Messrs Stephen King, John Gosling and William Tanner in December 1822. Gosling became a trustee of several Tent Methodist chapels but this

---

4   Barnett, *Memorials*, p.34. Barnett was accompanied by a friend, 'Brother Kent', who does not otherwise appear in Tent Methodist records.

5   Barnett, *Memorials*, pp.41-42.

6   *Baptist Handbook* (1878), p.331.

7   Evans, *As Mad as a Hatter*, p.120.

was the only one where his financial support is documented.[8] While use of the chapel was provided to other Nonconformists in 1826, the formal Notice of Deficiency relating to income was not served until May 1829. On three Sundays that month Samuel Smith, described as the 'officiating minister', read the notice to 'the congregations assembled at the Chapel within mentioned on Sunday 3rd May 1829 and two following Sabbaths'.[9] It is possible, therefore, that the Tent Methodist congregation was joined by the Tabernacle seceders in 1826 who, together, continued to worship for a further three years, rather than be replaced by them. A study of the Wesleyan membership statistics for the Dursley circuit (Appendix G), however, shows that after several years without significant change in numbers up to 1825, a small increase occurred in 1826 and a further 13% rise, from 530 to 600, was achieved in 1827. That may tentatively suggest, nothing more, that some at least of the Tent Methodists joined, or reverted to, the Wesleyans during 1826 and 1827. However, the fact that Wesleyan membership then declined for two years is confirmation that no firm conclusions can be drawn.

In any event the financial burden to the former Tent Methodists remained an unfortunate legacy for many years. The mortgage was transferred to George Hamley, a trustee, in June 1829 presumably when he repaid King, Gosling and Tanner, and ownership was acquired by him in early 1830 only days before he died. His son, also George, sold it to a Charles Vizard for just £140 in September 1838.[10] It was still referred to as a chapel in documents completed in 1851 and 1856, but it was subsequently used as a warehouse and later as a garage, the purpose it still had in 1964[11] and retained in 1999.

Samuel Smith, like Barnett, continued in the full-time Christian ministry. He was one of the three leaders who left Wesleyanism in early 1820, having by then been a local preacher for eleven years. By profession, according to various chapel trust documents, he was a 'poulterer', but in June 1825 he was shown as a 'Dissenting Minster' in a document relating to the Ancoats chapel in Manchester.[12] Sometime after 1829 but before August 1834 he had emigrated to Canada where he served as an 'Itinerant Preacher' in 'the Township of Kildare in the province of Lower Canada'.[13] Unfortunately, it has not been established

---

8   Indenture and other documents relating to Hill Road Chapel, Dursley. The building still remains and is now used as a garage.

9   Endorsement to the Notice of Deficiency of Income and for the Sale of the Chapel, 2 May 1829.

10   Sundry documents held at GRO.

11   Alderson, *Dursley Methodist Church Centenary*, p.10.

12   Stocks, *A Reply*, p.11.

13   Samuel Smith, Power of Attorney authorising 'James Rees, surgeon, and Henry Moore Pocock, Esquire, both of the City of Bristol, my true and lawful Attornies', dated

which denomination, if any, he had joined. His name does not appear among those who served with the Baptist Missionary Society, nor in a directory of Primitive Methodists who first arrived in Toronto in 1829,[14] nor in a commentary of mainstream Methodism in Canada.[15] O'Bryan, on his departure from the Bible Christians also went to Canada in 1829, and his former spiritual colleagues first sent missionaries to that country in 1831, and achieved considerable success,[16] but there is no record of a Samuel Smith working as a Bible Christian. The Congregationalists, through the London Missionary Society, failed to establish any meaningful presence there during the relevant period.

Nothing is directly known about the demise of the society at Wotton-under-Edge which was closely associated with the one at Dursley. A former Baptist chapel was acquired by the Tent Methodists in 1821 but its later use is uncertain. With Barnett's transfer of allegiance to the Baptists it might be that the society folded, or went with him to form part of the Wotton-under-Edge Baptist community under Mr Thomas, its pastor. The latter seems unlikely as it was felt expedient for Barnett to move away from the area to begin his Baptist ministry in Leicestershire rather than accept an invitation to the pastorate at Sodbury, eight miles to the south.[17] An article in the *Wesleyan Methodist Magazine* for 1827 might provide an explanation. There it was stated that a Wesleyan society in Wotton-under-Edge had been in existence for over twenty years but 'of late the work of God has revived, so that the Chapel became too small'.[18] That revival might have resulted from the attraction to the society of the former Tent Methodists.

The Tent Methodist society at Tetbury which was formed in 1823, a later date than for many societies, might also have formed the nucleus of a Wesleyan group. No Wesleyan chapel existed until February 1827 and the timing of its opening suggests that it was prompted by the Tent Methodist demise following Barnett's departure to the Baptists. However, the Wesleyan community had only reached twenty-eight in 1851.[19] Barnett had been a regular preacher in Tetbury which would have been

---

27 August 1834. James Rees was married to one of George Pocock's daughters, and Henry Moore Pocock was one of his sons.

14   William Leary, *Ministers and Circuits in the Primitive Methodist Church* (Loughborough: Teamprint, 1990).

15   Alexander Sutherland, *Methodism in Canada* (London: Charles H. Kelly, 1903).

16   Davies *et al* (eds), *A History of the Methodist Church*, II, p.303.

17   Barnett, *Memorials*, p.40.

18   *Wesleyan Methodist Magazine*, September 1827, p.632.

19   R.B. Pugh (ed.), *The Victoria History of the Counties of England: Volume 11. Gloucestershire* (London: Institute of Historical Research, University of London, 1976), p.281.

en route to Marlborough and his former home at Mildenhall, just a mile to the east.

Nearer to Bristol from the cluster of societies in south Gloucestershire there were certainly societies at Coalpit Heath and Frampton Cotterell, and there might have been others in the vicinity. No surviving records have been found to determine the fate of any of the groups in that locality except Frampton Cotterell. Here there is conclusive evidence that the Tent Methodist chapel, which was built and used for worship from the end of 1821, did become Wesleyan and several Tent Methodists became, or reverted, to Wesleyanism. John Hollister, a Tent Methodist trustee of the building became a Wesleyan trustee in April 1832[20] and the chapel steward in 1834. A formal record maintained by the Wesleyan stewards for several years from the final quarter of 1831 shows four other former Tent Methodist trustees as members. A Mrs Hollister, Mrs Foote, and Mr and Mrs Long all transferred their allegiance, although Mr and Mrs Long who had not paid pew rents in 1831 or 1832 were no longer members in 1833. By then sixty-one names appeared as members compared with twenty-nine a year earlier.[21] Precisely when the demise of the Tent Methodist cause in Frampton Cotterell occurred cannot be determined but September 1827 is the most likely date. In that month a sale of the chapel seems to have been agreed, although not directly to the Wesleyans. It was not until June 1831 that a Notice of Deficiency was formally delivered to the deacons.[22] One of the local Tent Methodists who joined the Wesleyans, Joseph Foote, emigrated to Australia in 1847 where his son, John Clark Foote, later achieved high public office in Queensland.[23] Another indication that the demise of Tent Methodism might have occurred in 1827 comes from knowledge that Samuel Bryant, who had become the leader of the group in Frampton Cotterell, died in January 1827, eight months before the sale of the premises was negotiated. His death might have left a leadership vacuum that nobody was able to fill.

Closer still to the centre of Bristol were several societies and chapels in the Kingswood area. These societies survived considerably beyond 1827.

---

20   Indenture between fourteen trustees of the Tent Methodist Chapel and thirteen Wesleyan trustees, 12 April 1832.

21   *Stewards Account Book for Frampton Cotterell Chapel* from fourth quarter of 1831 until 1833.

22   Indenture of Bargain and Sale, registered in Chancery 19 September 1827, and Notice of Income Deficiency 19 June 1831. These documents, and that in n.20 above, form part of the title documents relating to 153 Church Road, Frampton Cotterell which now has the Registered Title No. AV149486. I am grateful to Jeffrey Spittal, Mr and Mrs Page, who owned the property in April 1997, and to National Westminster Bank Home Loans, who all helped me to gain access to those old documents.

23   C. Jeffrey Spittal, *Notes on the Local History of the Free Churches of Frampton Cotterell* (n.p., [c.1992]).

Pyer, on a visit to Bristol following his brother's death on 17 February 1827, commented that large congregations were present at Colliers' Temple and in other local places, probably at Hanham, Rose Green and Jeffrey's Hill among others. He did not return to Manchester until the end of March and in those six weeks or so he was 'everywhere received with heartiest welcome, and, in some instances, crowds were disappointed in their attempts to gain admission where he preached'.[24] There were at least twelve Tent Methodist preachers in that locality in 1827 as that number were present at Samuel Bryant's funeral service. On the day of his funeral there was 'an immense train of weeping friends' and 'there were three thousand persons gathered to witness his burial'.[25] Although not all those would have been Tent Methodist members, the figures and the number of local preachers suggests an active local group of societies. A local history of the area written at the end of the nineteenth century with the help of some who had known George Pocock and one of his daughters, recorded that Colliers' Temple 'flourished for a long time, but finally the congregation dwindled and went to other places of worship'.[26]

When the decline affected the Kingswood area and central Bristol societies is, again, not known precisely, but much information is available. Pocock may have had little involvement for several years in other parts of the country, but his evangelical effort and commitment in this part of the Bristol area remained undiminished. He, and one at least of his daughters, were frequent visitors, often using one of his kite driven vehicles that were, by the second half of the decade, a familiar sight to many people in the locality. No records appear to have survived about the groups that were established in the St Philip's area in the city centre of Bristol, at Rose Green in Kingswood, and in Fishponds. The Rose Green society still existed in January 1827, but might have folded soon afterwards following the death of Samuel Bryant who was the class leader there as well as fulfilling the same responsibilities at Frampton Cotterell, Colliers' Temple and, probably, at Fishponds. In the cases of the Pithay chapel in the centre of Bristol, Colliers' Temple, Hanham, Staple Hill and Jeffrey's Hill, material has survived that makes it possible to make a reasonable assessment of when the demise came. In a letter that Pyer wrote to John Barnett in April 1832 he reported that he had met Pocock in London the previous November. 'Mr Pocock...has disposed of the Pithay to some Welsh Baptists,—holds Jeffries [sic] Hill; the rest, I believe, are gone to the Methodists'.[27] There is some supporting evidence for all those statements.

---

24   Russell, *Memoirs of Rev John Pyer*, p.128.

25   Anon., *Memoirs of the Life and Character of Samuel Bryant*, p.24.

26   A. Emlyn Jones, *Our Parish, Mangotsfield* (Bristol, 1899), p.72.

27   Barnett, *Memorials*, p.68.

Firstly, the *Mathew's Bristol Directories* show identical records for Tent Methodist occupation of Pithay Chapel, Bristol, from 1822 to 1826. Four services were held every Sunday, at 7.00 am, 10.30 am, 2.30 pm and 6.00 pm, with a midweek meeting on Wednesdays at 7.00 pm. The congregation had no one settled minister as the *Directories* show 'ministers changeable'. In 1826, reported in the 1827 edition, the midweek service had been discontinued but four Sunday services were still held. It is the 1832 *Directory* that first records that Welsh Baptists held services at Pithay, having moved from Black Friars, Merchant Street. They continued there until just before publication of the 1842 edition by which time they had moved again, this time to Upper Maudlin Street.[28] Two local histories that include details of Pithay Chapel indicate that the Welsh Baptists were in fact a secession from a congregation worshipping at Counterslip in Bristol. About forty-nine people left to form the new group, which bought the Pithay building for £800, £100 less than Pocock paid for it in 1820.[29] The Pithay building continued to be used by various dissenting groups until towards the end of the nineteenth century. It was demolished in 1907. It can be stated with reasonable accuracy, therefore, that Tent Methodism lasted at Pithay, Bristol, until 1831, but it is not known where the former Tent Methodists later worshipped. They might have returned to Wesleyanism several years before Pocock himself was re-united with his former friends.

By that time the activity at Hanham and Staple Hill had probably ceased. Both chapels were to be 'Sold by Auction (without reserve) by Mr Keyser, on Thursday 19th April 1832'.[30] The outcome as it related to Staple Hill is uncertain, but the sale of the Hanham property was completed on 2 April 1833. The formal Indenture recorded 'and whereas previous to March 1829 and from then to September 1831 the said Thomas Galley was the sole Deacon resident in Bristol', and that in March 1831 there was 'a deficiency in the income of the Chapel'. The property was sold at the auction to a George Mowbray Gilbert for £295 which was less than the £455 owing to George Pocock at the time of

---

28   The annually published *Mathew's Bristol Directories* provide valuable information about all the religious institutions in Bristol. William Mathew was the first publisher up to 1820, then Joseph Mathew published them up to 1833 before he was succeeded by Mathew Matthew up to 1850.

29   J.G. Fuller, *Memoir of Rev Thomas Roberts MA* (Bristol, 1842), p.111, and Hamlin, 'Pithay Chapel, Bristol', p.378, both describe the events after the Tent Methodists ceased worshipping there.

30   Handbill giving notice of the sale of Freehold Chapels and Land, by way of auction, on 19 April 1832 at the Rose & Crown Inn, Kingswood Hill.

completion of the sale.[31] Intriguingly, Gilbert was George Pocock's son-in-law, having married one of Pocock's daughters, Sarah Rose Pocock, in St Michael's Church, Bristol, on 3 September 1828, Sarah's twentieth birthday.[32] At least one of Pocock's daughters had accompanied him on occasions to Hanham when he took services, and it might have been this that prompted a desire to retain the property within the family's ownership. Another possible explanation is that Gilbert, who ran a school at Goodenough House in Ealing, London, might have wished to establish one, in a suitably sized building, in Hanham. Another son-in-law, James Rees, a London surgeon who also married a Pocock daughter, was also named in the sale documentation, but he had only a minor role in the transaction. The use of the building from just before completion of the sale until 1840 cannot be discovered with certainty as the evidence appears to be contradictory. On the one hand, a history of Bristol Congregationalism gives 1829 as the founding date for the Hanham Tabernacle, but the same book and an earlier, substantial volume, both record that a member of the Wills family bought the former Tent Methodist building, probably in 1840, and then gave it to the Congregationalists.[33] The existence of copies of the legal documentation of 1833 does not clarify the issue unless the Congregationalists of the Hanham Tabernacle used a completely different building until about 1840. The Tent Methodist chapel building was later incorporated into what is now Hanham United Reformed Church, but the Tent Methodist congregation probably joined a new Wesleyan congregation. The *Wesleyan Methodist Magazine* for January 1828 reported that 'on Monday 29th October [1827], a neat and well built Methodist Chapel was opened in this village...the congregations were large and attentive'. The chapel dimensions were 34 feet by 30 feet, the cost was £320, and 'this "labour of love" was not confined to our own Members, but others cheerfully joined in the undertaking'.[34] These 'others' might have been former Tent Methodists.

The Colliers' Temple in Soundwell Road, Kingswood, served an active community in early 1827. The history of the building and the society immediately after that is not known but it, too, might have become a

---

31   Indenture 2 April 1833 between the trustees of the Hanham Chapel and George Mowbray Gilbert. I am, again, indebted to Mrs Diane Comley who provided copies of the documents referred to in nn.30-31 (see also ch. 5 n.52).

32   *Bristol Marriages 1800-1837* (Bristol and Avon Family History Society, 1982), Part 2. 'Females married at St Michael's Bristol', entry number 386, and Portland Chapel Register of Baptisms, entry number 123.

33   Ignatius Jones, *Bristol Congregationalism, City and County* (Bristol, 1847), pp.7 and 63, and George Eayrs, *Wesley and Kingswood and Its Free Churches* (Bristol: J.W. Arrowsmith, 1911), p.168.

34   *Wesleyan Methodist Magazine* (January,1828), pp.45-46.

Wesleyan congregation. A minute book for the Kingswood circuit reports on 2 April 1832: 'Sunday evening preaching given up' at Soundwell, but the absence of any Wesleyan minute records for the period before September 1829 means that the date when preaching began cannot be established.[35] The building is shown on an 1843 tithe map but by 1882 it had been converted into two cottages. It might have ceased being used as a chapel in 1845 when a new Wesleyan building was opened less than a quarter of a mile away.[36] The Wesleyan membership figures for the Kingswood circuit, after remaining static for several years up to 1827, showed a large increase from 520 to 640 in 1828 which could be partially explained by the inclusion of former Tent Methodists (Appendix G).

Although Tent Methodist services elsewhere in the vicinity had ceased by 1832 at the latest, evangelical activity continued at Jeffrey's Hill, Hanham and Kingswood for several more years. Pocock clearly had a particularly high level of concern for the local inhabitants which had begun in 1814 and lasted for twenty-one years. That this is so can be demonstrated from a fascinating letter that he wrote to the Rev. H.T. Ellacombe, rector of Bitton, the parish in which Kingswood was situated. The content provides a valuable insight into several aspects of the Tent Methodists' work. Writing in October 1842, only a year before his death, he used the opportunity to express his feelings on a number of issues. As far as Jeffrey's Hill was concerned, his evangelical work continued until 'the summer of 1835 at the close of which year I ceased my poor efforts'.[37] 'It was in 1836 I gave up visiting the Highways and Hedges of Hanham—And I now leave my old Hill for ever', he wrote in moving terms.[38] In 1840 he had subscribed to the cost of building a 'new Church, Parsonage and School...at Hanham, on Jefferies [sic] Hill, naturally and spiritually a wild and uncultivated spot. It has long been thickly populated by poor people'.[39] Pocock did not seek to overestimate the extent of his evangelical successes when he wrote a poem to mark 'The Erection of Christ-Church, Jeffrey's Hill Hanham' which included the following verse:

> And though much zeal has wrought around
> Uncultivated still
> Has lain this sad unhallowed ground,
> This long neglected Hill.[40]

---

35 *Minute Book for Kingswood Circuit Local Preachers* from 28 September 1829.
36 Martindale, 'The Architecture and History', pp.8.2.1 and 8.2.3.
37 George Pocock, letter to Rev. H.T. Ellacombe, 13 October 1842, p.2.
38 George Pocock, letter to Rev. H.T. Ellacombe, 13 October 1842, p.3.
39 *Felix Farley's Bristol Journal* Saturday 15 February 1840.
40 H.T. Ellacombe, *The Parish of Bitton* (Exeter, 1881), p.223.

Jeffrey's Hill was, therefore, the last place where evangelical activity took place which could be regarded as a Tent Methodist venture. It was, by then, very much a personal Pocock evangelical crusade.

If the Tent Methodist membership in the Bristol district began to decline from about 1826 onwards, Wesleyan Methodist experience was also a disappointment to their authorities. Bristol circuit membership was virtually static throughout the 1820's with an increase of just 2% in the ten years compared with a 30% rise nationally. Joseph Entwisle was a Wesleyan itinerant in Bristol between 1826 and 1829 and was 'sometimes much discouraged about the state of religion in this circuit. I fear our society retrogrades. We have no active leaders...we hear of few conversions'.[41] Membership rose for some years after 1830 although pessimistic observations were again made in the mid 1830's.

It has not been established whether a Tent Methodist society was ever formed in Cheltenham. Certainly there is no reference to the sect in two local histories, one written in 1912 to mark the celebration of Wesleyanism's 100 years of activity in the town, and the other published in 1996. Both publications, however, identify a marked increase in preaching activity in the district up to 1829. Neither is there any reference to a Mr Rose, who invited Pyer to Cheltenham in 1820, on Wesleyan preaching plans of 1822 or 1829. In the absence, therefore, of information to the contrary it must be presumed that no Tent Methodist society was ever formed in or around Cheltenham, a town where the population expanded greatly in the early nineteenth century.[42]

Regrettably, too, no material has been found to indicate the details of the demise of Tent Methodism in the part of south Wales that Pyer visited before travelling to Cheltenham. Wesleyanism had difficulties in maintaining progress in Wales during the early nineteenth century, being short of preaching resources and cash which led to chapel closures and societies disbanding. Tent Methodism's rapid decline in the late 1820's was an experience later mirrored, and for probably the same reasons, by Welsh Wesleyans. It has been written about the Wesleyans in the 1840's that 'the work had spread too far afield for its resources in ministers and funds. In their zeal and enthusiasm the early Methodists had built chapels through faith, but many of them had forgotten to arrange means of meeting the expenses'.[43] Primitive Methodism reached Monmouthshire

41   J. (Junior) Entwistle, *Memoir of the Rev Joseph Entwistle* (Bristol, 1848), p.429.

42   G.H. Bancroft Judge, *The Origin and Progress of Wesleyan Methodism in Cheltenham and District in1912*. 'A Souvenir of the Cheltenham Methodist Circuit' (n.p., [c.1912]), and Dorothy Myatt, 'The Development of Methodism in Cheltenham', pp.1-20.

43   E. Tegla Davies, 'Welsh Wesleyan Methodism', in Harrison *et al* (eds), *Methodist Church*, pp.168-169. See also W.J. Townsend, H.B. Workman and G. Eayrs

in the 1820's, but in a district in the north east of the county not, it would seem, in the small area missioned by the Tent Methodists. It cannot be assumed, therefore, that the Tent Methodist society formed the nucleus of either a Wesleyan or a Primitive Methodist group. The absence of any known Welsh speaking preachers would have been a distinct disadvantage in that part of Wales.

At Bath it is likely, from an examination of the local directories, that Tent Methodism had ceased by the time, probably in late 1825, that the 1826 *Keene's Bath Directory* was prepared for publication. No reference is made in that year's directory to a chapel in Wells Road. It should be noted, however, that no Primitive Methodist meeting place is recorded in the late 1820s' directories, although they had certainly established a presence in 1828. In June of that year 'Frome Primitives...decided to appoint the Rev N. Towler to live in Bath and establish a mission there and in the surrounding neighbourhood'.[44] In 1829 the Wesleyan minister Joseph Sutcliffe complained in a letter that sixteen or eighteen Wesleyans had transferred their allegiance, and in the same year the Primitive Methodists reported their first Bath membership of forty-eight. It is probable that the Tent Methodist activity had closed down by then, although with only a short interval before the Primitive Methodists arrived it is possible that some former members joined them in 1828. The Wesleyan membership which had grown steadily throughout the early 1820's became static in 1825 and then fell for the following four years (Appendix G), so it would seem the Tent Methodist presence neither harmed the Wesleyans, nor benefited them when they disbanded.

While, as Chandler's analysis shows, the Tent Methodists were registering buildings in Wiltshire for services up to November 1825, there were by then signs of decline. John Sweetapple was, in January of that year, apparently keen to join the Wesleyans and bring with him a significantly sized group of societies. A letter written to Jabez Bunting by Harry Noyes, a leading local Wesleyan to whom Sweetapple was related by marriage, reveals some intriguing information. Noyes had written to Bunting about Sweetapple before, but in this letter he told him that Sweetapple, who was 'a very useful preacher indeed whose labours God has abundantly blest—wishes very much to join the Methodists and to become a Travelling Preacher'. He had 217 members spread among six chapels with eight local preachers to assist him. The societies were

---

(eds), *A New History of Methodism* (2 vols; London: Hodder & Stoughton, 1909), I, p.401.

44   Bruce Crofts (ed.), *At Satan's Throne: The Story of Methodism in Bath* (Bristol: White Tree Books, 1990), p.68, and also Petty, *History of Primitive Methodist Connexion*, p.179, where Mr Towler's initial is correctly shown as 'W', not 'N', as it was probably this William Towler who later went to the United States of America as a missionary.

'contiguous to Devizes and would make that a good Circuit'.[45] There is
no record of Sweetapple becoming a Wesleyan itinerant, but Devizes did
become a separate circuit in 1825, albeit with a modest membership of
101 which, when added to the number at Melksham from which it was
separated, was not much larger than the year before. However, one of the
Sweetapple chapels was at Salisbury which would certainly not have been
included in the Devizes statistics. It would seem, therefore, that
Sweetapple's following had largely deserted him by the end of 1826.

If this Salisbury chapel related to a meeting place in Freemasons Hall,
George Yard, High Street, Salisbury, registered for dissenter worship in
December 1823, then it only had a short life as a Tent Methodist place of
worship. Exactly two years later it was occupied by 'the New Jerusalem in
the Revelations'.[46] This sect spread to England in about 1770, and
initially followed the teachings and writings of Emanuel Swedenborg, a
Swedish scientist who was in London when he died in 1772. He believed
Christ had returned to this world in 1757. The New Jerusalem Church
formed congregations in various parts of England, mainly in the North
and Midlands. The Salisbury group was led by John Harbin, a former
Wesleyan local preacher, and while it is not known whether any Tent
Methodists joined the new occupants of the building they had used for
worship, services were soon 'attended by a crowded congregation'[47]
which suggests they might have done so. Some Methodist groups in other
parts of the country did become Swedenborgian, including one in St
Osyth and Brightlingsea in Essex, and another at Westhoughton,
Lancashire. However, in 1825, there were only eleven Swedenborgian
societies outside Lancashire and Yorkshire with a combined membership
of 734.[48] It is just possible that another local Tent Methodist preaching
place was taken over by the New Jerusalem in the Revelations group. In
September 1823, a garden and premises were registered for Tent
Methodist use at Fisherton Anger, not far from Salisbury, and in October
1829, the New Jerusalem in the Revelations sect did the same. Whether
there was any connection between the two registrations is uncertain, but it
would be a strange coincidence if there was not.

45   Harry Noyes, letter to Jabez Bunting, 19 January 1825.
46   Chandler (ed.), *Wiltshire Dissenters' Meeting House Certificates and Registrations*, No. 1053 on pp.101-102, and No.1145 on p.110.
47   Robert Hindmarsh, *Rise and Progress of the New Jerusalem Church in England, America and other parts* (London, 1861), p.440. This book was edited by Rev. Edward Madeley after Hindmarsh's death. See also Watts, *Dissenters*, II, p.82.
48   P.J. Lineham, 'The English Swedenborgians 1770-1840' (PhD thesis, University of Sussex, 1978), pp.353, 360, and Appendix 1. See also W.R. Ward, 'Swedenborgians: Heresy, Schism or Religious Protest', paper presented to the 1972 Meeting of Ecclesiastical History Society.

By the end of 1825 John Gosling could have severed his links with Tent Methodism. Barnett records in his diary of 25 May 1823 after returning from Marlborough that 'Mr G—has lost his humility. "The old man" in him seems to conquer now... If he should leave our Church, I shall no more preach in that town'.[49] In fact Barnett did continue to travel to Marlborough and Gosling was still providing premises for Tent Methodist use up to November 1825. At that time, and into 1826, there were many banking failures which badly affected the country's financial state and it would be entirely understandable if he had decided to concentrate his time and energy into ensuring his own banking partnership's survival, which he succeeded in doing. It might be that he also chose to give priority to his interests in providing for day schools in that part of Wiltshire, especially if he perceived that Pocock was also pursuing his educational interests more actively. Bearing in mind that Gosling had left the Church of England in about 1817, and was a member of the Wesleyans for only three years before joining the Tent Methodists, he was not noted for the longevity of his loyalty to religious causes.

There is evidence that no Tent Methodist chapels or societies were active in Wiltshire by 1829. In that year, 'in pursuance of a Resolution of the House of Commons, dated 19th June, 1829', a return of all Dissenter meeting places was to be made by the parish church authorities. The Wiltshire returns survive and at Milton Lilbourne, where, in 1825, a Tent Methodist registration had been made of a 'newly erected chapel', the chapel congregation was, by 1829, described as Wesleyan, but the building was still known locally as the 'Tent Methodist' chapel. No other definite references to Tent Methodists appear, although at the small hamlet of Hilcot, a 'Methodist Independent' congregation is certified by the church wardens to still be in existence in 1829.[50] At the very end of 1828, Joseph Sutcliffe, then superintendent of the Bath circuit, in a wide-ranging letter to Jabez Bunting, reported in a section referring to various 'local agitations of the connection', 'I believe all is peace in the West of England'.[51] With only the limited exception of a few societies in and around the Kingswood district of Bristol and Pithay Chapel itself, he was probably correct if he was referring to Tent Methodism.

The view has been expressed that the demise of Tent Methodism in Wiltshire and in west Berkshire around Newbury, coincided with the

---

49   Barnett, *Memorials*, p.25.
50   Poster headed 'Wilts Trinity Sessions, 1829', and signed by the 'Clerk to the Peace of the County of Wilts', relating to a return of Nonconformist places of worship. The return from the parish of Milton Lilbourne is signed by William Kingstone, Churchwarden, and Richard Litten, Overseer.
51   Ward (ed.), *Early Correspondence of Jabez Bunting*, pp.192-93, letter from Joseph Sutcliffe to Jabaz Bunting, 26 December 1828.

advent of the Primitive Methodists. Several volumes of the *Victoria County History* series covering Wiltshire make erroneous references to the Primitive Methodists appearing several years before they actually arrived. For example, one volume makes two mistakes when it states that 'William Sanger...certified premises at Manton for Primitive Methodists in 1817', and that 'In 1818 John Gosling, another Primitive Methodist, registered a field of 3a in Preshute'.[52] It might be these references that prompted another researcher to suggest 'they [Primitive Methodists] may have arrived in the south just in time to be the heirs to the declining fortunes of the Tent Methodists'.[53] However, a study of several histories of the early period of Primitive Methodist expansion in Wiltshire reveals that their work began in 1824 in areas to the north and west of the county, a considerable distance from where Tent Methodism was established, and did not expand into the Marlborough district for several years. Indeed, Petty's history of the Primitive Methodists recorded that it was 1830 before they established a presence in Salisbury, 1831 in Newbury, and as late as 1838 in Marlborough where, in 1833 they abandoned attempts because 'persecution was so violent'.[54] There was, then, unlikely to have been a connection between Tent Methodism's decline and Primitive Methodism's progress in the part of Wiltshire where the Tent Methodists made a significant impact.

There is the specific knowledge that one Wiltshire chapel, at least, was taken over by the Wesleyans, the suggestion that Sweetapple wished to become a Wesleyan and take his chapels with him, and the general contemporary statement by John Pyer that most chapels 'are gone to the Methodists'.[55] The Salisbury Wesleyan circuit membership increased significantly in 1827, as did the Hungerford circuit between 1829 and 1830, which included Marlborough and outlying villages. Most of the evidence, therefore, seems to point to the Wesleyans, not the Primitive Methodists, being the beneficiaries of Tent Methodist decline, to the extent that the members did join another denomination. There is, however, just the possibility that two individual Tent Methodists, at least, might have joined groups other than the Wesleyans. A William Drew occupied a house in East Harnham, near Salisbury, that was registered for Tent Methodist use in September 1823, and a man with the same name, in May 1825, occupied a house in Overton and signed a registration request

---

52   See Pugh (ed.), *The Victorian History of the Counties of England: 'Wiltshire'*, Vol. 6, p.160, and Vol. 12 p.183. There are other errors. George Pocock is described as 'one of Wesley's Bristol friends' in Vol. 12 p.226, but Pocock did not become a Methodist until 1797, was only seventeen when John Wesley died, and it is highly unlikely that the two ever met, let alone became friends.

53   Vickers, 'Methodism and Society in Central Southern England', p.279.

54   Petty, *History of Primitive Methodist Connexion*, p.284.

55   Barnett, *Memorials*, p.68.

on behalf of the Independents. Similarly, a Sarah Jones occupied a house in Cherhill registered for Tent Methodist worship in January 1823, and a woman with an identical name occupied a property in October 1829 registered for use by the Primitive Methodists.[56]

London and Birmingham

Very little information is available to describe the demise of Tent Methodism in London, but tentative suggestions can be made. One of the local preachers on the only Tent Methodist preaching plan for London that has been found may have become a Wesleyan local preacher for a short time. There is a 'Rawlins' shown on the 1822 Tent Methodist plan and the same name appeared on the London East circuit plan for January to April 1826, but not on one for the period between 27 July and 10 August 1828. To the extent that a substantial fillip to Tent Methodist evangelical activity came from those who left the Christian Community after the dispute between 1818 and 1820, a report that the Community 'gradually got back to its old status'[57] by 1827 might be significant. Some of those involved in that valuable activity may have reverted to their former roles. There is some circumstantial evidence that one of the earliest Tent Methodist preaching places was taken over by the Primitive Methodists. Pyer laid the foundation stone of a Sunday School at Cooper's Gardens, an area which consisted of extremely poor living accommodation, in November 1820, but there was no reference to it on the Tent Methodist 1822 preaching plan. While Hugh Bourne, one of the founders of the Primitive Methodists, visited London for two weeks in 1810, the denomination's permanent presence did not begin until December 1822. The two missionaries sent then were Paul Sugden and William Watson and they took over 'a small chapel in Cooper's Gardens, near Shoreditch Church'.[58] Being an existing building it could have been the one established by the Tent Methodists only two years earlier.

A further possible explanation of the decline might be found in the establishment and growth of the Home Missionary Society, or perhaps the founding of the London Christian Instruction Society in 1825. When the Tent Methodists began in London at the end of 1820, 'their labours

---

56 Chandler (ed.), *Wiltshire Dissenters' Meeting House Certificates and Registrations*, pp.90, 100, 107 and 118.

57 Rayner, *Story of the Christian Community*, p.56.

58 Petty, *History of Primitive Methodist Connexion*, p.157; H.B. Kendall, *The Origin and History of the Primitive Methodist Church* (2 vols; London: Edward Dalton, [c.1910]), II, p.252, describes the chapel as 'almost square...being about twenty feet each way', with three galleries and the 'pulpit stuck against the left or eastern wall'. The chapel lasted until 1835 before being replaced.

in the Tent...were countenanced by the Home Missionary Society, and arrangements made to assist in the work'.[59] The Home Missionary Society, which had been founded in 1819, was led, in the main, by Independent ministers. The work prospered for a while, in London and in the provinces, often in rural communities. George Charles Smith, the Baptist who had worked with the Tent Methodists in the docks area of Bristol in 1820, had a connection with the society. He was one of the founding leaders of it, being a member of the Corresponding Committee, and proposed a motion concerned with rules and regulations at its inaugural meeting. The missionary enterprise also used the name 'The Albion Union' according to a letter published in the *Evangelical Magazine* which announced its formation.[60]

The Home Missionary Society's work in London was taken over by the Christian Instruction Society which was established in 1825. Its main purpose was the visitation, on a regular and formal basis, of the poor and disadvantaged and 'bringing the poor, who crowd our alleys and garrets, under the stated ordinances of religion'.[61] Part of its evangelical activity was to 'promote and encourage tent preaching in any part of the metropolis'.[62] During the latter part of the 1820's tents were used beyond the localized east end of London where Tent Methodists had been active. As early as 1822 an aim had been 'to procure a tent for preaching on the Surrey side of the bridges',[63] and by 1824 tents were being used in Camden Town, Pentonville Fields, and Kingsland Green. The first annual meeting of the Christian Instruction Society was held in June 1826 when it was reported that 'the Home Missionary Society has presented to this Institution, the three tents formerly employed by them'.[64] Could these, indeed, have been the Tent Methodist tents which were certainly in London and used by them during the second half of 1822? While there would be a logic to the Tent Methodists' work being

---

59   Russell, *Memoirs of Rev John Pyer*, p.119.

60   The *Evangelical Magazine* carried regular reports of the annual meetings of the Home Missionary Society. The letter announcing its formation, signed by Thomas Thompson, treasurer, among others was published in Vol. 27 (1819), p.336. See also the *Congregational Magazine* September 1819, p.572, and Andrew Mearns, *England for Christ: A Record of The Congregational Church Aid and Home Missionary Society* (London, 1886), pp.17, 41 and 54.

61   *Evangelical Magazine* Vol. 4 (1826), p.109.

62   G.C. Smith, *Preaching in the Open Air, and the Origin of the Christian Instruction Society: being a Collection of Interesting and Important Documents....* (London, 1830), p.47. Smith was a prolific writer of pamphlets, many defending himself from criticism. His special concern was the spiritual welfare of seamen.

63   Smith, *Preaching in the Open Air*, p.24.

64   Mearns, *England for Christ*, p.56, see also *Evangelical Magazine* 4 (1826), p.384.

taken over by the Home Missionary Society or the Christian Instruction Society, and could have made Pyer's later appointment to the London Christian Instruction Society understandable, no link has been found. None of the names that appear on the 1822 Tent Methodist preachers' plan are to be found in any of the lists of committee members during the subsequent years where records have survived: 1824, 1830, and 1831.

The Wesleyan London East circuit membership numbers fluctuated significantly between 1822 and 1831 and do not provide any pointers to the direction of former Tent Methodists. While the Methodist New Connexion, the Primitive Methodists and the Bible Christians were all attempting, but with only limited success, to establish firm footholds in the relevant part of London, none of the histories suggest any connection with the Tent Methodist demise. The Bible Christians, though, did open a chapel in Old Street Road, Shoreditch, in April 1826, close to the place where Catherine Reed assisted the Tent Methodists in 1821.[65]

If little is known about the cessation of activity in London, there is no material that has been found to explain what happened in Birmingham. The only record of substance comes from J.P. Barnett's biography of his father, and this paints a wholly depressing picture. Barnett was 'very unhappy since I left home', was unable to obtain registration of land where it was intended to preach next to the chapel used in Birmingham, and was subjected to 'a rabble' that prevented him from preaching on several occasions. The negative reaction of the Lichfield diocesan authorities to a request to register land was quite different to the experience in Wiltshire where several permissions were granted to use land, such as fields and orchards, for worship. The 'Lord Bishop of Lichfield', in September 1823, claimed he was 'not authorised to certify any piece of waste ground as a place of Religious Worship, unless there is a Building upon it'.[66] Both the authorities, and local people, caused difficulties for Tent Methodists in Birmingham. The tent was damaged and had to be dismantled quickly to be saved from destruction by a hostile group of people. Despite the fact that a local preacher, William Williams, seemed to be prepared to stay in Birmingham as he had the prospect of secular employment, the most likely outcome was that the society based in a chapel in Rea Street survived for a very short time only.[67] Indeed, a comprehensive listing of all nonconformist chapels in Birmingham does not mention any chapel in Rea Street. It was a street just south of the town centre with much building of mills taking place alongside the river Rea with, no doubt, poor living conditions. This perhaps explains why the Tent Methodists attempted to mission the area,

---

65   Pyke, *Golden Chain*, copy of poster facing p.46.
66   William Matt (Registrar of the Bishop of Lichfield and Coventry), letter to Thomas Smith, dated 9 September 1823, quoted in Barnett, *Memorials*, p.26.
67   Barnett, *Memorials*, pp.25-28.

but they clearly failed to make any meaningful progress. The Methodist New Connexion had opened a chapel nearby in 1811, and the Primitive Methodists, at about the same time as the Tent Methodists, established a preaching place even closer to the centre of Birmingham. This initially made some impact but subsequently struggled to achieve any advance for several years.[68]

Manchester and Liverpool

The demise of Tent Methodism in Manchester is better documented than for any other place. The dispute which led to the chapel in the Ancoats district being sold and a further building being acquired was the subject of two pamphlets issued in February 1830 by Samuel Stocks, Jr, a Manchester cotton merchant, and the reply by John Pyer dated 30 June 1830. The hostilities were also extensively reported in the biography of Pyer. There was at least one earlier document prepared by Pyer in January 1830 to which the Stocks pamphlet is a reply. The pattern of argument and response is similar to the exchanges in Bristol ten years earlier which led to Pocock's, Pyer's and Samuel Smith's departure from Wesleyanism.

Samuel Stocks was a man of some influence in the Manchester area in the 1820's. In addition to his business interests, he was a trustee of Manchester Athenaeum,[69] and, despite his apparent severing of a connection with the Wesleyans at the end of 1821, he was believed to be a 'Country Member' of the Wesleyan Missions Committee in 1823 and 1824, but not in 1825. In addition he was a member of the General Committee and Chapel Building Committee in 1824. It might be, however, that these contributions to national Wesleyan affairs were provided by the father of Samuel Stocks, Jr, as the suffix 'junior' does not appear in the Wesleyan Methodist records.

The troubles in Manchester appear to have begun in 1824 at a time when Pyer was dividing his time between several other places as well as being the principal preacher at the Ancoats chapel. Pyer claimed that at Christmas 1823 'he left a large congregation and a flourishing society, of more than 300 members'.[70] Pyer's version of the events after that was that Mr and Mrs Stocks caused antagonism with local preachers who led the worship in his absence. Stocks, however, maintained that in a period

---

68   R.B. Pugh (ed.), *The Victoria History of the Counties of England: Volume 7. Warwickshire* (London: Institute of Historical Research, University of London, 1964), pp.460-74.

69   Quoted in a letter to the author from Manchester Central Library, 10 December 1996.

70   Pyer, *Six Letters*, p.5.

up to June 1825 'great difficulty was found in raising an adequate congregation' and blamed 'the want of ability in the local preachers'.[71] It is difficult to establish which of the two versions regarding the progress, or lack of it, is the more accurate. On the one hand Pyer's biographer records that in 1824 'congregations and interest generally at Canal Street somewhat declined',[72] and the minutes of a special church meeting held on 14 April 1825 record that it was attended by only thirty-three male members.[73] Conversely, the same meeting 'reported the acceptance by Mr Pyer of the call of the church...at a salary of £120 per annum, together with the rent free provision of a house'.[74] Furthermore, approval was given to build a gallery to increase the capacity of the chapel, construct a room for Sunday School purposes, build a house for Pyer's occupation, and four cottages. These plans were not indications that the work was in decline. Stocks financed, or procured the finance, for the additional buildings and the chapel was re-opened in June 1826 when there were two preachers, the Rev. John Ely and the Rev. R.S. McCall. Both these ministers were Congregationalists, a fact that was to become significant in the following few years.

A further sign of later developments took place in January and February 1825 when three meetings considered, and later agreed, that 'the church declares itself independent of any other whatsoever, and forms rules and regulations for its own government'. A footnote in one of the pamphlets records that 'The Society still retains its original name of Tent Methodists, as evidenced by the subsequent Society Tickets renewed quarterly, and the Preachers Plans'.[75] It is difficult to determine why that step was taken, but could indicate a souring of the relationship with Pocock, who appeared to show little interest at this time with activity so far away from Bristol, south Gloucestershire and Wiltshire. Bearing in mind that church meetings were held monthly, and deacons were part of the chapel's management structure, the decision two and a half years later to join the Congregational denomination would not have been a great surprise. This was so despite the fact that in April and June, probably in 1827, Pyer had been a party to two interviews with Jabez Bunting to consider whether he should rejoin the Wesleyans. Pyer decided that 'there existed insuperable obstacles to my uniting with the Methodists'.[76] Stocks recorded a quite different version of the encounters with Bunting.

---

71 Stocks, *A Reply*, p.4.
72 Russell, *Memoirs of Rev John Pyer*, p.120.
73 Stocks, *A Reply*, p.17.
74 Stocks, *A Reply*, p.17, 'Minutes of Church Meetings', 10 March 1825, and 14 April 1825.
75 Stocks, *A Reply*, p.16.
76 Pyer, *Six Letters*, p.14.

He claimed that when Bunting consulted other Wesleyan itinerant ministers who had known Pyer 'they strongly objected to him'.[77]

By November 1827 Pyer had concluded, following frequent discussions with leading Congregationalists, including Roby and Raffles as well as McCall, that he had a 'determination to place the Church at Canal Street on a Congregational foundation'. Roby considered that 'we...formed ourselves into an Independent Church in February 1825, and that an ordination service was all that would be necessary'.[78] McCall was a highly respected Congregational minister in the north west of England for many years until his death in 1838, being described as a 'loveable, able gentleman' and 'a prince of preachers'.[79] He had guided Pyer for several years from the first involvement in Manchester.

Stocks was still causing extreme difficulties for Pyer. Firstly, he was attempting to recover some of the money he had provided towards the building of the Canal Street chapel and the subsequent enlargements and additions. In effect his claim was that he had lent the money to the chapel authorities and, therefore, demanded it back plus interest. Several different amounts are recorded by Stocks as being due to him, including £3,651.18s.3d as at 26 December 1826. He went on to claim that since that time Pyer had received rents—presumably pew rents and from the four cottages that had just been built—but that Stocks 'made a great variety of payments on account of the trust, and my account now amounts to over £6,000'.[80] This was a huge sum of money in relative terms. By that time his business was in a poor financial state and he was seeking to raise a mortgage of £3,000 against the chapel premises, although a lesser sum of £1,100 was later sought. Stocks had moved away from central Manchester and became a much less frequent attender at the chapel services and meetings. It might have been his absence for long periods that caused him to be unaware of the intention that the society, led by Pyer, should become Congregational. This became the second cause of the hostility with Stocks, but although he succeeded in delaying Pyer's ordination, he did not prevent it for long. Pyer's *Memoirs* record that the ordination arrangements 'so auspiciously made, were however, suspended through the unworthy interference of their new opponent, Mr S, who contended that the trust deed would not allow of the change'.[81] By the end of November 1827, however, the congregation, and Pyer, had joined the Congregationalists.

That it was not, by then, a substantial congregation can be suggested by a lack of a record of the events in any histories of the Congregationalists

---

77   Stocks, *A Reply*, p.8.

78   Russell, *Memoirs of Rev John Pyer*, p.135.

79   William Leach, *Manchester Congregationalism* (London, 1898), pp.56-57.

80   Stocks, *A Reply*, p.6.

81   Russell, *Memoirs of Rev John Pyer*, p.137.

in Manchester or Lancashire, despite the involvement of several leading ministers. In addition, Pyer's own admission later that in the two years before he left the pastorate in 1830 only 'seventeen individuals...were received to the fellowship of the Church',[82] does not immediately indicate a flourishing society. The decision to join the Congregationalists was made by passing a resolution to 'form ourselves into a church of the Congregational faith and order'.[83] Sixty-three voted in favour, none against, and four abstained. The formal termination of Tent Methodism in Ancoats, then, took place at the end of November 1827 but for two years before that the internal squabbling, mainly it would seem with Stocks alone, was undermining the spiritual work. The work in the Stretford area of Manchester had probably ceased before 1827.

It is not known whether the whole congregation transferred their allegiance with Pyer in 1827. The population of the Ancoats district of Manchester was growing very fast in the second half of the 1820s and both the Wesleyans and Primitive Methodists began evangelical activity during that decade. Agreement to build a Wesleyan chapel in Great Ancoats Street was given in 1825. The expected cost was to be £3,214, of which £2,000 was to be collected beforehand by way of subscriptions.[84] It was opened in 1826 and 'for quite a while the Chapel attracted large congregations, and the Sunday School overflowed with young people'.[85] The initial impetus might have been helped by the attraction of former Tent Methodists. Primitive Methodism's involvement in Manchester began in the middle of 1820 when 'a tap room over an old factory up an entry in Ancoats...locally known as the "Long Room"'[86] was used. Ann Brownswood, an early Primitive Methodist travelling minister, recorded in her journal for 30 July 1820 that she preached 'at six in the room at New Islington. It was crowded from end to end'.[87] New Islington was close to where the Tent Methodist chapel was built, as was Jersey Street where the first Primitive Methodist chapel was opened in 1824. This chapel was, for many years 'the nerve centre of our denominational life in the City of Manchester'.[88] The 1827 Primitive Methodists' annual meeting was held in Manchester in May suggesting that by then there existed a number of well established societies. The Methodist New Connexion had four or five

---

82   Pyer, *Six Letters*, p.11.

83   Russell, *Memoirs of Rev John Pyer*, p.136.

84   *Register Book for Chapels, built, enlarged or purchased since the Conference held at Sheffield in 1817* (n.p., n.d.), entry No. 36 for 1825.

85   Anon., *Souvenir Brochure of the Opening and Dedication of the New Methodist Chapel, Ancoats*, Saturday 30 May 1964, p.5.

86   Kendall, *Origin and History of the Primitive Methodist Church*, II, p.17.

87   Barker, *Mother Church*, p.16; also quoted in Petty, *History of Primitive Methodist Connexion*, p.89.

88   Barker, *Mother Church*, p.25.

chapels, five or six societies, and a membership which ranged between 393 and 484 in the 1820's. That peak figure was reached in 1821 after which numbers fell for several years, although there was a significant increase between 1826 and 1827 when a further society was formed. Bearing in mind, also, that Wesleyan membership in the Manchester circuits increased substantially in the middle years of the decade, it is reasonable to suppose that some in the Tent Methodist Ancoats congregation might have transferred, not to the Congregationalists with Pyer, but to either the Wesleyans or the Primitive Methodists.

Pyer appeared to become more settled in his mind during 1828, feeling an affinity with the Congregational ministers in and around Manchester. In addition, an apparent lessening of the day to day aggravation between him and Stocks would have been greatly welcome. Nonetheless, Pyer found it necessary in 1830 to explain why all of the 'official characters' connected with the Ancoats chapel when it was re-opened after enlargement in 1826, had left by December 1828.[89] In 1829, Pyer's 'attention was arrested by an advertisement for a "City Missionary and General Agent for the London Christian Instruction Society"'.[90] He successfully applied for the post and he took up the appointment with the group which was then led by Congregational and Baptist ministers. His last service at the Canal Street chapel was on 10 January 1830 and he left Manchester the next month with the following words recorded in his diary: 'To be obliged to leave Manchester, cost me more uneasiness than perhaps any event of my life. I struggled against it for full three years'.[91] The London Christian Instruction Society had grown since it formation in 1825 and by the time of the 1830 annual report the society was able to record fifty-four 'associations', 1,100 'visitors', and the use of three tents during the summer months in London as well as the regular conduct of services and meetings in chapels.[92] In the earliest years the workers were all unpaid. Pyer was the first full-time, paid employee, although fifteen full-time missionaries were working by 1839.[93]

He worked in London for four years before accepting an invitation to the pastorate of South Molton Congregational Chapel in north Devon in the middle of 1834. Then followed two other ministerial appointments, the second one to Devonport at the end of 1839 where he remained until his death on 7 April 1859. His two surviving children also lived in

89   Pyer, *Six Letters*, pp.12-13.

90   Russell, *Memoirs of Rev John Pyer*, p.148.

91   Russell, *Memoirs of Rev John Pyer*, p.154.

92   *Home Missionary Magazine* (1830), p.193, report of the 5th Anniversary Meeting of the Christian Instruction Society.

93   H.D. Rack, 'Domestic Visitation: A Chapter in Early Nineteenth Century Evangelism', *Journal of Ecclesiastical History* 24.4 (1973), pp.365-367.

Devonport until at least 1844, by which time they were about thirty years of age. In retrospect, his time with the Tent Methodists was extremely important to him as his *Memoirs* record that as late as 1856: 'In the evening read "Tent Methodist Magazine" and was humbled in reviewing the past'.[94] This specific reference to John Pyer's reminiscences of events that occurred thirty years earlier indicates the significance to him of the Tent Methodist evangelizing work.

The position with the Canal Street premises continued to cause great difficulty after Pyer's departure in 1830. Indeed, the chapel's 'promoters were consigned to the tender mercies of the Court of Chancery',[95] and Pyer himself had to return to Manchester in the summer of 1831 in connection with the property. Interestingly, Fisher and Sons 1833 detailed map of 'Manchester, Salford and their Environs' still showed the building on the corner of Canal Street and Horne Street as a Methodist chapel, but later the premises were 'purchased in 1835 by Robert Gardner, and...opened as an Anglican church in 1837'[96] called St Jude's. The church continued in use there until a new building was opened nearby in April 1866 to replace the Canal Street premises. Meanwhile, in November 1836, a 'new Congregational chapel was opened in Every Street, Ancoats...erected by "the members of the Christian Church formerly connected with Canal Street Chapel, Ancoats, kindly aided by some of their friends in Manchester"'.[97] The chapel accommodated 400 people and there was also a school capable of holding the same number. The buildings were, therefore, much smaller than those at Canal Street where the chapel alone could seat more than 1,300 people. Nonetheless, after many years of turmoil the Ancoats district of Manchester, partly as a result of early Tent Methodist evangelical effort, provided many different places of worship for the growing population.

The cessation of the Tent Methodist work in Liverpool is relatively straight forward to describe and explain. George Smith, while initially guided by Pocock and then Pyer, would have found himself isolated from events elsewhere in Tent Methodist circles, except Manchester. The tents were latterly used in the southern half of England and Smith's congregation met in a room in Heath Street. Increasingly, his mentor was Dr Raffles, an eminent Congregational minister who conducted a highly successful ministry in Liverpool, held office as Chairman of the Congregational Union, and was Secretary of the Lancashire Congregational Union from 1826 to 1863. With Pyer, his nearest Tent Methodist colleague, becoming Congregational by persuasion, it was

---

94 Russell, *Memoirs of Rev John Pyer*, p.273.
95 Bunting, *Life of Jabez Bunting*, II, p.531.
96 Details of Manchester parish churches: St Judes, Ancoats.
97 Nightingale, *Lancashire Nonconformity*, V, p.182.

understandable that Smith would also turn to Dr Raffles for even more support and advice. The Congregationalists had only one church in Liverpool for many years, but in 1811 Dr Raffles became minister of Great George Street Chapel, which seated a congregation of 2,000, a role he undertook 'with outstanding success'.[98] Not being an ex-Wesleyan, Smith had no particular distinctive loyalty to Tent Methodism as others, such as Pocock, Pyer and Samuel Smith, had.

Smith, and his congregation, formally became Congregational on Friday 27 October 1827, at a service attended by forty-two members. 'Rev Dr Raffles preached on the nature of the Christian Church, and gave to the persons there meeting the right hand of fellowship'.[99] Dr Raffles also conducted a communion service at which Pyer was present and spoke to the congregation. At a separate service on Friday, 16 November 1827 Smith was officially ordained as a Congregational minister with Dr Raffles again taking a leading part in that service. The congregation left Heath Street and moved to a building only 200 yards away on the corner of Mill Street and Warwick Street, which became known as Hanover Chapel. Although it is shown by name on a map published in 1834, prepared presumably over the previous few years, it is not so identified on earlier Liverpool plans of 1825 and 1829. Smith's work in Liverpool was successful, both with his own congregation and in his active endeavours on behalf of the anti-slavery movement, of which he became secretary. He left Liverpool in 1831, eventually becoming Secretary of the Congregational Union of England and Wales in 1852, an office he held for eighteen years.

Smith retained his contact with and, probably, the friendship of Pyer for many years as there is a record of Pyer staying with Mr and Mrs Smith at Plymouth in 1833[100] and Smith conducted the funeral service of Pyer's daughter, Elizabeth, who died at South Molton in north Devon in January 1837 at the age of 20.[101] Smith developed a deeply pious approach to his ministry and published a profound book which consisted of thirteen chapters covering different aspects of 'spiritual life'.[102] His ministry to and for Tent Methodists in Liverpool might well have been an extremely important apprenticeship for his later noted work, particularly

---

98   Sellers, 'Liverpool Nonconformity 1786-1914', p.86.

99   *Congregational Magazine* (1828), p.390.

100   Russell, *Memoirs of Rev John Pyer*, p.183.

101   Memorial Stone on south side of the west wall of the former South Molton United Reformed Church. The building was, in August 1996, in a dilapidated state, and for sale at an asking price of £25,000. It is situated only twenty yards from the west door of the parish church.

102   George Smith, *Life Spiritual* (London, 1855). The book is based on a series of lectures given to his congregation while he was minister of Trinity Chapel, Poplar, in east London.

his long ministry to the congregation in Poplar in east London. Smith died on 13 February 1870 having served the church faithfully and with great distinction for exactly fifty years. Liverpool had not been easy ground for any of the Methodist denominations in the 1820s. Wesleyan membership, for example, in 1820 was larger than in Manchester but by the end of the decade it had not grown at all and was only half the Manchester number [Appendix G].

George Pocock's Lessening Interest

So far in this chapter the process of decline has been charted and analysed in relation to the different parts of the country where Tent Methodism established a presence. It has been shown to be a complex pattern with various factors playing a role, not all of which were apparent in each place. The outcome of the demise was also disparate, occurring at different times beginning in 1825 or 1826. It is now necessary to ascertain, and then examine, the reasons for the decline and ultimate disappearance of the Tent Methodists. In doing so a comparison will be made with the experience of the Methodist New Connexion, the Primitive Methodists and the Bible Christians. All three had become well established by 1820 and continued in separate forms until 1907 or 1932. Why did they retain an independent presence within Methodism for very many years when Tent Methodism did not? Although their initial progress was encouraging, the Tent Methodists were unable to capitalize on and extend the early advances that were achieved.

The quality of leadership in any organization is a key factor in its success or failure, and this is particularly the case in the formative stage. Once a certain size and momentum has been reached then it might be that it is the local management that becomes paramount, although the overall direction of the institution remains vitally important. The attributes required of the individual leaders will depend upon the precise circumstances, but in cases of fledgling nonconformist religious groups of the early nineteenth century, a number were needed in all cases. A determination to pursue the main issues despite much hostility from opponents was critical. Perseverence was a natural corollary as the disputes were long lasting as well as bitter, and frequently took place in a public forum in the presence of a committee which met on several occasions, or by an exchange of pamphlets. Sometimes both occurred at the same time. Stubbornness and inflexibility were often two other characteristics that were in evidence, both having similarities with the qualities of determination and perseverance. A willingness to devote much time to the cause and, probably, almost limitless energy were also prerequisites. It was a great advantage if the leader was an accomplished public speaker and had an ability to express views well in writing. To find all these qualities in one person would be remarkable, and there was, therefore, a pattern in the first quarter of the nineteenth century that two leaders emerged, not necessarily equal in terms of authority, but to share the work and utilize complementary skills. Before pursuing this thesis, it needs to be noted, of course, that in the case of the Wesleyans in the eighteenth century, John Wesley, once he had parted company with George Whitefield over a fundamental doctrinal matter, was and remained the undisputed leader right up to his death in 1791. Even so, in the earliest years Whitefield shared the leadership role to a significant extent, and Charles Wesley also had a substantial part to play in certain aspects of the early growth. It is interesting to test this dual leadership thesis against the experience of the various Methodist groups, and especially the Tent Methodists.

The undoubted leader and founder of the Tent Methodists was George Pocock. Far more is known about his achievements, which were very many, substantial, and diverse, than his personal characteristics. There is no autobiography by him, or any full length contemporary review of his life and work, with the result that any real idea of his personality during the particularly relevant period has to be pieced together from many different sources. Inevitably some opinions are contradictory, but it is possible to obtain a reasonably accurate profile of him. Apart from the fact that he was the son of a Hungerford clergyman and he went to live in Frome, Somerset, with his elder brother and a sister in about 1795, nothing else is known about his early life up to the age of twenty-one. He joined the Methodist society in Frome while his brother was curate at the parish church, married Elizabeth Rose, and may have opened a school in Bristol in 1795 while still living in Frome.[103] He had a genuine love of children, both his own, who numbered at least thirteen, and his pupils, about whom he frequently spoke and wrote with affection. Academically he had much talent: mathematics was his main subject, but he later produced what was a succinct history revision document,[104] and became a prolific writer of poems and hymns. He was a competent organist and several of his children also had musical talent and later ran their own schools. In looks Pocock is said to have had dark hair and eyes, a broad brow and a straight nose. An engraving of him in about 1823 (Appendix 1a) shows him to be of impressive appearance, and he was described in the same year as a 'strong man'.[105] Despite the fact that his school

---

103 G.H. Gibbs, *George Pocock—Schoolmaster and Inventor* (Bristol: Bristol Postscript Series, [c.1988]), p.72 suggests this is so. It proved to be unsuitable and he acquired what became known as Prospect Place Academy in 1800.

104 George Pocock, *A Sketch of English History for the use of the Young Gentlemen at Mr Pocock's Academy* (Bristol, 1832).

105 *TM Magazine*, p.98.

mainly served the children of the Bristol business community, he developed a real concern for the education of the poor—children and adults. He adopted a dogged stance to issues he felt strongly about. As can be judged by the events of 1819 and 1820 he would have been a formidable opponent. In later life, particularly, he was regarded with great fondness, being known as 'Grandfer' Pocock, but Pyer's biographer was not wholly complimentary about the period of his leadership of the Tent Methodists. She believed 'that authority was too largely vested in one individual, who, with all his excellencies (and they were many) was yet considered impulsive, and at times somewhat capricious'.[106] There is no supporting evidence that he was unpredictable in his behaviour, although one of the pamphlets issued in 1820 accused him of having 'eccentricities'.[107] He was certainly a man, up to 1822 or so, of great physical energy, but after that, not surprisingly as he was approaching fifty years of age, his enthusiasm was focused in other directions than solely his evangelical work.

Pocock became a wealthy man, not it is thought from any significant inheritance, but from his business activities, firstly his school and later from his inventions, some of which had commercial success. In 1832, during the course of a letter written to Barnett, Pyer expressed the view that Pocock was 'making money' from his inventions, and hoped 'he has not lost his zeal, but I have my fears'.[108] These two comments provide one of the main explanations for Tent Methodism's rapid decline and demise. Pocock's commitment to the continuing expansion of the sect waned against the competing demands on his time, enthusiasm, and money. He was not a young man and there is little indication that he wished to participate in the evangelical work away from the Bristol area. It might, indeed, be that he was unable to control the expansion which, for a short time, gained a momentum of its own. There is no evidence, for example, that he wished to become embroiled in efforts to resolve the serious difficulties in Manchester. George Smith's introduction to Liverpool probably followed Pyer's, not Pocock's, initial evangelical foray, and apart from his first visit to London at the end of 1820 there is no record of any subsequent Pocock journey to the capital. That he would wish to remain reasonably near his home is entirely understandable, for personal, business and social reasons. His children required his time, especially as several of them were setting up and running schools of their own, his academy was large and successful, and he was increasingly involved in developing various inventions.

---

106 Russell, *Memoirs of Rev John Pyer*, p.79.
107 Wood *et al*, *A Correct Statement of Facts*, p.9.
108 Barnett, *Memorials*, p.69.

Apart from his Tent Methodist evangelical work which was of contemporary interest to only a few, it was for his inventions that George Pocock became famous. He had designed and built the tents that were used for preaching, at an early age he played and started experimenting with kites, and he devoted an increasing amount of thought to these and other inventions. Significantly, it seems that 1822 was the year when he began to give substantially more time to them. Not only had he designed some relatively sophisticated refinements to simple concepts, he spent much time in experimentation, and writing about them. By 1822 he had invented a ferule, defined as a 'flat ruler with widened pierced end'. It was designed as a means of corporal punishment for wayward pupils, but was used, presumably, only occasionally. By 1829 he had invested in an inflatable globe for his school's geography lessons. This development was sufficiently noteworthy for him to be invited to present a paper on it to the Bristol Philosophical Institute in November 1829. In it he described his 'sphere made of paper, on the surface of which appear what of land and what of water compose our terraqueous globe. The simplicity of its construction, its portability, expansion, and extent of surface are the peculiarities which have obtained notice'.[109] While the globe's weight, when inflated, was only three ounces, its circumference measured twelve feet. It was clearly an enormous and most impressive teaching aid. An original paper globe, now over 170 years old, carefully folded, is retained in the Bristol Record Office. It is too fragile to handle and examine but it shows, for example, the course of Captain Cook's journeys in 1772 and 1775, and much other detail. The globe, which Pocock described as a 'Terrestrial Globe' is an extraordinary example of one of the talents that Pocock possessed.

It was his development of kites using the air and wind as a means of transport that particularly sparked his imagination, and people's interest in his work. His mathematical knowledge was an important factor and he devised several uses for the variety of refinements he developed. The one which became exceptionally notable, and noticeable, was the use of kites to provide the power to drive carriages, thus obviating the need for horses and, thereby, the payment of toll charges on turnpike roads. He was able to develop the means to control the speed and, particularly importantly, the direction of the carriage if the wind was not following or was very light. In addition to driving carriages, kites were designed to supplement sails in boats, as a means of transporting boat passengers to shore if shipwrecked, and for certain military purposes. There were times when Pocock spent many hours in practical experiments, three weeks at a stretch in the Bristol Channel, for example, and in some cases members of

---

109 George Pocock, *An Accompaniment to Mr G Pocock's Patent Terrestrial Globe* (Bristol, 1830), p.7.

his family had a role to play as 'guinea pigs'. They must have had impressive confidence in their father's ability.[110] By 1828 Pocock had designed and built a sufficiently sophisticated version of his kite to have it demonstrated, drawing a carriage, at the Ascot race course to King George IV who was, it was reported, greatly impressed.[111] Development of Pocock's kites continued and later examples were shown at the laying of the foundation stone of the Clifton Suspension Bridge, Bristol, in 1836.

Pocock also became a prolific writer of verse. He contributed an unknown number of hymns to the sect's hymn book published in 1825, included several poems in an 1827 publication concerning his inventions, and in 1838 published a special collection of verse for his pupils.[112] While it must remain a subjective judgement, there appears to be a quality about his writing that makes it somewhat surprising that none survived for more than a few years. He did, however, have a tendency to what can now only be regarded as plagiarism. For example, one hymn identified and claimed as being his work was a barely disguised version of two verses of a John Newton hymn. A two verse Pocock hymn is:

> Tis a point I long to prove;
> Oft it causes anxious thought;
> Gracious Lord, my doubts remove;
> Am I thine, or am I not?

> Now decide the dubious case;
> Rise on me, thou Glorious Sun;
> Shine upon thy work of grace;
> Finish what thou hast begun.

There are only very minor differences between those lines and the first and eighth verses of Newton's hymn which must have been written earlier as Newton died in 1807:

> verse 1   Tis a point I long to know,
> Oft it causes anxious thought—
> Do I love the Lord, or no?
> Am I his, or am I not?

---

110 George Pocock, *Navigation in the Air by the use of Kites, or Buoyant Sails* (Bristol, 1827). This fascinating document details the theories behind the inventions, experiences with them, and the reactions of those who had heard of them.

111 John Latimer, *Annals of Bristol* (Bristol, 1887), III, pp.121-122.

112 George Pocock, *Sacred Lyrics for Youth* (London, 1838).

verse 8   Lord, decide the doubtful case;
                   Thou who art thy people's sun,
                   Shine upon thy work of grace,
                   If it be indeed begun.[113]

It was, then, not unexpected that all these other activities restricted the time, and possibly the inclination, for Pocock's Tent Methodist work from about 1823 onwards.

John Pyer, who was appointed a full-time, paid home missionary in 1819, increasingly became the person most involved in the day to day management of the sect. He did, though, always seek Pocock's permission before major decisions were implemented, such as becoming pastor to an individual congregation at Wotton-under-Edge, and, before accepting the appointment as full-time minister in Manchester in 1825. It was not, then, an equal leadership role that he shared with Pocock.[114] Robert Currie expressed the view that Pocock and Pyer 'eventually quarrelled',[115] but no conclusive evidence for this has been discovered. It is apparent, though, that Pyer's responsibilities in Manchester would not have enabled him to take over the direction and policy making of the group, even if that would have been acceptable to the membership and to Pocock. The two men kept in touch with each other throughout the late 1820's and into the 1830's at least but not, apparently, for genuine consultation about the sect's management. A lack of decisive full-time leadership supporting and directing the various activities after about 1825 was undoubtedly an important factor in the rapid decline of Tent Methodism.

Comparison with other Methodist Off-shoots

It is relevant, now, to compare the leadership experience of the Tent Methodists with that of the three major offshoots of Wesleyanism in the period. The initial driving force behind the Methodist New Connexion was Alexander Kilham who had a 'brash doctrinaire approach' coupled with an 'evangelical passion with a zeal for constitutional reform, but lacked the tact and discrimination needed to change Wesleyan

---

113   The John Newton version is to be found in many nineteenth-century hymn books, including *The Open Air Preaching Hymn Book* selected by G.C. Smith in 1830, hymn No. 97 on p.88, and consisting of nine verses. The George Pocock version appears in the Tent Methodist *Collection of Hymns*, No. 622 on p.327, and No. C1 on p.109 of Pocock's *Sacred Lyrics for Youth*.

114   *TM Magazine*, p.199, details two examples indicating Pyer's acknowledgement that Pocock was the real decision maker, up to 1825 at least.

115   Currie, *Methodism Divided*, p.56.

Methodism from within'.[116] Kilham died at the end of 1798, within eighteen months of the secession from Wesleyanism, but the other joint leader, William Thom, formerly a Wesleyan preacher and a member of the 'Legal Hundred', showed 'constructive statesmanship', had a 'calm, steady character' and displayed 'orderliness and culture'.[117] Kilham and Thom had quite different personalities and, it could be thought, possessed between them complementary skills which contributed enormously to the establishment of the group and its early management. Perhaps its failure to expand as rapidly as the Primitive Methodists reflected the fact that for many years from 1799 Thom had to shoulder the leadership without one highly competent deputy.

The two joint leaders of the Primitive Methodists also had contrasting characteristics and talents. Hugh Bourne had 'a strong, rugged nature' and was 'constitutionally shy and serious'.[118] William Clowes, on the other hand, after his conversion to Wesleyanism in 1805, 'made each Sabbath a day of unremitting yet gladsome toil'.[119] Following his expulsion in 1811 he joined his classes with the groups already established by Bourne, although the two had no immediate ambition to develop a separate denomination. Indeed, it was written about the early days of Primitive Methodism, that it 'rose undesigned of men, and its infant prospects appeared weak and feeble'.[120] While the beginnings were modest in terms of membership, fine progress was later made in many parts of the country, and by the time that both Bourne and Clowes retired in 1842 they had presided over many successful years of splendid spiritual growth. Bourne would not have imagined when he began his endeavours that the membership would have reached 110,000 by the year of his death in 1852. The probability is that the combined skills of him and Clowes were necessary to achieve those results. Both dedicated their lives, full-time and without any distractions, to the conversion of many thousands of people, the leadership of a substantial number of preachers, and the organization of a significant religious body.

In William O'Bryan and James Thorne, the Bible Christians, too, benefited from the different attributes of contrasting characters. O'Bryan, expelled twice from Wesleyanism in Cornwall, 'was a man of restless temperament'[121] who, with exceptional energy, began preaching in parts of east Cornwall and west Devon where there was little religious activity. He very soon met James Thorne, then a young man of twenty years of

---

116 E. Alan Rose, 'Kilham, Alexander' (unpublished 1992), pp.1 and 3.

117 Davies *et al* (eds), *A History of the Methodist Church*, II, p.290.

118 Kendall, *Origin and History of the Primitive Methodist Church*, I, pp.7-8.

119 Kendall, *Origin and History of the Primitive Methodist Church*, I, p.55.

120 *Primitive Methodist Deed Poll*, 4 February 1830, Preface.

121 Davies *et al* (eds), *A History of the Methodist Church*, II, p.295.

age, who was 'noted for his strength and wisdom'.[122] After O'Bryan left the denomination in acrimonious circumstances in 1829, it was Thorne's abilities 'as preacher, editor, theologian, controversialist, debater and statesman'[123] that enabled the Bible Christian denomination to grow, aided by a number of particularly committed and capable preachers who were able to share the leadership responsibilities.

There were, then, several differences between the experiences of the Methodist New Connexion, the Primitive Methodists and the Bible Christians on the one hand, and the Tent Methodists on the other. Those three denominations had leadership which was able to draw on many talents, and often shared among several people who were prepared to devote themselves wholeheartedly to their chosen cause. It would seem that George Pocock had superior academic ability to any of those in the other Wesleyan offshoots, but he could not find enough people to help shoulder the increasing burdens, or was not prepared, in the early 1820's, to share the leadership role. He lost the inclination, if he ever had it, to attempt to develop a distinct national sect. He retained his individual ambition to save souls but was, later on, not willing to work to the exclusion of his other interests.

Declining Preaching Resources

Apart from the question of leadership, the quantity and quality of preaching and pastoral resources was also a crucial factor in Tent Methodism and the other sects. In 1820 the indications were that the overall personnel resource requirement was met by the existing tent preachers supplemented by those who then resigned from the Wesleyans and joined the group. As time went on, however, the numbers of local preachers declined. In particular, the deaths of Victory Purdy in June 1822 and Samuel Bryant in January 1827 were severe blows. They had been active, highly respected people in the Kingswood area. The transfer of allegiance of John Barnett to the Baptists in March 1826 was a major loss as he was a principal local leader not only in Dursley and Wotton-under-Edge, but also in other parts of south Gloucestershire and Wiltshire. Only two months earlier he had agreed to become a full-time missionary and Tent Methodist morale would have suffered from his fundamental change of heart and mind. The ordination and induction of John Pyer and George Smith into Congregational churches in 1827, while not unexpected, was a further important step in the sect's demise. Even before those events Pyer and Barnett both had periods of ill health

---

122 Pyke, *The Golden Chain*, p.28.
123 Pyke, *The Golden Chain*, p.31.

that prevented them from being fully effective from time to time. Pyer had 'a severe illness during his sojourn in Liverpool' and in 1832 he almost despaired of retaining good health. 'Feeble and frail is this mortal frame of mine; subject to great weakness and exhaustion'.[124] Attempts to maintain, if not to expand, the scope of evangelical preaching would have been adversely affected by the reduced availability of preachers.

As far as is known none of the Tent Methodist preachers had any formal ministerial training, or university or academy education. However, although unlike some Bristol academies, Pocock's did not advertise that it would offer any religious instruction, he undoubtedly gave much guidance to Barnett and George Smith, and perhaps to others. With evangelical activity expanding in all the Methodist groups it was a high priority to have preachers available all the time, and it was difficult to allow some to be absent from duty to receive the benefit of formal training. From the second decade of the nineteenth century onwards, however, the nonconformist denominations increasingly felt the need for theological training. The first Wesleyan institution at Hoxton was not opened until 1834, but the 'strongest argument of all for formalising ministerial preparation was born out of the growing realisation that the general expansion of educational provision in the first four decades of the nineteenth century was producing more knowledgeable congregations who might well be dissatisfied with men of mediocre academic attainment'. It has been calculated that 'almost 80 per cent of the Congregationalists and just under 50 per cent of the Baptists who entered the ministry between 1820 and 1849 had been educated at an academy, a college, or even a university'.[125] Tim Macquiban, in the Wesley Historical Society lecture of 1995, charted the development of thinking, both in America and Britain, towards the general acceptance by 1830 that more education of Wesleyan preachers was needed. Whether that greater training was to be in-service or through a college based course was still being debated.[126] It cannot be known with certainty if the apparent absence of any formal training played a part in the Tent Methodist demise but Pyer's biographer claimed that 'too little regard was paid to the education of the preachers'.[127] Barnett and George Smith were certainly young and inexperienced, both being only seventeen when they first met Pocock and began their Tent Methodist work. Their

---

124 Russell, *Memoirs of Rev John Pyer*, pp.119 and 180.

125 Kenneth D. Brown, *A Social History of the Nonconformist Ministry in England and Wales 1800-1930* (Oxford: Clarendon Press, 1988), p.58.

126 T.S.A. Macquiban, 'Practical Piety or Lettered Learning', *Proceedings of WHS* 50.3 (October, 1995), pp.83-97. See also Macquiban's 'John Hannah and the Beginning of Theological Education in Methodism', address to the WHS Bristol Branch, *Bulletin* 65 (March 1993), pp.1-36.

127 Russell, *Memoirs of Rev John Pyer*, p.79.

responsibilities, under far less supervision, at Dursley and Liverpool respectively, began when they were aged twenty. It is difficult to judge whether a lack of experience contributed significantly to Tent Methodism's demise, particularly as many Wesleyan itinerants also received their first appointments while in their very early twenties. Pyer, Barnett and George Smith were all regarded as excellent preachers and it is more likely that it was a numerical shortage that caused the difficulties. This would have been aggravated by the fact that, unlike the Primitive Methodists and the Bible Christians, women did not appear to have any preaching role.

Lack of Geographical Coherence

A contributory factor in the demise of Tent Methodism was the lack of a coherent geographical pattern to the work, which was in marked contrast to the development of the three main Wesleyan offshoots of the period. Not only did this mean that resources were dissipated over a wide area, but with long travelling times the ability of the principal preachers to meet together was limited. The opportunities for the leadership to discuss strategic matters and to encourage mutual local support to counteract difficulties were hard to find. Pyer, particularly, up to 1825 was spending considerable time just travelling between Bristol, Manchester and Liverpool in one direction, and to London in another, in addition to occasional excursions to south Wales and, probably, into Wiltshire and west Berkshire. While the road network between major centres of population was improving it still took two full days by coach to reach Manchester from Bristol in 1821. Quite apart from the unproductive time while travelling from place to place there would, inevitably, be costs incurred which, if there was a regional rather than a national coverage, would have been less. In addition, problems would have arisen if concentration of resources was needed for a special evangelical mission, or even a regular meeting for all the officials or members.

The Methodist New Connexion, the Primitive Methodists and the Bible Christians did not suffer from this problem to anything like the same extent. While all three groups did expand beyond their original bases, it was generally a steady progression and undertaken only when they had achieved a solid foundation in their home territories. Nonetheless, the Bible Christian extension to Kent and London, Primitive Methodist missionary activity into Wiltshire, and the Methodist New Connexion expansion into Cornwall were examples during the 1820's of a degree of, superficially, illogical use of scarce resources. By the time these geographical 'jumps' occurred, however, there were in existence formal, central structures in each that consisted of a membership which could debate and decide these matters. The Tent Methodists never really had a proper hierarchy or consultation process which, despite the problems associated with them, might have curbed unwise expansion. The strength of the argument for a more concentrated base for the evangelical work, rather than the spreading of resources too thinly, is well illustrated by the experience of the Bible Christians and the Methodist New Connexion. Both denominations concerned themselves from time to time with internal discussions as to the benefits, or otherwise, of opening up mission stations outside the regions where their initial progress in the United Kingdom had originated. The perceived problems associated with broadening the evangelical work led directly to discussions that were intended to result in an amalgamation of the two denominations in 1870 or thereabouts. As one eminent writer on Bible Christian affairs wrote in 1915: 'It is useless now to dwell upon the large sums of money which since that date [1815] the Bible Christians have spent on the barren struggle to establish themselves firmly in the North of England, where the New Connexion had so many flourishing circuits'.[128] Those negotiations were abortive but union between the two was achieved in 1907 which indicated, among other things, that the creation of national coverage like the Wesleyans achieved was always going to be a hard, if not intractable, task to attain alone. The Tent Methodists never got anywhere near managing it.

Congregational Influences

Another possible reason for this branch of Methodism to fail was that, in several ways, it was always congregational in its outlook, and some individual societies, being independent and not capable of inclusion in a circuit structure, fitted more naturally among other self governing congregations. Manchester and Liverpool were the two best examples. In fact, from the very early days there was a significant Independent influence in the activities of tent preaching, especially by Pyer. 'While quite a youth, he was introduced to the Rev J. Thorp[e], and received much kindness and valuable help from that eloquent and distinguished preacher of the gospel, both in the loan of books and conversational instruction'.[129] Whether this was before or after Pyer had joined the Wesleyans in 1803 when he was thirteen is not known. The Tent Methodist philosophy was, initially, opposed to the highly disciplined, centrally directed Wesleyan hierarchy, particularly one made up of

---

128 Pyke, *The Golden Chain*, p.198.
129 Russell, *Memoirs of Rev John Pyer*, p.4; the reference should probably be to the Rev. William Thorp of Bristol, not a Rev. John Thorp(e) whom Pyer met much later when he was in Manchester.

people that Pyer and Pocock had little time for. This was partly because there were not enough societies to exercise central control over, but mainly because the preachers wanted to concentrate, especially in the early stages of the sect's development, on their evangelical preaching, going where they wished and when they were invited, rather than be subjected to a rigorous planned format of preaching. When the rules were drawn up, terminology associated with the Congregationalists was used. Certainly, individual members had more protection from expulsion than the Wesleyans did, and the word 'deacon' was used, a term familiar to Congregationalists but not to Methodists. The formal meetings in Manchester in January 1825 by a committee excluding, incidentally, Pyer, 'to consult together on the proposed change of the constitution of the church', and the subsequent decision of the congregation to become 'independent of any other',[130] was a clear indication of the future adoption of a Congregational mode of government. Bearing in mind that Pocock, ten years later was to return to Wesleyanism, it might have been this decision in Manchester and, later in Liverpool, that caused him to fall out with Pyer, withdraw from any sectarian leadership and concentrate his evangelical efforts on his local communities.

One of the few features that distinguished the Tent Methodists from other Wesleyan offshoots was the deployment of tents as a means of reaching their intended congregations. There were, it seems, never more than three tents under their direct control, one of which was smaller than the others, and the wide geographical spread would also have caused transport difficulties in moving the equipment around the country. As the 1820's progressed there was less and less reliance on tents, with the increasing number of towns and villages where preaching took place needing more permanent places for regular worship. A conceivable reason for decline could have been the infrequency of worship opportunities if the various communities had to wait until one of three tents could be made available, particularly in periods of bad weather or the winter months. In considering George Whitefield's open air and field preaching eighty years or so earlier, H.D. Rack wrote: 'As always with this type of preaching, especially if not followed up with a tighter organisation than Whitefield ever developed, the results were bound often to be ephemeral'.[131] The same could be said of the Tent Methodists who certainly did not have an effective organisation to provide the necessary pastoral care locally between visits of a tent. Even when the use of chapels and other meeting places was obtained, the structure of the sect was not sufficient to prevent much of the influence achieved being transitory.

---

130 Stocks, *A Reply*, p.16.
131 H.D. Rack, *Reasonable Enthusiast: John Wesley and the Rise of Methodism* (London: Epworth Press, 1989), p.193.

Pocock, with obvious sadness, in the letter he wrote to the Rev. H.T. Ellacombe in October 1842 referred to the time when his 'fellow labourers grew weary of gratuitous and outdoor preaching'.[132] The words 'and outdoor' were inserted as an afterthought into the text. In earlier years, Barnett, while he was living in Pocock's home, as part of his duties, organized the movement, erection and dismantling of the tents. When he moved to Dursley the burden of that exacting responsibility would have to fall on other shoulders. If no one person was found to manage that exercise, problems would certainly have arisen and resulted, perhaps, in less than the most effective use of what had been valuable assets in the evangelizing activity.

Chapel Management

The management of chapels and meeting houses was no less onerous. The ownership and control of chapels was, of course, one of the two key issues that prompted Pocock and the Wesleyan authorities to part company. All the Tent Methodist chapels for which documentation has been found have Pocock as the first named trustee and, bearing in mind the financial contribution he would have made, he would have insisted on retaining practical, if not legal, control. If the Tent Methodist rules were complied with, however, he would not have contributed the entire amount which he certainly did for the Pill Wesleyan chapel just before he was expelled. So as to concentrate his time and energies on the Tent Methodist expansion in the early years 'he had relinquished the management'[133] at Pill by August 1822, but he kept complete control of the Tent Methodist chapels. The requirements regarding chapels in the Tent Methodist rules changed between the 1820 and 1824 versions with the earlier edition having three simple clauses concerning chapels and trustees. One half of the expected cost of any chapel building had to be raised beforehand by subscription, and a special meeting of 'Official Characters' would choose the trustees. This should have reduced Pocock's personal contribution towards the initial capital costs. The 1824 version did not contain any specific requirement about funds being contributed or committed before building began, although approval to acquire a chapel had to be given by 'either of a quarterly or special meeting of official characters'.[134] It might be that Pocock had, by then, already given up financing additional chapels. The ownership and

---

132 George Pocock, letter to Rev. H.T. Ellacombe, Bristol, 13 October 1842.

133 Skitt (Mr) letter to Mr Jno Hall of Broadmead, Bristol, (Steward at Pill Methodist Church), 24 August 1822.

134 *TM Rules* (1820), Section 6, clauses 33, 34, and 35 on p.7, and *TM Rules* (1824) Section 7, clauses 29 to 32 on pp.11-12 of the 1824 edn.

administration of the chapels and the tents was an increasing burden with inadequate resources and expertise to handle all the issues involved. Legal complications, maintenance of buildings, shortage of money, and difficulties in obtaining registration under the terms of the Toleration Acts, as in Birmingham, for example, all added to the time consuming aspects of chapel management. There is no real evidence that Tent Methodists suffered, in this respect, any more than the other Methodist groups. The buildings were, by and large, modest, but it is clear that Pocock personally suffered financial loss when the buildings were sold. Problems with buildings were, in the main however, a result of decline, not a cause of it.

The Impact of Economic Conditions

There have been, and still are, historians who have sought to link directly the periods of relative growth and decline in Methodism with periods of the country's economic prosperity and depression. While it is valuable to attempt to form a judgement using the Tent Methodists as an example and consider attributing Tent Methodism's demise to the country's economic performance, it is not possible to draw any firm conclusions. In the first place while it is reasonable to consider the overall economic situation during the relevant years, the position did, in fact, vary significantly from region to region. For example, any rise or fall in the price of grain, which fluctuated substantially, affected some people very differently from others. Those employed in the agricultural regions probably suffered from reduction in wages when farmers received less income from low grain prices, while those living and working in urban locations would not have been so adversely affected. Indeed, they may well have had extra disposable income for other things, such as clothes, when grain prices fell. Tent Methodists, of course, had involvement in both types of community. Secondly, the Tent Methodist sect, as a sample of Methodism, was a very small one and would not have been representative of the denominations as a whole, particularly as it existed for a relatively few years.

Addresses at Wesleyan annual conferences included comment on the economic climate within which Methodism operated. The references made in 1825 and 1826 reveal how quickly that environment could change. 'He [God] hath not only made wars to cease...but hath filled our borders with plenteousness. Fruitful seasons, commercial prosperity'[135] were confident statements in the 1825 address. Just one year later,

---

135 *Minutes of Methodist Conference* (1825), p.71, 'The Annual Address', 5 August 1825; Joseph Entwisle, President; Jabez Bunting, Secretary.

however, the writers acknowledged 'unexampled distress which has, during the past year, overwhelmed or embarrassed so many merchants, manufacturers, and tradesmen, and plunged so many thousands of our labouring classes into penury and want'.[136] A complete change of sentiment in so short a time. At the micro level within Tent Methodism there were at least two supporting examples of the financial and economic difficulties in 1826. In September of that year Barnett returned to Dursley and found that 'trade was quite gone from the neighbourhood, and every cloth factory was shut up. The people had neither money, nor work'.[137] Stocks, critically describing events in Manchester when he accused Pyer of extravagance, wrote that 'most trades-people know what sort of a year 1826 was'.[138] Certainly there is evidence of an 1825 boom, followed dramatically by a slump the next year. Hand-loom weavers in the Manchester area suffered especially severely, and agricultural workers in the south often received much lower wages than those, for example, in East Anglia. These economic conditions, coming at a time when population growth was peaking in the two decades from 1811, could indicate possible support for a thesis that Tent Methodist decline mirrored a severe economic downturn in 1826.[139] What cannot be substantiated is whether the economic crisis, which did seem to be severe in those areas where Tent Methodism was active, caused the demise, or whether it was purely coincidental.

Indeed, there are two quite opposite schools of thought regarding the connection between denominational growth and decline, and economic upturns and downturns. One is that in periods of economic depression people sought the support and comfort of the churches 'in order to benefit from religious philanthropy'.[140] As an example, when cotton crop disease led to severe disruption to the Lancashire cotton industry in the middle of the nineteenth century, Wesleyan membership in a large part of the county increased at more than five times the national rate.[141] The other is that the day to day requirement of survival meant that many

---

136 *Minutes of Methodist Conference* (1826), p174, 'The Annual Address', 8 August 1826, Richard Watson, President; Jabez Bunting, Secretary.

137 Barnett, *Memorials*, p.41.

138 Stocks, *A Reply*, p.5.

139 Mathias, *First Industrial Nation*, chs 6 'The Human Dimension' and 7 'Economic Fluctuations', both describe the differing conditions in terms of cycles of time, the stages of the industrializing process, and the employment prospects. Evans, *Britain Before the Reform Act*, p.141, links an unemployment crisis for agricultural workers in southern England with declining wages and a significant rise in population, particularly between 1815 and 1830.

140 Currie, Gilbert and Horsley, *Church and Churchgoers*, p.105.

141 R.B. Walker, 'The Growth of Wesleyan Methodism in Victorian England and Wales', *Journal of Ecclesiastical History* 24.3 (1973), p.270.

people, especially those on low incomes, did not see association with a
church or chapel as a way of improving their lot, and, in any event, could
not afford to contribute financially to the churches' needs. The balance
of the views of religious historians, including W.R. Ward, probably
supports the argument that there is a link, with periods of slowing growth
or reduction in church membership coinciding with economic recession.
Tent Methodism's experience might, albeit tentatively, provide a degree
of evidence to sustain that view, but it is hard to disagree with D.W.
Bebbington when he records that 'no consistent correlation between
economic and religious cycles emerges'.[142]

Overall, by 1826 there was little that was distinctive about Tent
Methodism which would attract members, either from other
denominations or sects, or those who were coming new to the Christian
faith. The impressive appearance of a large tent coming into a locality
was less common, relative to the size and geographical extent of the
group. There would seem to have been, other than Pocock, no
particularly outstanding preachers or pastors once Pyer, George Smith
and Barnett had left. The doctrinal characteristics were not noticeably
different from other Methodist groups. In addition, other Methodist
offshoots, and Wesleyanism itself, were soon to come into areas where
Tent Methodism had faced little competition.

The difficulties faced by Pocock and his colleagues were not unique. A
comment made in a book to mark the centenary of the Methodist New
Connexion could equally have applied to the Tent Methodists. The
Methodist New Connexion 'had to labour where its adherents were
widely scattered, and under the disadvantage of difficulty in finding
suitable preachers, and in obtaining chapels or commodious rooms for
worship. The preachers received sadly insufficient allowances, and the
work they had to do was frequently in excess of their strength; and hence,
as well as for other reasons, many desisted, occasioning, time after time,
perplexity and discouragement'.[143] Pocock, perhaps anticipating the
disappointments that would be associated with a declining cause, sought
to reunite with the Wesleyans and take his chapels with him. An unknown
writer of a manuscript history of Portland Chapel—possibly Mark Guy
Pearse, who was a minister there between 1883 and 1886—recorded that
Pocock 'offered to return with all his chapels burdened with debt to the
connexion, but the offer was declined as far as the chapels and their debts

---

142 D.W. Bebbington, *Evangelicalism in Modern Britain: A History from the
1730s to the 1980s* (London: Unwin Hyman, 1989), p.114.
143 T.D. Crothers *et al* (eds), *The Centenary of the Methodist New Connexion 1797
-1897* (London, 1897), p.91.

were concerned'.[144] Bearing in mind that Pocock began the disposal of chapels in and around Bristol in 1831 and 1832, this approach was probably in 1830, by which time the sect's demise was well under way. The Wesleyan authorities' action delayed the reconciliation with Pocock by at least five years. Certainly, the disintegration process occurred much more rapidly than the growth phase. There were many contributing factors to the demise, but the turning point, after which the decline was both quick and painful, came when the leaders, principally Pocock, but also Pyer and Barnett, lost whatever inspiration they ever had to develop Tent Methodism into a substantial force in nonconformity, focusing particularly on the poor in both rural and urban communities.

---

144 Anon., *A Short History of Portland Street Wesleyan Chapel, Bristol, and its surroundings with brief notes of some of the principal persons and events connected with Methodism in the City* (n.p., n.d.), p.32.

CHAPTER 8

The Contribution of Tent Methodism to the Religious Life of the Early Nineteenth Century

The Social and Religious Contexts

It is now possible to make an assessment of the significance of Tent Methodism from the time of its inception, as a part of Wesleyanism, in April 1814 until its demise. The life span of the sect was about eighteen years until 1832. That is a much longer period than has been recognized hitherto, but it is necessary to qualify the year of termination. 1832 has been used as it was the year that three of the chapels were disposed of, but in most parts of the country the work had ceased a few years earlier. On the other hand, George Pocock himself continued with his own individual evangelical endeavours for a further three years after 1832. The fact is that the sect made a much greater contribution to the life of Nonconformity than those people who have included reference to the group in their written work have been aware of from the sources they used. During the course of the research for this book substantial quantities of additional primary, and near contemporary, material has been found to contain relevant information. This has proved of great value, particularly relating to the later years. Biographies of men involved to a greater or lesser extent with Tent Methodism have provided an insight into the sect that was not possible to achieve from the material which, up to then, had been studied. A comprehensive biography of John Pyer by a daughter, had been used as source material for many years, but no previous knowledge of the group had been gleaned from memorials, obituaries or biographies written of John Barnett especially, but also of Edward Griffith, Samuel Bryant, George Smith and Victory Purdy.

This assessment is, however, still hindered by the lack of any national statistical information. There were serious flaws in the religious membership surveys undertaken in the eighteenth and early nineteenth centuries, but an equivalent one producing, in the 1820's, even the rudimentary and only partially accurate measurements that John Evans prepared between 1715 and 1718, Josiah Thompson achieved in 1772 and 1773, and Messrs Bogue and Bennett recorded in 1812, would have been helpful. By the time of the comprehensive, though still deficient, survey that Horace Mann undertook in 1851, Tent Methodism had ceased to exist for some twenty years. The absence of any statistics, or surviving minutes of meetings, that could throw light on the numbers of members, preachers, congregations or chapels adds to the difficulty of judging the significance of the sect. Despite the problems associated with the unavailability of information, the substantial amount of primary material that has been uncovered, coupled with much useful secondary material, has provided a good opportunity to assess the role played by the Tent Methodists, in their own right and in the context of other Wesleyan offshoots that emerged during the first quarter of the nineteenth century.

A full and detailed appraisal needs to be made using both religious and social perspectives. The religious impact is crucial. Throughout the period of Tent Methodism's existence, there were many aspects of their Christian witness that impacted on the spiritual life of the parts of the country where they were active. Their relationships with Wesleyanism, before and after the formal establishment of the sect, and the increasing importance of the contact with other nonconformist denominations permeates the whole story. However, it was the personalities involved that influenced the actions and behaviour of the Tent Methodist movement itself and the association with other nonconformist groups. That interaction has to be examined against the social climates of the period. In this context, 'social' includes both economic and political factors. It might be that in the past religious and social assessments were made with each having little regard for the other. Increasingly, though, there has been a recognition that the two are inextricably linked. W.R. Ward draws immediate attention, in the introduction to his book, *Religion and Society in England 1790-1850*, to the importance of the social scene, not only in England, but also in parts of mainland Europe, to the religious developments here between those dates.[1] David Bebbington also acknowledges the need to set the history of British Evangelicalism within the context of the many strands of society.[2] A further example of the recognition that both religious and social perspectives need to be considered together can be found in John Wolffe's study of women and community in the nineteenth century. Wolffe states his aim is to examine 'the character of Evangelicalism as a religious movement' and that a secondary objective is to recognize that it is 'not a study of a religious moment in isolation, but rather an investigation of the interactions between that movement and the society and culture around it'.[3]

---

1   Ward, *Religion and Society in England 1790-1850*, pp.1-4.

2   Bebbington, *Evangelicalism in Modern Britain*, pp.ix-x.

3   John Wolffe, *Evangelicals, Women and Community in Nineteenth-Century Britain* (Course A425; Milton Keynes: Open University Study Guide, 1994), pp.7-8.

Many sociologists, while not focusing specifically on the role of Christianity on social events, do increasingly underline the importance of 'agency' (the role of individuals) rather than 'structure' (the role of institutions) in their assessment of societal matters. A.H. Halsey is one who has articulated this view in recent years as he developed the theme of 'citizenship' as a concept which is useful in examining various social issues, including class and equality of wealth.[4] Tent Methodism operated in societies that had long experienced inequalities of wealth that were, arguably, becoming greater all the time. Formal class divisions, however, were relatively new phenomena, becoming more pronounced as the Industrial Revolution developed, especially so in some of the places where Tent Methodists worked. Perhaps the most thorough examination so far of the context within which church history—of all eras and not confined to Great Britain alone—is written, was undertaken by John Kent who described the various positions taken by church and social historians. He expressed the view that in the last forty years or so 'social historians...began to interest themselves...in the part which religion had played in the formation of the modern world'.[5] Indeed, William Gibson believes that 'from 1760 onwards the challenges that confronted the Church came from social and economic changes'.[6]

As far as Tent Methodism is concerned, religious and social issues were certainly inter-connected in such a way that it is not possible, nor justified, to separate the religious and social factors. Tent Methodist preachers attempted to address the very real practical concerns with a different emphasis than the Wesleyans did during the period under review. The day to day living experiences of many early nineteenth-century people were so severe that Tent Methodists, and others, strived to bring a spirituality to ease harsh conditions. If the preaching and pastoral care was not able to relieve the social and economic pain, it might just have provided a deeper dimension to the lives of thousands of ordinary people—a benefit that was sorely needed, if not always readily recognized.

'One soweth, and another reapeth'

In one outstanding way the Tent Methodist contribution to the growth of Nonconformity was far greater than is immediately obvious. It might also be said of other sects and denominations, but in a very real sense what

---

4   A.H. Halsey, *Change in British Society* (Oxford: Oxford University Press, 1986), pp.60-76.

5   John Kent, *The Unacceptable Face: The Modern Church in the Eyes of the Historian* (London: SCM Press, 1987), p.8.

6   Gibson, *Church, State and Society*, p.1.

Tent Methodism sowed, others reaped. Even ignoring the impact that Pocock and Pyer had on some, like Elijah Waring, John Irving and George Hadfield who never actually joined the sect, Tent Methodism's role in influencing several men who went on to provide many years of dedicated Christian service in other denominations is not to be underestimated.

George Pocock himself is an example. Not only did he significantly influence two others, particularly, who gave many distinguished and committed years to other denominations, he returned to Wesleyanism and shared his spiritual gifts for several more years up to his death in 1843. By then he was sixty-nine years of age and in the final years of his life he became, once again, a local preacher in the Bristol North circuit, and contributed financially to the fund to support Kingswood and Woodhouse Grove schools. He did not, however, appear to make any donations either to the 'Theological Institution' fund, or, not surprisingly, to the 'Chapel Fund'.[7] He also published a volume of hymns and poems prepared particularly for young people, and contributed to the cost of a new Church of England building erected in the parish of Bitton where much of his evangelical labours had been conducted. While the reunion with his former Wesleyan friends was not, apparently, initially universally welcomed, it was said he was in the company of the denomination's leadership when they met in Bristol for the centenary conference in 1839.[8] In fact, it was the 1838 conference that was held in Bristol. The centenary one, a year later, took place in Liverpool. His reinstatement as a member of the Wesleyan community was an event significant enough for Jacob Stanley to make specific reference to it in a letter from Bristol to his long standing friend Henry Moore. Stanley was in the habit of writing each year to Moore to mark his birthday in December, and in 1839 when Moore became eighty-eight he wrote, 'Your old friend George Pocock has been reunited to us and is now on our Plan as a Local Preacher. Much opposition was made to his readmission, but now I believe the general feeling is that of gratitude for his return. He seems in a humble and friendly state of mind'.[9] After his reconcilation with Wesleyanism, and once the initial reluctance to accept him back was overcome, he was, apparently, 'honoured by all for his goodness and loved for his generous spirit'.[10] The same letter from Stanley to Moore made it clear, as other preachers did, that for several years before 1839 'the Society [Wesleyan] has been in a perturbed and

---

7   *Circuit Schedule Book for Bristol North Circuit, 1839-1845* (n.p., n.d.).

8   W. Symons, 'Portland Chapel, Bristol and the Tent Methodists', *Cornish Methodist Recorder* (January, 1893), p.4.

9   Jacob Stanley, letter to Henry Moore, 20 December 1839.

10   Lambert, *Chapel on the Hill*, p.54.

declining state' with much 'hallowed strife and bitterness'.[11] That
situation had improved, partly it might be hoped, because of the
reconciliation with Pocock. Despite Moore's friendship with Pocock and
his knowledge of Tent Methodism, he makes no reference to either in his
autobiography.[12] George Pocock, then, began and finished his Christian
discipleship with the Wesleyans and the denomination greatly benefitted
from his very many talents. The pity was that neither Pocock nor the
Wesleyan leadership could reconcile their respective idiosyncrasies
during the middle period of Pocock's evangelical activity.

A hymn reproduced below, written by Pocock, probably near the end
of his life and not found in any book other than the one he wrote for his
pupils, reveals an intensity of inner spiritual feeling that he shared for the
benefit of others for nearly fifty years, both before and after his twenty
years or so as a Tent Methodist. Significantly, the hymn is headed,
'Giving all to God'.

What shall I render to the Lord
For all his benefits to me?
My soul, say what canst thou afford
For all the Lord has done for thee?

Me thinks, my soul, I hear thee say
To him I owe immortal praise;
And fain would I his love repay,
With songs as endless as my days.

My body, what canst thou impart?
Give Him thy feet, thy hands, thy head:
But ah! if thou withhold thy heart
Vain is thy toil: thy works are dead.

My Lord, my God, accept thine own;
Nought that I am, or have, is mine;
My ransomed powers be thine alone;
My wealth, my life, my heart, be thine.[13]

---

11   Jacob Stanley, letter to Henry Moore, 20 December 1839.

12   Henry Moore, *The Life of the Rev Mr Henry Moore* (London, 1844). This work
was completed by Mrs Richard Smith as Moore suffered from a disability which prevented
him continuing with his autobiography after about 1833.

13   This hymn appeared in Pocock's *Sacred Lyrics for Youth*, No. 95, p.103. It was
a collection of verse that showed much evidence of his real love for, and interest in,
young people.

It is not possible to fully quantify Pocock's contribution to Nonconformity during his life, and his death, sadly, did not result in even the briefest of mentions in the *Wesleyan Methodist Magazine*, or in the minutes of the annual conference. It can be said with certainty that very many people far beyond the confines of Tent Methodism were affected for good by the spiritual, academic, and social beliefs and gifts that he had. He died of bronchitis at his home on 9 November 1843. His funeral service was held on 14 November 1843 at Portland Chapel, Bristol, and was conducted by the Rev. John Smith who was, partly at least, instrumental in guiding Pocock back to Wesleyanism.[14] This dedicated Wesleyan itinerant, who became known as John Smith III, died in London at the age of forty-seven, little more than a year after he had officiated at George Pocock's funeral. George Pocock sowed the seeds of Christian witness in many of the 2,000 or so pupils who had attended his academy over a period of more than forty years, countless others, and in two men particularly who were later to bring to the Congregational and Baptist denominations the benefit of their commitment and service.

George Smith served the Congregationalists for no less than forty-three years after he had left Tent Methodism in 1827. It was Pocock who provided Smith with a home and spiritual guidance when he was only seventeen. He was to exercise a dedicated ministry in several places but he is especially noted for his pastoral oversight at Poplar in east London, and as General Secretary of the Congregational Union of England and Wales for eighteen years. In addition, he became a Director of the London Missionary Society, was a firm advocate of anti-slavery, acted as Secretary of the Christian Witness Fund which was particularly concerned with easing the lot of the poor in society, and became Secretary of the Irish Evangelical Society. He undertook many official positions, yet retained a deep affinity for his pastoral responsibilities, and published several religious works.[15] It can be reasonably claimed that as his conversion was a result of Pocock's influence, Congregationalists reaped where Tent Methodists sowed.

Similarly, John Barnett, who moved from Wiltshire to live with Pocock for three or four years in Bristol soon after his acceptance of Methodism at the age of about twenty, became a valued Baptist minister in 1826 and served that denomination for another fifty years. He was regarded as an excellent preacher, despite periods of personal spiritual doubt, and it was a great pleasure to him that he guided his son, who he had named John Pyer Barnett, into the Baptist ministry. Though not accepting high office in the Baptist Union he diligently served several pastorates in Leicestershire right up to his death in 1876. Here again his formative

---

14 *Portland Chapel Register of Burials*, entry No. 1470, 14 November 1843.
15 *Congregational Year Book* (1871), pp.346-349, obituary of Dr George Smith.

Christian beliefs were developed while he worked exceedingly hard for the Tent Methodists in Gloucestershire and parts of Wiltshire.[16]

The other main personality whose contribution to church life continued long after his departure from Tent Methodism was John Pyer. He had little difficulty in arousing the bitterness of some but it does seem that he had, by the time he was forty and had become a Congregational minister, mellowed to a degree. His biographer accepts that he retained an 'outward mask of sternness' and that his 'natural temper was quick and passionate',[17] but by the time of his death in 1859 he had been a valued Congregational minister for over thirty years. A Wesleyan minister willingly agreed to take a part in his funeral service, suggesting reconciliation from the bitterness of earlier years. Barnett, in a letter to Pyer's daughter on hearing of his death, wrote: 'the noble, sanctified spirit has fled, and that fine, tall, well-built, robust frame, which was full of majesty, especially in the pulpit, when he was before his people in the fullness of the blessing of the gospel of Christ, and his eye was brilliant and sparkling with the fire of heavenly love'.[18] Pyer had suffered more than his share of personal domestic tragedy. There were the deaths of two brothers and a daughter, all in their twenties or thirties, and a severe illness which afflicted his wife from the birth of their second child and which deprived him of 'the softening influence of a happy wedded life'. 'Patiently and bravely did he endure this long fight of affliction'.[19] Pyer was also actively associated with the teetotal movement, beginning his assistance at a time when Congregationalism's official line was not supportive of the movement's aims.[20] Here, again, is an example of a man who gave fifteen years or so to Tent Methodism, but a further thirty to another Nonconformist denomination.

The Significance of the Use of Tents

By adopting the use of portable structures for worship, particularly in the early years, Tent Methodists were ahead of their time. Tents had been deployed to provide shelter at camp meetings from about 1807, organized by those who later formed the Primitive Methodists, but the Tent Methodists developed the use in a particular way. They became a central feature of missionary effort and were transported to many

---

16   *Baptist Handbook* (1878), pp.330-334, 'Memoirs of Ministers', obituary of John Barnett.

17   Russell, *Memoirs of Rev John Pyer*, pp.299-300.

18   Barnett, *Memorials*, p.170.

19   Russell, *Memoirs of Rev John Pyer*, p.300.

20   P.T. Winskill, *The Temperance Movement and its Workers* (London, 1892), II, p.45; also *Congregational Magazine* (November, 1836), p.692.

different locations. Portability was seen as a benefit to overcome the
shortage of buildings, and of money to acquire permanent premises. In
addition, tents were felt to be less intimidating than chapels to some of the
people who Tent Methodists sought to reach. They may also have
directly influenced others to use an identical practice. Only a few years
after Pocock's first tent was built, both the Home Missionary Society and
the Christian Instruction Society in their evangelical activities in parts of
London during the 1820's were making extensive use of tents. It is
entirely possible that it was Pocock's inspired idea that prompted others
to see the benefits and to acquire tents of their own.

London Wesleyan Methodists were not, it appears, active in either the
Home Missionary Society or the Christian Instruction Society, but twenty
years later some provincial Wesleyans had accepted the principle of
portable structures. To overcome continuing difficulties in finding
suitable sites to erect chapels because of the refusal of landowners to co-
operate, portable chapels were used. While no further records have been
found of tents being used in the way that Tent Methodists employed
them in the United Kingdom, Nottinghamshire Methodists, in the 1840's,
adapted the Tent Methodist idea. They provided 'a truly original and
elegant moveable wooden chapel upon wheels made by Mr Clifton,
builder, Bingham, at a cost of £60, and capable of seating of nearly 130
persons. This chapel is for the accommodation of a group of small
villages or hamlets in their circuit where no site can be obtained, the land
being the property of noblemen or other large landed proprietors'.[21]
Similarly, and at about the same time, Primitive Methodists acquired a
boat on which services were held at Shelford, a village on the river Trent
seven miles east of Nottingham, and elsewhere in the vicinity.[22] There is
no evidence in either of these cases that Tent Methodist experience was
known about and followed, but the examples suggest that if ways had
been found to retain the Tent Methodist leaders within Wesleyanism, the
denomination as a whole would have greatly benefited. Further
justification for the view that Tent Methodist thinking and practice was
subsequently accepted by the Wesleyans can be found in Jabez Bunting's
biography. In volume 1 his son wrote that the use of tents 'is not an
uncommon practice in these times'.[23] The deployment of tents was, then,
accepted as being useful. Unsurprisingly, there is no acknowledgement
that had the previous generation of Wesleyans recognized that a
significant secession could have been prevented, and Wesleyanism could
have kept for itself a valuable evangelical resource. Flexibility was not

21   R.C. Swift, 'A Chapel on Wheels', *Proceedings of WHS* 28 (June, 1952),
pp.122 and 123, quoting *Nottingham Review* 5 July 1844.
22   Watts, *Dissenters*, II, p.117.
23   Bunting, *Life of Jabez Bunting*, I, p.170.

often evident in the management of Wesleyan spiritual or administrative activity.

The missionary work of Tent Methodists, especially in the rural areas of south Gloucestershire and east Wiltshire, was soon followed by Wesleyans, but local preachers, not full-time itinerants.[24] That this should be the case provides further evidence for the view that Tent Methodists were in advance of future Wesleyan thinking. In parts of southern England, at least, Wesleyan concentration of effort on established urban congregations had begun to lessen by the end of the 1820's. It was not, however, until 1841 that Bunting himself was able to say, 'fewer chapels and more horses would save more souls' and 'we should preach in barns, the cottages of the poor, and out of doors'.[25] It was a great pity that his conversion to the thinking of Tent Methodists, and others, took so long.

The original Tent Methodist practice of using tents was not confined to England. It would be presumptuous, and probably unjustified, to claim that George Pocock's idea of worship in portable tents spread directly to America, but in several parts of the United States tents were built and used for services. Many years after Pocock's tent was first taken to a site just outside Bristol, a much larger and more sophisticated structure, though still portable, was dedicated for worship on 1 May 1858 in Philadelphia. It was an ecumenical project supported by ten denominations and during the following six months 416 meetings were held in six different places.[26] The Young Men's Christian Association was heavily involved in the management of it, as it was also with what was known as the 'Gospel Tent' in Brooklyn in 1876. The same name was given to yet another tent used in New York for the first time on 11 June 1876, built at a cost of less than $2,000.[27] In all cases the intention, like that of the early tent preachers in and around Bristol, was to attract those people who would not feel comfortable worshipping in a church or chapel. The tents were also helpful in parts of America because the churches became unbearably hot in the main summer months and because of this were simply not used. They were capable of holding about 3,000 people and, partly as a result of that, were cumbersome to dismantle and erect elsewhere. There is no evidence that these later American evangelists were aware of Pocock's introduction of tent worship much earlier in the nineteenth century, but what the Tent Methodists undertook was also provided to

---

24   Vickers, 'Methodism and Society in Central Southern England', pp.159-160, and 173.

25   Benjamin Gregory, *Side Lights on the Conflicts of Methodism* (London, 1898), p.315.

26   Edwin M. Long, *The Union Tabernacle, or Movable Tent-Church* (Philadelphia, 1859), pp.97 and 107.

27   William B. Mucklow, *Under Canvas, or, Tent Worship in Summer Months* (New York, 1876), pp.10-14.

many thousands of others in the fullness of time. Ironically, the only denomination to object to the New York venture was the American Methodists. At a conference of Methodist ministers a paper was presented by one member which 'contained the most reckless and sweeping statements regarding the tent services, which were...mere claptrap and excitement with the view of cheaply earning popularity'.[28] Nonetheless, in a mirroring of the experiences of Pocock and his colleagues fifty years earlier, especially in Manchester, some individual Methodists and many from other denominations were most supportive.

There is no evidence that the employment of tents for public worship, or other meetings, by the Tent Methodists was considered to be a significant parallel to the use of tents and tabernacles as described in the books of the Old and New Testaments. The *Tent Methodist Magazine* for 1823 includes nineteen biblical quotations, fourteen of them from the New Testament, but none make reference to any of the biblical passages which contain the word 'tent' or 'tabernacle', mainly found in the Old Testament, especially Exodus and Numbers. In particular, it is not apparent that the Tent Methodist preachers, either before or after the secession from the Wesleyans, gave any indication that they felt that their evangelical campaigns with the tents were similar to the journeys of the Israelites to the 'Promised Land'. The 'itinerant temples' of the Tent Methodists were much simpler than the elaborate and precise design and fitting of the Israelites' 'tabernacle of the congregation' (Exodus 27:21, KJV).

Concern for the Poor in Urban and Rural Areas

Another fact that needs to be recognized in any assessment of Tent Methodism's contribution to Christian endeavours is that some of the towns and villages where Tent preachers worked were significantly larger than they subsequently became. Wotton-under-Edge, for example, was a Gloucestershire market town with a population that was growing rapidly in the early nineteenth century, reaching 5,482 in 1831, but which had declined to 2,979 by 1901. Dursley, too, had a population that had increased up to 1831, but had declined by one third seventy years later. Both these places were in Gloucestershire where the overall county population had nearly doubled in the first thirty years of the nineteenth century. A similar picture emerges from an analysis of some of the Wiltshire places. Great Bedwyn, for instance, was 'formerly a market town of some importance, and until the Reform Act of 1832 was a rotten

---

28   Mucklow, *Under Canvas*, p.15.

borough regularly sending its two members to Parliament'.[29] Urchfont, Enford and Ogbourne St George were all busy rural communities that became just small villages as depopulation affected parts of the county. Marlborough and Salisbury were, and remain, significant places situated on main roads. Elsewhere, Tent Methodists were at work in inner city locations where living and working conditions were often appalling. It would be inaccurate, therefore, to emphasize that Tent Methodists were only to be found in the small backwater places where little real evangelical impact was achieved.

Another important feature of Tent Methodism was that it attempted to make a meaningful contribution to evangelical effort in places where poor families lived. Often those places were in city centres, such as the parishes of St James and St Phillips in Bristol, where population growth was rapid in the early nineteenth century. It was about this part of Bristol that the Rev. George Charles Smith, the Baptist minister, wrote that the Tent Methodist preachers were conducting missionary services despite being ordered to stop by the civil authorities. Furthermore, a local Baptist minister, referring to the squalid living conditions of the area, advised his congregation to 'keep their children from that sink of iniquity'.[30] Kingswood was regarded as 'the haunt of some of the most depraved and desperate race of men living, often becoming a pest and annoyance',[31] and other places in the vicinity had similar reputations. Yet, here for nearly twenty years, Tent Methodists were active. Highly urbanized districts of east London, Manchester, Liverpool and Birmingham also received the attention of the Tent Methodists. While it has tended to be assumed that the city centres and the rapidly growing centres of the Industrial Revolution were the places where poverty was most acute, many rural areas and market towns and villages also suffered. In Dursley and other nearby towns, for example, bitter hostility regularly occurred between the weavers and their employers when the factory owners imposed wage cuts on an already underpaid workforce. Poverty increased and more than one hundred workers were imprisoned for their protestations. For four years between 1821 and 1825, during which time the Tent Methodists were at their most active, the dispute raged. Low agricultural wages in parts of Wiltshire led to much economic and social distress among many in the rural communities. There is, then, much evidence of Tent Methodism's concern to bring the Christian gospel to the least fortunate members of the communities where they were present.

It is not easy to substantiate any claim that Tent Methodists, and Primitive Methodists and Bible Christians, were more concerned with the

---

29   Michael Marsham, *The Wiltshire Village Book* (Newbury: Countryside Books, 1987), pp.19-20.

30   G.C. Smith, *Bristol Fair but no Preaching!* (Bristol, 1823), pp.24-32.

31   William Arthur, *The Successful Merchant* (London, 1852), p.275.

spiritual welfare of the poorer classes than Wesleyanism, or for that matter, the Church of England. Certainly, the leaders who produced the two sets of Tent Methodist rules in 1820 and 1824 exhibited a recognition that the disadvantaged among the membership needed special support. There are, though, considerable difficulties in producing a satisfactory understanding of who, in the 1820's, constituted the 'disadvantaged'. Henry Rack, among others, draws attention to John Wesley's concern, in the second half of the eighteenth century, for the poor when he wrote that 'he [Wesley] was peculiarly sensitive to the feelings of the poor and recipients of charity'.[32] Rack later acknowledged 'that the category of "the poor" in the eighteenth century is itself an imprecise term'.[33] The same was true in the early nineteenth century as a formalized way of categorizing the growing class divisions from the impact of the Industrial Revolution had not, by then, been established. It is tempting to use the word 'underclass' which would indicate that the people of concern to the Tent Methodists were not the artisans or self-employed who, nonetheless, often struggled to make ends meet. 'Underclass', 'pauperism' and 'primary poverty' are words increasingly used by sociologists to reflect a class below, in sociological terms, a working class category.[34] There are benefits in attempting to define 'poor' more closely, and 'underclass' may accurately describe the people who lived in squalor, in cities and rural communities, rarely earned a living, and received no meaningful education. Tent Methodist leaders' graphic references, for example, to the conditions of the miners in south Wales, and those living in inner city Bristol and London, do suggest a very real concern for those right at the bottom of the social ladder.

It might be that the particular people attracted to Tent Methodism simply did not possess, or develop, the gifts needed to enable them to share the burden of local pastoral leadership or the management of buildings used for worship. There is a school of thought which suggests that one of the features of Methodism generally in the nineteenth century was its ability to produce men and women of stature from humble origins because it provided opportunities for service and local leadership.[35] Significant numbers of people accepted those chances and, at the same time, improved their own position in society by developing, for example,

---

32   Rack, *Reasonable Enthusiast*, p.363.

33   Rack, *Reasonable Enthusiast*, p.441.

34   Royle, *Modern Britain*, pp.156-65; Mathias, *First Industrial State*, pp.344-45; and Peter Ackroyd, *London: The Biography* (London: Chatto & Windus, 2000), pp.599-617.

35   Bebbington, *Evangelicalism in Modern Britain*, p.111; Ritson, *Romance of Primitive Methodism*, pp.177-89, 191-93; and Thomas Shaw, *A History of Cornish Methodism* (Truro: D. Bradford Barton, 1967), p.114.

their ability to read and speak in public. Tent Methodism does not seem to have been a beneficiary of that experience.

The Primitive Methodists and Bible Christians did, however, draw to their ranks working class people who served their respective denominations with great distinction. During the decade of the 1820's alone, many examples can be found. For the Primitive Methodists, apart from the national leaders, men such as John Oxtoby, Thomas Batty and Robert Key have special places among the annals. The same position was apparent for the Bible Christians in the same period. Billy Bray, who has become a celebrity to those interested in Bible Christian or Cornish affairs, and Edmund Warne, were two who, from humble backgrounds, were called to serve the young church with great enthusism and commitment. The missionary activity of both these denominations was concentrated more than Wesleyanism on the materially poorer sections of communities. Early Primitive Methodism has always been particularly associated with evangelizing the working class at a time when, in R.A. Soloway's words, 'each passing year revealed that the gaps between rich and poor were growing wider'.[36] Robert F. Wearmouth is clear that the Primitive Methodists 'can be described as a working-class association'.[37] John Petty, however, one of the earliest writers of the denomination's history, felt moved to write in 1860: 'Look at London, Portsmouth, Bristol, Plymouth, Liverpool, Manchester, Birmingham, Leeds, Bradford, Newcastle-on-Tyne, and several other large towns and cities! How little has the Connexion done for them compared with their pressing wants'.[38] K.S. Inglis, claiming only modest success for the Primitive Methodists, wrote: 'it is clear that the proportion of working-class people reached by Primitive Methodism was small'.[39] Bible Christian experience was similar in the West Country counties. The needs of the poor were great. 'The working men were often little better off than serfs. Their complete lack of education, and the meagre pittance which they received for their labour, both contributed to the abject hopelessness in which most of them passed their lives'.[40] It was among these folk that the early Bible Christian preachers concentrated their efforts.

The commitment, then, to attempts to provide spiritual guidance to the lower classes in society can be readily identified from the histories of the Primitive Methodists and the Bible Christians. In that endeavour the Tent Methodists worked equally hard. What is much more difficult to judge is

---

36   R.A. Soloway, *Prelates and People: Ecclesiastical Social Thought in England 1783-1852* (London: Routledge and Kegan Paul, 1969), p.233.

37   Wearmouth, *Methodism and the Working-Class Movement*, p.167.

38   Petty, *History of Primitive Methodist Connexion*, p.386.

39   K.S. Inglis, *Churches and the Working Classes in Victorian England* (London: Routledge and Kegan Paul, 1963), p.12.

40   Pyke, *The Golden Chain*, p.14.

the extent of the overall success. In any event, how can 'success' in this context be measured? Information regarding the breakdown of the social groupings of denominational membership became more available as the nineteenth century progressed, but in the 1820's comprehensive statistical data of this kind was not collected. It is possible to suggest, albeit only tentatively, that the strenuous work among the disadvantaged in society by Primitive Methodists, Bible Christians and the Tent Methodists achieved modest success which was probably greater than that achieved by other dissenting groups. The progress made, however, was not to the extent that made it easily recognizable to social or religious historians.

It was clear, however, that the leaders of the Tent Methodist movement showed concern for the disadvantaged sections of communities beyond their involvement with the local societies to whom they ministered. George Smith was not afraid to demonstrate publicly his opposition to slavery—a view sure to find many opponents in Liverpool, a west coast shipping port with a vested interest in the continued exploitation of slaves. John Pyer embraced the teetotal movement because he believed that even the very limited consumption of alcoholic drink would severely affect the health and wealth of the poor. The lifetime involvement and interest of George Pocock and John Gosling in education included the provision of facilities for children who received few other opportunities to write as well as read.

The Wesleyan hierarchy of the time showed far less official anxiety for these social conditions. Up to 1825 the Wesleyans did not support anti-slavery measures. Indeed, the 1824 Wesleyan annual conference censured and removed two missionaries serving the West Indies because they criticized slavery.[41] Although many individual Wesleyans were among the earliest advocates of the teetotal movement, the hierarchy was not supportive. In Cornwall, for example, a secession occurred in 1841 on this very issue.[42] As far as education in general and writing in particular was concerned, the official Wesleyan line for a long time was that reading, but not writing, was to be taught in Wesleyan Methodist Sunday schools.[43] To bring children to a knowledge and belief in Christian discipleship and Wesleyan churchmanship it was not, apparently, beneficial that they should learn to write on Sundays.

To a very modest, though conscious, extent, then, Tent Methodists formed a part of the growing, but often uncoordinated, movement

---

41   Watts, *Dissenters*, II, pp.445-46.

42   John K. Lander, 'The Early Days of Teetotalism in Cornwall', *Journal of the Royal Institution of Cornwall* (2002), pp.85-100, and Michael S. Edwards, 'The Teetotal Wesleyan Methodists', *Proceedings of WHS* 33 (September-December, 1961), pp.63-70.

43   Ward, *Religion and Society in England*, pp.135-40; and Gowland, *Methodist Secessions*, p.141.

throughout the country to improve the lot of those who lived in the poorest circumstances. Tent Methodist preachers sought to respond, almost forty years later, to the message contained on a medallion produced by Josiah Wedgwood in 1787 and widely used for many years to promote the emerging campaign for the abolition of slavery. Around a figure of a kneeling black slave was inscribed the question, 'Am I not a man and a brother?'[44] Tent Methodism was principally a movement that addressed religious matters, but it did not avoid the practical, material aspects of day to day life, and sought to improve the circumstances of their 'brothers'.

The Wesleyan emphasis at this time appears to be rather different than that shown by John Wesley himself. Perhaps little can be inferred from an extract of a letter that Thomas Allan, Wesleyanism's principal solicitor in the early nineteenth century, wrote in March 1840 to Edmund Grindrod, then superintendent of the London (City Road) circuit. The statement that 'it has long been obvious that the lower classes generally speaking will not attend our chapels'[45] seems to portray a lack of much concern and indicates an air of resignation among Wesleyans. The 1820 Wesleyan Conference had, however, exhorted the preachers to 'try to open new places; let us try again places which have not been recently visited', and also to have recourse 'to the practice of preaching out of doors'. This was in response to the question 'What measures can we adopt for the increase of spiritual religion among our Societies and congregations, and for the extension of the work of God in our native country?'[46] In some areas, no doubt, genuine attempts were made by Wesleyans to evangelize in unfamiliar territory, but Victory Purdy, a loyal and highly respected Wesleyan for many years before becoming a Tent Methodist for the final two years of his life, bemoaned the lack of local Wesleyan preaching resources for existing places in the Downend circuit of south Gloucestershire. He feared that unless more preachers were found 'must not several of the places be entirely shut up on the Sabbath?'[47] Certainly the starting point for Pocock's initial ideas for his first tent was to reach communities that did not, up to then, receive any Wesleyan ministry. The whole tenor of Tent Methodism's evangelical witness was one of highly dedicated, hard working preachers proclaiming the Christian message to people who had rarely come into contact with it. Unfortunately, when their supply of preachers became depleted the work quickly declined and ceased. That was not a situation unique to the Tent Methodists.

---

44   Jenny Uglow, *The Lunar Men. 'The Friends who made the Future: 1730-1810'* (London: Faber and Faber, 2002), pp.411-13.

45   Hempton, *Religion of the People*, p.126.

46   *Minutes of Methodist Conference* (1820), p147, answers 6 and 7 to question 26.

47   Victory Purdy, *Thoughts on the case of the Local Preachers in the Methodist Connexion* (Bristol, 1820).

Clyde Binfield made no distinctions between the various Nonconformist denominations when he wrote that 'the real problem was their failure to replenish their stock'[48] of preachers and members. The Bible Christians in their Devonport circuit were concerned in 1820, that 'there are a great many attentive hearers but they do not join Society'.[49] The Primitive Methodists found that in many places initial success did not continue and societies ceased to function. The difference, though, between the experience of Primitive Methodists and Bible Christians on one hand, and the Tent Methodists on the other, was that the Tent Methodists did not succeed in reaching a critical mass of members, societies and leaders that enabled them to survive disappointments in some places because there were other places where progress was being achieved. Bible Christians, in particular, seemed to have attracted several generations of the same families into their work, coupled with which there was considerable marriage between the main families which served to produce an even greater degree of commitment and loyalty. Apart from a daughter who regularly accompanied Pocock to his preaching appointments, no other children were ever mentioned as Tent Methodists. Some daughters became associated with parish churches, and a grand-daughter married a Church of England clergyman. There was, then, no family succession to carry on Tent Methodism's evangelical work.

Wesleyan Methodism, too, suffered a loss of membership in the 1820's as the reference to Joseph Entwisle's experience as a Wesleyan itinerant in Bristol in the previous chapter showed. Bristol Wesleyan leaders during the following decade also gave expression to several concerns. A letter from William Leach to Jabez Bunting in 1831 suggested that little ministerial attention was given to rural areas[50] where many poor lived. Another letter two years later clearly showed that the position of trustees continued to cause friction,[51] and in 1841 a minister claimed that attendances at meetings were small and concluded, 'we are far from being in a healthy state of religion in this city'.[52] In September 1835, Joseph Fowler, another leading Wesleyan itinerant, wrote to a great personal friend following that year's conference. He had just taken up an appointment in Bristol, but was already moved to write, 'I have itinerated sufficiently to make very painful and depressing discoveries. Never in my

---

48   Clyde Binfield, *So Down to Prayers* (London: J.M. Dent, 1977), p.9.

49   Thomas Shaw, *The Bible Christians 1815-1907* (London: Epworth Press, 1965), p.35.

50   Ward (ed.), *Early Victorian Methodism*, pp.7-8, letter from William Leach to Jabez Bunting, 14 February 1831.

51   Ward (ed.), *Early Victorian Methodism*, pp.37-38, letter from James Wood to Jabez Bunting, 6 June 1833.

52   Ward (ed.), *Early Victorian Methodism*, pp.252-53, letters from Abraham E. Farrar to Jabez Bunting, 15 February 1841 and 5 April 1841.

whole course did I meet with a society so uniformly dead... We have two places in the country called chapels; but, alas! they are almost without congregations. We are minus eighty of the number of members printed in the Minutes'.[53] Clearly the Wesleyan experience in Bristol during the 1820s and 1830s was not a universally happy one.

Other Methodist denominations, too, complained of lack of progress from time to time. In his history of the Bible Christians, R. Pyke asked 'Why should it have been that the Denomination practically ceased to open up any new territory at home after the first few years of its existence?'[54] Similarly, H.B. Kendall, in his substantial, two volume history of the Primitive Methodist Church, recounted the failures and disappointments as well as the successes.[55] The Methodist New Connexion had many problems to overcome, some of which proved intractable. For example, some of the chapels acquired from the Wesleyans had to be returned as a result of legal proceedings, and difficulties were encountered with preachers such as a Joseph Barker who was expelled and then attempted to cause much dissension.[56] Other dissenting denominations, notably the Quakers and Presbyterians, at certain times in the early nineteenth century and in certain districts, were in steady, if not rapid, decline. Despite the fact that the United Kingdom's population doubled in the first half of the nineteenth century, Quaker membership fell in that period continuing a trend that began in the previous century.[57] A similar pattern was evident among Presbyterians and Unitarians, thus failing to share in the general increase in membership among other denominations, especially the Methodists.[58]

Wesleyan Reaction to Secessions

It is relevant to assess the Wesleyan reaction to the Tent Methodism secession. Jabez Bunting's biographer used somewhat patronizing language in describing the Tent Methodists. The preachers were claimed to be 'zealous and heady' but 'doubtless did a great deal of good', although 'there is much danger of irregular agencies interfering with the ordained and systematic work'. Similar wording was employed to

---

53   Joseph Fowler, letter to Francis West dated 29 September 1835, quoted in Gregory, Benjamin, *Side Lights on the Conflicts of Methodism* (London, 1899), p.20.

54   Pyke, *The Golden Chain*, p.205.

55   Kendall, *Origin and History*, I, pp189-90, 196-98, 363.

56   Ward, *Religion and Society in England*, pp.273-75.

57   Watts, *Dissenters*, II, pp.98-99; and Currie *et al*, *Churches and Churchgoers*, p.156.

58   Currie *et al*, *Churches and Churchgoers*, pp.139-41, 156, 216; and Watts, *Dissenters*, II, pp.41, 96-97.

denigrate the activity in Ancoats, Manchester. The supporters were said to be 'malcontents' and later 'the place and its promoters were consigned to the tender mercies of the Court of Chancery'.[59] The local Wesleyan reaction in Bristol was at first equally bitter although Moore expressed the view soon afterwards that the secession should not have been allowed to happen. However, the opposition in certain quarters to Pocock's return to Wesleyanism fifteen years later showed that the hostility survived a long time in some people's minds. Few modern writers have made any reference to Tent Methodism, although John Bowmer states that the group was 'a loose federation of free-lance evangelists',[60] a dismissive statement simply suggesting a lack of discipline. There was no acknowledgement by him of any effective evangelism being achieved, either in the eighteen years to 1832, or later when the preachers worked in other denominations.

The lack of much Christian charity towards the Tent Methodists was also apparent in public utterings about other offshoots of Wesleyanism. John Gaulter, an itinerant from 1785, in a sermon preached in the early 1820's, referred to secessions as events that 'floated like a bubble on the water, but soon broke to pieces'.[61] While the annual address at the 1824 Wesleyan conference congratulated the denomination on the absence of divisions, a few years later the Organ Case events in Leeds in 1827 prompted an outburst in the annual address the following year prepared by Bunting as President and Robert Newton as Secretary. The departure from Wesleyanism of those who objected to the denomination's handling of the issue was described in that address as 'so infinitely beneath the noble and generous spirit of the Gospel; so obviously opposed to reason and moderation; so contrary to the example of the holiest and best of Christians...and is so clearly a snare of Satan'.[62] No recognition then that a contrary view might just have some validity. A leading writer on Bible Christian affairs has written that 'the nineteenth century was notoriously the period of Methodist disunion and there were those who feared that its fissiparousness was endemic'.[63] It might, of course, be entirely coincidential, but it is interesting to note that very soon after the Tent Methodist secession, the *Methodist Magazine*, the name used since 1798, changed to the *Wesleyan-Methodist Magazine* in January 1822. The 'Prospectus of the Third Series', as the new format was described, included an explanation that the word 'Wesleyan' was incorporated in

---

59 Bunting, *Life of Jabez Bunting*, II, pp.170-171.
60 Bowmer, *Pastor and People*, p.80.
61 Shaw, *Bible Christians*, p.26.
62 *Minutes of Methodist Conference* (1828), p.409.
63 Shaw, *Bible Christians*, p.74.

the title 'partly for the sake of more perfect distinction',[64] although there was no reference to any specific schism or secession.

The Tent Methodists were not alone in being a group that became established but then struggled to survive as an independent sect. In the city of Bristol, where the Tent Methodists originated, a French Huguenot group had acquired a chapel in Orchard Street but had ceased to worship in 1825. The Bible Christians early in their existence established a Bristol circuit, but by 1827 numbers had fallen to only fifty and by 1829 'the work in Bristol had ceased completely'.[65] It was many years later before the denomination gained a secure foothold in the city. A little known group called the 'Revivalist Methodists' were active in parts of Derbyshire, Shropshire, Staffordshire and Leicestershire and lasted a few years from about 1821. In 1823 'they had 13 circuits, 25 travelling preachers, and 71 local preachers'. They were likened to the Primitive Methodists, held their first conference in 1821 at Northampton, but seemed to have ceased to exist by 1827.[66] The Wesleyan Methodist Association was formed in 1835 with a membership that was concentrated in south Lancashire, but they also founded a society in Camelford, and elsewhere in Cornwall.[67] A few years earlier a splinter group that became known as the Arminian Methodists was established in Derby and spread to parts of the Peak District, Leicester, Nottingham, and a few other places in the Midland counties.[68] Most of their societies joined the Wesleyan Methodist Association in 1836 or 1837. In these cases a major cause of the disagreement was the perceived authoritarian leadership style of Wesleyanism in general and Bunting in particular. Secessions occurred, too, in north Wales in 1831 at Tregarth, and at about the same time at Towyn, Merioneth.[69] The Swedenborgians attracted a Wesleyan Society in Brightlingsea and St Osyth, Essex, as well as an Independent Methodist society based in Westhoughton, near Manchester.[70]

It should not be thought, however, that it was only Wesleyanism that suffered secessions. William O'Bryan severed his connection with the Bible Christians after he had led them for fourteen years. Again, principally, it was the degree of power being exercised by one man that was the underlying dispute. While his splinter group rejoined the main body six years later, O'Bryan himself did not. The Primitive Methodists

64   *The Wesleyan-Methodist Magazine for the Year 1822* (London, 1822), p.3.

65   Leslie M. Wollen, 'An Early Bible Christian Minute Book', *WHS Proceedings* 36 (1967-68), p.124.

66   Hulbert, *Religions of Britain*, p.288.

67   Watts, *Dissenters*, II, pp.466-467.

68   William Parkes, *The Arminian Methodists: The Derby Faith; A Wesleyan Aberration in Pursuit of Revivalism and Holiness* (Cannock: Charles H. Goodwin, 1995).

69   Watts, *Dissenters*, II, p.34.

70   Lineham, 'English Swedenborgians', pp.353 and 360.

suffered a minor, short-lived, secession in 1822 when a Mr W. Wildbur, who had been sent to Lincoln in 1819, fell out with the authorities in the Nottingham circuit and persuaded seventy members in Norfolk to secede.[71] Other offshoots of Primitive Methodism emerged in Nottinghamshire in 1828 over the question of ministerial stipends, and about ten years later a splinter group was formed that took the title 'Original Methodists', attracting members from some of the societies on the Nottinghamshire and Derbyshire border.

Tent Methodism—Methodist or Congregational?

At this stage it is useful to attempt to assess to what extent the Tent Methodist sect was, indeed, Methodist at all. References have been made earlier in this book to the influences of, and likenesses to, Congregationalism, but how strong were the links?

Before 1820 the tent preachers felt themselves to be a valuable arm of the Wesleyans, evangelizing in areas not then reached by the denomination. In addition, they used an entirely appropriate means to do so. Subsequently, the *Tent Methodist Magazine* for 1823 followed a very similar format to the *Wesleyan Methodist Magazine*, and the *Collection of Hymns* compiled by Pocock and Pyer contained material entirely consistent with other Methodist hymn books. The report of the Tent Methodist annual meeting held in 1823 indicated that the sect was organized along Methodist lines as there were references to classes, societies, circuits and districts. The only religious periodical to carry an advertisement for the *Tent Methodist Magazine* was the *Wesleyan Methodist Magazine*. There was an annual address to all members written by the chairman and secretary, very similar in style and content to Wesleyan ones.

There were, however, two fundamental differences between the 1823 Tent Methodist annual meeting and the Wesleyan Methodist annual conferences. The Tent Methodist meeting held in Manchester was not only attended by ministers of other denominations, but several of them spoke and proposed or seconded resolutions. Congregationalists, Baptists and a member of the Church of England all took part.[72] Secondly, all Tent Methodist society members were entitled to attend the annual meeting. At Wesleyan Methodist annual conferences at this time in the nineteenth century, only the chosen 100 itinerant ministers were entitled to take a decision-making part in the proceedings.

---

71   Petty, *History of Primitive Methodist Connexion*, p.174. Also see R.W. Ambler, 'Preachers and the Plan-Patterns of Activity in Early Primitive Methodism', *WHS Proceedings* 46, (1987-88), pp.21-31.

72   *TM Magazine*, pp.149-156.

As time went by, Congregational influences became more and more important. For example, the 1824 version of the rules, prepared mainly if not entirely by Pyer, contained a specific requirement that church meetings of all societies were to be held quarterly, but the 1820 rules makes no such stipulation. Church meetings played a central role in both Congregational and Baptist church life. It is possible that as George Pocock took a less important part in the life of the sect, John Pyer's authority increased. As has been shown, Pyer was influenced by a number of Congregational ministers in Bristol and latterly in Manchester, and he eventually became one of their number. It is likely that the Tent Methodist churches in Manchester and Liverpool became 'congregational' several years before they joined the Congregational Union in 1827. There is no evidence, though, that any formal decision was taken to accept the Calvinist principles of Congregationalism. It was a matter of polity, not doctrine, and gave Pyer much needed support from fellow Nonconformists.

Elsewhere, with several Tent Methodist societies in close proximity to one another and not subject to Pyer's day to day involvement from 1826, the Methodist circuit and district system prevailed throughout the sect's existence. The likelihood was, though, that each circuit would have had greater autonomy than under a Wesleyan regime. Furthermore, out of necessity the authority and influence of local preachers and lay members was much more significant. While the Wesleyan Methodist Association, and later the United Methodist Free Church, came nearest to the Tent Methodists in polity, the Tent Methodists, if their rules were scrupulously followed, gave much greater freedom to individual members. Tent Methodism, in its later years, was not dominated by Pocock and Pyer in the same way that the Rev. Robert Eckett controlled the Wesleyan Methodist Association—a reason perhaps for Tent Methodism's failure to capitalize on a promising start. Other than in Manchester and Liverpool, most of the Tent Methodists seemed to choose a variety of Methodist groups to join when the sect declined and then folded in the six years to 1832. Unlike the Protestant Methodists who survived as an independent sect for eight years before its 4,000 members joined the Wesleyan Methodist Association in 1836,[73] the Tent Methodists, probably because there was no regional concentration anywhere, dispersed in many different directions.

---

73   John A. Vickers (ed.), *A Dictionary of Methodism in Britain and Ireland* (Peterborough: Epworth Press, 2000), pp.105, 106 and 283; and Currie, *Methodism Divided*, pp.220-222.

Conclusion: The Impact of Tent Methodism

One of the early twentieth-century histories of Methodism, referring to the offshoots of Wesleyanism, recorded that 'by far the greater number have long since passed away and been forgotten. They perished quickly'.[74] Indeed they did, but this study has shown that Tent Methodism's influence and contribution to Nonconformist evangelical effort has been underestimated by twentieth-century historians. John Bowmer claimed that the Tent Methodists 'did no damage to the Wesleyan cause'.[75] Similarly, David Gowland, referring only to the Manchester work, dismissed the efforts as 'singularly unsuccessful',[76] and W.R. Ward wrote that the Tent Methodists 'soon proved dismally unsuccessful'.[77] Frank Baker merely records that the Tent Methodists, among other groups, 'are remembered only by queer names in particular localities'.[78] It is harder now to substantiate these inadequate assessments in the light of the material that has become available. Inaccuracies, such as quoting 1825 as the date of the Tent Methodist withdrawal from Wesleyanism in *The History of the Methodist Church in Great Britain*,[79] should not recur. The greater knowledge of Pocock should prevent him being described in the future as simply 'a quaint messenger' or an 'eccentric'.[80] The fact is that for a short time and in a few places the Tent Methodists made a significant impact, and this understanding can now be more widely acknowledged.

On the other hand, the value of Tent Methodism should not be exaggerated. It did not survive as an independent sect for more than about ten years and there were very many parts of the country where it established no presence at all. It failed to reach a critical mass in any particular region of the country which, if accomplished, might just have enabled the group to overcome the disappointments and frustrations that resulted in a rapid decline. Like other offshoots of Wesleyanism, the preachers worked exceptionally hard in an environment which was often not conducive to achieving progress. The antagonism they faced from Wesleyans in Bristol and Manchester, and mobs in Birmingham, were just examples of difficulties they faced that finally prompted them to give up the work. The lack of permanency was heightened by Pocock's apparent conclusion that he did not wish to pursue any long term ambitions, and

---

74   Townsend, Workman and Eayrs (eds), *New History of Methodism*, II, p.557.
75   Bowmer, *Pastor and People*, p.81.
76   Gowland, *Methodist Secessions*, p.24.
77   Ward, *Religion and Society in England*, p.83.
78   Frank Baker, *A Charge to Keep* (London: Epworth Press, 1947), p.40.
79   Davies *et al* (eds), *A History of the Methodist Church*, II, p.213.
80   R.B. Pugh (ed.), *The Victoria History of the Counties of England: Volume 3. Wiltshire* (London: Institute of Historical Research, University of London, 1976),p.142.

Barnett's and Pyer's respective decisions to join the Baptist and Independent denominations. The sect was simply too weak to be able to cope with the loss of the three principal actors, and the two Smiths, Samuel and George. The group did not develop an inherent loyalty, or sense of community togetherness, which, if achieved, may have resulted in new leaders emerging to take the sect forward. Instead the membership probably either reverted to Wesleyanism, or transferred with the leaders to their newly found denominations, or drifted and attached themselves to no other Christian community.

It is difficult to disagree with a retrospective comment about the Methodist divisions of the late eighteenth and first half of the nineteenth centuries included in a history written in 1897 of the first 100 years of the Methodist New Connexion: 'If the concessions already made in Wesleyan Methodism could have been conceded a hundred years ago, no secession would have taken place, and English Methodism might not have had any divisions in it today'.[81] In later years Wesleyans changed their collective minds about such issues as the role of lay members, the acceptability of open air and tent meetings for worship, and the use of unfermented wine at communion services. Had they done so earlier, the secessions of the early nineteenth century might not have occurred.

The demise of the Tent Methodists, albeit that many members undoubtedly joined and served other denominations, did not lessen the need for evangelical activity in the country as a whole. Indeed, in 1830, by which time Tent Methodist influence was drawing to a close, Charles Blomfield, then Bishop of London and particularly concerned for urban parishoners, was moved to write an impassioned 'letter' to the inhabitants of his diocese. In it he abhorred 'the profanation of the Christian Sabbath..,[which] seems to threaten the destruction of all religious habits in the lower classes of society'.[82] He complained of the opening on Sundays of many businesses selling food and drink, the scarcity of places of worship, drunkenness, prostitution, and the gathering of 'youthful profligates of both sexes, for the purpose of fighting, pigeon-shooting, gambling, and all kinds of improper pastimes'.[83] Laws to control and prevent the perceived abuses were, he claimed, ineffective, and the clergy were, also, unable to persuade 'the poor lamented sinners...in the abatement of those evils'.[84] The need for the dedication of people like Pocock and Pyer was no less urgent in the 1830's as it had been in the previous fifteen years. That this was so was tacitly acknowledged by the Wesleyan authorities, judged by the content of the

---

81   Packer (ed.), *Centenary of the Methodist New Connexion*, p.64.

82   C.J. Blomfield, *A Letter on the neglect of the Lord's Day addressed to the inhabitants of London and Westminster* (London, 1830), p.4.

83   Blomfield, *A Letter on the neglect*, p.14.

84   Blomfield, *A Letter on the neglect*, p.18.

annual addresses to conference members. In 1832, for example, each member was exhorted 'to bear his testimony against all the vices which meets his eye and revolt his heart... It would shame transgressors; and Sabbath-breaking, intemperance, and other open sins, would scarcely be so prevalent among us as they are...unconcern in religious matters could scarcely exist for any length of time in its present deplorable degree'.[85] Here, then, is evidence that the Church of England and the Wesleyan Methodists were both concerned in the 1830s at the sinful nature of English society, a theme frequently focused upon by the Tent Methodists.

It is inevitable that any academic study of this kind concentrates on the firm, visible evidence of the material that has been found, and the interpretation of it. G.M. Trevelyan, one of the most important of social historians of the twentieth century, noted that 'historians and antiquarians have amassed by patient scholarship a great sum of information, and have edited innumerable records, letters and journals...yet even this mass of knowledge is small indeed compared with the sum total of social history'.[86] Most of the documentation on Tent Methodism is subjective in its nature—for example, pamphlets were written with great intensity of feeling revealing the author's views, obituaries concentrate on certain aspects, and private manuscript letters reveal personal thoughts not found in written material for public perusal. Even the minutes of annual conferences and official records of meetings are not objective. Yet all this material that has survived is 'small indeed' compared with the contemporary evidence that has been lost.

The requirements of any in-depth analysis of this kind are to find and test the evidence, discuss alternative explanations, compare experiences, place the subject matter in the context of wider religious and social issues of the period, and produce an assessment. All this has been done, but that does not quite complete the work on Tent Methodism. The evangelical fervour and dedication is sometimes, unfortunately, allowed to appear of lesser significance and is more difficult to express. During the period of Tent Methodist existence from 1814 to 1832, the movement touched the hearts and minds of many people, some of whom were never members. A few of those who met Tent Methodism but did not embrace it have been mentioned in this work—many more have not for they are simply unknown. They have disappeared into history without a memorial of any kind. Those parts of inner Bristol, Manchester, London and Liverpool where Tent Methodists worked for several years, are now quite different than they were in the 1820s. For example, Canal Street and Horne Street,

---

85   *Minutes of Methodist Conference* (1832), p.182, 'The Annual Address', 6 August 1832, Robert Newton, President; Edmund Grindod, Secretary.
86   G.M. Trevelyan, *English Social History* (London: Longman, 1944), p.viii.

Ancoats, Manchester, on the corner of which once stood a large chapel used to further Christian influence for Tent Methodism, no longer exist. Current maps show much of that area as simply 'Ancoats, Central Retail Park'.[87] The houses in streets such as Allum Street, Pot Street, Factory Street and Back Cotton Street, all conjuring impressions of an industrial past, which in total contained many thousands of working-class souls, have long since been demolished. Nonetheless, the successors of the families who once lived there may now be providing Christian service totally oblivious to the history of their forebears 180 years ago.

The evidence in this work indicates that the Tent Methodist movement, albeit briefly, assumed significance in Britain, but equally certainly it can be stated that the known impact was multiplied in ways that can never be fully appreciated. The influence and Christian service of Pocock, Pyer, George Smith and Barnett, among many others, continued among Wesleyans, Congregationalists and Baptists respectively, and with Samuel Smith emigrating to Canada and Henry Payne, a trustee of Dursley Tent Methodist chapel, moving to the United States of America, a part of Tent Methodism went into other denominations, even far beyond these shores, well after the sect had ceased to exist—hence the sub-title to one of the sections in this chapter from John 4.37: 'one soweth, and another reapeth'. All this can, doubtless, be said about the other groups that grew from Wesleyanism after John Wesley's death in 1791, but Tent Methodism did seem to have an influence among people far greater than might have been expected. It is to be hoped that more can be uncovered about the group so as to extend still further the knowledge of its life, work, and the Christian evangelistic influence of its preachers.

Rupert Davies, one of Methodism's leading twentieth-century historians, presented, in 1991, a paper on the history of *Methodism in Bedminster*, an area of Bristol he knew very well. The information given about Tent Methodism in that address appears to have come entirely from a cursory study of the *Tent Methodist Magazine* published in monthly parts during 1823. He did not seem to have noticed from that magazine that for several years before 1820 Bedminster was chosen as the place to begin the evangelical 'season' in a tent and that there were reports of much blessing to those who attended the special opening services. He concluded his reference to Tent Methodism: 'The later history of Tent Methodism is wrapped in obscurity, so far as I know'. One of the ambitions for this work is that the word 'obscurity' will no longer be an appropriate one to use in relation to Tent Methodism. As Rupert Davies correctly said in his paper: 'the little-chronicled Tent Methodists...do not rate a mention in either the old or the new official

---

87   *AZ Street Plan Manchester and Salford City Centres* (Sevenoaks: Geographers A-Z Map Company, n.d. [c.1996]), grid reference N7.

histories of Methodism'.[88] His successors, presenting future histories, will, hopefully, find it relevant to make reference to the activities, for eighteen years, of a group which is worthy of greater recognition for the spiritual concern it showed for people, particularly those who suffered especially harshly in the parts of England and Wales where Tent Methodists worked.

88   Rupert E. Davies, 'Methodism in Bedminster', address to the WHS Bristol Branch, 26 October 1991, *Bulletin* 62 (1991), pp.4-5.

Appendix A

Branwhite delt.   Woodman sculpt.

M.ʳ GEORGE POCOCK,

BRISTOL.

George Pocock (1774–1843)
Picture from the *Tent Methodist Magazine* (1823), inside front cover.

REV? JOHN PYER.

John Pyer (1790–1859)
Picture courtesy of the National Library of Scotland

Appendix B

Places known to have been visited by tent preachers 1814-1819

Almonsbury, Gloucestershire	1818
Andover, Hampshire	1818
Arlingham, Gloucestershire	1819
Backwell, Somerset	1816
Barrow, Somerset	1814, 1815
Bath, Somerset	1814
Bedminster, Somerset	1814, 1815, 1816, 1817, 1818
Berkeley, Gloucestershire	1819
Bishop Sutton, Somerset	1816
Bishport, Somerset	1815, 1816
Brislington, Somerset	1814, 1815
Cam, Gloucestershire	1819
Cambridge, Gloucestershire	1819
Charlton, Hampshire	1818
Chew Magna, Somerset	1815
Cleeve Wood, Gloucestershire	1816
Coaley, Gloucestershire	1819
Coalpit Heath, Gloucestershire	1818
Cockroad, Gloucestershire	1817
Collingbourne, Berkshire	1814
Compton Greenfield, Gloucestershire	1816
Dursley, Gloucestershire	1819
Eastington, Gloucestershire	1819
Elberton, Gloucestershire	1817
Fishponds, Gloucestershire	1818
Framilode, Gloucestershire	1819
Frampton Cotterell, Gloucestershire	1818, 1819
Halmore, Gloucestershire	1819
Hodson, Wiltshire	1817
Hungerford, Berkshire	1814, 1817, 1818
Inkpen, Berkshire	1814
Iron Acton, Gloucestershire	1817
Jeffrey's Hill, Gloucestershire	1815, 1816, 1817
Kendleshire, Gloucestershire	1817
Kingsclere, Hampshire	1818
Kintbury, Berkshire	1814
Lambourn, Berkshire	1818
Littleton, Gloucestershire	1814

Lower Wallop, Hampshire	1818
Marlborough, Wiltshire	1817, 1818
May's Hill, Gloucestershire	1818
Meare, Somerset	1816
Milbury Heath, Gloucestershire	1816, 1818
Mumbles, Glamorgan	1819
Neath, Glamorgan	1819
Newbury, Berkshire	1817
Newport, Isle of Wight	1818
North Dibley, Gloucestershire	1819
Olveston, Gloucestershire	1816, 1818, 1819
Pill, Somerset	1817
Rangeworthy, Gloucestershire	1817, 1818
Rose Green, Gloucestershire	1815
Rudgeway, Gloucestershire	1816, 1817
Ryde, Isle of Wight	1818
Shepton Mallet, Somerset	1816
Shirehampton, Gloucestershire	1817
Sison Common, Gloucestershire	1817
Soundwell, Gloucestershire	1819
Southampton, Hampshire	1818
Stanley, Gloucestershire	1819
Stockbridge, Hampshire	1818
Swansea, Glamorgan	1819
Swindon, Wiltshire	1817
Thornbury, Gloucestershire	1816, 1817
Tockington, Gloucestershire	1816, 1817
Trooper's Hill, Gloucestershire	1815
Uley, Gloucestershire	1819
Vernham, Hampshire	1818
Wanborough, Wiltshire	1814
Wantage, Oxfordshire	1818
Wells, Somerset	1816
Westbury-on-Severn, Gloucestershire	1819
Westbury-on-Trym, Gloucestershire	1816
Weyhill, Hampshire	1818
Whitchurch, Somerset	1814, 1819
Whitehall, Gloucestershire	1814
Wickwar, Gloucestershire	1817
Winchester, Hampshire	1818
Wotton-under-Edge, Gloucestershire	1819
Wroughton, Wiltshire	1817
Wycomb Heath, Berkshire	1818

Appendix   C

Additional places known to have been visited by Tent Methodist preachers from 1820 onwards

Abercairne, Monmouthshire
Bedwyn Common,Wiltshire
Box, Wiltshire
Birmingham, Warwickshire
Bradford on Avon, Wiltshire
Bristol: Brandon Hill
               Docks
               Pithay Chapel
               Poyntz Pool
               St PhilipsWest Street
Broad Hinton, Wiltshire
Cheltenham, Gloucestershire
Cherhill, Wiltshire
Chisenbury, Wiltshire
Clay Hill, Kingswood, Gloucestershire
Compton Bassett, Wiltshire
Cwm Dws, Monmouthshire
Ditchampton, Wiltshire
East Harnham, Wiltshire
Enford, Wiltshire
Fisherton Angar, Wiltshire
Fyfield, Wiltshire
Lockeridge, Wiltshire
London: Cooper's Gardens
               Hare Street Fields
               Webb Square, Shoreditch
Manchester, Ancoats, Lancashire
Milford, Wiltshire
Milton Lilbourne, Wiltshire
Newport, Monmouthshire
Nibley, Gloucestershire
Oare, Wiltshire
Ogbourne St George, Wiltshire
Preshute, Wiltshire
Ruckley, Wiltshire
Rushton, Wiltshire
Salisbury, Wiltshire
Staple Hill, Gloucestershire

Stinchcomb Hill, Gloucestershire
Tetbury, Gloucestershire
Thornhill, Hampshire
Upavon, Wiltshire
Urchfont, Wiltshire
Warminster, Wiltshire
Waterly Bottom, Gloucestershire
Wilsford, Wiltshire
Winterbourne, Wiltshire
Wootton Bassett, Wiltshire
Wootton Rivers, Wiltshire

Appendix D

List of known Tent Methodist preachers and dates

Peter Arrivé (1817-1825?)
John Barnett (1819-1826) became a Baptist minister
Samuel Bryant (1820-1827) died 12 January 1827
William Bryant (1820-?)
Brother D. (1820-?)
John Gosling (1818-?)
Brother H. (1820-?) possibly Henry Hall, or George Hamley, or John
    Hollister
Samuel Long (1820-?)
Brother M. (1820-?) probably William Merrifield
Henry Payne (1820-?) emigrated to America
George Pocock (1814-1835/36) rejoined Wesleyans
Mr Pring (1820-?)
Victory Purdy (1820-1822) died 28 June 1822
John Pyer (1814-1827) became a Congregational minister
Henry Roberts (1817-?)
James Roberts (1814-?)
George Smith (1820-1827) became a Congregational minister
Samuel Smith (1817-1829) emigrated to Canada
Brother S...y (1820-?)
John Sweetapple (1821?-?)
William Williams (1822?-?)

London

The 'Independent or Tent Methodists' preaching plan for London covering the period from 28 April 1822 to 25 August 1822 shows the following preachers: Messrs Cooper, Dennis, Geary, Gunn, Jeffs, Jones, Lefevre, Linsey, Palmer, Rawlins, Trendel and Woodland; and the following exhorters: Messrs Freeman, Meek, Parkhouse, Steward and Vary. There were twenty five prayer leaders, some of whom were also exhorters.

Appendix E

Places where societies were known to have been formed

Bath		1820
Birmingham		1823?
Bristol:	Pithay	1820
	St Philip's	1820
Chisenbury, Wiltshire		1821
Coalpit Heath, Gloucestershire		1820
Cwm Dws, Monmouthshire		1821
Dursley, Gloucestershire		1820
Frampton Cotterell, Gloucestershire		1820
Kingswood:	Hanham	1821
	Rose Green	1820
	Soundwell	1820 known as Colliers' Temple
	Staple Hill	1820
Liverpool		1823
Lockeridge, Wiltshire		1820
London:	Dalston	1822?
	Dockhead	1822?
	Dunk Street	1822?
	Hare Street Fields	1821
	Lambeth	1822?
	Saunders' Gardens	1822?
	Squirries Street	1821?
	Twig Folly	1822?
	Webb Square	1820
Manchester: Ancoats		1821
Marlborough, Wiltshire		1821
Milton Lilbourne, Wiltshire		1823
Newbury, Berkshire		1824
Preshute, Wiltshire		1823?
Ruckley, Wiltshire		1821
Salisbury, Wiltshire		1823
Tetbury, Gloucestershire		1823
Urchfont, Wiltshire		1822
Wotton-under-Edge, Gloucestershire		1820

Appendix F

Bristol and South Gloucestershire

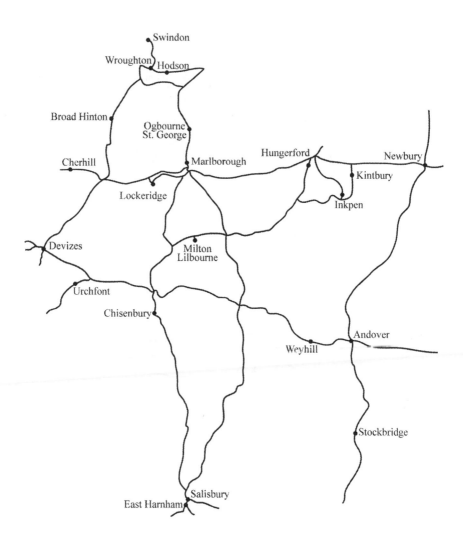

Wiltshire

England and Wales

Appendix G
Wesleyan Circuits: Membership

Date	National GB Membership	Bristol	Kingswood	Downend	Dursley	Bath
1819	196,605	2,690	490	460	345	825
1820	191,217	2,523	460	432	406	780
1821	200,354	2,545	480	460	471	800
1822	211,392	2,580	480	430	510	950
1823	219,398	2,610	500	430	504	1,140
1824	226,939	2,620	500	453	490	1,280
1825	228,646	2,580	515	457	500	1,290
1826	231,045	2,570	520	457	530	1,230
1827	237,239	2,542	520	440	600	1,200
1828	245,194	2,598	640	447	600	1,200
1829	247,529	2,590	650	450	560	1,190
1830	248,592	2,590	850	424	505	1,260
1831	249,119	2,705	850	442	520	1,218

Notes:
1) Includes London North from 1823 when the London East cicuit split.
2) Includes Manchester North and South from 1825, and a total of four circuits from 1828.
3) Includes Liverpool North and South from 1827.
Source:
Annual Conference Minutes.

Hungerford	Salisbury	London East (1)	Manchester (2)	Liverpool
340	600	4,400	3,170	3,250
355	500	4,500	3,025	3,250
339	550	4,484	3,050	3,800
350	575	4,669	3,206	3,700
345	600	3,862	3,283	3,550
353	600	4,013	3,288	3,468
338	615	4,110	3,550	3,420
350	610	4,134	4,000	3,000
338	645	4,290	4,600	3,132
334	650	4,230	6,560	3,032
350	680	4,398	6,225	3,134
420	690	4,240	5,955	3,270
360	744	4,175	6,012	3,455

Bibliography

Primary Sources

a) Manuscript

(I) BRISTOL RECORD OFFICE

Anon., *A Short History of Portland Street Wesleyan Chapel, Bristol, and its surroundings with brief notices of some of the principal persons and events connected with Methodism in the City* (n.d., BRO 21780/37(a)).

— *Circuit Schedule Book for Bristol North Circuit 1839-1845* (BRO 21780(23)).

Pocock, George, Letter to Rev. H.T. Ellacombe dated 13 October 1842.

Mr Skitt, Letter to Mr Jno Hall dated 24 August 1822.

Stewards Account Book for Frampton Cotterell Chapel [Wesleyan].

Wood, James and William Phillips, Letter to Circuit Stewards of Bristol South Circuit, 12 June 1833.

(II) DREW UNIVERSITY, MADISON, NEW JERSEY, USA

Stanley, Jacob, Letter to Rev. Henry Moore dated 20 December 1839.

(III) FROME PARISH CHURCH REGISTERS

Marriage Register entry No. 1125 recording marriage of George Pocock and Elizabeth Rose on 27 April 1797.

(IV) GLOUCESTERSHIRE RECORD OFFICE

Indenture: Purchase of land for chapel in Dursley, 17 July 1821 (GRO D2719/2-3).

(V) JOHN RYLANDS UNIVERSITY LIBRARY OF MANCHESTER

Benson, Joseph, Letter to William Smith and Michael Longridge, 8 November 1796 (JR PLP/7/9/12).

Benson, Joseph, Letter to Walter Griffiths (?), 20 July 1813, (JR PLP/7/11).

Coke, Thomas, Letter to Mr Gridley, 4 June 1782.

— Letter to Ezekiel Cooper, 12 January 1799.

Noyes, Harry, Letter to Jabez Bunting, 19 January [July?] 1825.

Register Book for Chapels, built, enlarged or purchased since the Conference held at Sheffield in 1817 (JR DDPD 58).

(VI) PUBLIC RECORD OFFICE

Indenture: Purchase of land for chapel at Hanham, 23 August 1822 (C54/10086).
Last Will and Testament of George Pocock, 25 November 1842.

(VII) WILTSHIRE RECORD OFFICE

Minutes of Monthly Meetings of Wiltshire Quakers from 1801 to 1818 (WRO 854/18).
Returns to Wiltshire Trinity Sessions, 1829 [Re: Dissenter Meeting places].

b) Printed

Anon. ('A trustee and layman'), *An Apology for the Methodists of the New Connexion illustrating the origin of the Division in 1797; its commencement, progress, present state, influence and prospects.* Conference Office [of MNC] (Hanley, 1815).

Anon., *A Parochial Minister's Affectionate Expostulation with those inhabitants of his parish who neglect the public worship of Almighty God* (Bristol, 1819).

Anon., *Plan devised by some preachers and Trustees of the Gloucester, Stroud, Cheltenham and Dursley circuits, at Gloucester, 5th June 1832*

Anon., *Some Account of the Life, Ministry and Writings of Victory Purdy, the Kingswood Collier* (Bristol, 1822).

Anon., *Memoirs of the Life and Character of Samuel Bryant, a Kingswood Collier* (Bristol, 1827).

Anon., *A short Narration or Circumstances connected with the life and death of John Horwood who was executed at Bristol, Friday, April 13, 1821 aged eighteen years and two days* (n.p., n.d.).

Arminian Magazine (May and June, 1790).

Ashmead, G.C., *Plan of the City of Bristol and its Suburbs* (Bristol, 1828).

Bielby, Knott and Bielby, *This Map of Birmingham Engraved from a minute Trigonometrical Survey made in the years 1824 and 1825* (Birmingham, 1828).

Blomfield, C.J., *A letter on the neglect of the Lord's Day addressed to inhabitants of London and Westminster* (London: B. Fellowes, 1830).

— *Bristol Poll Book being a list of the Freeholders and Freemen who voted at General Election, for Members to Serve in Parliament for the City and County of Bristol* (October, 1812).

Bristol Weekly Newspapers between 1800 and 1847.

— *Felix Farley's Bristol Journal*

— *Bristol Mirror and General Advertiser*
— *Bristol Gazette*
— *Bristol Mercury*
Bunting, Jabez, *An Appeal to the Members of the Wesleyan Methodist Societies in Great Britain* (Leeds, 1827).
Congregational Magazine (1819, 1830, 1831).
Dix, T., *A New Map of the County of Monmouth Divided into Hundreds* (London: William Dalton, 10 February 1821).
Douglas, James, *The System of Methodism Further Exposed, and the Wiles of Priestcraft Investigated* (Newcastle, 1814).
Evangelical Magazine and Missionary Chronicle (1819, 1822, 1824, 1826, 1831, 1832).
Fletcher, Joseph, *The Funeral Sermon on the death of Rev W Thorp, delivered at Castle Green Chapel, Bristol, on Lord's Day Morning, May 26, 1833* (London: Westley and Davies, 1833).
— *Address given on the occasion of Rev John Pyer's 'Public Designation to the Office of City Missionary' in the Christian Instruction Society* (London, 21 April 1830).
Gosling, John and Thomas Hall, *Letter of Agreement* (2 December 1816).
Greenwood, C. and J., *Map of the County of Gloucester from an actual survey made in the year 1823* (London, 22 November 1824).
Gye's Bath Directory (1822 and 1824).
Hill, William, *An Alphabetical Arrangement of all the Wesleyan-Methodist Preachers and Missionaries* (London, 1824, 1827 and 1841).
Home Missionary Magazine, or Record of the Transactions of the Home Missionary Society (vols 5, 11, and 12; London: Richard Baynes, 1824, 1830 and 1831).
Horwood, Richard, *Plan of the Cities of London and Westminster* (London: William Faden, 3rd edn, 1813).
Hulbert, Charles, *The Religions of Britain: or a view of its various Christian Denominations;.....* (Shrewsbury, 1826).
Indenture: Re: chapel at Frampton Cotterell (19 September 1827).
Indenture: Lease of property in High Street, Marlborough (28th May 1831).
Indenture: Re: property on the south side of Oxford Street, Marlborough (2 July 1811).
Keene's Bath Directories (1819, 1824, 1826, 1829 and 1837).
Mathews' Bristol Directories (1793-1832).
Member of the Old Methodist Society, *An Exposition of the Proceedings of the Old Methodist Conference* (Bristol, 1820).
Minutes of Independent Methodist Yearly Meetings (1813 and 1835).

Minutes of Methodist New Connexion Annual Conferences (1810-1835).

Minutes of Wesleyan Methodist Annual Conferences (1806 onwards).

O'Bryan, William, *A Collection of Hymns for Arminian Bible Christians* (Stoke Damarel: S. Thorne, 1825).

Pigot, J. *A Plan of Manchester and Salford with the recent improvements* (Manchester, 1821, 1825 and 1833).

— *Commercial Directories; Cumberland, Lancashire, Westmorland; 1828 - 1829. Commercial Directory of Wiltshire* (1822, 1830, 1842).

Pocock, George, *A sketch of English History for the use of the young Gentlemen at Mr Pocock's Academy* (Bristol, 1832).

— *A Statement of Facts connected with the ejectment of Certain Ministers from the Society of the Wesleyan Methodists in the City of Bristol in February and March 1820* (Bristol, 1820).

— 'An Accompaniment to Mr G Pocock's Patent Terrestrial Globe', paper read to Bristol Philosophical Institution, 23 November 1829.

— Handbill '....Whereas ....' re-Charles Greenly, 23 March 1820.

— Poster 'The Tent', notice of public meetings, 29 March 1820.

— *Sacred Lyrics for Youth* (London: Sherwood Gilbert and Piper, 1838).

— *The aeroplaustic art, or navigation in the air by the use of kites or buoyant sails* (London, 1827).

Pocock, George *et al, Facts Without a Veil; or A Further Account of the Circumstances...* (Bristol, 19 May 1820).

Pocock, George and John Pyer (eds), *A Collection of Hymns* (Bristol: Albion Press, 1825).

— *Portland Chapel Register of Baptisms* (1792-1823).

— *Portland Chapel Register of Burials* (1810-1830).

— *Portland Street Journal Minutes of Trustees Meetings 1794-1860*.

— *Primitive Methodist Deed Poll* (February 1830).

Purdy, Victory, *Thoughts on the case of the Local Preachers in the Methodist Connexion* (Bristol, 1820) (quoted as Vicary).

— *Register of Bristol Society 1808-1820* [Wesleyan Methodists].

— *Report of the Committee of the Home Mission established among the Methodists of the New Connexion for the year ended 1st June 1819* (Hanley, 1819).

Reynolds, Joseph, *A Selection of Hymns and Spiritual Songs, devised for a body of Independent Methodists* (Cambridge, 1822).

Robinson, Mark, *Observations on the system of Wesleyan Methodism; to Rev R Johnson* (London: Stationers' Hall, 1824).

— *Rules of the Tent-Methodists or Agrarian Society for Extending Christianity at Home* (Bristol, 1820).

— *Rules of the Tent-Methodists' Society* (Bristol: Albion Press, 1824).

— *Rules for the Regulation of a Society denominated The Community; (belonging to the London East Circuit)* (London, 1817).

Sherwood, W.S., *A Plan of the town and township of Liverpool with the Environs, 1825 and 1829* (Liverpool: J. Gore and Son, 1829).

Smith, G.C., *Bristol Fair but no Preaching!* (Bristol: T.D. Clark, 1823).

— *Preaching in the Open Air, and the origin of the Christian Instruction Society; being a Collection of Interesting and Important Documents...* (London: W.K. Wakefield, 1830).

Stocks, S. Junior, *A Reply to the Rev John Pyer's 'Few Plain and Indisputable Testimonies' Explanatory of the Affairs of Canal Street Chapel* (Manchester, 1830).

Taylor, Thomas, *Plan of Liverpool* (Liverpool, 1834).

— *Tent Methodists' Magazine and Register of Events Connected with the Spread of the Gospel at Home* (Bristol, 1823).

— *A Plan for the Preachers, Exhorters, & Prayer Leaders of the Independent or Tent Methodists, London* (28 April - 25 August [1822]).

— *The Imperial Magazine* 4 (1822).

Toase, William, 'Memoir of Mrs Elizabeth Arrivé', *Methodist Magazine* (April 1820 and May 1820), pp.290-98 and 368-79.

Tuck, Stephen, *Wesleyan Methodism in Frome* (Frome: Frome Quarterly Meeting, 1837).

Welch, Charles, *An Investigation of Mr Mark Robinson's 'Observations on the System of Wesleyan Methodism'* (Hull, 1825).

— *Wesleyan Methodist Magazine* (1820 onwards) (formerly *Methodist Magazine* up to 1821).

— *Wesleyan Methodist Preaching Plans* (Bristol and Kingswood circuits, March to June 1817 and December 1819 to March 1820).

— *Wesleyan Methodist Preaching Plan* (Bristol North Circuit, September to November 1840).

— *Wesleyan Methodist Preaching Plan* (London East, February to June 1819, June 1819 to January 1820, November 1819 to April 1820, April to September 1823).

— *Wesleyan Methodist Preaching Plan* (Manchester, January to April 1821).

Wood, Thomas, *A Biographical Sketch of the life and character of the late Mr James Bundy* (Bristol, 1818).

Wood, Thomas, *The Spirit of Calumny, Detected and Exposed; with suitable advices* (Bristol: Albion Press, 1820).

Wood, Thomas *et al*, *A Correct Statement of Facts, connected with what Mr George Pocock has termed the ejectment of Certain Ministers from the Society of Wesleyan Methodists in the City of Bristol'* (Bristol: Leaders' Meeting, 27 April 1820).

Theses

Lineham, P.J., 'The English Swedenborgians 1770-1840' (PhD thesis, University of Sussex, 1978).

Macquiban, T.S.A., 'Ministerial or Lay Aristocracy' (MA thesis, University of Bristol, 1986).

Sellers, Ian, 'Liverpool Nonconformity 1786-1914' (PhD thesis, University of Keele, 1969).

Vickers, John A., 'Methodism and Society in Central Southern England' (PhD thesis, University of Southampton, 1987).

Secondary Sources

a) Books

Ackroyd, Peter, *London: The Biography* (London: Chatto & Windus, 2000).

Anderson, James, *et al* (eds), *Society and Social Change: A Reader* (Milton Keynes: Open University, 1994).

Andrews, J.R., *George Whitefield: A Light Rising in Obscurity* (London: Morgan and Chase, [c.1865]).

Arthur, William, *The Successful Merchant* (London: Hamilton Adams, 1852).

Baker, Frank, *A Charge to Keep* (London: Epworth Press, 1947).

— *Baptist Handbook* (1864 and 1878).

Barber, B. Aquila, *A Methodist Pageant* (London: Holborn Publishing House, 1932).

Barnett, J.P. (ed.), *Memorials of the late Rev John Barnett of Blaby 'Faithful unto Death'* (Leicester: James Vice, 1878).

Bebb, E.D., *Nonconformity and Social and Economic Life 1660-1800* (London: Epworth Press, 1935).

Bebbington, D.W., *Evangelicalism in Modern Britain: A history from the 1730s to the 1980s* (London: Unwin Hyman, 1989).

Bett, Henry, *The Spirit of Methodism* (London: Epworth Press, 1937).

Binfield, Clyde, *So Down to Prayers: Studies in English Nonconformity 1780-1920* (London: J.M. Dent, 1977).

Booth, Frank, *Robert Raikes of Gloucester* (Redhill: National Christian Education Council, 1980).

Bourne, F.W., *The Bible Christians: Their Origin and History (1815-1900)* (London: Bible Christian Book Room, 1905).

Bowmer, John C., *Pastor and People* (London: Epworth Press, 1974).

— *Bristol Marriages 1800-1837: Part II. Bristol and Avon* (Bristol: Family History Society, 1982).

Brontë, Charlotte, *Shirley* (London: Penguin Books, 1974).

Brown, Kenneth D., *A Social History of the Nonconformist Ministry in England and Wales 1800-1930* (Oxford: Clarendon Press, 1988).

Brownlee, W. Methven, *W.G. Grace* (London: Iliffe & Son, 1887).

Bunting, T.P., *The Life of Jabez Bunting* (Vol. 1; London: Longmans, 1859; Vol. 2; London: T. Woolmer, 1887).

Catling, Christopher and Alison Merry, *Gloucestershire and Hereford and Worcester* (Harmondsworth: New Shell Guides, 1990).

Cavendish, Richard (ed.), *AA Road Book of Britain* (Basingstoke: Automobile Association, 1995).

Chadwick, Owen, *The Victorian Church: Part One 1829-1859* (London: SCM Press, 1987).

Chandler, J.H. (ed.), *Wiltshire Dissenters' Meeting House Certificates and Registrations 1689-1852* (Gloucester: Alan Sutton, 1985).

— *Congregational Year Book* (1846, 1860 and 1871).

Crittall, Elizabeth (ed.), *The Victoria History of the Counties of England: Volume 2. Wiltshire* (London: Institute of Historical Research, University of London, 1959).

Crofts, Bruce (ed.), *At Satan's Throne* (Bristol: White Tree Books, 1990).

Crothers, T.D. *et al* (eds.), *The Centenary of the Methodist New Connexion 1797-1897* (London: Geo. Burroughs, 1897).

Crowley, D.A. (ed.), *The Victoria History of the Counties of England: Volume 2. Gloucestershire* (London: Institute of Historical Research, University of London, 1983).

Currie, Robert, *Methodism Divided: A Study of the Sociology of Ecumenicalism* (London: Faber and Faber, 1968).

Currie, R., A. Gilbert and L. Horsley, *Churches and Churchgoers: Patterns of Church Growth in the British Isles since 1700* (Oxford: Clarendon Press, 1977).

Davies, Horton, *The English Free Churches* (London: Oxford University Press, 1963).

Davies, R.E., *Methodism* (London: Epworth Press, 1987).

Davies, R., A.R. George and G. Rupp (eds), *A History of the Methodist Church in Great Britain*, Vol. 2 (London: Epworth Press; 1978).

Davis, A.P., *Isaac Watts* (London: Independent Press, 1948).
— *Dictionary of Quaker Biography* (Library of the Society of Friends, forthcoming).
— *Dictionary of Welsh Biography down to 1940* (London: Honourable Society of Cymmrodorion, 1959).
Dowley, T. (ed.), *The History of Christianity* (Oxford: Lion, 1990).
Dresser, Madge and P. Ollerenshaw (eds), *The Making of Modern Bristol* (Bristol: Redcliffe Press, 1996).
Dyson, John B., *Methodism in the Isle of Wight* (Ventnor: George M. Burt, 1856).
Eayrs, G., *Wesley and Kingswood and its Free Churches* (Bristol: J.W. Arrowsmith, 1911).
Edwards, Maldwyn L., *After Wesley: A Study of the Social and Political Influence of Methodism in the Middle Period (1791-1849)* (London: Epworth Press, 1935).
Ellacombe, H.T., *The History of the Parish of Bitton in the County of Gloucester* (Exeter, 1881).
England, *The Story of 'The Christian Community', an interdenominational society for the preaching of the Gospel in Poor Law Institutions, hospitals and infirmaries... A brief survey of 250 years of service; 1685-1935* (London: n.p., 1935).
Entwisle, William, *Memoir of the Rev Joseph Entwisle* (Bristol, 1848).
Evans, David, *As Mad as a Hatter! Puritans and Whitefieldites in the History of Dursley and Cam* (Gloucester: Alan Sutton, 1982).
Evans, Eric, *Britain Before the Reform Act: Politics and Society 1815-1832* (London: Longman, 1989).
— *The Forging of the Modern State* (Harlow: Longman, 1983).
Gay, John D., *The Geography of Religion in England* (London: Gerald Duckworth, 1971).
Gibson, William, *Church, State and Society, 1760-1850* (London: Macmillan, 1994).
Gilbert, A.D., *Religion and Society in Industrial England: Church, Chapel and Social Change* (London: Longman, 1976).
Gill, Derek J., *Frome Schooldays: A History of Schools in Frome up to the Second World War* (Frome: 1300 Publications, 1985).
Goring, J. and R., *The Unitarians* (London: Pergamon Press, 1984).
Gowland, D.A., *Methodist Secessions: The Origins of Free Methodism in Three Lancashire Towns* (Manchester: Chetham Society, 1979).
Grace, W.G., *'W G' Cricketing Reminiscences and Personal Recollections* (London: James Bowden, 1899).
Graham, Winston, *Poldark* (11 vols; various publishers, 1976-91).
— *The Twisted Sword* (London: Guild Publishing, 1990).

Gregory, Benjamin, *Side Lights on the Conflicts of Methodism during the Second quarter of the nineteenth century 1827-1852* (London: Cassell, 1899).

Halsey, A.H., *Change in British Society* (Oxford: Oxford University Press, 1986).

Harrison, A.W. *et al.*, *The Methodist Church: Its Origin, Divisions and Reunion* (London: Methodist Publishing House, 1932).

Hempton, David, *The Religion of the People: Methodism and Popular Religion c1750-1900* (London: Routledge, 1996).

— *Methodism and Politics in British Society 1750-1850* (London: Hutchinson, 1987).

Hindmarsh, Robert, *Rise and Progress of the New Jerusalem Church in England, America and other Parts* (ed. Edward Madeley; London: Hodson & Son, 1861).

Horne, C.S., *A Popular History of the Free Churches* (London: James Clarke, 1903).

Inglis, K.S., *Churches and the Working Classes in Victorian England* (London: Routledge and Kegan Paul, 1963).

Ives, A.G., *Kingswood School in Wesley's Day and Since;* (London: Epworth Press, 1970).

Jay, Elisabeth (ed.), *The Journal of John Wesley: A Selection* (Oxford: Oxford University Press, Oxford, 1987).

Jones, Ignatius, *Bristol Congregationalism, City and Country* (Bristol: J.W. Arrowsmith, 1947).

Kendall, H.B., *The Origin and History of the Primitive Methodist Church* (2 vols; London: Edward Dalton, [c.1910]).

Kent, John, *The Unacceptable Face: The Modern Church in the Eyes of the Historian* (London: SCM Press, 1987).

Lambert, A.J., *The Chapel on the Hill* (Bristol: St Stephen's Press, 1929).

Latimer, John, *Annals of Bristol.* Vols 2 and 3 (Bristol: W. & F. Morgan, 1887).

Leach, Charles, *Manchester Congregationalism* (London: Woodford Fawcett, 1898).

Lewis, Donald M., *Lighten their Darkness: The Evangelical Mission to Working-Class London, 1828-1860* (New York: Greenwood Press, 1986).

Little, Bryan, *The City and County of Bristol* (London: Warner Laurie, 1954).

Long, Edwin M., *The Union Tabernacle, or Moveable Tent-Church* (Philadelphia: Parry & McMillan, 1859).

Low, Robert, *W.G.* (London: Richard Cohen Books, 1997).

Macquiban, T.S.A. (ed.), *Methodism in its Cultural Milieu*, The Centenary Conference of the Wesley Historical Society in

Conjunction with the World Methodist Historical Society, 26-30 July 1993 (Westminster Wesley Series, Applied Theology Press, 2; 1994).

Marsham, Michael, *The Wiltshire Village Book* (Newbury: Countryside Books, 1987).

Mathias, Peter, *The First Industrial Nation* (London: Routledge, 1983).

Matthews, Ronald, *English Messiahs* (London: Methuen, 1936).

McGarvie, Michael, *The Book of Frome* (Buckingham: Barracuda Books, 1980).

Mingay, G.E., *Rural Life in Victorian Britain* (London: Heinemann, 1977).

Moore, Henry and Mrs Richard Smith, *The Life of the Rev Mr Henry Moore* (London: Simpkin, Marshall, 1844).

Morris, William, *Swindon Fifty Years Ago (More or Less)* (Swindon: 'Advertiser' Office, 1885).

Mounfield, Arthur (ed.), *A Short History of Independent Methodism* (London: Independent Methodist Book Room, 1905).

Mucklowe, William B., *Under Canvas; or Tent Worship in Summer Months* (New York: Atlantic Publishing and Engraving, 1876).

Nicholls, J.F. and John Taylor, *Bristol Past and Present: Volume 2. Ecclesiastical History* (Bristol: J.W. Arrowsmith, 1881).

Nichols, Reginald (ed.), *Monmouthshire Medley*, Vols 2 and 3 (Pontypool: Reginald Nichols, 1977 and 1978).

Nightingale, B., *Centenary of the Lancashire Congregational Union 1806-1906* (Manchester: Lancashire Congregational Union, 1906).

— *Lancashire Nonconformity*, Vols 5 and 6 (Manchester: J. Heywood, 1890 and 1893).

O'Dea, Thomas F., *The Sociology of Religion* (New Jersey: Prentice-Hall, 1966).

Oliver, Robert W., *The Strict Baptist Chapels of England: Volume 5. The Chapels of Wiltshire and the West* (London: R.F. Chambers, 1968).

Page, William (ed.), *The Victoria History of the Counties of England: 'Gloucestershire'*, Vol. 2 (London: Institute of Historical Research, University of London, 1907).

Packer, G. (ed.), *The Centenary of the Methodist New Connexion, 1797-1897* (London, 1897).

Parker, P.D. (ed.), *The Heart of Wesley's Journal* (Grand Rapids, MI: Kregal, 1989).

Petty, John, *History of Primitive Methodist Connexion to 1860* (London: R. Davies, 1864).

Pocock, W.W., *A Sketch of the History of Wesleyan Methodism in Some of the Southern Counties of England* (London, 1885).

Powell, A.G. and S.C. Caple, *The Graces, E.M.; W.G; and G.F.* (Bath: Cedric Chivers, Portway, 1974).

Pressnell, L.S. *Country Banking in the Industrial Revolution* (Oxford: Clarendon Press, 1956).

Prothero, I.J., *Artisans and Politics in Early Nineteenth-Century London* (London: W.M. Dawson & Son, 1979).

Pugh, R.B. (ed.), *The Victoria History of the Counties of England: Volume 2. 'Gloucestershire'* (London: Institute of Historical Research, University of London, 1956).

— *The Victoria History of the Counties of England: Volume 3. 'Wiltshire'* (London: Institute of Historical Research, University of London, 1976).

Pyer, C.S., *Wild Flowers; or Poetic Gleanings from Natural Objects, and topics of Religious, Moral, and Philanthropic Interest* (London: John Snow, 1844).

Pyke, R., *The Golden Chain* (London: Henry Hooks, [c.1915]).

Rack, Henry D., *Reasonable Enthusiast: John Wesley and the Rise of Methodism* (London: Epworth Press, 1989).

Rayner, Edward C., *The Story of the Christian Community, 1685-1909* (London: Memorial Hall, [c.1910]).

Redford, Arthur, *The History of Local Government in Manchester*, Vols 1 and 2 (London: Arthur Longmans, Green, 1939 and 1940).

Rees, T. Mardy, *A History of the Quakers in Wales* (Carmarthen: W. Spurrell & Son, 1925).

Ritson, Joseph, *The Romance of Primitive Methodism* (London: Edward Dalton, 1909).

Robinson, W.G., *A History of the Lancashire Congregational Union 1806-1956* (Manchester: Lancashire Congregational Union, 1955).

Royle, Edward, *Modern Britain: A Social History 1750-1985* (London: Edward Arnold, 1987).

Russell, K.P., *Memoirs of Rev John Pyer* (London: John Snow, 1865).

Sale, Richard, *The Visitors' Guide to the Cotswolds* (Ashbourne: Moorlands, 1987).

Scarf, Betty R., *The Sociological Study of Religion* (London: Hutchinson, 1970).

Sellers, Ian, *Nineteenth-Century Nonconformity* (London: Edward Arnold, 1977).

Semmell, B., *The Methodist Revolution* (London: Heinemann, 1974).

Shaw, Thomas, *A History of Cornish Methodism* (Truro: D. Bradford Barton, 1967).

— *The Bible Christians 1815-1907* (London: Epworth Press, 1965).

Smith, George, *History of Wesleyan Methodism: Volume 1. Wesley and His Times* (London: Longman, Brown, Green, Longman and Roberts, 1859); *Volume 2. The Middle Age* (London: Longman, Green, Longman and Roberts, 1862); *Volume 3. Modern Methodism* (London: Longman, Green, Longman and Roberts, 1862).

Smith, George, *Life Spiritual* (London, 1855).

Soloway, R.A., *Prelates and People: Ecclesiastical Social Thought in England 1783-1852* (London: Routledge and Kegan Paul, 1969).

Stell, Christopher, *Nonconformist Chapels and Meeting Houses in South West England* (London: HMSO, 1991).

Stevens, Abel, *History of Methodism*, Vol. 3 (London: Wesleyan Conference Office, 1878).

Stevenson, George J., *City Road Chapel, London and its Associations* (London: George J. Stevenson, 1873).

Stevenson, George J., *Methodist Worthies: Characteristic Sketches of Methodist Preachers of the Several Denominations, with Historical Sketch of each Connexion* (6 vols; London: Thomas C. Jack, 1884-86).

Stevenson, John, *Popular Disturbances in England 1700-1832* (London: Longmans, 1992).

Stone, G.F., *Bristol: As it was—and as it is: A Record of Fifty Years' Progress* (Bristol: Walter Reid, 1909).

Sutherland, Alexander, *Methodism in Canada* (London: Charles H. Kelly, 1903).

Thompson, E.P., *The Making of the English Working Class* (Loondon: Penguin, 1980).

Thorne, James, *A Jubilee Memorial of Incidents in the Rise and Progress of the Bible Christian Connexion* (Shebbear: Bible Christian Bookroom, [c.1865]).

Townsend, W.J., H.B. Workman and George Eayrs (eds), *A New History of Methodism* (2 vols; London: Hodder & Stoughton, 1909).

Trevelyan, G.M., *British History in the Nineteenth Century and After 1782-1919* (London: Longmans, 1922).

— *English Social History* (London: Longmans, 1944).

Turner, J.M.., *Conflict and Reconciliation: Studies in Methodism and Ecumenism in England 1740-1982* (London: Epworth Press, 1985).

Uglow, Jenny, *The Lunar Men. 'The Friends who made the Future: 1730-1810'* (London: Faber and Faber, 2000).

Valenze, Deborah M., 'Charity, Custom and Humanity: Changing Attitudes towards the poor in Eighteenth Century England', in

Jane Garnett and Colin Matthew (eds), *Revival and Religion since 1700* (London: Hambleton Press, 1993), pp.1-46.

— *Prophetic Sons and Daughters: Female Preaching and Popular Religion in Industrial England* (Princeton: Princeton University Press, 1985).

Vickers, James, *History of Independent Methodism* (Manchester: Independent Methodist Bookroom, 1920).

Vickers, John A. (ed.), *A Dictionary of Methodism in Britain and Ireland* (Peterborough: Epworth Press, 2000).

Vidler, Alec R., *The Church in an Age of Revolution* (Harmondsworth: Penguin Books, 1961).

Waddy, Adeline *The Life of the Rev Samuel D Waddy DD* (London: Wesleyan Conference Office, 1878).

Ward, W.R. (ed.), *The Early Correspondence of Jabez Bunting, 1820-1829* (London: Royal Historical Society, University College, London, 1972).

Ward, W.R. (ed.), *Early Victorian Methodism: The Correspondence of Jabez Bunting, 1830-1858* (Oxford: Oxford University Press, 1976).

Ward,. W.R., *Religion and Society in England 1790-1850* (London: B.T. Batsford, 1972).

Watts, Michael R. *The Dissenters: Volume II. The Expansion of Evangelical Nonconformity 1791-1859* (Oxford: Clarendon Press, 1995).

Wearmouth, R. F., *Methodism and the Common People of the Eighteenth Century* (London: Epworth Press, 1945).

— *Methodism and the Working-Class Movement of England 1800-1850* (London: Epworth Press, 1937).

Werner, J.S., *The Primitive Methodist Connexion: Its Background and Early History* (Madison, Wisconsin: University of Wisconsin Press, 1984).

Wicks, G.H., *Free Church Life in Bristol from Wycliffe to Wesley* (Bristol: n.p., 1910).

Williams, William R., *'The Prisoners' Friend', The Life of Mr James Bundy of Bristol* (London: Wesleyan Conference Office, 1880).

Willis, A.J., *A Hampshire Miscellany: Part III. 'Dissenter Meeting House Certificates in the Diocese of Winchester 1702-1844* (4 vols; Folkestone: A.J. Willis, 1963-67).

Winskill, P.T., *The Temperance Movement and its Workers* (4 vols; Edinburgh: Blackie, 1890-92).

Wolffe, John, *Evangelicals, Women and Community in Nineteenth-Century Britain* (Study Guide; Milton Keynes: Open University, 1994).

Yarrow, William H., *The History of Primitive Methodism in London from its commencement in 1822 to the year 1876* (London: John Dickenson, 1876).

Young, David, *Origin and History of Methodism in Wales* (London: Charles H. Kelly, 1893).

b) Articles, Booklets, Letters, and Pamphlets

Alderson, James, *Dursley Methodist Church Centenary, Historical Souvenir 1864-1964* (n.p., n.d. [c.1964]).

Ambler, R.W., 'Preachers and the Plan—Patters of Activity in Early Primitive Methodism', *Proceedings of WHS* Vol. 46 (1987-88), pp.21-31.

Anon., *A Short History of Portland Street Wesleyan Chapel, Bristol, and its surroundings with brief notices of some of the principal persons and events connected with Methodism in the City* (unpublished MS, n.d. [c.1880]).

Anon., *Historical Sketch of the Christian Community AD 1818-1826* (London: Geo J. Stevenson, 1868).

Anon., *Ryde Methodist Church 1883-1983* (Ryde, Isle of Wight: n.p., 1983).

Anon., *Rangeworthy Methodist Church 1820-1970: 150 Years of Christian Worship* (n.p., n.d. [c.1970]).

Anon., *History of Bunhill Fields Burial Ground* (London: City Lands Committee of the Corporation of London, 1887).

Anon., 'Obituary of George Hadfield', *Manchester Guardian* 22 April, 1879.

Anon., *Souvenir Brochure of the Opening and Dedication of the New Methodist Church, Ancoats: Saturday 30th May 1964* (n.p., n.d.).

Barker, William, *The Mother Church of Manchester Primitive Methodism* (Manchester: n.p., 1928).

Bates, E. Ralph, 'Portland Chapel, Bristol', WHS Bristol Branch *Bulletin* Vol. 40 (1983), pp.1-16.

Brown, Kenneth D., 'An Unsettled Ministry? Some Aspects of Nineteenth Century British Nonconformity', *Church History* 56.2 (June, 1987), pp.210-26.

Brown, Peter, *Bristol and South Gloucestershire Coalfield* (n.p., n.d. [c.1994]).

Butler, J.F., 'John Wesley's Defence before Bishop Butler', *Proceedings of WHS* Vol. 20 (1940), pp.63-66.

Carter, E.R., *History of Bath Road, Methodist Church, Swindon 1880-1980* (Swindon: E.R. Carter, 1981).

Cox, Marjorie, *William Wood of Bowden: Champion of Climbing Boys* (Manchester: Lancashire and Cheshire Antiquarian Society, 1995).

Currie, Robert, 'A Micro-Theory of Methodist Growth', *Proceedings of WHS* Vol. 36 (October, 1967), pp.65-73.

Davies, Rupert E., 'Methodism in Bedminster', WHS Bristol Branch; *Bulletin* Vol. 62 (1991), pp.1-16.

Dresser, Madge, 'Sisters and Brethren: Power, Propriety and Gender among the British Moravians, 1746-1833', *Social History* 21.3 (October, 1996), pp.304-29.

Edwards, John B., 'A Methodist Country Circuit in the First Half of the Nineteenth Century: The Downend Circuit 1804-1859', WHS Bristol Branch Occasional Paper No. 7 (January, 1992), pp.1-8.

— 'Ebenezer, Midland Road, and Primitive Methodism in Bristol', (WHS Bristol Branch; *Bulletin* No. 48 (1987), pp.1-16.

— *Victory Purdy, 'The Kingswood Collier'* (Bristol: The New Room, 1984).

Edwards, Michael S., 'The Teetotal Wesleyan Methodists', *Proceedings of WHS* 33 (September-December, 1961), pp. 63-70.

Fuller, J.G., *A Memoir of Rev Thomas Roberts M.A.* (Bristol, 1842).

Gibbs, George H., *George Pocock—Schoolmaster and Inventor* (Bristol: Bristol Postcript Series, [c.1988]).

Hamlin, A. Gordon, 'The Pithay Chapel, Bristol', *Baptist Quarterly* 15 (1953-54), pp.378-84.

Hearle, D.C., 'The Growth in Methodism in the Frome Valley and South Gloucestershire' (WHS Bristol Branch, *Bulletin* Vol. 63 (1992), pp.1-19.

Hobbs, Laura., *A Story of Methodism in Westbury on Trym, 1805-1989* (n.p., n.d.).

Jefferies, Brian, *This House in Bedminster* (Bristol: W.G. Williams, 1975).

Jones, A. Emlyn, *Our Parish, Mangotsfield* (Bristol: W.F. Mack, 1899).

Jones, P., *Gentlemen and Players* (Bristol: Downend Local History Society, 1989).

Jordan, Christopher, *Olveston Methodist Church* (Bristol: C. Jordan, 1979).

Judge, G.H. Bancroft, *The Origin and Progress of Wesleyan Methodism in Cheltenham and District: 'A Souvenir of the Cheltenham Methodist Circuit'* (n.p., n.d. [c.1912]).

Kaines-Thomas, E.G., 'Along the Road by Kite', *Country Life* 10 June 1949, n.p..

Kilby, W.M., *Yonder Country is Ours* (n.p., 1986).

Lander, John K., 'The Early Days of Teetotalism in Cornwall', *Journal of the Royal Institution of Cornwall* (2002), pp.85-100.

Leary, William, *Ministers and Circuits in the Primitive Methodist Church* (Loughborough: Teamprint, 1990).

Macquiban, T.S.A., 'John Hannah and the Beginning of Theological Education in Methodism', WHS Bristol Branch, *Bulletin* Vol. 65 (1993), pp.1-7.

— 'The Sacramental Controversy in Bristol in the 1790s', WHS Bristol Branch, *Bulletin* Vol. 60 (1991), pp.1-20.

— 'Practical Piety or Lettered Learning', *Proceedings of WHS* Vol. 50 (October, 1995), pp.83-107.

Martindale, Ron, 'Architecture and History of the Nonconformist Chapels and Meeting Houses in Kingswood' (unpublished MS, n.d. [c.1990]).

Mignot, Arthur, *The Beginnings of Methodism in Guernsey with special reference to the family Arrivé* (unpublished MS, 1994).

Myatt, Dorothy, 'The Development of Methodism in Cheltenham' (WHS Bristol Branch, *Bulletin* Vol. 74 (1996), pp.1-20.

Parkes, William, *The Arminian Methodists: The Derby Faith; A Wesleyan Aberration in Pursuit of Revivalism and Holiness* (Cannock: The Wesley Fellowship, 1995).

Powell, W.R., *The Society of Friends in Wiltshire* (n.p.: WRO, W.R. Powell, 1950).

Pyer, John, *The Position of the Church and the Work of the Pastor; address delivered at ordination of Rev J P Allen at Falmouth, Cornwall 12th October 1858* (London: John Snow, 1858).

Rack, H.D., 'Domestic Visitation: A Chapter in Early Nineteenth-Century Evangelism', *Journal of Ecclesiastical History* 24.4 (October, 1973), pp.358-75.

Ralph, Elizabeth, 'People Matter "Mary Carpenter"', *St Stephen's Review*, Bristol, December 1961, pp.6-7.

— 'People Matter "George Pocock"', *St Stephen's Review*, Bristol, September 1962), pp.6-8.

Rose, E.A., 'Kilham, Alexander' (unpublished MS, 1992).

— *Tell It as It Was: 'Oldham Street 1781-1883* (Manchester: n.p., 1981).

Sheard, Michael, *Primitive Methodism in the Manchester Area 1820-1830* (Manchester: WHS Lancashire and Cheshire Branch, 1976).

Spittal, C. Jeffrey, *Heavenly Impulses: The Life of George Pocock* (Bristol: University of Bristol, 1984).

Spittal, C. Jeffrey, *Notes on the Local History of the Free Churches of Frampton Cotterell* (unpublished, [c.1992]).

— 'The History of Methodism in the Environs of Old Market Street, Bristol 1739-1985' (WHS Bristol Branch, *Bulletin* No. 45 (1986), pp.1-32.

Swift, R.C., 'A Chapel on Wheels', *Proceedings of WHS* 28 (June, 1952), pp.122-23.

Symons, W., 'Highways and Byways of the Connexion', *Bible Christian Magazine* (April, 1884), pp.179.

— 'Portland Chapel, Bristol and the Tent Methodists', *Cornish Methodist Record* (January, 1893), pp.3-4.

Tanner, William, *Three Lectures on the Early History of the Society of Friends in Bristol and Somersetshire* (London: n.p., 1858).

Tidwell, S.C., *Pill Methodist Church 1757-1982* (Pill: S.C. Tidwell, 1982).

Vintner, Dorothy, *More Kingswood Stories: 'The Cleft in the Rock'* (Kingswood, Bristol: Central Press, 1951).

Walker, R.B., 'The Growth of Wesleyan Methodism in Victorian England and Wales', *Journal of Ecclesiastical History* 24.3 (1973), pp.262-78.

Walsh, Elizabeth., *With Buoyant Sails, They Fly* (Bristol: n.p., 1948).

Ward, W.R., *Swedenborganism: Heresy, Schism or Religious Protest?* (London: Cambridge University Press, 1972).

Williams, T.M., *A Short History of Old King Street Baptist Church, Bristol* (Bristol: n.p., 1955).

Wollen, Leslie M., 'An Early Bible Christian Minute-Book', *Proceedings of WHS* Vol. 36 (1967), pp.124-28.

Index

Studies in Evangelical History and Thought
(All titles uniform with this volume)
Dates in bold are of projected publication

Andrew Atherstone
Oxford's Protestant Spy
The Controversial Career of Charles Golightly
Charles Golightly (1807–85) was a notorious Protestant polemicist. His life was dedicated to resisting the spread of ritualism and liberalism within the Church of England and the University of Oxford. For half a century he led many memorable campaigns, such as building a martyr's memorial and attempting to close a theological college. John Henry Newman, Samuel Wilberforce and Benjamin Jowett were among his adversaries. This is the first study of Golightly's controversial career.
2006 / 1-84227-364-7 / approx. 324pp

Clyde Binfield
Victorian Nonconformity in Eastern England
Studies of Victorian religion and society often concentrate on cities, suburbs, and industrialisation. This study provides a contrast. Victorian Eastern England—Essex, Suffolk, Norfolk, Cambridgeshire, and Huntingdonshire—was rural, traditional, relatively unchanging. That is nonetheless a caricature which discounts the industry in Norwich and Ipswich (as well as in Haverhill, Stowmarket and Leiston) and ignores the impact of London on Essex, of railways throughout the region, and of an ancient but changing university (Cambridge) on the county town which housed it. It also entirely ignores the political implications of such changes in a region noted for the variety of its religious Dissent since the seventeenth century. This book explores Victorian Eastern England and its Nonconformity. It brings to a wider readership a pioneering thesis which has made a major contribution to a fresh evolution of English religion and society.
2006 / 1-84227-216-0 / approx. 274pp

John Brencher
Martyn Lloyd-Jones (1899–1981) and Twentieth-Century Evangelicalism
This study critically demonstrates the significance of the life and ministry of Martyn Lloyd-Jones for post-war British evangelicalism and demonstrates that his preaching was his greatest influence on twentieth-century Christianity. The factors which shaped his view of the church are examined, as is the way his reformed evangelicalism led to a separatist ecclesiology which divided evangelicals.
2002 / 1-84227-051-6 / xvi + 268pp

Jonathan D. Burnham
A Story of Conflict
The Controversial Relationship between Benjamin Wills Newton and
John Nelson Darby
Burnham explores the controversial relationship between the two principal leaders of the early Brethren movement. In many ways Newton and Darby were products of their times, and this study of their relationship provides insight not only into the dynamics of early Brethrenism, but also into the progress of nineteenth-century English and Irish evangelicalism.
2004 / 1-84227-191-1 / xxiv + 268pp

Grayson Carter
Anglican Evangelicals
Protestant Secessions from the Via Media, c.1800–1850
This study examines, within a chronological framework, the major themes and personalities which influenced the outbreak of a number of Evangelical clerical and lay secessions from the Church of England and Ireland during the first half of the nineteenth century. Though the number of secessions was relatively small—between a hundred and two hundred of the 'Gospel' clergy abandoned the Church during this period—their influence was considerable, especially in highlighting in embarrassing fashion the tensions between the evangelical conversionist imperative and the principles of a national religious establishment. Moreover, through much of this period there remained, just beneath the surface, the potential threat of a large Evangelical disruption similar to that which occurred in Scotland in 1843. Consequently, these secessions provoked great consternation within the Church and within Evangelicalism itself, they contributed to the outbreak of millennial speculation following the 'constitutional revolution' of 1828–32, they led to the formation of several new denominations, and they sparked off a major Church–State crisis over the legal right of a clergyman to secede and begin a new ministry within Protestant Dissent.
2007 / 1-84227-401-5 / xvi + 470pp

J.N. Ian Dickson
Beyond Religious Discourse
Sermons, Preaching and Evangelical Protestants in Nineteenth-Century
Irish Society
Drawing extensively on primary sources, this pioneer work in modern religious history explores the training of preachers, the construction of sermons and how Irish evangelicalism and the wider movement in Great Britain and the United States shaped the preaching event. Evangelical preaching and politics, sectarianism, denominations, education, class, social reform, gender, and revival are examined to advance the argument that evangelical sermons and preaching went significantly beyond religious discourse. The result is a book for those with interests in Irish history, culture and belief, popular religion and society, evangelicalism, preaching and communication.
2005 / 1-84227-217-9 / approx. 324pp

Neil T.R. Dickson
Brethren in Scotland 1838–2000
A Social Study of an Evangelical Movement
The Brethren were remarkably pervasive throughout Scottish society. This study of the Open Brethren in Scotland places them in their social context and examines their growth, development and relationship to society.
2003 / 1-84227-113-X / xxviii + 510pp

Crawford Gribben and Timothy C.F. Stunt (eds)
Prisoners of Hope?
Aspects of Evangelical Millennialism in Britain and Ireland, 1800–1880
This volume of essays offers a comprehensive account of the impact of evangelical millennialism in nineteenth-century Britain and Ireland.
2004 / 1-84227-224-1 / xiv + 208pp

Khim Harris
Evangelicals and Education
Evangelical Anglicans and Middle-Class Education in
Nineteenth-Century England
This ground breaking study investigates the history of English public schools founded by nineteenth-century Evangelicals. It documents the rise of middle-class education and Evangelical societies such as the influential Church Association, and includes a useful biographical survey of prominent Evangelicals of the period.
2004 / 1-84227-250-0 / xviii + 422pp

Mark Hopkins
Nonconformity's Romantic Generation
Evangelical and Liberal Theologies in Victorian England
A study of the theological development of key leaders of the Baptist and Congregational denominations at their period of greatest influence, including C.H. Spurgeon and R.W. Dale, and of the controversies in which those among them who embraced and rejected the liberal transformation of their evangelical heritage opposed each other.
2004 / 1-84227-150-4 / xvi + 284pp

Don Horrocks
Laws of the Spiritual Order
Innovation and Reconstruction in the Soteriology of Thomas Erskine of Linlathen
Don Horrocks argues that Thomas Erskine's unique historical and theological significance as a soteriological innovator has been neglected. This timely reassessment reveals Erskine as a creative, radical theologian of central and enduring importance in Scottish nineteenth-century theology, perhaps equivalent in significance to that of S.T. Coleridge in England.
2004 / 1-84227-192-X / xx + 362pp

Kenneth S. Jeffrey
When the Lord Walked the Land
The 1858–62 Revival in the North East of Scotland
Previous studies of revivals have tended to approach religious movements from either a broad, national or a strictly local level. This study of the multifaceted nature of the 1859 revival as it appeared in three distinct social contexts within a single region reveals the heterogeneous nature of simultaneous religious movements in the same vicinity.
2002 / 1-84227-057-5 / xxiv + 304pp

John Kenneth Lander
Itinerant Temples
Tent Methodism, 1814–1832
Tent preaching began in 1814 and the Tent Methodist sect resulted from disputes with Bristol Wesleyan Methodists in 1820. The movement spread to parts of Gloucestershire, Wiltshire, London and Liverpool, among other places. Its demise started in 1826 after which one leader returned to the Wesleyans and others became ministers in the Congregational and Baptist denominations.
2003 / 1-84227-151-2 / xx + 268pp

Donald M. Lewis
Lighten Their Darkness
The Evangelical Mission to Working-Class London, 1828–1860
This is a comprehensive and compelling study of the Church and the complexities of nineteenth-century London. Challenging our understanding of the culture in working London at this time, Lewis presents a well-structured and illustrated work that contributes substantially to the study of evangelicalism and mission in nineteenth-century Britain.
2001 / 1-84227-074-5 / xviii + 372pp

Herbert McGonigle
'Sufficient Saving Grace'
John Wesley's Evangelical Arminianism
A thorough investigation of the theological roots of John Wesley's evangelical Arminianism and how these convictions were hammered out in controversies on predestination, limited atonement and the perseverance of the saints.
2001 / 1-84227-045-1 / xvi + 350pp

Lisa S. Nolland
A Victorian Feminist Christian
Josephine Butler, the Prostitutes and God
Josephine Butler was an unlikely candidate for taking up the cause of prostitutes, as she did, with a fierce and self-disregarding passion. This book explores the particular mix of perspectives and experiences that came together to envision and empower her remarkable achievements. It highlights the vital role of her spirituality and the tragic loss of her daughter.
2004 / 1-84227-225-X / xxiv + 328pp

Don J. Payne
The Theology of the Christian Life in J.I. Packer's Thought
Theological Anthropology, Theological Method, and the Doctrine of Sanctification
J.I. Packer has wielded widespread influence on evangelicalism for more than three decades. This study pursues a nuanced understanding of Packer's theology of sanctification by tracing the development of his thought, showing how he reflects a particular version of Reformed theology, and examining the unique influence of theological anthropology and theological method on this area of his theology.
2005 / 1-84227-397-3 / approx. 374pp

Ian M. Randall
Evangelical Experiences
A Study in the Spirituality of English Evangelicalism 1918–1939
This book makes a detailed historical examination of evangelical spirituality between the First and Second World Wars. It shows how patterns of devotion led to tensions and divisions. In a wide-ranging study, Anglican, Wesleyan, Reformed and Pentecostal-charismatic spiritualities are analysed.
1999 / 0-85364-919-7 / xii + 310pp

Ian M. Randall
Spirituality and Social Change
The Contribution of F.B. Meyer (1847–1929)
This is a fresh appraisal of F.B. Meyer (1847–1929), a leading Free Church minister. Having been deeply affected by holiness spirituality, Meyer became the Keswick Convention's foremost international speaker. He combined spirituality with effective evangelism and socio-political activity. This study shows Meyer's significant contribution to spiritual renewal and social change.
2003 / 1-84227-195-4 / xx + 184pp

James Robinson
Pentecostal Origins
Early Pentecostalism in Ireland in the Context of the British Isles
Harvey Cox describes Pentecostalism as 'the fascinating spiritual child of our time' that has the potential, at the global scale, to contribute to the 'reshaping of religion in the twenty-first century'. This study grounds such sentiments by examining at the local scale the origin, development and nature of Pentecostalism in Ireland in its first twenty years. Illustrative, in a paradigmatic way, of how Pentecostalism became established within one region of the British Isles, it sets the story within the wider context of formative influences emanating from America, Europe and, in particular, other parts of the British Isles. As a synoptic regional study in Pentecostal history it is the first survey of its kind.
2005 / 1-84227-329-1 / xxviii + 378pp

Geoffrey Robson
Dark Satanic Mills?
Religion and Irreligion in Birmingham and the Black Country
This book analyses and interprets the nature and extent of popular Christian belief and practice in Birmingham and the Black Country during the first half of the nineteenth century, with particular reference to the impact of cholera epidemics and evangelism on church extension programmes.
2002 / 1-84227-102-4 / xiv + 294pp

Roger Shuff
Searching for the True Church
Brethren and Evangelicals in Mid-Twentieth-Century England
Roger Shuff holds that the influence of the Brethren movement on wider evangelical life in England in the twentieth century is often underrated. This book records and accounts for the fact that Brethren reached the peak of their strength at the time when evangelicalism was at it lowest ebb, immediately before World War II. However, the movement then moved into persistent decline as evangelicalism regained ground in the post war period. Accompanying this downward trend has been a sharp accentuation of the contrast between Brethren congregations who engage constructively with the non-Brethren scene and, at the other end of the spectrum, the isolationist group commonly referred to as 'Exclusive Brethren'.
2005 / 1-84227-254-3 / xviii+ 296pp

James H.S. Steven
Worship in the Spirit
Charismatic Worship in the Church of England
This book explores the nature and function of worship in six Church of England churches influenced by the Charismatic Movement, focusing on congregational singing and public prayer ministry. The theological adequacy of such ritual is discussed in relation to pneumatological and christological understandings in Christian worship.
2002 / 1-84227-103-2 / xvi + 238pp

Peter K. Stevenson
God in Our Nature
The Incarnational Theology of John McLeod Campbell
This radical reassessment of Campbell's thought arises from a comprehensive study of his preaching and theology. Previous accounts have overlooked both his sermons and his Christology. This study examines the distinctive Christology evident in his sermons and shows that it sheds new light on Campbell's much debated views about atonement.
2004 / 1-84227-218-7 / xxiv + 458pp

Kenneth J. Stewart
Restoring the Reformation
British Evangelicalism and the Réveil at Geneva 1816–1849
Restoring the Reformation traces British missionary initiative in post-Revolutionary Francophone Europe from the genesis of the London Missionary Society, the visits of Robert Haldane and Henry Drummond, and the founding of the Continental Society. While British Evangelicals aimed at the reviving of a foreign Protestant cause of momentous legend, they received unforeseen reciprocating emphases from the Continent which forced self-reflection on Evangelicalism's own relationship to the Reformation.
2006 / 1-84227-392-2 / approx. 190pp

Martin Wellings
Evangelicals Embattled
Responses of Evangelicals in the Church of England to Ritualism, Darwinism and Theological Liberalism 1890–1930
In the closing years of the nineteenth century and the first decades of the twentieth century Anglican Evangelicals faced a series of challenges. In responding to Anglo-Catholicism, liberal theology, Darwinism and biblical criticism, the unity and identity of the Evangelical school were severely tested.
2003 / 1-84227-049-4 / xviii + 352pp

James Whisenant
A Fragile Unity
Anti-Ritualism and the Division of Anglican Evangelicalism in the Nineteenth Century
This book deals with the ritualist controversy (approximately 1850–1900) from the perspective of its evangelical participants and considers the divisive effects it had on the party.
2003 / 1-84227-105-9 / xvi + 530pp

Haddon Willmer
Evangelicalism 1785–1835: An Essay (1962) and Reflections (2004)
Awarded the Hulsean Prize in the University of Cambridge in 1962, this interpretation of a classic period of English Evangelicalism, by a young church historian, is now supplemented by reflections on Evangelicalism from the vantage point of a retired Professor of Theology.
2006 / 1-84227-219-5 / approx. 350pp

Linda Wilson
Constrained by Zeal
Female Spirituality amongst Nonconformists 1825–1875
Constrained by Zeal investigates the neglected area of Nonconformist female spirituality. Against the background of separate spheres, it analyses the experience of women from four denominations, and argues that the churches provided a 'third sphere' in which they could find opportunities for participation.
2000 / 0-85364-972-3 / xvi + 294pp

Paternoster
9 Holdom Avenue,
Bletchley,
Milton Keynes MK1 1QR,
United Kingdom
Web: www.authenticmedia.co.uk/paternoster

July 2005

ND - #0074 - 270225 - C0 - 229/152/16 - PB - 9781842271513 - Gloss Lamination